UNIFYING PSYCHOTHERAPY

Jeffrey J. Magnavita, PhD, ABPP, FAPA, is a licensed psychologist and marriage and family therapist in active clinical practice. A diplomate in both counseling and clinical psychology of the American Board of Behavioral Psychology and fellow of the American Psychological Association (APA), he is the recipient of the Award for Distinguished Professional Contribution to Independent or Institutional Practice in the Private Sector for 2006 from APA for his work in unifying psychotherapy and personality systematics. Dr. Magnavita authored *Restructuring Personality Disorders: A Short-Term Dynamic Approach; Relational Therapy for Personality Disorders, Personality-Guided Relational Psychotherapy: A Unified Approach; Theories of Personality: Contemporary Approaches to the Science of Personality;* and was the volume editor for the *Comprehensive Handbook of Psychotherapy: Psychodynamic/ Object Relations: Volume I, Handbook of Personality Disorders: Theory and Practice,* and *Evidence-Based Treatment of Personality Disorders: Principles, Methods, and Processes.* He recently authored *Theories of Personality,* an undergraduate text. He is the co-founder and co-editor-in-chief of the *Journal of Unified Psychotherapy and Clinical Science.* He served as the president of the Division of Psychotherapy in 2010 and has previously made a highly acclaimed DVD demonstrating his approach in a single session, as well as one on *Psychotherapy Over Time* (six sessions). Most recently he was the founder of the Unified Psychotherapy Project and has created a task force to map the current methods and techniques of psychotherapy called *psychotherapedia*™. He is the creator and producer of a video series *Psychotherapists Fact-to-Face,* a production of the APA Division of Psychotherapy. He was recently appointed lecturer at Yale University in the Department of Psychiatry.

Jack C. Anchin, PhD, FAPA, is adjunct professor of psychology at SUNY at Buffalo and a clinical psychologist engaged in full-time private practice for over 25 years. Dr. Anchin is also co-editor of the *Handbook of Interpersonal Psychotherapy* and has published articles and chapters on the theory and practice of interpersonal psychotherapy, as well as on psychotherapy integration and psychotherapy unification. His publications also include invited commentaries on relational psychoanalysis; the unification of knowledge across the natural sciences, social sciences, and humanities; and integrative research methodology in the scientific study of interpersonal psychotherapy. Dr. Anchin has been an associate editor of the American Psychological Association (APA) *Journal of Psychotherapy Integration* and is currently a member of the editorial board. He has also served on the inaugural advisory council of APA's *Clinician's Research Digest: Briefings in Behavioral Science,* and on the editorial boards of the *Journal of Integrative and Eclectic Psychotherapy* and the APA journal *Psychotherapy: Theory, Research, Practice, Training.* With Dr. Magnavita, he is co-founder and co-editor of the electronic *Journal of Unified Psychotherapy and Clinical Science.* Dr. Anchin is an invited charter member of the Society for the Exploration of Psychotherapy Integration. He is a Fellow of the APA and is the 2011 recipient of the APA Division of Psychotherapy's Distinguished Psychologist Award for contributions to psychology and psychotherapy.

UNIFYING PSYCHOTHERAPY
Principles, Methods, and Evidence From Clinical Science

Jeffrey J. Magnavita, PhD, ABPP, FAPA
Jack C. Anchin, PhD, FAPA

SPRINGER PUBLISHING COMPANY
NEW YORK

Springer Publishing Company, LLC
11 West 42nd Street
New York, NY 10036
www.springerpub.com

Acquisitions Editor: Sheri W. Sussman
Composition: Techset Composition (P) Ltd., Bangalore and Chennai, India.

ISBN: 978-0-8261-9982-9
e-book ISBN: 978-0-8261-9983-6

13 14 15 16 / 5 4 3 2 1

The author and the publisher of this Work have made every effort to use sources believed to be reliable to provide information that is accurate and compatible with the standards generally accepted at the time of publication. The author and publisher shall not be liable for any special, consequential, or exemplary damages resulting, in whole or in part, from the readers' use of, or reliance on, the information contained in this book. The publisher has no responsibility for the persistence or accuracy of URLs for external or third-party Internet websites referred to in this publication and does not guarantee that any content on such websites is, or will remain, accurate or appropriate.

Library of Congress Cataloging-in-Publication Data

Magnavita, Jeffrey J.

 Unifying psychotherapy : principles, methods, and evidence from clinical science / Jeffrey J. Magnavita and Jack C. Anchin.

    pages cm

 Includes bibliographical references and index.

 ISBN 978-0-8261-9982-9

1. Psychotherapy--Philosophy. 2. Clinical psychology--Philosophy. 3. System theory. 4. Self-organizing systems. I. Anchin, Jack C. (Jack Charles), 1951- II. Title.

 RC480.5.M3145 2014

 616.89'14--dc23

                             2013025373

Printed in the United States of America by McNaughton & Gunn.

I dedicate this book to my dear, sweet Chris; you are everything beautiful and precious to me

— Jack C. Anchin

This book is also dedicated to Dr. Charles and Josephine Gardner who passed away before this volume was published. Their presence is missed but their spirits live on in their family, friends, and students

— Jeffrey J. Magnavita

CONTENTS

PREFACE

This volume, *Unifying Psychotherapy: Principles, Methods, and Evidence From Clinical Science*, represents a joint effort that has come to fruition after germinating over the course of more than a decade-long relationship. We have spent considerable time discussing our notions about how to advance our effectiveness by taking the best of clinical science and theory. We believe that the time for unifying clinical science and psychotherapy is upon us, and hope this volume generates broader interest in unification, as well as provides a new paradigm for clinicians. It is important to share with our readers the roots and context of our unifying perspective, and why we think we have something unique to contribute. We realize there are many professional books available and appreciate that you are considering reading this one, and believe it will at least pique your curiosity. We have enjoyed and grown from our scholarly explorations and collaboration. It is important to state that our primary commitment is to our psychotherapeutic work—we both maintain full-time independent practices—that between us amounts to almost six decades. We believe that theory and practice, supported by relevant research, are essential to our effectiveness, and one of the reasons why people seek our service. We share Cummings and Cummings's (2013) admiration for and perspective of the great physician Sir William Osler, who said:

> He who studies medicine without books sails an uncharted sea. But he who studies medicine without patients does not go to sea at all.

Cummings and Cummings (2013) write that psychotherapy shares similar features with medicine and comment on Osler's perspective:

> This is as true for the practice of psychotherapy as it is for the practice of medicine, but unfortunately too many books on the practice of psychotherapy are written by academic clinicians

who may be good teachers and researchers, but they do not see patients.

We believe that researchers and academic clinicians bring much to our clinical science, but as psychotherapists, with decades of clinical experience, we have something unique to offer our readers. Clinicians know, as we do, that facing those in suffering, on a daily basis, is not for the faint hearted, heavy with responsibility and often lonely. We make complex decisions every day with limited empirical evidence to guide us. Clinical decision making in our view cannot be learned from a book, a research journal, or a manual, but rather requires clinical experience to appreciate the complexity of human nature and the skills of being a healer. Sometimes a novelist is able to say things in a way that deeply resonants with us. Michael Robotham's (2010) protagonist, a psychologist-psychotherapist, describes this way of processing information in his novel *Bleed for Me*:

> Sometimes we know things even if we don't know we know them. Maybe all we have is a fluttering sensation in our stomachs or a nagging sense of doubt or an unexplained certainty that something has happened.
>
> Call it intuition or perception of insight. There is no sixth sense—it is a simple mental process where the brain takes in a situation, does a rapid search of its files, and among the sprawl of memories and knowledge it throws up an immediate match, a first impression. (pp. 153–154)

Malcolm Gladwell in *Blink* calls this phenomenon "thin splitting." This rapid instinctive response, called intuition, is too often overlooked or dismissed as unscientific. We are beginning to understand more about the various information processing systems of the brain, which suggest both a rational, more deliberative one and a rapid, emotional one. "Genuine intuition" is based on a solid foundation of knowledge and exercised by experience. Assimilation of knowledge is essential and separates professionals from psychics. This knowledge blended with experience provides the basis for complex pattern recognition, which is one of the hallmarks of effective psychotherapy and an important aspect of a unified approach. We attempt this by drawing on multiple and converging areas of science and knowledge to guide our pattern recognition.

In Search of the "Holy Grail"

The field of psychotherapy has long been engaged in a search for the "Holy Grail—the most potent therapeutic approach—with applicability to the widest array of psychological disorders and expressions of human suffering" (Anchin & Magnavita, 2006, p. 26). We are propelled to find the psychotherapeutic approach that will help us attain the "pure gold" of mental health—character change and permanent symptom alleviation. Many pioneers have offered their approaches with a promise of redemption from suffering if one adopts and adheres to their model. Most of these figures have both nourished our hope and disappointed us. We, along with our professional colleagues, have experienced many forms of treatment that we practice in our own hope for enlightenment and to alleviate suffering. We or our family members are likely to be mental health consumers at one time or another. We are no exception on this seemingly noble quest for the most potent and enduring approach for our families, our patients, and ourselves. The pathway each of us has traversed has not been different from that of many other psychotherapists. Indeed, the route we—and we suspect many others—have taken has been more akin to a maze than a singular road forward. Sometimes working as a psychotherapist feels more like living in a Kafkaesque-inspired labyrinth between navigating the health care system and the Tower of Babel in our field, and the competition from renegade practitioners who offer pathways to change using unfounded methods.

We have studied and been trained in various systems of psychotherapy, each of which shine light on something we didn't know or understand, illuminating and crystallizing our perspective. We are excited when new approaches offer us novel ways to conceptualize our psychotherapeutic work, or teach us new techniques and methods to utilize when our treatment is stuck and the trusted strategies in our clinical toolkit prove ineffective. We find these experiences to be remoralizing, when we can't find what works with some of the people we treat, and a novel approach or perspective offered inspires hope. We also have experienced disappointment when so many of the approaches that we have studied and learned failed to deliver what they promised. Looking back over our professional and personal journey, we each seem to have taken what we found to be innovative and of clinical utility and continued our search for the Holy Grail. We maintain hope that science and practice working in synchrony can advance our knowledge of human behavior and refine how we can help those who need our services. We believe that the search for the Holy Grail of clinical science and psychotherapy rests on a foundation of unification. This book is not a final stage but a beginning in a continuing evolution toward unifying clinical science and psychotherapy.

The Current State of Affairs—Alphabet Soup

There are currently over 1,000 different names for approaches to psychotherapy (Garfield, 2006), and to no small extent our field has become an alphabet soup of acronyms for different therapeutic schools and approaches, some major and some minor. I (JJM) have contributed to proliferating approaches, believing at the time that these offered something unique. Yet, in retrospect, these are variations, not new approaches. It seems as if psychotherapy suffers from acrynomia—an addiction to acronyms. Our therapeutic soup now includes RET, CBT, FFT, STDP, ISTDP, ACT, ISTDP, AEP, EMDR, and the list goes on and on. To add to the confusion, many approaches have their own often-esoteric language, which creates a Tower of Babel. Oftentimes, a similar phenomenon is described with different terms, contributing to confusion and fragmentation in the field. Dollard and Miller (1950) were some of the original investigators to address this issue of theoretical confusion in the 1950s when they translated psychoanalytic terms into behavioral ones, demonstrating how different language can be used to describe similar phenomena. Are there really substantive differences among the vast array of current approaches to psychotherapy and their respective constructs? How can clinicians reasonably be expected to select among the range of approaches, techniques, and modalities of treatment to formulate a treatment package for each patient system? We believe unifying psychotherapy better addresses these concerns.

A goal of many innovators has been to develop their own school or approach and then find adherents who can disseminate what they have developed; recruiting and training other clinicians in one's own model has become big business for our field. Oftentimes, when we examine approaches it appears that the similarities often outweigh the differences, except in the case of certain uniquely distinctive approaches even these share the fundamental core processes with others. Along with the many approaches to psychotherapy, there are many therapeutic tribes, and we belong to a few ourselves. There is often a reification of constructs as if they without doubt represent "reality." At one conference, panelists talked about "punitive superegos" as if these are real entities and not just metaphorical terms. At another, we heard panelists dismiss the notion of an unconscious mind or its relevance to psychotherapists and clinical scientists.

Does having all these separate approaches harm or help our work? Research efforts may suffer as a result of this proliferation of so many brands of therapy that might have only minor differences. Accumulating evidence for an approach is thwarted because independent efforts validating an approach that only has minor differences is going to weaken the evidence base and waste precious resources. This phase of differentiation of psychotherapeutics, with so many approaches being promulgated, many with only minor differences, was likely a necessary phase in the development of our field. A new stage in the evolution of psychotherapy seems apparent and necessary. As we shall learn in this volume, differentiation is a normal phase of development in any complex system, with integration and synthesis coming during later stages, but never ceasing as more information is gathered and science advances.

The field of psychotherapy has all too often been preoccupied with pitting one approach to psychotherapy against another to see which one is best. We are still thrilled when we discover a new perspective that seems to better guide our conceptual and clinical efforts—but is holding racehorses among approaches the best way to advance knowledge? The perspective we offer in this volume is of a unified psychotherapy based firmly on the best available evidence from clinical science, and we have found it to be highly useful. Unified psychotherapy is a multiperspective approach that provides the clinician with a framework to select from an array of technical interventions based on an understanding of relational principles. There are other problems when we become overly adherent to any approach—we want to fit everybody into our Procrustean bed.

If You Only Have a Hammer—Everything Looks Like a Nail

The therapeutic approach offered by a clinician is typically based on the type of training the clinician has received, and his or her philosophical beliefs and therapeutic preferences. Recently, one of us evaluated a patient who had made a severe suicide attempt and was hospitalized. Initially she had consulted a mental health professional and told him that she was suicidal; he prescribed medication and asked her to pray. She later made an almost lethal suicide attempt. She said he never asked her about what she was experiencing or what led to her despair. She stated, "I needed to talk but no one seemed interested in listening." There are many devoted and excellent therapists who practice in challenging settings and get good results. There are also many who believe that what they do is the only way to address issues, and if their approach doesn't work it was the patient's fault because he or she wasn't cooperative or ready. In one of my (JJM) recent cases, a woman came in for treatment after having a tree fall on her car and being trapped. Her first psychotherapist never asked her any questions, he just sat and waited for her to talk. After six months the patient asserted herself and told the therapist that this approach was not working, to which the therapist replied "it works with my other patients." There was never any offer of a first-line evidence-based exposure therapy that should have been considered. In this case it seemed that if one only has one therapeutic hammer, every patient's issues look like a nail.

How Clinicians Make Sense out of Complexity

How can clinicians be expected to select among the range of approaches, techniques, and modalities of treatment? With over 1,000 approaches to psychotherapy, and many more for the treatment of mental disorders, how can clinicians operate with this level of complexity and expect to be effective? Are there really substantive differences among the approaches to psychotherapy? How can we reasonably be expected to select among the range of approaches, techniques, and modalities of treatment? Treatments for mental disorders range from biological to spiritual, with every conceivable combination in between. Some clinicians believe single-photon emission computed tomographys (SPECT) scans of an individual's brain hold the key to diagnosis and treatment planning, and yet others believe in the healing capacity of existential–humanistic or mindful experiences.

The Challenge for Mental Health Consumers

Putting aside for the moment our own challenges as mental health professionals and psychotherapists, consider what mental health consumers have to deal with when they seek treatment. Consulting various mental health clinicians for a psychological disturbance such as anxiety or depression may result in being prescribed psychotropic medication, cognitive–behavioral therapy, psychodynamic therapy, spiritual counseling, experiential therapy, or an array of other therapies. We are only now beginning the process in North America of developing treatment guidelines based on empirical evidence to hopefully guide us as well as the public in answering these questions of what approach works for whom (APA Treatment Guidelines Initiative). With so much branding, what are consumers supposed to do to find effective treatment? What if all approaches were different ways of approaching a problem and could be understood as working at different domain levels of a complex system?

One senior clinician told us that she was not concerned with what consumers had to deal with. How can this not be our concern? Limited access to mental health services is a major international issue that causes much suffering. The fragmentation in the field is difficult enough to untangle for those who are professionals. How can the public possibly choose what is appropriate with so many approaches from which to choose? Clinical science and its related disciplines does itself harm when we present such a chaotic state of affairs.

Challenge to Psychotherapy and Clinical Science

Practitioners who have either begun or continued their personal journey of growth as a psychotherapist in this first quarter of the 21st century do so in a daunting environment. These are difficult times in the United States, with increasing demands being placed on mental health professionals and expectations that may be unrealistic. For example, with the increasing incidence of gun-related violence, some believe that we should be able to predict and stop these horrific incidents. The challenge of providing quality mental health services is a common theme among psychotherapists who do complex work requiring advanced education and training, but whose services are undervalued by insurance companies who view mental health providers as technicians. We think that unification guided by science offers a brighter future because there will be less fragmentation.

We agree with Kendler (2005), who called for psychiatry—and in our reading, by implication clinical science—"to move from a prescientific 'battle of paradigms' toward a more mature approach that embraces complexity along with empirically rigorous and pluralistic explanatory models" (p. 433). We hope that this volume proves engaging and thought provoking. Our sincere wish is that this volume assists you in doing your clinical work with greater hope, patience for yourself and, most of all, greater clinical utility.

ACKNOWLEDGMENTS

This volume is the result of over a decade of fertile collaboration. We believe that the model we present in this volume is an amalgam of our combined six decades of clinical experience and our passion for trying to understand the complexity of conducting psychotherapy in a way that makes sense given the correspondingly daunting complexities of the human being. We first met at a yearly Society for the Exploration of Psychotherapy Integration (SEPI) conference and immediately felt like we were kindred spirits in sharing a passion for conducting psychotherapy as our major career choice, as well as pursuing similar lines of intellectual inquiry regarding the next stage in the evolution of psychotherapy. At our first introduction, we immediately clicked and were struck by our similar vision for unifying clinical science and psychotherapy, which we present in its most current form in this volume. We have both enjoyed this stimulating intellectual and scholarly journey and have felt a true mind blend when working out the issues we struggled with as this model evolved. Our friendship and respect have been the foundation of our collaboration. From this deep synergy has emanated a number of publications and symposia presentations exploring the topic of unification. We are also proud to have launched the *Journal of Unified Psychotherapy and Clinical Science* (JUPCS) with our collaborator Dr. Steve Sobelman, who is also a dear friend and innovator in many areas and from whom we have learned much.

There are many people who have shared this journey with us along the way, some of whom we have known on a personal level and others through intensively studying their scholarly, scientific, and clinical work. We have learned from some of the great masters and have explored many forms and approaches to psychotherapy and healing. Here I (JCA) wish to express my special gratitude to Dr. Donald J. Kiesler. I was indeed blessed to have Don as my major professor and mentor throughout graduate school. Departed but never forgotten, Don's kindness and graciousness, his powerfully motivating belief in me, the breadth and depth of knowledge he imparted about interpersonal psychotherapy and psycho-therapy research, and ways of thinking, conceptualizing, and integrating that I absorbed through the incredible good fortune of being his student are inscribed deep within me.

Of the many people who have influenced us on this long journey toward unification, some have shared our view and, as importantly, others have challenged the notion of unification, offering a number of credible points that sharpened our thinking. Among the many people we want to thank is Dr. Arthur Staats, who was one of the pioneering figures in the unification of psychology and who graciously came to Washington, DC to participate in a symposium we presented on unification. We also have been shaped and influenced by many pioneers from the psychotherapy integration movement to whom we express our appreciation, including Drs. Marvin Goldfried, Stanley Messer, George Stricker, and Paul Wachtel. Dr. Theodore Millon has been a significant psychological and interpersonal presence over the course of our work, and we extend our sincere gratitude for his abiding influence and support. We would also like to express appreciation to David Barlow for his influence and interest in our work, and, for JCA, his indelible role modeling early in my career of what it means, at its very best, to be a scientist-professional. We also want to thank the members of the editorial board of *JUPCS*, an exceptionally talented, diverse mixture of scholars who, in agreeing to serve on the journal's board, have provided validation and support that means more to us than they may know. Dr. David Allan, another of our collaborators, was the first to begin using the term unified psycho-therapy and his work continues to be very influential and challenging of the status quo.

There has been a small and growing group of incredibly smart and iconoclastic scholar clinicians who have urged us on and acutely shared our vision, including Drs. Gregg Henriques, Craig Shealy, Timothy Melchert, Ken Critchfield, Michael Alpert, Tom Sexton, Jay Lebow, Howard Liddle, and Andre Marquis. We are grateful to each of you. We would also like to thank many of our friends and colleagues from the Division of Psychotherapy and the Society for Psychotherapy Research. I (JCA) would also like to extend my appreciation to Drs. Frank Fincham, J. Gayle Beck, Craig Colder, John Roberts, Leonard Simms, and Stephen Tiffany, academicians par excellence, for their explicit support over the course of my involvement with the University at Buffalo's (UB) distinguished doctoral program in clinical psychology. I would like to thank, as well, the many outstanding graduate students in UB's clinical program to whom I have been been privileged to provide clinical supervision for well over a decade and counting. Your keen intellects, refreshing openness to different ways of clinically thinking and working, and enthusiasm for learning the art and science of psychotherapy have, in multiple ways, contributed to my own growth and development as a psychotherapist.

I (JJM) also want to express my sorrow and that of the professional community over the loss of Dr. Dan Galper whose untimely death has been hard for many of us. Dan was a great teacher and friend who taught us so much about developing practice guidelines.

Many of our close friends and colleagues have also provided unflagging support. Special thanks goes to a close friend and passionate psychiatrist Dr. Vincent Stephens, whose untimely death occurred before the publication of this volume. Dr. William Alder has been a support over two decades supplying JJM with valuable references and new developments from his extensive library. Dr. Frank Knoblauch should also be recognized as a stalwart support over the years, always adding a fresh perspective during our many hours over the past two decades reviewing videotapes of our psychotherapy sessions and offering advanced training in psychotherapy. Dr. Daniel Trigoboff, a soaring intellect, has been and continues to be a source of enormous support for JCA; our nearly three-decade-long friendship and the multitude of rich conversations we have had over this time on topics ranging from philosophy, psychotherapy, and science to history, culture, and indeed the cosmos, have enriched my being and my thinking immeasurably.

We would also like to express our appreciation to Sheri W. Sussman, Executive Editor extraordinaire. Her excited belief in this project, insightful editorial feedback, and unswerving patience throughout have been invaluable in this volume's coming to fruition. We are appreciative, as well, to Katie Corasaniti, Associate Editor, for the many beneficial forms of input and help she provided as this project unfolded and moved toward production.

Lastly, we are indebted to our families for the numerous ways—past and present—that they have contributed to this book's becoming a reality. My (JCA's) parents, Edward and Anita, may they rest in peace, are profoundly loved internalized others to whom I return time and again. How I wish I could share this book with them. I also extend deep appreciation to my two brothers, Steve and Marv, with whom I share a cherished closeness. To my two wonderful sons, Scott and David, I say, with appreciation that is really beyond words, "thank you" for your love and all that you bring to my life. Now with families of your own, may you experience the joy that I have known and continuously experience in the gift of having you as my sons. I (JJM) would also like to thank my three beautiful and intelligent daughters, Elizabeth, Emily, and Caroline who often accompany me on my professional trips making my work much more fun and interesting. We also want to thank our amazing patients who we learn so much from and who are so affirming of our endeavors to move the field forward. Most importantly we wish to thank our wives

Anne G. Magnavita and Chris Anchin for their loving support, tolerance, and understanding in accepting the stress and strain of both of us writing and teaching, while conducting full-time private practices. The life of a doctor of the mind has its tremendous privilege but also carries with it considerable strain associated with the responsibility that goes along with caring for those in states of emotional suffering that at times seem more than anyone should bear.

INTRODUCTION

Allan N. Schore

You are about to encounter a fresh, challenging, and indeed bold treatise on not only the current status but also the future of psychotherapy. The two authors of this groundbreaking volume are not only extremely well versed in integrating large bodies of current research over a number of disciplines, but also expert psychotherapists with decades of clinical experience. This dual expertise allows them to explore the essential realm that lies both within and between research and clinical practice. Over the following chapters they not only present but also synthesize very recent clinical and scientific data to assert that the field is now experiencing a paradigm shift, and that a new phase of unified psychotherapy is emerging from these rapid advances in our knowledge.

The book represents a significant expansion of the biopsychosocial model of health and illness, first elaborated by George Engel (1977, 1980) at the University of Rochester Medical School, and later incorporated into medicine, psychiatry, and clinical psychology. This model continues to provide an over-arching, holistic, and integrative conception of the human experience by postulating hierarchically arranged yet interacting biological, psychological, and sociocultural domains within the individual. The authors describe how the biopsychosocial perspective has significantly increased our understanding of human development and functioning across the life span, and has acted to elucidate the deeper mechanisms that underlie both healthy adaptive states and pathological maladaptive states. Here, following recent trends in a number of disciplines, they expand the biopsychosocial construct by integrating current relational conceptions into the core of the model. They state, "At every level of the biopsychosocial system, the influence of the relational matrix on development, functioning, and change is ubiquitous. Indeed, the pervasive relationalism in which biopsychosocial structures and processes are awash may well be the ultimate unifying principle of personality, psychopathology, and psychotherapy."

In the following pages, Magnavita and Anchin describe the manifestations of the current paradigm shift:

> Perhaps reflecting the quiet yet growing influence of systemic perspectives on mainstream thinking, theoretical and empirical lenses in both clinical and basic psychological science have been expanding beyond the reductionistic metapsychology that dominated the 20th century. The direction has been toward achieving a more holistic understanding of complex interrelationships among clusters of domains constituting human structure, process, and functioning along the continuum from psychopathological to healthy states. Influential examples include (a) Schore's (1994, 2003a, 2003b, 2012) interdisciplinary work linking such domains as neuroscience, developmental neurochemistry, interpersonal processes (including the centrality of attachment), unconscious mechanisms of affect regulation and dysregulation, and the self. …

Over the past two decades my contributions to the emergent field of interpersonal neurobiology have been firmly grounded in the biopsychosocial perspective in part because I did my undergraduate work at the University of Rochester. In this Introduction, I will offer a number of applications of my theoretical models to various developmental and clinical phenomena. I will focus on my latest book, *The Science of the Art of Psychotherapy*, including its Introduction, "Toward a New Paradigm of Psychotherapy." That work expands upon a plenary address I delivered to the American Psychological Association's 2009 Annual Convention, "The Paradigm Shift: The Right Brain and the Relational Unconscious" (Schore, 2009a). My expositions of "affect regulation theory," which integrate biology and psychology and focus on the "holistic" right brain, are an example of what Magnavita and Anchin describe as translational theoretical research, "the purpose of which is to translate findings from basic scientific research into applications within the applied clinical realm." The forthcoming chapters of this volume masterfully present a large number of authors who describe in some detail the essential relational, holistic processes that are activated in both the developmental and psychotherapeutic contexts. At various points, I cite these updated psychological formulations, focusing specifically on attachment, the therapeutic alliance, and transference-countertransference phenomena, and then offer my work on the neurobiological mechanisms that underlie these essential biopsychosocial phenomena.

I also discuss the recent advances in neuroscience in conceptions of brain laterality. A large body of research shows that "the right and left human brain hemispheres differ in macrostructure, ultrastructure, physiology, chemistry, and control of behavior" (Braun et al., 2002, p. 97). It is now accepted that functional lateralization is crucial for brain efficiency because it enhances neural capacity by allowing separate, parallel, and specialized processing in the two hemispheres (Vallortigara, 2006). Indeed in the most comprehensive review of the massive body of laterality research, McGilchrist (2009) concludes that the differences between the two hemispheres are profound, and that each expresses not only a distinct mode of functioning but also wholly different perspectives on the world. These updated ideas about brain asymmetry translate into clinical constructs of an analytical, rational left-lateralized conscious explicit self (a conscious mind), and a holistic, emotional right-lateralized unconscious implicit self (an unconscious mind). Throughout, my purpose is to demonstrate that clinicians need to be aware of the advances in neuroscience, and that this knowledge can significantly enhance their understanding of not only their patients, but also their own subjectivity in facilitating therapeutic changes, especially in the patient's right-lateralized brain/mind/body.

INTERPERSONAL NEUROBIOLOGY OF ATTACHMENT: INTERACTIVE REGULATION AND THE MATURATION OF THE RIGHT BRAIN

As the reader will note, one of the fundamental themes of the ongoing paradigm shift and this book is attachment. Indeed, Magnavita and Anchin boldly assert, "the impact of attachment theory on conceptualizations of personality, psychopathology, psychological health, and psychotherapy over the past several decades has been nothing short of explosive." Overviewing current advances in the field, they conclude that attachment

> ... is a biologically hard-wired motivational system that from the moment of birth onward impels the human being to seek contact with others—and as such, the attachment system operates as the infrastructural foundation of all interpersonal relationships and the building block of larger relational constellations. The early attachment system is one of the building blocks of personality, as well as influential in the structuralization of the brain.

Underscoring its essential biopsychosocial functions, they further note that evolution has imprinted into the human being several behavioral systems designed to optimize survival and the individual's adaptation to life.

Over four volumes and numerous articles and chapters, I have utilized an interdisciplinary perspective to describe the developmental psychological, biological, and neurochemical processes that underlie the formation of an attachment bond of emotional communication between the infant and primary caregiver (Schore, 1994, 2003a, 2003b, 2012). Throughout my work, I have offered a large body of research and clinical data that underscores the centrality of this evolutionary mechanism for all later aspects of human development, especially adaptive social–emotional functions that are essential for survival. Building upon and expanding John Bowlby's (1969) pioneering work that integrated psychology, biology, and psychoanalysis, the biopsychosocial perspective of modern attachment theory (Schore & Schore, 2008) incorporates current advances in developmental and affective neuroscience to offer an overarching theoretical model of the relational, psychobiological origins of attachment dynamics. A major purpose of this interpersonal neurobiological theory is to generate both heuristic experimental research and clinically relevant models of human social–emotional development. I now offer a succinct summary of the model, first proposed in 1994, and subsequently expanded over the last two decades.

A central principle of modern attachment theory dictates that an essential evolutionary and developmental task of the first 2 years of human life is the co-creation of an attachment bond of emotional communication between the infant and the primary caregiver. Building upon prenatal communications between mother and fetus, in ensuing perinatal and postnatal periods, affective transactions are rapidly transmitted within the dyad using more and more complex nonverbal sensoriaffective communications. To facilitate this emotional communication, the mother must be psychobiologically attuned to the dynamic shifts in the infant's bodily based internal states of central and autonomic arousal. Although initially these communications are expressed in olfactory, gustatory, and tactile modalities, by the end of the second month, the dyad utilizes more integrated visual and auditory channels of communications in mutual gaze episodes.

The early developing attachment mechanism represents the primordial expression of what Magnavita and Anchin term "the relational matrix," which imparts a "ubiquitous influence of social-interpersonal processes at every level of human development, functioning, and change." In the first year of life, the sensitive primary caregiver perceives and appraises nonverbal expressions of the infant's more and more intense states of positive and negative affective arousal. Through these communications, the primary caregiver can then regulate the infant's postnatally developing central nervous system (CNS) and autonomic nervous systems (ANS). The attachment relationship thus mediates the dyadic regulation of bodily based emotional arousal. In this ongoing co-created dialogue, the "good enough" mother and her infant co-construct multiple cycles of both "affect synchrony" that upregulates positive affect (e.g., joy-elation, interest-excitement) and "rupture and repair" that downregulates negative affect (e.g., fear, sadness). These cycles of inter- and intrasubjective attunement/misattunement/re-attunement represent a preverbal psychobiological relational matrix that forms the core of the infant's emerging implicit corporeal self.

There is now an agreement that emotion is initially regulated by others, but over the course of infancy it increasingly becomes self-regulated as a result of neurophysiological development and actual lived experience. Such adaptive capacities are central to the emergence of self-regulation, the ability to flexibly regulate an expanding array of positive and negative psychobiological states in various dynamic relational contexts, thereby allowing for the assimilation of various adaptive emotional–motivational states into a coherent and integrated self-system. Optimal relational experiences that engender a secure attachment with the primary caregiver thus facilitate both types of self-regulation: interactive regulation of emotions accessed while subjectively engaged with other humans in interconnected contexts, and autoregulation of emotions activated while subjectively disengaged from other humans in autonomous contexts. This model is consonant with Mitchell's (1988) description of "self-regulatory" and "field regulatory" processes: "the mind operates with motivations concerning self-regulation as well as regulation of the interpersonal field" (p. 9). Developmental studies clearly show that both modes of self-regulation are generated in optimal attachment dynamics of interactive psychobiological regulation. Modern attachment theory defines emotional well-being as nonconscious yet efficient and resilient switching between these two modes (interconnectedness and autonomy), depending upon the relational context. Internal working models of attachment encode both of these modes of coping strategies of affect regulation. At the most fundamental level, modern attachment theory is a regulation theory.

Affectively charged relational attachment dynamics represent the biopsychosocial mechanism by which we are sociophysiologically connected to others to coregulate our internal homeostatic affective states. Attachment, the interactive regulation of emotion, thus represents the regulation of biological synchronicity between and within organisms (Bradshaw & Schore, 2007; Schore, 1994). At all points of the life span, this interactive psychobiological regulation supports the survival functions of the human implicit (unconscious) self-system (Schore, 2003a, 2003b). This principle is echoed in current developmental brain research, where Ovtscharoff and Braun (2001) report,

> The dyadic interaction between the newborn and the mother
> ... serves as a regulator of the developing individual's internal

homeostasis. The regulatory function of the newborn–mother interaction may be an essential promoter to ensure the normal development and maintenance of synaptic connections during the establishment of functional brain circuits. (p. 33)

In this manner, dyadic attachment regulatory transactions impact the development of psychic structure, that is, they generate brain development (Schore, 1994).

In a number of contributions, I have elucidated how the maturation of the emotion processing limbic–autonomic circuits of, specifically, the infant's developing right brain are influenced by implicit intersubjective affective transactions embedded in the attachment relationship with the primary caregiver (Schore, 1994, 2003a, 2011, 2012). Implicit processing underlies the quick and automatic handling of nonverbal affective cues in infancy, and it is "repetitive, automatic, provides quick categorization and decision-making, and operates outside the realm of focal attention and verbalized experience" (Lyons-Ruth, 1999, p. 576). The nonconscious joint processing of these attachment communications is the product of the operations of the infant's right brain interacting with the mother's right brain. Representations of attachment experiences are incorporated into right-lateralized implicit–procedural memory as an internal working model that encodes nonconscious strategies of affect regulation. The regulatory functions of mother–infant social–emotional interactions thereby imprint right brain circuits in critical periods of infancy (Ammaniti & Trentini, 2009; Cozolino, 2002; Henry, 1993; Schore, 1994, 2003a, 2012; Siegel, 1999).

Confirming this model, neuroscientists now document that the right hemisphere shows an earlier maturation than the left in prenatal and post-natal stages of human development (Gupta et al., 2005; Sun et al., 2005), that the strong and consistent predominance for the right hemisphere emerges postnatally (Allman, Watson, Tetreault, & Hakeem, 2005, p. 367), and that the mother's right hemisphere is more involved than the left in emotional processing and mothering (Lenzi et al., 2009). Studying structural connectivity asymmetry in the perinatal brain with newborn infants at the beginning of the first year, Meaney and his colleagues conclude,

[I]n early life the right cerebral hemisphere could be better able to process ... emotion (Schore, 2000; Wada and Davis, 1977). This idea appears consistent with our findings of rightward asymmetry in ... limbic structures ... These neural substrates function as hubs in the right hemisphere for emotion processes and mother and child interaction. (Ratnarajah et al., 2013, p. 193)

Tronick's recent research on infants in the middle of the first year reports 6-month-old infants use left-sided gestures generated by the right hemisphere to cope with the stressful face-to-face–still-face paradigm. They interpret these data as being "consistent with Schore's (2005) hypotheses of hemispheric right-sided activation of emotions and their regulation during infant–mother interactions" (Montirosso, Cozzi, Tronick, & Borgatti, 2012, p. 826). Using near-infrared spectroscopy to study infant–mother attachment at the end of the first year, Minagawa-Kawai et al. (2009) observed, "Our results are in agreement with those of Schore (1999, 2000) who addressed the importance of the right hemisphere in the attachment system" (p. 289).

Implicit attachment transactions thus shape the experience-dependent maturation of right (and not left) cortical–subcortical systems, and in this manner they impact later personality development and functions. Magnavita and Anchin emphasize that the "processes associated with the self and those associated with being in relationship with others is always implicit." The implicit (unconscious) self-system of the right brain that evolves in preverbal stages of development thus represents the biological substrate of Freud's dynamic unconscious (Schore, 2002a). A growing body of studies report that unconscious processing of emotional information is mainly subsumed by a right hemisphere subcortical route (Gainotti, 2012), that unconscious emotional memories are stored in the right hemisphere (Gainotti 2006), and that this hemisphere is centrally involved in maintaining a coherent, continuous, and unified sense of self (Devinsky, 2000; McGilchrist, 2009). From infancy throughout all later stages of the lifespan, this right-lateralized system's rapidly acting emotional processes are centrally involved in the control of vital functions supporting survival, in enabling the organism to cope with stresses and challenges, and thus in emotional resilience and well-being. Indeed, a body of research now indicates that right- (and not left-) lateralized prefrontal systems are responsible for the highest-level regulation of affect and stress in the brain (Cerqueira, Almeida, & Sousa, 2008; Perez-Cruz et al., 2009; Schore, 1994; Stevenson, Halliday, Marsden, & Mason, 2008; Sullivan & Gratton, 2002; Wang et al., 2005).

Right Brain Attachment Communications Within the Therapeutic Alliance

It is important to note that early social–emotional experiences may be either predominantly regulated or dysregulated, imprinting secure or insecure attachments, respectively. Developmental neuroscience now clearly demonstrates that all children are not "resilient," but "malleable," for better or worse (Leckman & March, 2011). In marked contrast to an optimal attachment scenario, in a relational growth-inhibiting early environment of abuse and/or neglect, the primary caregiver of an insecure disorganized–disoriented infant induces traumatic states of enduring negative affect in the child (Schore, 2001a, 2002b). This caregiver is too frequently emotionally inaccessible and reacts to her infant's expressions of stressful affects inconsistently and inappropriately (massive intrusiveness and/or massive disengagement), and therefore shows minimal or unpredictable participation in the various types of arousal regulating processes. Instead of modulating, she induces extreme levels of stressful stimulation and arousal, very high in abuse and/or very low in neglect. Because she provides little interactive repair, the infant's intense negative affective states last for long periods of time.

Watt (2003) observes, "If children grow up with dominant experiences of separation, distress, fear and rage, then they will go down a bad pathogenic developmental pathway, and it's not just a bad psychological pathway but a bad neurological pathway" (p. 109). More specifically, during early critical periods, frequent dysregulated and unrepaired organized and disorganized insecure attachment histories are "affectively burnt in" the infant's early developing right brain (Schore, 1994, 2003a, 2009b). Less than optimal early relational experiences, including the "relational trauma" of abuse and neglect (Schore, 2001a), are imprinted into right cortical–subcortical systems, and these insecure internal working models are nonconsciously accessed at later points of interpersonal emotional stress. Affect regulation theory suggests that these right-lateralized insecure working models are a central focus of the affectively focused treatment of early forming self-pathologies and personality disorders. Such right brain relational deficits are described by Feinberg and Keenan (2005):

> The right hemisphere, particularly the right frontal region, under normal circumstances plays a crucial role in establishing the appropriate relationship between the self and the world ... dysfunction results in a two-way disturbance of personal relatedness between the self and the environment that can lead to disorders of both under and over relatedness between the self and the world. (p. 15)

All forms of therapy currently view affect dysregulation and associated relational deficits as fundamental elements of every psychiatric disorder, including personality disorders, and therefore share a common goal of improving the effectiveness of emotional self-regulatory processes (Schore, 2001b, 2009c, 2102).

Bowlby (1988), a psychoanalyst, asserted that the reassessment of nonconscious internal working models of attachment is a primary goal of any psychotherapeutic encounter. These interactive representations of early attachment experiences encode strategies of affect regulation, coping mechanisms for maintaining basic regulation and positive affect in the face of stressful challenges from the social environment. Acting at levels beneath conscious awareness, this internal working model is accessed to appraise, interpret, and regulate social–emotional information and guide action in familiar and especially novel relational interpersonal environments. Following Bowlby's interdisciplinary perspective, my work indicates that the patient's unconscious internal working model of attachment, whether secure or insecure, is reactivated in right-lateralized implicit–procedural memory and reenacted in the psychotherapeutic relationship.

The implicit attachment mechanism is a relational affect communicating and regulating system of the right hemisphere, which I have suggested is the biological substrate of the human unconscious. Neuroscientists now contend that "the left side is involved with conscious response and the right with the unconscious mind" (Mlot, 1998, p. 1006), and that the right hemisphere processes unconscious emotional material, while the left is involved in the conscious processing of emotional stimuli (Wexler, Warrenburg, Schwartz, & Janer, 1992). In my own work, in the discipline of neuropsychoanalysis, I have described the structural and functional properties of a "relational unconscious," whereby "one unconscious mind communicates with another unconscious mind" (Schore, 2003a, p. xvi). This interpersonal neurobiological mechanism, a primary vector of what Magnavita and Anchin term "the relational matrix," mediates right-brain-to-right-brain communications across an intersubjective field embedded within the therapeutic alliance (Schore, 1994, 2002a, 2012). Thus, in contributions on the central role of attachment dynamics in psychotherapy, I have focused not on the verbal narratives expressed between the left brain conscious minds of the patient and the therapist, but on the moment-to-moment nonverbal dialogues between the right-brain unconscious minds of both members of the therapeutic dyad. Affectively focused, relationally oriented therapeutic contexts that activate right-brain intersubjective communications attempt to explore and alter inefficient nonconscious insecure internal working models of the self and the world.

In light of the commonality of implicit intersubjective right-brain-to-right-brain emotion communicating and regulating mechanisms in the caregiver–infant relationship and the therapist–patient relationship, developmental attachment studies have direct relevance to the treatment process. Across the life span, the right hemisphere is dominant for non-verbal communication (Benowitz et al., 1983) and subjective emotional experiences (Wittling & Roschmann, 1993), and so the implicit, unconscious communication of affective states between the right brains of the members of the patient–therapist dyad is best described as "intersubjectivity." Decety and Chaminade's (2003) characterization of higher functions of the right brain is directly applicable to the psychotherapy of disorders of the self: "Mental states that are in essence private to the self may be shared between individuals ... self-awareness, empathy, identification with others, and more generally intersubjective processes, (and) are largely dependent upon … right hemisphere resources, which are the first to develop" (p. 591).

In "heightened affective moments" within a psychotherapy session, the attachment bond at the psychobiological core of the therapeutic alliance acts as a communication channel for the patient's right brain "relational unconscious." In optimal therapeutic contexts, this right-lateralized system that unconsciously processes social and emotional information is activated on both sides of the therapeutic alliance. These implicit clinical dialogues convey much more essential organismic information than left brain explicit, verbal information. Rather, right-brain interactions beneath the words nonverbally communicate critical nonconscious bodily based affective relational information about the inner world of the patient (and therapist). Decety and Chaminade's assertion that "mental states that are in essence private to the self may be shared between individuals" clearly describes the intimate context of psychotherapy.

This model applies to all patients, but especially those with early attachment disorders. The operational principle in this work is, just as the left brain communicates its states to other left brains via conscious linguistic behaviors, so the right nonverbally communicates its unconscious states to other right brains *that are tuned to receive these communications.* In his recent book on psychotherapy with developmental trauma, Philip Bromberg (2011) concludes,

> Allan Schore (2003a) writes about a right brain-to-right brain channel of affective communication—a channel that he sees as "an organized dialogue" comprised of "dynamically fluctuating moment-to-moment state-sharing" (p. 96). I believe it to be this process of state-sharing that … allows … "a good psychoanalytic match." (p. 169)

Writing on working with borderline patients who present with a history of attachment trauma and right-brain deficits (Meares, Schore, & Melkonian, 2011), Russell Meares (2012) suggests, "an important component of this approach is a form of therapeutic conversation that can be conceived … as a dynamic interplay between two right hemispheres."

Psychobiologically attuned communications of the right-lateralized "emotional brain" of the patient and the empathic therapist allow for rapid moment-to-moment, right-brain-to-right-brain "state sharing," an organized, co-created, dynamically changing dialogue of mutual influence. As in early development, in this intersubjective matrix, both partners simultaneously adjust their patterns of social attention, stimulation, and accelerating/decelerating arousal in response to the partner's signals, thereby matching the dynamic contours of different emotional–motivational self-states. According to Bromberg (2011),

> Self-states are highly individualized modules of being, each configured by its own organization of cognitions, beliefs, dominant affect and mood, access to memory, skills, behaviors, values, actions, and regulatory physiology. (p. 73)

I suggest that, with clinical experience, psychotherapists of all schools become experts in these relational intersubjective processes, and that this increased "implicit relational knowledge" (Stern et al., 1998) enhances therapeutic effectiveness (for recent clinical examples of right-brain-to-right-brain tracking see Bromberg, 2011; Gantt & Badenoch, 2013; Kalsched, 2013; Marks-Tarlow, 2012; Meares, 2012; Montgomery, 2013; Schore, 2012).

Affect regulation theory offers a deeper understanding of the mutual psychobiological processes that underlie any clinical encounter, whatever the verbal content. It is now accepted that the "nonverbal, pre-rational stream of expression that binds the infant to its parent continues throughout life to be a primary medium of intuitively felt affective-relational communication between persons" (Orlinsky & Howard, 1986, p. 343). Lyons-Ruth (2000) characterizes the affective exchanges that communicate early implicit relational knowledge within the therapeutic alliance. She observes that most relational transactions rely on a substrate of affective cues that give an evaluative valence or direction to each relational communication. These occur at an implicit level of bidirectional cueing and response that occurs much too fast for verbal processes and conscious reflection. Neuroscience now characterizes the fundamental role of the right brain in these rapid nonverbal face-to-face affective communications. At all stages of the life span, "The neural substrates of the perception of voices, faces, gestures, smells and pheromones, as evidenced by modern neuroimaging techniques, are characterized by a general pattern of right-hemispheric functional asymmetry" (Brancucci, Lucci, Mazzatenta, & Tommasi, 2009, p. 895).

In forthcoming chapters, Magnavita and Anchin assert that "the clinician needs to serve in a pattern recognition function, achieved through continually identifying and bringing the patient's attention to these patterns, as well to the limitations they impose and the costs they exact." They cite Millon (2000), who states, "Our task as therapists is not to see how we can blend intrinsically discordant models of therapeutic technique, but to match the pattern of features that characterize each patient, and then to select treatment goals and tactics that mirror this pattern optimally." Neuroscience demonstrates that the clinician's right and not left brain is involved in this critical therapeutic function. Van Lancker Sidtis (2006) concludes, "Pattern recognition and comprehension of several types of stimuli, such as faces, chords, complex pitch, graphic images, and voices, has been described as superior in the normal right hemisphere" (p. 223).

In the clinical literature, Scaer (2005) describes essential implicit communication patterns embedded within the therapist–patient relationship:

> Many features of social interaction are nonverbal, consisting of subtle variations of facial expression that set the tone for the content of the interaction. Body postures and movement patterns of the therapist ... also may reflect emotions such as disapproval, support, humor, and fear. Tone and volume of voice, patterns and speed of verbal communication, and eye contact also contain elements of subliminal communication and contribute to the unconscious establishment of a safe, healing environment. (pp. 167–168)

These implicit nonconscious right brain/mind/body nonverbal communications are bidirectional and thereby intersubjective. On the other side of the therapeutic alliance, Meares (2005) observes,

> Not only is the therapist being unconsciously influenced by a series of slight and, in some cases, subliminal signals, but also is the patient. Details of the therapist's posture, gaze, tone of voice, and even respiration are recorded and processed. A sophisticated therapist may use this processing in a beneficial way, potentiating a change in the patient's state without, or in addition to, the use of words. (p. 124)

This bidirectional mechanism underlies Casement's (1985) proposal,

> It is usual for therapists to see themselves as trying to understand the unconscious of the patient. What is not always acknowledged is that the patient also reads the unconscious of the therapist, knowingly or unknowingly. (p. 3)

These right-brain-to-right-brain communications, more so than conscious verbalizations, reveal the personality of the therapist as well as the client (see Schore, 2003b, for a right-hemisphere-to-right-hemisphere model of projective identification, a fundamental process of deep implicit communication between the relational unconscious systems of patient and therapist).

Affect regulation theory emphasizes the clinician's shift from constricted left hemispheric attention that focuses on local detail to more widely expanded right hemispheric attention that focuses on global detail (Derryberry & Tucker, 1994), a characterization that fits with Freud's "evenly suspended attention." In any session, the empathic therapist is consciously, explicitly attending to the patient's verbalizations to objectively diagnose and rationalize the patient's dysregulating symptomatology. However, the therapist is also listening and interacting at another level, an experience-near subjective level, one that implicitly processes moment-to-moment attachment communications and socioemotional information at levels beneath awareness. An essential relational element of any treatment encounter is how we work with what is being communicated, but not symbolized with words. How we understand and relate to an unexpressed unconscious emotion depends on our capacity to receive and express nonverbal communications.

In discussing "presymbolic" processing, Bucci (2002) observes, "We recognize changes in emotional states of others based on perception of subtle shifts in their facial expression or posture, and recognize changes in our own states based on somatic or kinesthetic experience" (p. 194). These bodily based implicit communications are expressed within the therapeutic alliance between the patient's and therapist's right brain/ mind/body systems. McGilchrist (2009, p. 437) observes, "The right hemisphere, is ... more closely in touch with emotion and the body (therefore with the neurologically 'inferior' and more ancient regions of the central nervous system)..." (p. 437). Dorpat (2001) describes reciprocal "primary process communication," and suggests that, "The primary process system analyzes, regulates, and communicates an individual's relations with the environment" (p. 449). Furthermore, Dorpat concludes, "Affective and object-relational information is transmitted predominantly by primary process communication. Nonverbal communication includes body movements (kinesics), posture, gesture, facial expression, voice inflection, and the sequence, rhythm, and pitch of the spoken words" (p. 451).

Writing on therapeutic "nonverbal implicit communications" Chused (2007) asserts, "It is not that the information they contain cannot be verbalized, only that sometimes only a nonverbal approach can deliver the information in a way it can be used, particularly when there is no conscious awareness of the underlying concerns involved" (p. 879). These ideas are echoed by Hutterer and Liss (2006), who state that nonverbal variables such as tone, tempo, rhythm, timbre, prosody, and amplitude of speech, as well as body language signals, may need to be reexamined as essential aspects of therapeutic technique. It is now well established that the right hemisphere is dominant for nonverbal (Benowitz et al., 1983) and emotional communication (Blonder, Bowers, & Heilman, 1991), as well as emotional prosody (George et al., 1996). The right hemisphere is thus important in the processing of the "music" behind the patient's words.

It has long been assumed in the psychotherapeutic literature that all forms of language reflect left hemispheric functioning. Current neuroscience now indicates that this is incorrect. Indeed, in a recent review, Ross and Monnot (2008) conclude, "Thus, the traditional concept that language is a dominant and lateralized function of the left hemisphere is no longer tenable" (p. 51). They report,

> Over the last three decades, there has been growing realization that the right hemisphere is essential for language and communication competency and psychological well-being through its ability to modulate affective prosody and gestural behavior, decode connotative (non-standard) word meanings, make thematic inferences, and process metaphor, complex linguistic relationships, and non-literal (idiomatic) types of expressions. (p. 51)

Neurobiological data suggest, "While the left hemisphere mediates most linguistic behaviors, the right hemisphere is important for broader aspects of communication" (van Lancker & Cummings, 1999, p. 95). Intersubjective, relational affect-focused psychotherapy is not the left brain "talking cure," but the right brain "communicating cure."

In this intersubjective dialogue, the psychobiologically attuned intuitive clinician tracks the nonverbal moment-to-moment rhythmic structures of the patient's internal states from the first point of contact, and is flexibly and fluidly modifying his/her own behavior to synchronize with that structure. This, in turn, co-creates with the patient a growth-facilitating context for the establishment of an attachment bond of emotional communication and the dyadic organization of the therapeutic alliance. The attachment connection between them is thus established and deepened over time, allowing for the reexpression of unconscious socioemotional experiences that resonate with the original infant–mother attachment history. Over the ensuing stages of the treatment, the sensitive, empathic clinician's monitoring of unconscious psychobiological process, rather than conscious verbal content, calls for right brain attention to match the patient's implicit affective-arousal states. The empathic intuitive therapist also resonates with the client's simultaneous implicit expressions of engagement and disengagement within the co-constructed intersubjective field (for interpersonal neurobiological discussions of right-brain clinical intuition, see Marks-Tarlow, 2012; Schore, 2012). These neurobiological mechanisms directly relate to Magnavita and Anchin's description of Beutler and Clarkin's (1990) clinical work: "An effective therapist intuitively is able to respond to the unique characteristics and needs of the patients, and in this process to apply a variety of interventions that encourage movement and enhance the persuasive power of the interpersonal experience of psychotherapy" (p. 265).

Transference–Countertransference and Right-Brain-to-Right-Brain Mechanisms of Therapeutic Change

Affect regulation theory's right-brain perspective of the treatment process allows for a deeper understanding of the critical intersubjective factors that operate at implicit levels of the therapeutic alliance, beneath the exchanges of language and explicit cognitions. An essential therapeutic context for this nonconscious mechanism is the transference–countertransference relationship. There is now a growing consensus that despite the existence of a number of distinct theoretical perspectives in clinical work, the concepts of transference and countertransference represent a common ground. Magnavita and Anchin describe the fundamental process of transference, originated in psychodynamic theories but now accepted in all schools of psychotherapy. They state,

> In this process, the patient unconsciously transfers onto the therapist certain schemas of self and others, including embedded expectancies, emotions, and motivations, that have been developed on the basis of relational experiences with previous significant others and overtly plays these out through in-session enactment of his or her intimately related maladaptive interpersonal patterns.

The neuropsychoanalytic perspective of affect regulation theory describes the central role of implicit right-brain-to-right-brain nonverbal communications (facial expression, prosody-tone of voice, gesture), in unconscious transference–countertransference affective transactions, which revive earlier attachment memories, especially of intensely dysregulated traumatic affects. Gainotti (2006) observes, "the right hemisphere may be crucially involved in those emotional memories which must be reactivated and reworked during the ... treatment" (p. 167). In discussing the role of the right hemisphere as "the seat of implicit memory," Mancia (2006) notes: "The discovery of the implicit memory has extended the concept of the unconscious and supports the hypothesis that this is where the emotional and affective—sometimes traumatic— presymbolic and preverbal experiences of the primary mother–infant relations are stored" (p. 83). These implicit procedural memories are expressed in "heightened affective moments" as transferential right-brain-to-right-brain nonverbal communications of fast-acting, automatic, regulated, and especially dysregulated bodily based stressful emotional states. Transference has been described as "an expression of the patient's implicit perceptions and implicit memories" (Bornstein, 1999, p. 170).

Recent psychoanalytic models of transference now contend that "no appreciation of transference can do without emotion" (Pincus, Freeman, & Modell, 2007, p. 634), and that "transference is distinctive in that it depends on early patterns of emotional attachment with caregivers" (p. 636). Clinical theoreticians describe transference as "an established pattern of relating and emotional responding that is cued by something in the present, but oftentimes calls up both an affective state and thoughts that may have more to do with past experience than present ones" (Maroda, 2005, p. 134). This conception is echoed in descriptions of right-brain functions in neuroscience, about which Shuren and Grafman (2002) assert:

> The right hemisphere holds representations of the emotional states associated with events experienced by the individual. When that individual encounters a familiar scenario, representations of past emotional experiences are retrieved by the right hemisphere and are incorporated into the reasoning process. (p. 918)

Other researchers report that the right hemisphere is fundamentally involved in the unconscious processing of emotional stimuli (Mlot, 1998) and in autobiographical memory (Markowitsch et al., 2000).

In classical writings, Racker (1968) proposed, "Every transference situation provokes a countertransference situation." Translating this into modern neuropsychoanalytic terms, transference–countertransference transactions are expressions of nonconscious, bidirectional, affectively charged right brain–mind–body nonverbal communications between patient and therapist. These reciprocal psychoneurobiological exchanges reflect activities of both the CNS and the ANS. Behaviorally, the patient's transferential communications are expressed in spontaneous nonverbal, visual, and auditory affective cues that are rapidly expressed from the face and voice of the patient. Countertransference is similarly defined in nonverbal implicit terms as the therapist's "autonomic responses that are reactions on an unconscious level to nonverbal messages" (Jacobs, 1994, p. 749). In my first book I stated,

> Countertransferential processes are currently understood to manifest in the capacity to recognize and utilize the sensory (visual, auditory, tactile, kinesthetic, and olfactory) and affective qualities of imagery which the patient generates in the psychotherapist ... countertransference dynamics are appraised by the therapist's observations of his own visceral reactions to the patient's material. (Schore, 1994, p. 451).

Consonant with this conception, Magnavita and Anchin cite Gelso and Hayes' (2007) definition of countertransference: "the therapist's internal and external reactions that are shaped by the therapist's past or present emotional conflicts and vulnerabilities" (p. 130).

As she monitors her somatic countertransferential responses, the empathic clinician's psychobiologically attuned right-brain tracks, at a preconscious level, not only the patterns of arousal rhythms and flows of the patient's dysregulated affective states, but also her own stressful somatic countertransferential, interoceptive, bodily based affective responses to the patient's implicit right brain facial, prosodic, and gestural transferential communications. Updated models of psychotherapy describe the clinical importance of "making conscious the organizing patterns of affect" (Mohaupt, Holgersen, Binder, & Nielsen, 2006). Once again, neuroscience reveals the psychoneurobiological mechanisms that underlie psychotherapy. Recall, "transference is distinctive in that it depends on early patterns of emotional attachment with caregivers" (Pincus et al., 2007). Neuroscientists now assert, "Simply stated, the left hemisphere specializes in analyzing sequences, while the right hemisphere gives evidence of superiority in processing patterns" (Van Lancker & Cummings, 1999, p. 95).

Through these right brain mechanisms, the intuitive psychobiologically attuned therapist, on a moment-to-moment basis, nonconsciously focuses her right brain countertransferential broad attentional processes (Derryberry & Tucker, 1994) upon patterns of rhythmic crescendos/decrescendos of the patient's regulated and dysregulated states of affective autonomic arousal. Freud's (1915) dictum, "It is a very remarkable thing that the *Ucs* of one human being can react upon that of another, without passing through the Cs" (p. 194, italics added) is thus neuropsychoanalytically understood as a right brain-to-right brain communication from one relational unconscious to another. In this manner, "The right hemisphere, in fact, truly interprets the mental state not only of its own brain, but the brains (and minds) of others" (Keenan et al., 2005, p. 702).

Right brain-to-right brain transferential–countertransferentail communications, especially of unconscious negative emotion (Sato & Aoki, 2006) and dissociated affects (Schore, 2012), accompany reexpressions of relational attachment trauma in enactments. Magnavita and Anchin cite Brown and Lane's (2000) clinical description of enactment, which acts both as a defense against unbearable feeling and an attempt to communicate one's untold story:

> Unable to communicate through language, the traumatized, severely disturbed patient may draw the therapist into situations that symbolize his or her traumatic experience. The interaction mirrors the patient's past and may evoke the patient's

disowned, dissociated feelings and conflicts in the therapist, inducing the therapist to respond in ways that feel alien (pp. 71–72).

According to Borgogno and Vigna-Taglianti (2008),

> In patients whose psychic suffering originates in … preverbal trauma … transference occurs mostly at a more primitive level of expression that involves in an unconscious, way … not only the patient but also the analyst … These more archaic forms of the transference–countertransference issue—which frequently set aside verbal contents—take shape in the analytical setting through actual mutual enactments. (p. 314)

Ginot (2007, p. 317) notes, "Increasingly, enactments are understood as powerful manifestations of the intersubjective process and as inevitable expressions of complex, though largely unconscious, self-states and relational patterns" (see chapter 5 in Schore, 2012 for an extensive interpersonal neurobiological model of working within clinical enactments).

The intensely negative affects communicated in enactments were neither shared nor interactively regulated by the original attachment object in the historical context, but now the patient has the possibility of a reparative relational experience. In these potentially "corrective emotional experiences" (Alexander & French, 1946), intensely dysregulated bodily based conscious and especially unconscious negative affects are communicated within the intersubjective field co-constructed by two individuals, an energy-transmitting field that includes not just two minds, but also two bodies (Schore, 1994, 2003a, 2003b, 2012). At the psychobiological core of the co-constructed intersubjective field is the attachment bond of emotional communication and interactive regulation. Implicit intersubjective communications are interactively regulated and dysregulated psychobiological processes that mediate shared conscious and unconscious emotional states, not just "mental" states. Affect regulation theory thus describes how beneath the exchanges of language, the implicit affects of the client are not only communicated to but also regulated by implicit systems of the therapist.

This relational enactment mechanism represents an interaction between the patient's emotional vulnerability and the clinician's emotional availability (the ability to "take" the transference). It is most fully operational during ruptures of the therapeutic alliance, described by Aspland et al. (2008) as "points of emotional disconnections between client and therapist that create a negative shift in the quality of the alliance" (p. 699), that act as "episodes of covert or overt behavior that trap both participants in negative complementary interactions" (p. 700). Although such ruptures of the alliance are the most stressful moments of the treatment, these "collisions" of the therapist's and patient's subjectivities allow not only for right brain communications but also for potentially interactive regulations of intensely dysregulated affective states.

The essential biological function of attachment communications in all human interactions, including those embedded in the psychobiological core of the therapeutic alliance, is the regulation of right brain/mind/body states. Aron (1998) observes,

> [P]atient and analyst mutually regulate each other's behaviors, enactments, and states of consciousness such that each gets under the other's skin, each reaches into the other's guts, each is breathed in and absorbed by the other ... the analyst must be attuned to the nonverbal, the affective ... to his or her bodily responses. (p. 26)

The importance of this intersubjective right brain/mind/body limbic-autonomic "deep contact" is stressed by Whitehead (2006):

> Every time we make therapeutic contact with our patients we are engaging profound processes that tap into essential life forces in our selves and in those we work with ... *Emotions are deepened in intensity and sustained in time when they are intersubjectively shared.* This occurs at moments of deep contact. (p. 624, italics added)

At moments of deep contact, intersubjective psychobiological resonance between the patient's relational unconscious and the clinician's relational unconscious produces an amplification of arousal and affect, and so unconscious affects are deepened in intensity and sustained in time. This dyadic increase of emotional intensity (energetic arousal) allows dissociated bodily based affects beneath levels of awareness to emerge into consciousness of both members of the therapeutic dyad (Schore, 2012).

In this manner, therapeutic "heightened affective moments" afford an opportunity for interactive regulation of dysregulated affects, including traumatic affects. Neuroscientists assert, "The ability to modulate emotions is at the heart of the human experience ... emotional self-regulatory processes constitutes the core of several modern psychotherapeutic approaches" (Beauregard, Levesque, & Bourgouin, 2001, p. RC165). Echoing this principle in the clinical literature, Ogden (2005) and her colleagues conclude,

> Interactive psychobiological regulation ... provides the relational context under which the client can safely contact, describe and eventually regulate inner experience ... It is the patient's experience of empowering action in the context of

safety provided by a background of the empathic clinician's psychobiologically attuned interactive affect regulation that helps effect ... change. (p. 22)

In a groundbreaking article in the clinical psychology literature, Greenberg (2007) describes a "self-control" form of emotion regulation involving higher levels of cognitive executive function that allows individuals "to change the way they feel by consciously changing the way they think" (p. 415). He proposes that this explicit form of affect regulation is performed by the verbal left hemisphere, and unconscious bodily based emotion is usually not addressed. This regulatory mechanism is at the core of verbal-analytic understanding and controlled reasoning and is heavily emphasized in models of cognitive behavioral therapy. In contrast to this conscious emotion regulation system, Greenberg describes a second, more fundamental implicit affect regulatory process performed by the right hemisphere. This system rapidly and automatically processes facial expression, vocal quality, and eye contact in a relational context. Therapy attempts not control but the "acceptance or facilitation of particular emotions," including "previously avoided emotion," to allow the patient to tolerate and transform them into "adaptive emotions." Citing my work, he asserts, "it is the building of implicit or automatic emotion regulation capacities that is important for enduring change, especially for highly fragile personality-disordered clients" (2007, p. 416).

In cases of early attachment failures and resultant self-pathologies, deep emotional contact, and implicit interactive affect regulation are central mechanisms of right-brain psychotherapy processes. Such work implies a profound commitment by both participants in the therapeutic dyad and a deep emotional involvement on the part of the therapist (Tutte, 2004). These types of cases, difficult as they may be, represent valuable learning experiences for the therapist, and they call for expert skills. In this challenging work, more so than cognitive understanding, relational factors lie at the core of the change mechanism; however, affect regulation theory's trans-theoretical clinical perspective that describes the basic interpersonal neurobiological mechanisms of therapeutic action applies to all patients, and all forms of psychotherapy.

Relevance of the Paradigm Shift in Brain Lateralization for a Unifying Biopsychosocial Model of Psychotherapy

In this last section of the Introduction, I want to offer some further thoughts about the contributions of interpersonal neurobiology to the central theme of this groundbreaking book, the emergence of a unifying paradigm of psychotherapy. In the chapters that follow, Magnavita and Anchin offer a wealth of interdisciplinary scientific and clinical data that support a biopsychosocial perspective of psychotherapy, a holistic framework for guiding psychotherapy unification. They cite Singer's (in press) observation that "the older therapeutic orientations of cognitive, behavioral, psychodynamic, humanistic, biological, and so on are breaking down and being replaced by a more integrated and less partisan vision of the person." Indeed, they put forth a compelling argument that a transtheoretical holistic framework can cohesively organize and interrelate our rapidly expanding knowledge about personality, psychological health, and pathology into more effective psychotherapeutic processes and methods. This, in turn, they say, is in line with the APA Task Force on Evidence-Based Practice (2006) conclusion that "clinical practice should be predicated on the best available research integrated with the clinician's expertise within the context of a particular patient" (Norcross, Hogan, & Koocher, 2008, p. xi).

I would strongly agree, but add that "the best available research" must include the rapid, if not spectacular advances of knowledge in neuroscience, and that this needs to be incorporated into psychotherapy training programs. Current information from developmental and affective neuroscience on the unique structure–function relationships of the right-brain not only directly supports but also operationalizes the biopsychosocial model. In addition, neuroscience, especially interpersonal neurobiology, can expand the model and serve as a theoretical and experimental source of a more complex and efficient model of treatment. The explicit knowledge we gain from studying the rapidly expanding amount of clinically relevant interdisciplinary information from literally every scientific discipline is essential to our professional growth. However, to be optimally effective in treating the regulatory and interpersonal deficits of both Axis l psychiatric and Axis ll personality disorders, the expert clinician must access not only the patient's left lateralized conscious mind and explicit self, but also even more importantly the patient's right lateralized unconscious mind and implicit, bodily based self. Neuroscience now confirms that the right hemisphere is dominant for implicit learning (Hugdahl, 1995), and that the left hemisphere is involved with conscious response and the right with the unconscious mind (Mlot, 1998).

In an extraordinary feat of neurobiological scholarship on human brain asymmetry, Iain McGilchrist (2009) synthesizes hundreds of studies to argue that the right and left hemispheres create coherent, utterly different, and often incompatible versions of the world, with competing priorities and values. He concludes,

> If what one means by consciousness is the part of the mind that brings the world into focus, makes it explicit, allows it to be formulated in language, and is aware of its own awareness, it is reasonable to link the conscious mind to activity, almost all of which lies ultimately in the left hemisphere. (p. 188)

On the other hand,

> The right hemisphere, by contrast, yields a world of individual, changing, evolving, interconnected, implicit, incarnate, living beings within the context of the lived world, but in the nature of things never fully graspable, always imperfectly known— and to this world it exists in a relationship of care. (p. 174)

He then discusses the unique integrative functions of the right hemisphere:

> I believe that the relationship between the hemispheres is not equal, and that while both contribute to our knowledge of the world, which therefore needs to be synthesized, one hemisphere, the right hemisphere, has precedence, in that it underwrites the knowledge that the other comes to have, and is alone able to synthesize what *both* know into a usable whole. (p. 177)

Indeed, McGilchrist cites a large body of neurobiological, neuropsychological, neuroanatomical, and neurochemical evidence indicating that the right hemisphere is "holistic" and nonlinear; is sensitive to context and "the relational aspects of experience;" and is dominant for empathy, theory of mind, emotional receptivity and emotional expressivity, self-awareness, and sense of self.

In parallel writings and consonant with my own work on the unique functions of the right-lateralized implicit self, Keenan, Gallup, and Falk (2003) assert,

> By casting the right hemisphere in terms of self, we have a revolutionary way of thinking about the brain. A new model of the brain, therefore, must take into account the primary importance of the right hemisphere in establishing and maintaining our sense of awareness of ourselves and others. (p. 252)

It is undoubtedly true that both brain hemispheres contribute to effective therapeutic treatment, but in light of "the primacy of affect," the right brain, the "emotional brain," is dominant in all forms of psychotherapy. Over the course of treatment, in an array of emotionally charged clinical "heightened affective moments," the skilled therapist is flexibly accessing a storehouse of right brain implicit relational knowledge and a wide range of affective experiences gained over the course of his or her career. Affect regulation theory dictates that at the most essential level, the intersubjective work of psychotherapy is not defined by what the therapist says to or does for the patient (left brain explicit focus). Rather, the key mechanism is how to be with the patient, especially during affectively stressful moments when the patient's subjectivity is disintegrating in real time (right brain implicit focus).

In the forthcoming chapters, Magnavita and Anchin propose that "the aim of unified psychotherapeutics is to increase differentiation and integration of component parts." I suggest that this biopsychosocial principle most directly applies to the growth and integration of hierarchical cortical and subcortical systems of the right brain (see Schore, 2012). Over the course of long-term treatment, a more complex structure evolves, which in turn can process more complex right brain functions (intersubjectivity, empathy, affect tolerance, and stress regulation). Ultimately, effective psychotherapeutic treatment of early evolving self-pathologies (including personality disorders) can facilitate changes of both increased integration and differentiation within the right brain, the biological substrate of the human unconscious, including alterations of the nonconscious internal working model and more effective coping strategies of affect regulation. This interpersonal neurobiological mechanism allows optimal treatment to potentially transform "insecure" into "earned secure" attachments. Characterological changes in what used to be termed "psychic structure" that ensue from deeper work alter not only the conscious left mind but also the unconscious right mind. The growth-facilitating relational environment of effective psychotherapy can thus promote the experience-dependent *bio-psycho-social* maturation of the right hemisphere, which is more closely linked to the *physiological* changes in the body (Spence, Shapiro, & Zaidel, 1996), and is dominant for processing *self*-awareness (Keenan & Gorman, 2007), and *social* interaction than the left (Decety & Lamm, 2007; Semrud-Clikeman, Fine, & Zhu, 2011).

In the following pages of this remarkable volume, the authors describe the psychobiological change mechanism of psychotherapy,

> ... the therapist and patient are collaboratively reworking the patient's memories, and thus the intrapsychic and interpersonal levels of change are inseparably tied to changes at the substrative neurobiological levels in which affectively charged memories are stored and from which they emerge. (see, e.g., Cozolino, 2006; Schore, 2012)

Indeed, a body of studies now indicates that psychotherapy induces changes in the brain (see Schore, 2012). Glass (2008) summarizes these findings: "Recent research in brain imaging, molecular biology, and neurogenetics has shown that psychotherapy changes brain function and structure. Such studies have shown that psychotherapy effects regional cerebral blood flow, neurotransmitter metabolism, gene expression, and persistent modifications in synaptic plasticity" (p. 1589). He further refers to the problem of "variability" in how well psychotherapy is done, "which is determined by training, experience, and natural ability. *There is an art, as well as a science, of doing psychotherapy*" (p. 1589, italics added).

As this Introduction ends, it is my pleasure to now hand you over to the creative minds of Jeffrey Magnavita and Jack Anchin. You are in for a rich amalgam of updated biopsychosocially based clinical theory that integrates the biological, psychological, and cultural realms, overarching summaries of research across a number of sciences and clinical disciplines, wide-ranging reviews of individual, couples, group, and family psychotherapy, and ultimately, I think, an intellectually stimulating and compelling argument for a unifying paradigm for psychotherapy.

REFERENCES

Alexander, F., & French, T. M. (1946). *Psychoanalytic therapy: Principles and application.* New York: Ronald Press.

Allman, J. M., Watson, K. K., Tetreault, N. A., & Hakeem, A. Y. (2005). Intuition and autism: A possible role for Von Economo neurons. *Trends in Cognitive Sciences, 9,* 367–373.

Ammaniti, M., & Trentini, C. (2009). How new knowledge about parenting reveals the neurobiological implications of intersubjectivity: A conceptual synthesis of recent research. *Psychoanalytic Dialogues, 19,* 537–555.

Aron, L. (1998). The clinical body and the reflexive mind. In L. Aron & F. Sommer Anderson (Eds), *Relational perspectives on the body* (pp. 3–37). Hillsdale, NJ: The Analytic Press.

Aspland, H., Llewelyn, S., Hardy, G. E., Barkham, M., & Stiles, W. (2008). Alliance rupture resolution in cognitive-behavior therapy: A preliminary task analysis. *Psychotherapy Research, 18,* 699–710.

Beauregard, M., Levesque, J., & Bourgouin, P. (2001). Neural correlates of conscious self-regulation of emotion. *Journal of Neuroscience, 21,* R165.

Benowitz, L. I., Bear, D. M., Rosenthal, R., Mesulam, M.-M., Zaidel, E., & Sperry, R. W. (1983). Hemispheric specialization in nonverbal communication *Cortex, 19,* 5–11.

Beutler, L. E., & Clarkin, J. (1990). *Systematic treatment section: Toward targeted therapeutic interventions.* New York: Brunner/Mazel.

Blonder, L. X., Bowers, D., & Heilman, K. M. (1991). The role of the right hemisphere in emotional communication. *Brain, 114,* 1115–1127.

Borgogno, F., & Vigna-Taglianti, M. (2008). Role-reversal: A somewhat neglected mirror of heritages of the past. *American Journal of Psychoanalysis, 68,* 313–328.

Bornstein, R. F. (1999). Source amnesia, misattribution, and the power of unconscious perceptions and memories. *Psychoanalytic Psychology, 16,* 155–178.

Bowlby, J. (1969). *Attachment and loss. Vol. 1: Attachment.* New York: Basic Books.

Bowlby, J. (1988). *A secure base* (2nd ed). New York: Basic Books.

Bradshaw, G. A., & Schore, A. N. (2007). How elephants are opening doors: Developmental neuroethology, attachment and social context. *Ethology, 113,* 426–436.

Brancucci, A., Lucci, G., Mazzatenta, A., & Tommasi, L. (2009). Asymmetries of the human social brain in the visual, auditory and chemical modalities. *Philosophical Transactions of the Royal Society of London Biological Sciences, 364,* 895–914.

Braun, C. M. J., Boulanger, Y., Labelle, M., Khiat, A., Dumont, M., & Mailloux, C. (2002). Brain metabolic differences as a function of hemisphere, writing hand preference, and gender. *Laterality, 7,* 97–113.

Bromberg, P. M. (2011). *The shadow of the tsunami and the growth of the relational mind.* New York: Routledge.

Brown, J. A., & Lane, R. C. (2000). Enactment, classical and relational perspectives: Definition, conceptualization, usefulness, and role in therapeutic process. *Journal of Psychotherapy of Independent Practice, 1,* 71–87.

Bucci, W. (2002). The referential process, consciousness, and the sense of self. *Psychoanalytic Inquiry, 5,* 766–793.

Casement, P. (1985). *Learning from the patient.* New York: Guilford Press.

Cerqueira, J. J., Almeida, O. F. X., & Sousa, N. (2008). The stressed prefrontal cortex. Left? Right! *Brain, Behavior, and Immunity, 22,* 630–638.

Chused, J. F. (2007). Nonverbal communication in psychoanalysis: Commentary on Harrison and Tronick. *Journal of the American Psychoanalytic Association, 55,* 875–882.

Cozolino, L. (2002). *The neuroscience of psychotherapy.* New York: W. W. Norton.

Cozolino, L. (2006). *The neuroscience of human relationships: Attachment and the developing social brain.* New York: W. W. Norton.

Decety, J., & Chaminade, T. (2003). When the self represents the other: A new cognitive neuroscience view on psychological identification. *Consciousness and Cognition, 12,* 577–596.

Decety, J., & Lamm, C. (2007). The role of the right temporoparietal junction in social interaction: How low-level computational processes contribute to meta-cognition. *The Neuroscientist, 13,* 580–593.

Derryberry, D., & Tucker, D. M. (1994). Motivating the focus of attention. In P. M. Niedentahl & S. Kiyayama (Eds.), *The heart's eye: Emotional influences in perception and attention* (pp. 167–196). San Diego: Academic Press.

Devinsky, O. (2000). Right cerebral hemispheric dominance for a sense of corporeal and emotional self. *Epilepsy & Behavior, 1,* 60–73.

Dorpat, T. L. (2001). Primary process communication. *Psychoanalytic Inquiry, 3,* 448–463.

Engel, G. (1977). The need for a new model: A challenge for biomedicine. *Science, 196,* 129–136.

Engel, G. (1980). The clinical application of the biopsychosocial model. *American Journal of Psychiatry, 137,* 535–544.

Feinberg, T. E., & Keenan, J. P. (2005). Where in the brain is the self? *Consciousness and Cognition, 14,* 661–678.

Freud, S. (1915). *The unconscious* (Standard Edition, Vol. 14, pp. 159–205). London: Hogarth Press.

Gainotti, G. (2006). Unconscious emotional memories and the right hemisphere. In M. Mancia (Ed.), *Psychoanalysis and neuroscience* (pp. 151–173). Milan: Springer Milan.

Gainotti, G. (2012). Unconscious processing of emotions and the right hemisphere. *Neuropsychologia, 50,* 205–218.

Gantt, S. P., & Badenoch, B. (2013). *The interpersonal neurobiology of group psychotherapy and group process.* London: Karnac.

Gelso, C. J., & Hayes, J. A. (2007). *Countertransference and the therapist's inner experience. Perils and possibilities.* Mahwah, NJ: Lawrence Earlbaum.

George, M. S., Parekh, P. I., Rosinsky, N., Ketter, T. A., Kimbrell, T. A., Heilman, K. M., Herscovitch, P., & Post, R. M. (1996). Understanding emotional prosody activates right hemispheric regions. *Archives of Neurology, 53,* 665–670.

Ginot, E. (2007). Intersubjectivity and neuroscience: Understanding enactments and their therapeutic significance within emerging paradigms. The empathic power of enactments. The link between neuropsychological processes and an expanded definition of empathy. *Psychoanalytic Psychology, 24,* 31–332.

Glass, R. M. (2008). Psychodynamic psychotherapy and research evidence. Bambi survives Godzilla? *Journal of the American Medical Association, 300,* 1587–1589.

Greenberg, L. S. (2007). Emotion coming of age. *Clinical Psychology: Science and Practice, 14,* 414–421.

Gupta, R. K., Hasan, K. M., Trivedi, R., Pradhan, M., Das, V., Parikh, N. A., & Narayana, P. A. (2005). Diffusion tensor imaging of the developing human cerebrum. *Journal of Neuroscience Research, 81,* 172–178.

Henry, J. P. (1993). Psychological and physiological responses to stress: The right hemisphere and the hypothalamo-pituitary-adrenal axis, an inquiry into problems of human bonding. *Integrative Physiological and Behavioral Science, 28,* 369–387.

Hugdahl, K. (1995). Classical conditioning and implicit learning: The right hemisphere hypothesis. In R. J. Davidson & K. Hugdahl (Eds.), *Brain asymmetry.* Cambridge, MA: MIT Press.

Hutterer, J., & Liss, M. (2006). Cognitive development, memory, trauma, treatment: An integration of psychoanalytic and behavioural concepts in light of current neuroscience research. *Journal of the American Academy of Psychoanalysis and Dynamic Psychiatry, 34,* 287–302.

Jacobs, T. J. (1994). Nonverbal communications: Some reflections on their role in the psychoanalytic process and psychoanalytic education. *Journal of the American Psychoanalytic Association, 42,* 741–762.

Kalsched, D. (2013). *Trauma and the soul. A psycho-spiritual approach to human development and its interruption.* New York: Routledge.

Keenan, J. P., Gallup, G. G., & Falk, D. (2003). *The face in the mirror: The search for the origins of consciousness.* New York: Harper Collins.

Keenan, J. P., Rubio, J., Racioppi, C., Johnson, A., & Barnacz, A. (2005). The right hemisphere and the dark side of consciousness. *Cortex, 41,* 695–704.

Keenan, J. P., & Gorman, S. (2007). The causal role of the right hemisphere in self-awareness: It is the brain that is selective. *Cortex, 43,* 1074–1082.

Leckman, J. F., & March, J. S. (2011). Editorial: Developmental neuroscience comes of age. *Journal of Child Psychology and Psychiatry, 52,* 333–338.

Lenzi, D., Trentini, C., Pantano, P., Macaluso, E., Iacoboni, M., Lenzi, G. I., & Ammaniti, M. (2009). Neural basis of maternal communication and emotional expression processing during infant preverbal stage. *Cerebral Cortex, 19,* 1124–1133.

Lyons-Ruth, K. (1999). The two-person unconscious: Intersubjective dialogue, enactive relational representation, and the emergence of new forms of relational organization. *Psychoanalytic Inquiry, 19,* 576–617.

Lyons-Ruth, K. (2000). "I sense that you sense that I sense…": Sander's recognition process and the specificity of relational moves in the psychotherapeutic setting. *Infant Mental Health Journal, 21,* 85–98.

Mancia, M. (2006). Implicit memory and early unrepressed unconscious: Their role in the therapeutic process (How the neurosciences can contribute to psychoanalysis). *International Journal of Psychoanalysis, 87,* 83–103.

Markowitsch, H. J., Reinkemeier, A., Kessler, J., Koyuncu, A., & Heiss, W. D. (2000). Right amygdalar and temperofrontal activation during autobiographical, but not fictitious memory retrieval. *Behavioral Neurology, 12*, 181–190.

Marks-Tarlow, T. (2012). *Clinical intuition in psychotherapy: The neurobiology of embodied response.* New York: W.W. Norton.

Maroda, K. J. (2005). Show some emotion: Completing the cycle of affective communication. In L. Aron & A. Harris (Eds.), *Revolutionary connections. relational psychoanalysis. Vol. II. Innovation and expansion* (pp. 121–142). Hillsdale, NJ: Analytic Press.

McGilchrist, I. (2009). *The master and his emissary.* New Haven, CT: Yale University Press.

Meares, R. (2005). *The metaphor of play: Origin and breakdown of personal being* (3rd ed.). London: Routledge.

Meares, R., Schore, A. N., & Melkonian, D. (2011). Is borderline personality a particularly right hemispheric disorder? A study of P3A using single trial analysis. *Australian and New Zealand Journal of Psychiatry, 45*, 131–139.

Meares, R. (2012). *A dissociation model of borderline personality disorder.* New York: W.W. Norton.

Millon, T. (2000). Toward a new model of integrative psychotherapy: Psychosynergy. *Journal of Psychotherapy Integration, 10*, 37–53.

Minagawa-Kawai, Y., Matsuoka, S., Dan, I., Naoi, N., Nakamura, K., & Kojima, S. (2009). Prefrontal activation associated with social attachment: Facial-emotion recognition in mothers and infants. *Cerebral Cortex, 19*, 284–292.

Mitchell, S. A. (1988). *Relational concepts in psychoanalysis.* Cambridge, MA: Harvard University Press.

Mlot, C. (1998). Probing the biology of emotion. *Science, 280*, 1005–1007.

Mohaupt, H., Holgersen, H., Binder, P.-E., & Nielsen, G. H. (2006). Affect consciousness or mentalization? A comparison of two concepts with regard to affect development and affect regulation. *Scandinavian Journal of Psychology, 47*, 237–244.

Montgomery, A. (2013). *Neurobiology essentials for clinicians: What every therapist needs to know.* New York: W.W. Norton.

Montirosso, R., Cozzi, P., Tronick, E., & Borgatti, R. (2012). Differential distribution and lateralization of infant gestures and their relation to maternal gestures in the face-to-face still-face paradigm. *Infant Behavior and Development, 35*, 819–828.

Norcross, J. C., Hogan, T. P., & Koocher, G. P. (2008). *Clinician's guide to evidence based practice: Mental health and the addictions.* New York: Oxford University Press.

Ogden, P., Pain, C., Minton, K., & Fisher, J. (2005). Including the body in mainstream psychotherapy for traumatized individuals. *Psychologist-Psychoanalyst, 25*(4), 19–24.

Orlinsky, D. E., & Howard, K. I. (1986). Process and outcome in psychotherapy. In S. L. Garfield & A. E. Bergin (Eds.), *Handbook of psychotherapy and behavior change* (3rd ed.). New York: Wiley.

Ovtscharoff, W., & Braun, K. (2001). Maternal separation and social isolation modulate the postnatal development of synaptic composition in the infralimbic cortex of octodon degus. *Neuroscience, 104*, 33–40.

Perez-Cruz, C., Simon, M., Czeh, B., Flugge, G., & Fuchs, E. (2009). Hemispheric differences in basilar dendrites and spines of pyramidal neurons in the rat prelimbic cortex: Activity- and stress-induced changes. *European Journal of Neuroscience, 29*, 738–747.

Pincus, D., Freeman, W., & Modell, A. (2007). A neurobiological model of perception: Considerations for transference. *Psychoanalytic Psychology, 24,* 623–640.

Racker, H. (1968). *Transference and countertransference.* New York: International Universities Press.

Ratnarajah, N., Rifkin-Graboi, A., Fortier, M. V., Chong, Y. S., Kwek, K., Saw, S. M., Godfrey, K. M., Gluckman, P. D., Meaney, M. J., & Qiu, A. (2013). Structural connectivity asymmetry in the neonatal brain. *NeuroImage, 75,* 187–194.

Ross, E. D., & Monnot, M. (2008). Neurology of affective prosody and its functional-anatomic organization in right hemisphere. *Brain and Language, 104,* 51–74.

Sato, W., & Aoki, S. (2006). Right hemisphere dominance in processing unconscious emotion. *Brain and Cognition, 62,* 261–266.

Scaer, R. (2005). *The trauma spectrum: Hidden wounds and human resiliency.* New York: W. W. Norton.

Schore, A. N. (1994). *Affect regulation and the origin of the self.* Mahwah, NJ: Erlbaum.

Schore, A. N. (2000). Attachment and the regulation of the right brain. *Attachment and Human Development, 2,* 23–47.

Schore, A. N. (2001a). The effects of relational trauma on right brain development, affect regulation, and infant mental health. *Infant Mental Health Journal, 22,* 201–269.

Schore, A. N. (2001b). Minds in the making: Attachment, the self-organizing brain, and developmentally-oriented psychoanalytic psychotherapy. *British Journal of Psychotherapy, 17,* 299–328.

Schore, A. N. (2002a). The right brain as the neurobiological substratum of Freud's dynamic unconscious. In D. Scharff (Ed.), *The psychoanalytic century: Freud's legacy for the future* (pp. 61–88). New York: Other Press.

Schore, A. N. (2002b). Dysregulation of the right brain: A fundamental mechanism of traumatic attachment and the psychopathogenesis of posttraumatic stress disorder. *Australian and New Zealand Journal of Psychiatry, 36,* 9–30.

Schore, A. N. (2003a). *Affect dysregulation and disorders of the self.* New York: W.W. Norton.

Schore, A. N. (2003b). *Affect regulation and the repair of the self.* New York: W.W. Norton.

Schore, A. N. (2005). Back to basics: Attachment, affect regulation, and the developing right brain: Linking developmental neuroscience to pediatrics. *Pediatrics in Review: 26,* 204–217.

Schore, A. N. (2009a, August 8). The paradigm shift: The right brain and the relational unconscious. Invited plenary address to the American Psychological Association 2009 Convention, Toronto, Canada. Retrieved September 16, 2009, from http://www.allanschore.com/pdf/SchoreAPAPlenaryFinal09.pdf

Schore, A. N. (2009b). Relational trauma and the developing right brain. An interface of psychoanalytic self psychology and neuroscience. *Annals of the New York Academy of Sciences, 1159,* 189–203.

Schore, A. N. (2009c). Right brain affect regulation: An essential mechanism of development, trauma, dissociation, and psychotherapy. In D. Fosha D. Siegel & M. Solomon (Eds.), *The healing power of emotion: Affective neuroscience, development, & clinical practice* (pp. 112–144). New York: W.W. Norton.

Schore, A. N. (2011). The right brain implicit self lies at the core of psychoanalysis. *Psychoanalytic Dialogues, 21,* 75–100.

Schore, A. N. (2012). *The science of the art of psychotherapy.* New York: W.W. Norton.

Schore, J., & Schore, A. (2008). Modern attachment theory: The central role of affect regulation in development and treatment. *Clinical Social Work Journal, 36,* 9–20.

Semrud-Clikeman, M., Fine, J. G., & Zhu, D. C. (2011). The role of the right hemisphere for processing of social interactions in normal adults using functional magnetic resonance imaging. *Neuropsychobiology, 64,* 47–51.

Shuren, J. E., & Grafman, J. (2002). The neurology of reasoning. *Archives of Neurology, 59,* 916–919.

Siegel, D. J. (1999). *The developing mind: Toward a neurobiology of interpersonal experience.* New York: W. W. Norton.

Singer, J. A. (in press). Lost in translation? Finding the person in the emerging paradigm of clinical science: Introduction to a special issue on personality psychology and psychotherapy. *Journal of Personality.*

Spence, S., Shapiro, D., & Zaidel, E. (1996). The role of the right hemisphere in the physiological and cognitive components of emotional processing. *Psychophysiology, 33,* 112–122.

Stern, D. N., Bruschweiler-Stern, N., Harrison, A. M., Lyons-Ruth, K., Morgan, A. C., Nahum, J. P., Sander, L., & Tronick, E. Z. (1998). The process of therapeutic change involving implicit knowledge: Some implications of developmental observations for adult psychotherapy. *Infant Mental Health Journal, 19,* 300–308.

Stevenson, C. W., Halliday, D. M., Marsden, C. A., & Mason, R. (2008). Early life programming of hemispheric lateralization and synchronization in the adult medial prefrontal cortex. *Neuroscience, 155,* 852–863.

Sullivan, R. M., & Gratton, A. (2002). Prefrontal cortical regulation of hypothalamic-pituitary-adrenal function in the rat and implications for psychopathlogy: Side matters. *Psychoneuroendocrinology, 27,* 99–114.

Sun, T., Patoine, C., Abu-Khalil, A., Visader, J., Sum, E., Cherry, T. J., et al. (2005). Early asymmetry of gene transcription in embryonic human left and right cerebral cortex. *Science, 308,* 1794–1798.

Tutte, J. C. (2004). The concept of psychical trauma: A bridge in interdisciplinary space. *International Journal of Psychoanalysis, 85,* 897–921.

Vallortigara, G. (2006). The evolutionary psychology of left and right: Costs and benefits of lateralization. *Developmental Psychobiology, 48,* 418–427.

Van Lancker, D., & Cummings, J. L. (1999). Expletives: Neurolinguistic and neurobehavioral perspectives on swearing. *Brain Research Reviews, 31,* 83–104.

Van Lancker Sidtis, D. (2006). Where in the brain is nonliteral language? *Metaphor and Symbol, 21,* 213–244.

Wada, J. A., & Davis, A. E. (1977). Fundamental nature of human infant's brain asymmetry. *Canadian Journal of Neurological Science, 4,* 203–207.

Wang, J., Rao, H., Wetmore, G. S., Furlan, P. M., Korczkowski, M., Dinges, D. F., & Detre, J. A. (2005). Perfusion functional MRI reveals cerebral blood flow pattern under psychological stress. *Proceedings of the National Academy of Sciences of the United States of America, 92,* 17804–17809.

Watt, D. F. (2003). Psychotherapy in an age of neuroscience: Bridges to affective neuroscience. In J. Corrigal & H. Wilkinson (Eds.), *Revolutionary connections: Psychotherapy and neuroscience* (pp. 79–115). Karnac: London.

Wexler, B. E., Warrenburg, S., Schwartz, G. E., & Janer, L. D. (1992). EEG and EMG responses to emotion-evoking stimuli processed without conscious awareness. *Neuropsychologia, 30,* 1065–1079.

Whitehead, C. C. (2006). Neo-psychoanalysis: A paradigm for the 21st century. *Journal of the Academy of Psychoanalysis and Dynamic Psychiatry, 34,* 603–627.

Wittling, W., & Roschmann, R. (1993). Emotion-related hemisphere asymmetry: Subjective emotional responses to laterally presented films. *Cortex, 29,* 431–448.

Part 1

THEORY AND EVIDENCE FOR UNIFYING PSYCHOTHERAPY

Chapter 1

THE EMERGENCE OF A UNIFYING PARADIGM FOR PSYCHOTHERAPY

A new phase of *unified psychotherapy* is emerging from rapid advances being made in clinical science and related disciplines. Technological innovations, new trends in health care, globalization, the flowering of neuroscience, and the prominence of multiculturalism, along with rapidly accumulating scientific evidence from many other disciplines, are changing the field. Entwined with these expansive changes, different realms of scientific and clinical activity are fathoming the multilevel, multidomain complexities and intricacies of human development, mental health, disorder, and change. This exciting coalescence of developments reflects a more holistic perspective, moving beyond the single-domain perspectives that dominated 20th-century clinical science and psychotherapeutics. It offers the tantalizing suggestion that, before our very eyes, the field is undergoing a profound shift, evolving from the previous century's pre-paradigmatic efforts toward development of a singular, comprehensive paradigm containing the potentiality to advance and accelerate integration and synthesis of multiple and diverse realms of knowledge and study. This movement toward developing a unifying psychotherapeutic paradigm is at once ambitious and pragmatic, linked ultimately by the goal of heightening the effectiveness of efforts at promoting mental health and preventing, diagnosing, and treating psychological disorders (Clinical Sciences Enterprise Task Force, 2006). In this first chapter, we lay the groundwork for the remainder of the volume by presenting fundamental issues and perspectives informing our work. As will become evident, principles and methods presented in subsequent chapters build heavily on these foundations.

THE PRE-PARADIGMATIC STASIS IN PSYCHOLOGY AND PSYCHOTHERAPY

Historical prescience for the intriguing, unifying developments taking place in psychology and psychotherapy resides in no less a figure than William James, the father of American psychology. James had a keen interest in the ever-growing diversity of phenomena and "knowledge elements" (Staats, 1991) encompassed by the rapidly emerging discipline of psychology, reflected in his definition of the latter as "the Science of Mental Life, both of the phenomena and their conditions. The phenomena are such things as we call feelings, desires, cognitions, reasonings, decisions, and the like; and superficially considered, their variety and complexity is such as to leave a chaotic impression on the observer" (p. 1). James was also fascinated with the issue of making sense of the endlessly kaleidoscopic composition of human experience and being—not to subjugate this staggering diversity of phenomena (for James, endless plurality was inherent to the human condition) but rather to seek the unifying chord that enabled understanding of how this plurality could be organized into a singular whole containing coherent meaning. For James, the critical issue was how to hit the balance between "the one and the many" (1907/1992, p. 71).

Within the variegated discipline of psychology, this quandary has resonated across the decades since James's seminal writings about the tension between plurality and unification, for the relevance of this issue never ceases. As the discipline has progressed, it has conspicuously differentiated into different fields of study (Henriques, 2011; Marquis, 2012), with mixed consequences. On the one hand, this intradisciplinary diversity has been critically valuable to the ever-greater breadth and depth of knowledge accumulated about mind and behavior. On the other hand, there are those who view this ever-growing mass of knowledge elements as counterproductively partitioned into disparate realms of understanding, insufficiently organized and interrelated, and consequently costly to the discipline's advancement and maturation as a science (see, e.g., Henriques, 2011). For some, this fractionation poses a threat to the discipline's very existence (see, e.g., Bandura, 2001). Consequent calls for the unification of psychology (see, e.g., Chao, 2002; de Groot, 1989; Gilgen, 1987; Henriques, 2003, 2004, 2011; H. Kendler, 1987, 2002; Koch, 1981; Royce, 1987; Staats, 1987, 1991, 1999; Sternberg, 2004; Sternberg & Grigorenko, 2001; Viney, 1989; Wertheimer, 1988; Yanchar & Slife, 1997; Yela, 1987) offer an array of arguments counterposing contentions that the discipline's disparate composition is not only inescapable but in fact beneficial—and the debate continues apace.

This abiding tension between "the one and the many" is fractally mirrored in the primary concern of this volume, the multifaceted field of psychotherapy. Over the course of the field's brief but eventful over 100-year history, theoretical and technical diversity has been the rule. Beginning with the psychoanalytic and psychodynamic orientation and proceeding through the overlapping emergence of behavioral, humanistic, cognitive, systemic, biomedical, multicultural, and integrative approaches (Anchin, 2012; Magnavita, 2012; Melchert 2013), the field has spawned multiple schools of thought about how best to psychotherapeutically treat human pain and suffering. These orientations have also each given rise to numerous other branches, such that we now have more than 400 specific approaches to psychotherapy (Corsini & Wedding, 2008). The plurality afforded by this multiplicity of approaches is pragmatically and functionally invaluable, given patients' seemingly inevitable complexities as the psychotherapeutic process unfolds. Morever, plurality has enabled the scientific examination of psychotherapy's effectiveness from diverse perspectives and with a cadre of empirical methods. From this 60-some years of psychotherapy research in the modern era (Anchin, 2008b), irreproachable evidence has accrued demonstrating that *psychotherapy works*; a vast array of within- and between-school investigations of psychotherapy demonstrates that psychotherapy can indeed effectively ameliorate numerous forms of psychological pain and suffering (see, e.g., Wampold, 2001). This conclusion has most recently been formally recognized in the American Psychological Association's (2013) Resolution on the Recognition of Psychotherapy Effectiveness.

Ironically, however, the enormous plurality of psychotherapeutic concepts, strategies, and techniques has spawned double-edged consequences. In an incisive analysis highly in sync with the spirit of the present volume, Melchert (2013) observed the persistent conflict and confusion stemming from the continuing prominence of "the traditional theoretical orientations" (p. 11) serving as the conceptual foundations of practice and education in professional psychology. Among problems elaborated by Melchert (2013) is the fact that each of these orientations offers an incomplete explanation of personality, psychopathology, and behavior change; different theoretical approaches continue to proliferate, despite disagreement as to the most appropriate approach to understanding human psychology; no single approach has yet to achieve dominance, with the largest number of adherents to any single approach, including integrative, remaining in the minority; and disagreements persist regarding the most appropriate training model for professional psychology. "Theoretical and conceptual confusion" (Melchert, 2013, p. 13) in the field thus persists.

Melchert (2013) also identified four issues underlying this vexing state of affairs: philosophically, many orientations are rooted in widely varying and discrepant foundational assumptions about human nature; many psychological theories are constructed in a way that renders them scientifically nonfalsifiable—that is, nonamenable to refutation—and hence they are poor theories in a scientific sense; none of the traditional theoretical orientations can fully accommodate the tremendous complexity of human mind, behavior, functioning, and development and their multicausal character; and until recently, scientific tools for penetrating and understanding this complexity have been of limited power and precision, perhaps making development of an array of theoretical explanations inevitable.

Interlaced with these issues are additional problems associated with the diversity of theoretical orientations underpinning psychological practice. To no small extent, a tribal mentality continues to exist among adherents to different theoretical orientations, whose different esoteric language systems contribute significantly to fractionation continuing to plague the field (Magnavita, 2008). Moreover, the overlap and even outright redundancy of phenomena encompassed by the staggering diversity of terms, concepts, and techniques spawned by different theoretical orientations are considerable, yet consensual bodies of knowledge have yet to be developed. Consequently, needless terminological confusion reigns, which impedes the creation of bodies of knowledge "that would be accepted as recognized knowledge, and that would serve to draw separate empirical-theoretical endeavors together" (Staats, 1987, p. 41). Conceptual redundancy's drag on the field's advancement is further compounded by enduring schisms, for example, determinism versus agency, empiricism versus constructivism/hermeneutics, and nomothetic versus idiographic methodologies.

All of these factors contribute to the field's continued stasis in a pre-paradigmatic state (Kuhn, 1970). Thus, we agree with Melchert's (2013) assessment that, while there can be no denying that the field has shown "remarkable growth and many achievements" (p. 11), the pace of continued maturation and advancement, especially in today's environment of rapid, technology-driven knowledge expansion, is constrained by continued reliance on "outmoded theoretical frameworks for education, practice, and research" (p. 12).

Perhaps, then, it is not surprising that recent efforts to advance the field are increasingly focusing on issues that encompass but also go beyond specific traditional orientations. Intensified efforts to bridge the gap between research and practice (Teachman, Drabick, Hershenberg, Vivian, Wolfe, & Goldfried, 2012); growing recognition of the value of both quantitative and qualitative methodologies in clinical research (e.g., Anchin, 2008a, 2008b; Shahar, Anchin, Gottdeiner, Levy, & Mor, 2012);

heightening interest in pantheoretical constructs, factors, and measures (e.g., Carter et al., 2012; Levitt & Williams, 2010; Lukowitsky & Pincus, 2011; Pincus, 2010; Spinhoven, Geisen-Bloo, van Dyck, Kooiman, & Arntz, 2007); and calls for a common language system (e.g., Norcross, 2005) all exemplify the growing shift toward identifying and addressing trans-theoretical issues as pivot points for propelling forward movement. In our view, identifying and grappling with these issues are vitals steps on the path to elevating psychotherapy's effectiveness and efficiency, but, like the traditional orientations, they too are at risk of becoming disparate areas of development, each yielding valuable insights and understandings that nevertheless remain segmented.

In appraising this state of affairs, we have come to believe, in agreement with a growing chorus of clinical scientists and practitioners (Henriques, 2011; Henriques & Stout, 2012; Mahoney, 2003; Mayer, 2004; Melchert, 2011, 2013; Marquis, in press; Constantino, Boswell, Barnecke, & Castonguay, in press; Millon & Grossman, 2012; Schore, 2012; Singer, 2005; Wolfe, 2008), that the field's progress can be accelerated through incorporating a *holistic* framework that can cohesively organize and interrelate our ever-accumulating multisource knowledge about personality, psychological health and pathology, and effective psychotherapeutic processes and methods. A holistic framework also provides a bridge that can help *connect* contemporary transtheoretical endeavors (see Tschacher, Junghan, & Pfammatter, in press). Indeed, since the latter are all focused on one facet or another of the complexity of phenomena that collectively compose the science and practice of psychotherapy, would the field not benefit from a way to cohesively interconnect the bodies of knowledge and understanding generated by these various debates?

A HOLISTIC PERSPECTIVE

Holism is a position within philosophy of science, a branch of philosophical inquiry that broadly deals with "the most fundamental assumptions and first principles of thought" (Miller, 1992, p. 6) that underlie scientific theories, research methodologies, and specific procedures for applying that knowledge in ways intended to be salutary. R. Elliott (2008) vividly conveyed the fundamentality of such assumptions in the science and practice of psychotherapy:

> underlying assumptions or implicit philosophies ... drive the whole therapeutic and research enterprise, with the force of unconscious moral imperatives. In other words, the assumptions are there, guiding what we do with clients in therapy and research, whether we are aware of them or not.... it is

these guiding assumptions that provide the moral grounding for our work, that justify what we do, and that supply
the scientific framework within which our work is ultimately
judged. (p. 41)

Slife and Williams (1995), Mahoney (2005), Miller (1992), Rychlak (1976),
and Woolfolk and Richardson (2008) are among others who have eloquently argued the case that no facet of scientific and clinical thinking
can escape the influence of underlying philosophical assumptions relative to the focus of interest—whether these are, for example, maladaptive
core beliefs, problematic interpersonal styles, or specific patterns of family
dysfunction. Therapeutic targets are anchored in theoretical systems—
cognitive therapy, interpersonal therapy, family therapy, and so on—
whose respective anchorings are "fundamentally predicational ... relying
upon assumptions, preferential biases, preferred paradigms, meaningful
worldviews, and so forth" (Rychlak, 1992, p. xvi).

As a fundamental assumption, "holism (from ὅλος, *holos*, a Greek
word meaning *all, whole, entire, total*)" (Wikipedia, 2010) maintains that a
complex system (exemplified by the human brain, a person, or a societal
institution) functions as a totality, a unified whole, that is *"more than or
different from the sum of its parts"* (Ostreng, 2007, p. 12) and manifests properties not contained in any of the parts themselves. A holistic perspective
holds that properties characterizing a given complex system (e.g., the
brain's plasticity; a person's resilience; a social institution's functions) are
emergent in that they develop out of *interrelationships*—the "interconnectedness, interdependencies and interactions" (Ostreng, 2007, p. 12)—that
continuously transpire between and among the whole's constituent parts.
As crystallized by Mabry, Olster, Morgan, and Abrams (2008), "Emergent
properties are those properties that can only be seen at the system level
and are not attributes of the individual components themselves (e.g., a
flock emerges when a group of birds flies together; it is a property of the
system, not of any individual bird)" (p. S218).

A holistic approach to understanding a complex system proceeds
through *synthesis*, "acknowledg[ing] the impact of multiple variables,
complex interactions among variables, and multiple levels of analysis"
(Haynes, 1992, p. xi). The concept of nonlinearity is embedded in the process of synthesis, and among its defining characteristics is the notion that
the directionality of influence processes between parts is reciprocal and
multidirectional. For example, in the case of a triad involving a therapist,
individual psychotherapy patient, and the latter's spouse, the therapist
and patient reciprocally influence each other within a given session in
verbal and nonverbal ways; by the same token, a multidirectional influence process unfolds when a change in the patient following a specific
session prompts the latter's spouse to call the therapist with expressions

of concern, which the therapist then shares with the patient in the next session, and based on their discussion, the patient asks her spouse to attend the next session.

The concept of part–whole relationships is also central to holistic understanding, in that a given part acquires meaning based on the role it plays in the total system—but by the same token, the total system cannot be comprehensively understood without reference to its heterogeneous, constituent parts and their interrelationships. In the same vein, thorough understanding of any particular constituent part is achieved only insofar as that understanding grasps how that part affects and is affected by other parts constituting the whole (Magnusson & Torestad, 1993).

Striking the chord of holism in composing a unifying framework for psychotherapy begs the question about the role occupied by *reductionism*, a position in the philosophy of science characteristically depicted as holism's polar opposite and hence as incommensurable. This issue of holism "versus" reductionism, indeed often characterized as "the debate over 'wholes' and 'parts'" (Corning, 1998, p. 134), is of no small importance to advancing the field, for it embodies two distinctly different approaches to understanding why and how things happen as they do in "the world of nature and the social world of humankind" (McClellan & Dorn, 2006, p. 129). As Malanson (1999) points out, this difference "is significant because the extremes lead to fundamentally different questions and to different answers to the same questions" (p. 746)—an issue that certainly pertains to the innumerable questions of interest to those working scientifically and clinically in the fields of personality, psychopathology, and psychotherapy.

Thus, in contradistinction to a holistic perspective, reductionism pursues understanding of a complex system, not through synthesis, but rather through *analysis*—that is, by breaking it down into its constituent parts and developing detailed knowledge about each of those parts and their respective properties (see Polkinghorne, 1983). In this perspective, the whole is understood as the additive effect of each of its elemental constituents; as classically stated, the whole is *equal* to the sum of its parts. Moreover, "it is a feature of reductionist explanation that parts are assumed to affect other parts in a linear or one-way manner, and interpretation proceeds from the parts to the whole" (Chandler, 1995, n.p.). Intimately related, a highly valued form of knowledge in this model is evidence of a one-way (unidirectional) cause–effect relationship between variables; thus, X (the therapist) exerts causal effects on Y (the patient), and Y causally affects Z (her spouse), but the direction of influence is always one way.

Although a holistic perspective is of primary importance in a unifying paradigm for clinical science and psychotherapy, eschewing reductionism is in point of fact not only inconceivable but also wholly undesirable. As critically pointed out by Malanson (1999, p. 746), in reality, a gradient exists between holism and reductionism, and therefore in applying a unifying frame for understanding a complex system, one need not choose between *either* a holistic perspective *or* a reductionist perspective. Rather, adopting a *both/and* perspective—that is, examining the interplay between both reductionistic analysis and holistic synthesis—is conceived as the optimal course in pursuing comprehensive understanding of a complex system. No intrinsic incommensurability exists between these two approaches to understanding, in that each concentrates on a distinctly different form of knowledge about the particular human system under consideration: "[reductionism] focuses on the *properties of parts*, [holism] on the *relationship between them*. Put together, they stand out as supplementary rather than conflicting, as inclusive rather than exclusive" (Ostreng, 2007, p. 12).

Pursuing understanding of a phenomenon or entity through tacking back and forth between alternative lenses, in this case reductionism and holism, is the essence of *dialectical thinking* (Anchin, 2008c; Rychlak, 1976)—fundamental to the process of unification (Anchin, 2008c; Marquis, in press). Though referencing the specific domain of environmental studies, Mebratu's (2001) perspective on the relationship between reductionism and holism has direct applicability to pursuing a unifying paradigm for the clinical sciences and psychotherapy:

> Fundamentally, the holistic view recognizes the validity of the reductionist way of thinking within the broader domain of the holistic view. In this context, disciplinary sciences, as reductionist as they are, will remain to be the best source of gaining in-depth knowledge about the parts. But, when it comes to complex systems, the limitation of the reductionist view needs to be rectified through the application of the holistic view. Recognizing the relationship between the holistic and reductionist view is one of the major challenges that must be addressed by the scientific community in its efforts of dealing with environmental issues. (n.p.)

We maintain the very same challenge confronts the scientific and clinical communities in their shared objective of unraveling and understanding the complexities of personality, psychopathology, psychological health, and psychotherapy. Ostreng (2007) concisely crystallized this dialectical challenge: "breaking complex systems down into their individual components by the method of reductionism is only a first approximation of the truth, and while it may afford many useful insights, it behooves scientists to put the pieces together again by way of holism" (p. 12).

BIOPSYCHOSOCIAL SYSTEMS METATHEORY: A HOLISTIC FRAMEWORK FOR GUIDING PSYCHOTHERAPY UNIFICATION

Undergirded by holism and its embedded dialectic between analysis and synthesis, unifying the clinical sciences and psychotherapy is centered on developing a singular paradigm capable of facilitating progress toward a set of ongoing and intertwined objectives; specifically:

- Identifying and investigating all of the domains and their composite structures and processes, which in thoroughly interdependent fashion comprise the individual as a living system and thus are essential to understanding the entire spectrum of human development and functioning from healthy, adaptive states to pathologic, maladaptive states

- Guiding theory and research on the generative interconnections and interdependencies among these different domains, structures, and processes

- Extending conceptual tendrils into other fields of study in order to optimize the breadth and depth of attainable knowledge

- Systematically organizing and interrelating these ever-expanding bodies of single and multidomain knowledge into a coherent narrative that has fidelity with the complexity of the human experience and brings meaning and intelligibility to this enormous diversity of knowledge elements

- Developing unifying strategies, principles, and methods of psychotherapeutic intervention in the service of maximizing beneficial utilitarian application of this knowledge

To the field's great advantage (see Anchin, 2012), a principal way forward for realizing these objectives is already before us in the form of *biopsychosocial systems metatheory.* This unifying framework, highly robust in composition and heuristically rich in implications, is innervated by holism, and hence the analysis–synthesis dialectic, in each of its component parts.

The Nature of Metatheory

Metatheory is definable literally as theory about theory, and while it has become a focus of scientific interest in its own right (see L'Abate, 2012; Wallis, 2010), in the present context we stress its totalizing structure and function. Metatheory can be understood as a comprehensive conceptual scaffold that organizes and integrates more specific theories that conceptually and empirically map different aspects of a given phenomenon, however simple or complex (Anchin, 2008c; cf. Wallis, 2010). Pursuing unification and its multifaceted objectives without the guidance provided by metatheory is unimaginable. Underscoring the massive complexities within and interconnecting personality, psychopathology, and psychotherapy, Melchert (2013) explained why this is so:

> it is not currently possible for a true unified theory of psychology to provide the foundation for unifying [professional psychology] around a single scientific approach—such a theory is unlikely to be discovered for a very long time (if ever). Instead, the solution to this problem is (naturally) the same as it was for the natural sciences. When it comes to discrete, less complex phenomena, scientific laws and theories are often able to explain the processes involved. Explanations of highly complex phenomena involving many variables and processes are frequently not yet available, however. As a result, metatheoretical frameworks and models are needed to integrate what is known and provide approximate explanations of these phenomena (Mitchell, 2009; Rodgers, 2010). Metatheoretical frameworks attempt to identify the most essential characteristics that need to be integrated to understand complex phenomena. ... (p. 15)

Metatheory, in its comprehensiveness, thus knits together into an overarching and coherent conceptual structure the different theories and their related scientific findings relative to a given phenomenon of interest in the servicing of advancing the study, understanding, and explanation of that phenomenon. Methatheory's viability rests strongly on dialectical thinking (Anchin, 2008d) in that, relative to mapping the territory of interest, a dialectical frame views any particular conceptual and/or empirically based datum as certainly important in its own right, reflecting metatheory's analytic, deconstructive dimension. However, by virtue of metatheory's supraorganizing purpose, the meaning of any given single piece of information ultimately derives from its contribution to apprehending the territory in its totality—an expression of metatheory's synthetic, reconstructive dimension (see Wallis, 2010). Abrams and Hogg (cited in Wallis, 2010) provided a wonderfully clear metaphor that captures this vitally important mapping function of metatheory:

> A metatheory is like a good travel guide—it tells you where to go and where not to go, what is worthwhile and what is not, the best way to get to a destination, and where it is best

to rest a while. Metatheoretical conviction provides structure and direction, it informs the sorts of questions one asks and does not ask, and it furnishes a passion that makes the quest exciting and buffers one from disappointments along the way. (p. 116)

Clinical practice is ultimately guided by theoretical systems, which provide pathways toward change and health. Metatheory comprises an overarching framework subsuming sets of pattern recognition tools that emerge from theories to map the clinical landscape as we traverse the clinical landscape.

The Biopsychosocial Model of Health and Illness

In pursuing unification, the biopsychosocial model of health and illness provides clinical scientists, practitioners, and educators with the all-important travel guide. Offered by George Engel (1977, 1980, 1997) to both medicine and psychiatry as a more comprehensive alternative to the prevailing biomedical approach to understanding and treating physical and mental health and illness (see also Fava & Sonino, 2008), the biopsychosocial model provides an all-inclusive, holistic conception of the human being through encompassing the hierarchically arranged biological, psychological, and sociocultural domains that in thoroughly interlocking fashion explain human psychology and behavior. Moreover, given human verbal and nonverbal experiencing of consciousness and internal subjectivity, the biopsychosocial model necessarily incorporates within its purview the vibrant domain of phenomenology, underscoring that, in real time, human biopsychosociality is a lived experience; as such, it is ineluctably entwined with such complex processes and elements as intentionality, agency, purpose, values, and meaning (Anchin, 2003, 2006, 2012; Henriques, 2011; Krippner, Ruttenber, Engelman, & Granger, 1985; Magnusson, 1995). Notable in this regard is the fact that, while the biopsychosocial model is a scientifically based framework, Engel "understood with remarkable clarity, depth and eloquence, that science and humanism are not dichotomies" (Ryff & Singer, 2000, p. 170). Thus, while he saw it as essential that the physician operate in an "observational [mode]" (p. 170) by using the biopsychosocial model to guide "reliable and informed scientific work in the clinical realm" (p. 170), he also recognized the vital importance of the "relational model," which

required attending to the human realm, in which language, symbols, thoughts, and feelings are the means by which private experience is organized and communicated. "It is through dialogue that the physician learns the nature and history of the patient's experiences and clarifies on the one hand what they mean for the patient, and on the other hand, what they might mean in terms of other systems of the natural hierarchy, be they biochemical and physiological, or psychological and social" ([Engel, 1998], p. 8). Engel's wisdom was in understanding that the two modes constitute not separate alternatives, but "a single integrated means for data disclosure, clarification, and interpretation" ([Engel, 1998], p. 8). (Ryff & Singer, 2000, p. 170)

Melchert (2013), confronting the critical question as to whether "enough is known to justify a transition away from the clearly incomplete and inadequate theories of the past to a single, unified, science-based [biopsychosocial] methatheoretical orientation" (p. 16), maintained that in point of fact "[t]he evidence…is overwhelming" (p. 16). In this respect, it is instructive to note that the biopsychosocial framework "has been adopted within several of the clinical specializations in [professional psychology] (e.g., in child, school, health, and addiction psychology, neuropsychology, and geropsychology; see Martin, Weinberg, & Bealer, 2007; Seagull, 2000; Shah & Reichman, 2006; Suls & Rothman, 2004; Williams & Evans, 2003)" (Melchert, 2013, p. 16). Further, evidence continues to amass that comprehensive understanding of psychological health and well-being (e.g., Ryff & Singer, 2000, 2006; Strack, 2005) and the development, onset, and maintenance of diverse adult psychopathologies (e.g., Gabbard, 2005; Gilbert, 2004; Kiesler, 1999; Zucker, 2006) *necessitates* the multidomain, multicausal explanations afforded by the biopsychosocial model. Collectively, these developments bring the truth to Kiesler's (1999) forward-looking assertion that "for the first time, it is possible for the mental health field and its respective scientific disciplines to converge and integrate their efforts under an identical theoretical umbrella" (p. xii).

Kiesler's use of an umbrella as a metaphor to capture the integrative and unifying function of the biopsychosocial model is itself noteworthy. Through placing a concept in another conceptual framework (Meyer, 2005), metaphor fleshes out important meanings in the former that may remain implicit or hidden; it helps us "better understand … by defining the less concrete by means of reference to a more concrete concept (Lakoff & Johnson 1980)" (p. 1601).

In this respect, Ryff and Singer (1998) draw on the ladder as another metaphor for depicting the biopsychosocial model, specifically to illuminate the pertinence of reductionist and holistic perspectives, analysis and synthesis, in studying the biopsychosocial composition of human life. Pointing out that "positive human health, with its emphasis on complex mind–body processes that must be tracked through time, is a daunting biopsychosocial agenda" (p. 23), they explain that "stratigraphic approaches, which differentiate layers of living into their cultural, social, psychological, and biological components (Geertz, 1973), are not sufficient for the task" (p. 23). Rather, it is necessary "to go beyond the separated layers into the synthesis of how they come together" (p. 23). Aware that "[s]uch agendas may evoke praise for their scope at the same time that they prompt contempt for their audacity" (p. 23), they revisit

> Melnechuk's wise admonishment that the scientific gains in precision (e.g., specificity of the physiological mechanisms of emotional responses) must be matched by a broadening of scope that reaches across a wide territory. The span from social events and human feelings to DNA and microbioelectric fields may seem long, but to those who seek a comprehensive understanding of health the analytical levels are as close together as a nested set of hollow Russian dolls. ... One can prefer to focus on a given level of this series and yet perceive the series as a ladder that can be climbed holistically up as well as reductionistically down (Melnechuk, 1988, p. 222). (Ryff & Singer, 1998, p. 23)

Still, a third metaphor—the holograph—provides a valuable representational frame for crystallizing the biopsychosocial model's embodiment of part–whole relationships. A holograph can be pictured as a three-dimensional map of a complex system that visually organizes an array of data culled from different lenses; this three-dimensional image encompasses multiple part–whole relationships expressed in unity. In holographically viewing an entity—however simple or complex—the observer's visual image changes as a function of such factors as the angle or perspective from which the holographic image is viewed, as well as the level of resolution applied (molecular to molar), but this percept, this image, is always part of the whole (Anchin, 2012). Thus, a holographic rendering of the complex biopsychosocial ecology in which the human experience is thoroughly encased allows us to vizualize simultaneously any given part within its totalistic context. To illustrate, if we imagine a crying toddler being comfortingly hugged by a loving mother in the kitchen of their home, a three-dimensional, holographic rendering of this situation visually "allows one to spin, zoom in or out, and fly over" (Stebly, 1998) this situation, thereby always seeing some particular part (e.g., the toddler's facial expression; mother embracing her child) but simultaneously in the context of the whole.

Systems Concepts and Principles

In his seminal paper introducing the biopsychosocial concept of health and illness, Engel (1977) explicitly tied the model to systems theory. He recognized that the latter offered a formal methatheoretical structure for encompassing the biological, psychological, and social levels interactively at play in the occurrence, manifestations, and experience of physical disease and psychiatric disorder, and he delineated advantages stemming therefrom:

> Since systems theory holds that all levels of organization are linked to each other in a hierarchical relationship so that changes in one affect change in the others, its adoption as a scientific approach should do much to mitigate the holist-reductionist dichotomy and improve communication across scientific disciplines. For medicine, systems theory provides a conceptual approach suitable not only for the proposed biopsychosocial concept of disease but also for studying disease and medical care as interrelated processes. (p. 134)

As discussed elsewhere (Anchin, 2012), Ludwig von Bertalanffy propelled systems thinking to prominence through his general systems theory, "an attempt to understand the universal rules and principles by which systems in general operate" (Magnavita, 2005, p. 36). Beginning with its articulation in the mid-20th century (von Bertalanffy, 1950) and through ensuing developments (von Bertalanffy, 1968), general systems theory introduced ground-changing conceptions into the science of living systems. Suffice it to say that over the 60-plus years since general systems theory first laid down roots, it has proven to be seminal—a spawning ground for the growth of different directions in systems thinking; these include cybernetics (Francois, 1999; Heylighen & Joslyn, 2001; Kenny, 2009; Pouvreau & Drack, 2007; Umpleby, 1990), chaos theory (Barton, 1994; Chamberlain, 1998; Kossman & Bullrich, 1997; Kiel & E. Elliott, 1996; Kautz, 2011; Werndl, 2009), nonlinear dynamical theory (Anchin, 2005; Burlingame & Hope, 1997; Guastello, 2001; Smith & Thelen, 2003; Thelen & Smith, 2006), and complex adaptive systems (Gell-Mann, 1994; Levin, 2003; Miller & Page, 2007; Morowitz & Singer, 1995). These different approaches to systems thinking have been fruitfully applied across the physical, life, and social sciences (see, e.g., Ashby, 1954, 1956; Barton, 1994; Bateson, 1972; Boulding, 1956; Byrne, 1998; Capra, 1996, 2005; Checkland, 1981; Glass & Mackey, 1988; Gottman, 1979; Haken, 1977; Kauffman, 1995; Lorenz, 1972; Maturana & Varela, 1980; Miller, 1978; Nicolis & Prigogine, 1977; Nowotny, 2005; Pumain, 2010; Senge, 1990; Simon, 1962; Vallacher & Nowak, 2007; Watzlawick, Beavin, & Jackson, 1967).

Systems theory—more accurately characterizeable as systems metatheory—puts meat on the bones of holism. By definition, the essence of any system is wholeness. Thus, we can beneficially divide any such system into the heterogeneous array of subsystems, or parts, of which it is composed and in which it is ecologically situated—and, we can focus in on any one of these subsystems in highly concentrated fashion. Nevertheless, in reflecting the understanding that this diverse array of subsystems is bound together into a singular whole form, a coherent unity, through complex processes of reciprocal influence and interdependence (Capra, cited in Funch, 1999; Joslyn, 1992; von Bertalanffy, 1968), the systems perspective forcefully reminds us of the "big picture" (Mabry, Olseter, Morgan, & Abrams, 2008; Magnavita, 2008), and that the system's properties as a whole emerge out of subsystems' interactions and interrelationships.

Additional key principles more or less shared by systems-oriented theorists, researchers, and clinicians, which will be elaborated in the context of different facets of the unifying approach discussed in ensuing chapters, include the following (Anchin, 2012):

- A living system is characterized by purposefulness and intentionality, an active agent motivated toward achievement of goals, attainment of desired states, and realization of valued ends (Carver & Scheier, 1999; Magnusson & Torestad, 1993; Mayer, 2004; Millon & Grossman, 2012; Singer, 2005)

- A living system is an open—as opposed to a mechanical and closed—system because, in order to live, it must "exchange information, energy, and material with the many other systems within which they are nested and which they themselves encompass" (Reis et al., 2000, p. 847)

- A living system is dynamic, which entails thinking in terms of movement, change, and activity over time, and in turn points to the centrality of *process* in systems thinking (Capra, 1996, p. 42)—paraphrasing Fay (1996), in real time the human organism is a verb, not a noun

- A systems perspective emphasizes the nonlinear nature of interrelationships between and among subsystems by directing attention to mutual effects, reciprocal interactions, feedback loops, networks, and cycles. Nonlinearity also holds that there can be a disproportionate relationship between the size of an input (e.g., small) and the magnitude of its effect (e.g., large).

- In systems thinking, every structure is seen as manifesting itself through processes (Capra, 1996); the organized configuration of relationships among subsystems and their specific features that can be mapped as having a particular structure unfolds, in real time, as a fluid process of interwoven multivariate activity

- Self-regulatory processes are characteristic of living systems (Bertalannfy, 1968; Capra, 1996; Carver & Scheier, 1999; Vallacher & Nowak, 1999)

- A "delicate balance between the forces of stability and the forces of instability" (Gleick, 1987, p. 309), between order and disorder, is inherent to living systems (see also Mahoney, 1991)

- The multilevel, nested structural composition of the human being as a complex system renders human processes thoroughly contextual in nature (Anchin, 2008c; Capra, 1996; Chu, Strand, & Fjelland, 2003; Kagan, 2012)

- Unpredictability is a major property of complex systems as a consequence of reciprocal interactions among a large number of interlocking elements, which are themselves in flux (Mahoney, 1991; Rihani, 2002)

- Whether due to endogenous and/or exogenous factors, disruptions in the balance between stability and instability in a complex system have the capacity to shift the latter into a phase of marked disequilibrium and turbulence denoted by the concept of chaos (Anchin, 2008c; Chamberlain, 1998; Kiel & Elliott, 1996)

- New order, reflected in structural and processural change that can range from adaptive to maladaptive, emerges from chaos by virtue of a living system's intrinsic capacity to engage in self-organization (Capra, 1996; Holland, 1995; Mahoney & Moes, 1997; Perna & Masterpasqua, 1997)

In its various iterations, systems theory has now been in existence for over 60 years, while the biopsychosocial model has been making its way through the life and social sciences for over 35 years. Integrating these rich, time-honored frameworks creates a metatheoretical paradigm that captures and defines in one fell swoop the enormous multilevel structural complexity of the human living system, while acknowledging the inherently unified manner in which this structure operates within the ecological sphere. This paradigm has sufficient breadth to encompass the vast plurality of phenomena, from microlevel domains to macrolevel domains, differentially mapped and to varying degrees empirically substantiated by current theoretical orientations. Importantly, however, this framework does not specify in an a priori way the specific terminology and concepts for mapping those domains and their composite subsystems, operating instead as an overarching scaffold that serves an organizing function. Biopsychosocial systems metatheory thus provides a unifying framework without the exclusionary processes associated with any single theory, which would otherwise place constraints on the structures and process of relevance to personality, psychopathology, and psychotherapy. To the extent that the field forges an increasingly interconnected body of psychotherapeutically related knowledge, casting this within a biopsychosocial systems metatheoretical framework thus seems all the more logical. At the same time, in spotlighting as a core postulate the intrinsic interrelatedness of phenomena that in real time is manifested in processural fashion, the biopsychosocial systems paradigm, in its philosophical foundations, is isomorphic with holism and its fundamental emphasis on the inter-woven nature of phenomena.

ADDITIONAL DEVELOPMENTS REFLECTING THE VALUE OF A UNIFYING PARADIGM FOR PSYCHOTHERAPY AND THE CLINICAL SCIENCES

These considerations operate as significant components of our rationale for proposing biopsychosocial systems metatheory as a viable frame-work for unifying psychotherapy and the clinical sciences. However, additional developments convergently point to unification as a building dynamism in the field's evolution and to advantages of biopsychosocial systems metatheory as the paradigm for organizing and synthesiz-ing these developments. These include limitations of the psychother-apy integration movement, burgeoning interest in interdependencies between multilevel structures and processes in human functioning, per-sonality and psychopathology, the evidence-based practice movement in psychology, and calls for addressing health problems through cross-disciplinary collaborations (Anchin, 2012).

Limitations of the Psychotherapy Integration Movement

Psychotherapy integration emerged as a formal movement beginning in the early 1980s, fostered by a number of developments:

1. Proliferation of therapies
2. Inadequacy of single theories and treatments
3. External socioeconomic contingencies
4. Ascendancy of short-term, problem focused treatments
5. Opportunity to observe various treatments, particularly for dif-ficult disorders
6. Recognition that therapeutic commonalities heavily contribute to outcome
7. Identification of specific therapy effects and evidence-based treatments
8. Development of a professional network for integration (Norcross, 2005, p. 5)

Driven by four main currents—technical eclecticism, the common factors approach, theoretical integration, and assimilative integration—the integrative movement has advanced the field significantly over the course of its 30-some years of evolution. Among the movement's consistent emphases have been identifying and explicitly harnessing into the treatment process key common therapeutic factors that operate across approaches, as well as systematically integrating and synthesizing specific principles, constructs, and techniques from two or more single-school approaches to create more encompassing, versatile, and effective therapeutic amalgams than any single approach taken alone. In the process, psychotherapy integration has dramatically reduced dogma, enhanced conceptual diversification, and emboldened clinical flexibility.

By the same token, a distinct limitation of psychotherapy integration is the relative lack of *personological comprehensiveness* characteristic of any given specific integrative approach. Because it characteristically begins at the level of theory associated with selected single-school approaches and then expands to the blending of techniques, any given integrative approach tends to cover only a limited number of the multiple domains and subsystems of the human personality system and psychopathology (Anchin & Magnavita, 2006). In his observation of debates among psychotherapy integrationists, Millon (2000) parsed out the central issue:

> These discussants have things backward so to speak, because they start the task of intervention by focusing first on technique or methodology. Integration does not adhere in treatment methods or in their theories, be they eclectic or otherwise. *Integration inheres in the person, not in our theories or in the modalities we prefer.* It stems from the dynamics and interwoven character of the patient's traits and symptoms. Our task as therapists is not to see how we can blend intrinsically discordant models of therapeutic technique, but to match the pattern of features that characterize each patient, and then to select treatment goals and tactics that mirror this pattern optimally. (p. 49)

Thus, from the outset, unified psychotherapy emphasizes organismic holism by encompassing all the major domain systems composing personality and psychopathology and their interconnections, in turn providing a more comprehensive, multiparadigmatic framework for psychotherapy (Anchin & Magnavita, 2006). Indeed, Stricker and Gold (2011), observing the appearance of unified approaches to conceptualization and intervention to be "a recent trend that has emerged in psychotherapy integration" (p. 478), adjudged that it "may in fact mark the end of psychotherapy integration as we know it" (p. 478).

Burgeoning Interest in Interdependencies Between Multilevel
Structures and Processes in Human Functioning, Personality,
and Psychopathology

Perhaps reflecting the quiet yet growing influence of systemic perspectives on mainstream thinking, theoretical and empirical lenses in both
clinical and basic psychological science have been expanding beyond
the reductionist metapsychology that dominated the 20th century. The
direction has been toward achieving more holistic understanding of
complex interrelationships among *clusters* of domains constituting
human structure, process, and functioning along the continuum from
psychopathological to healthy states. Influential examples include (a)
Schore's (1994, 2003a, 2003b, 2012) interdisciplinary work linking such
domains as neuroscience, developmental neurochemistry, interpersonal processes (including the centrality of attachment), unconscious
mechanisms of affect regulation and dysregulation, and the self; (b)
Andersen and colleagues' (e.g., Andersen & Chen, 2002; Andersen &
Przybylinski, 2012; Andersen & Saribay, 2003; Miranda & Andersen,
2010) theory and research on the intricate relationship between the
relational self and the phenomenon of transference through integrating concepts and methodologies from social cognition (e.g., mental
representations of self and others), emotion, motivation, and interpersonal behavior; (c) Cacioppo and colleagues' (e.g., Cacioppo, 2002;
Cacioppo, Bernston, Sheridan, & McClintock, 2000; Norman et al., 2010)
approach to understanding complex behavior and the mind through
theoretical and empirical multilevel integrative analyses focusing on
the intrinsic unity among the biological, cognitive, and social domains;
and (d) theory and research in the muldisciplinary field of "relationship science" (Berscheid, 1999; Reis, 2007), which center on studying
the interpersonal context of such phenomena as human evolution, brain
development, physical and mental well-being, cognition, and emotion
(see Reis, Collins, & Berscheid, 2000).

These examples of theory and research focused on *interrelationships* among different domain-level phenomena, in conjunction with still
other "compelling examples of behavioral research that integrates theory
and methods within and outside of psychology" (Eisenberg, Robertson,
& Sher, 2000, p. 805), are reshaping our ways of understanding human
development, functioning, psychological health, and psychopathology.
In this same vein, they provide firm footing for Eisenberg et al.'s (2000)
contention that "whereas much of the 20th century [in psychology] was
a period of division and segregation of intellectual interest, the 21st century promises to be one of convergence and integration" (p. 805). From
the still broader perspective of advancing collaboration between different
mental health professions, these more holistically oriented investigative

foci within clinical and basic psychological science are highly concordant with K. Kendler's (2005) call for psychiatry "to move from a prescientific 'battle of paradigms' toward a more mature approach that embraces complexity along with empirically rigorous and pluralistic explanatory models" (p. 433).

The Evidence-Based Practice Movement in Psychology

Evidence-based practice in psychology (EBPP) has been formalized as policy of the American Psychological Association (APA) (2006), and it provides further justification for the desirability, viability, and utility of a unifying paradigm for psychotherapy and clinical science. EBPP entails "the integration of the best available research with clinical expertise in the context of patient characteristics, culture, and preferences" (APA, 2006, p. 280).

In elaborating on this definition, the APA (2006) pointed out that "psychological services are most likely to be effective when they are responsive to the patient's specific problems, strengths, personality, sociocultural context, and preferences (Norcross, 2002)" (p. 278). This principle clearly asserts the importance of taking into account the complex and idiographic nature of the patient's personality and psychopathology in influencing treatment strategy, interventions, and outcomes; unified psychotherapy's multilevel, multidomained model of personality and psychopathology, anchored in biopsychosocial systems metatheory, provides an organizing, systematic framework for explicitly operationalizing this specificity principle. Indeed, as Gilbert (2004) pointed out, while the biopsychosocial approach is holistic, "it also recognizes the importance of individual differences ... how your systems interact may be different than mine" (p. 106).

Also notably consistent with the underlying philosophy of unified psychotherapy is APA's (2006) indication that "research suggests that sensitivity and flexibility in the administration of therapeutic interventions produces better outcomes than rigid application of manuals or principles (Castonguay, Goldfried, Wiser, Raue, & Hayes, 1996; Henry, Schacht, Strupp, Butler, & Binder, 1993; Huppert et al., 2001)" (p. 278). This collective finding from psychotherapy process and outcome research denotes the imperativeness of tailoring even evidence-based manuals and psychotherapeutic principles to the patient at hand, underscoring from another perspective the importance of therapist openness to and skill at drawing on the potential contributions of concepts, interventions, and processes of all the major approaches to psychotherapy on a case-by-case basis, among defining components of unified treatment (Anchin & Magnavita, 2006).

Calls for Addressing Health Problems Through Cross-Disciplinary Collaborations

In his preface to the 2007 strategic prospectus of the NIH Office of Behavioral and Social Sciences Research (OBSSR), Abrams (2007; see also Mabry, Olster, Morgan, & Abrams, 2008) summarized the framework and causal model (see Haynes, 1992; Haynes, O'Brien, Kaholokula, & Witteman, 2012) most appropriate for conceptualizing human health and illness based on growing bodies of research; he described an approach that places at center stage the complex biopsychosociality of both physical and mental health and illness and the corresponding shift toward an increasingly systemic causal model in the clinical and health sciences:

> Robust findings are mounting with evidence of how biology, behavior, and the social and physical environments are dynamically intertwined in the ways that they promote health or produce disease, disability, and death. The emerging view is that differences in patterns of health and disease represent the embodiment of a dynamic interaction of genes and environment over time. Two previously separate, often competing world views about health and illness may finally be converging: (1) the biomedical view of causation, and (2) the socio-behavioral-ecological view of causation. The biological "causes" and the socio-behavioral-ecological "causes of the causes" are two sides of the same coin. Historically powerful scientific models of linear causality and reductionism are giving way to the ideas of multiple causal pathways and "causal loops" within complex adaptive systems.

This shift toward a comprehensive complex-systems metamodel also undergirded OBSSR's emphasis on cross-disciplinarity as essential to advancing the understanding and successful treatment of pressing and persistent human health problems. Pointing to the need for "strong partnerships among the biological, social, behavioral, economic, and public health sciences", Abrams (2007) maintained that "solutions to some of our biggest health challenges may depend on whether scientists from different disciplines are able to learn each other's languages, listen across the gulfs that separate their sciences, and forge a new conceptual synthesis across their disciplinary boundaries."

In accord with this perspective, OBSSR (2007; Mabry et al., 2008) explicitly identified interdisciplinary research as among the major directions for meeting these challenges. In issuing this call, interdisciplinarity was defined in the terms put forth by Rosenfield (1992) in her influential differentiation of three modes by which scientific disciplines can unify their efforts to address complex health problems. As crystallized by Stokols, Hall, Taylor, and Moser (2008):

> **Multidisciplinarity** is a process in which scholars from disparate fields work independently or sequentially, periodically coming together to share their individual perspectives for purposes of achieving broader-gauged analyses of common research problems. Participants in multidisciplinary teams remain firmly anchored in the concepts and methods of their respective fields. **Interdisciplinarity** is a more robust approach to scientific integration in the sense that team members not only combine or juxtapose concepts and methods drawn from their different fields, but also work more intensively to integrate their divergent perspectives, even while remaining anchored in their own respective fields [Klein, 2008]. **Transdisciplinarity** is a process in which team members representing different fields work together over extended periods to develop shared conceptual and methodologic frameworks that not only integrate but also transcend their respective disciplinary perspectives. (pp. S78–S70)

Mabry et al. (2008) point out that much of the current work at OBSSR "involves moving from multidisciplinary to interdisciplinary science" (p. S212), and volumes by Higginbotham, Briceno-Leon, and Johnson (2002) and Kessel, Rosenfield, and Anderson (2003, 2008) amply illustrate the rich heurism and productive yield of this specific form of cross-disciplinarity. Cicchetti and Toth (2009) similarly discussed the centrality of interdisciplinary collaboration to "contributions, challenges, and future directions" (p. 16) of developmental psychopathology. Notably, in the context of discussing research on normal and maladaptive development, they, like OBSSR, observed the inseparable linkage between interdisciplinarity and a complex systems paradigm:

> When disciplines function in isolation, they run the risk of creating theories that ultimately will be incorrect because vital information from other disciplines has either been ignored or is unknown. As is true in systems neuroscience, it is essential that an integrative framework that incorporates all levels of analysis about complex systems in the development of psychopathology or in the promotion of resilience be utilized. Rather than adhering to a single domain or unitary disciplinary focus, striving for a multi-domain, multi-level synthesis may impel researchers to broaden their visions and thereby

lead to the formulation of integrative developmental theories that can elucidate both normal and abnormal forms of ontogenesis across developing systems. (p. 20)

Even as interdisciplinary work continues to grow, transdisciplinarity in the health sciences is also drawing increasing attention (see, e.g., Klein, 2008). For example, Mabry et al. (2008) expressed OBSSR's long-range projection that "over time, collaboration among diverse scientists may shift from multidisciplinary and interdisciplinary work to a full transdisciplinary synthesis that has the potential to produce new disciplines, as in psychoneuroimmunology, cognitive and social neurosciences, and behavioral genetics" (p. S216). The broadening and deepening understanding of human functioning, health, and illness contributed by these new disciplines provides powerful evidence of the advances in knowledge that can flow when two or more disciplines unify their efforts in ways that engender new conceptual and methodological syntheses that transcend unidisciplinary study of phenomena (see Stokols, 2006, n. 2).

Moreover, salient processes, methodologies, and issues characterizing interdisciplinarity and transdisciplinarity have become topics of study in their own right. Analyses and discussion have focused, for example, on specific factors that can impede or facilitate these different forms of collaboration (Stokols, 2006); generic principles for guiding research performance and evaluation (Klein, 2008); advances in the conceptualization, organization, and assessment of transdisciplinary research that may derive from deploying the concept of *heterarchy* (Kessel & Rosenfield, 2008), "defined as ... the 'relation of elements to one another when they are unranked or when they possess the potential for being ranked in a number of different ways'" (Crumley, cited in Kessel & Rosenfield, 2008, p. S231), as an alternative to the notion of hierarchy and its connotation of differential levels of power among elements; and ways in which systems thinking can facilitate the effective translation of transdisciplinary research findings to applied settings (e.g., clinical and community-wide practice; Leischow, Best, Trochim, Clark, Gallagher, Marcus, & Matthews, 2008).

SUMMARY

There is a growing consensus among many scholars, clinical researchers, theorists, and practitioners that psychotherapy and the clinical science on which it rests is moving to a phase of unification. William James, the father of American psychology, saw the need for unifying the multiple realms and domains of psychology. New developments in science and theory are paving the way for a new paradigm in clinical science and psychotherapy situated on a foundation of holism, systems theory, and biopsychosocial metatheory. Understanding the key principles of how complex living systems operate, foundational to which is the interrelatedness of the various domains of the human system, is critical to using a unified framework in practice. Employing the metaphor of a hologram we can depict the multiperspective image that emerges from simultaneously viewing the clinical phenomena through multiple lenses from the micro to the molar. This holographic representation achievable with a unified framework ensures that the holism of the individual as he or she is embedded in the layers of the biopsychosocial system are taken into consideration and that this information is used to guide treatment.

REFERENCES

American Psychological Association Presidential Task Force on Evidence-Based Practice. (2006). Evidence-based practice in psychology. *American Psychologist, 61,* 271–285.

American Psychological Association. (2013). Recognition of psychotherapy effectiveness. *Psychotherapy, 50,* 102–109.

Abrams, D. B. (2007). Preface. In the office of behavioral and social sciences research, *The contributions of behavioral and social sciences research to improving the health of the nation: A prospectus for the future.* The office of behavioral and social sciences research, NIH. Bethesda, MD: NIH. Retrieved December 11, 2011, from http://obssr.od. nih.gov/pdf/OBSSR_Prospectus.pdf

Anchin, J. C. (2003). Cybernetic systems, existential phenomenology, and solution-focused narrative: Therapeutic transformation of negative affective states through integratively oriented brief psychotherapy. *Journal of Psychotherapy Integration, 13,* 334–442.

Anchin, J. C. (2005, May). Using a nonlinear dynamical biopsychosocial systems paradigm to individually tailor the process of psychotherapy. In J. J. Magnavita & J. C. Anchin (Co-chairs), *Unified psychotherapy: Implications for differential treatment strategies and interventions.* Symposium presented at the 21st Annual Conference of the Society for the Exploration of Psychotherapy Integration, Toronto, Ontario, Canada.

Anchin, J. C. (2006). A hermeneutically informed approach to psychotherapy integration. In G. Stricker & J. Gold (Eds.), *A casebook of psychotherapy integration* (pp. 261–280). Washington, DC: American Psychological Association.

Anchin, J. C. (2008a). Comment: Integrating methodologies in the scientific study of interpersonal psychotherapy: A reaction to "Therapist immediacy in brief psychotherapy: Case study I and case study II". *Psychotherapy: Theory, Research, Practice, Training, 45,* 316–319.

Anchin, J. C. (2008b). Contextualizing discourse on a philosophy of science for psychotherapy integration. *Journal of Psychotherapy Integration, 18,* 1–24.

Anchin, J. C. (2008c). Pursuing a unifying paradigm for psychotherapy: Tasks, dialectical considerations, and biopsychosocial systems metatheory. *Journal of Psychotherapy Integration, 18,* 310–349.

Anchin, J. C. (2008d). The critical role of the dialectic in viable metatheory: A commentary on Henriques' Tree of Knowledge System for integrating human knowledge. *Theory and Psychology, 18,* 801–816.

Anchin, J. C. (2012). Prologue to unified psychotherapy and clinical science. *Journal of Unified Psychotherapy and Clinical Science, 1,* 1–20.

Anchin, J. C., & Magnavita, J. J. (2006). The nature of unified clinical science: Implications for psychotherapeutic theory, practice, training, and research. *Psychotherapy Bulletin, 41*(2), 26–36.

Andersen, S. M., & Chen, S. (2002). The relational self: An interpersonal social-cognitive theory. *Psychological Review, 109,* 619–645.

Andersen, S. M., & Przybylinski, E. (2012). Experiments on transference in relations: Implications for treatment. *Psychotherapy, 49,* 370–383.

Andersen, S. M., & Saribay, S. A. (2003). The relational self and transference: Evoking motives, self-regulation, and emotions through activation of mental represenations of significant others. In M. W. Baldwin (Ed.), *Interpersonal cognition* (pp. 1–32). New York: Guilford.

Ashby, W. R. (1954). *Design for a brain.* New York: Wiley.

Ashby, W. R. (1956). *An introduction to cybernetics.* London: Chapman & Hall.

Barton, S. (1994). Chaos, self-organization, and psychology. *American Psychologist, 49,* 5–14.

Bateson, G. (1972). *Steps to an ecology of mind: Collected essays in anthropology, psychiatry, evolution and epistemology.* Chicago, IL: University of Chicago Press.

Berscheid, E. (1999). The greening of relationship science. *American Psychologist, 54,* 260–266.

Boulding, K. E. (1956). General systems theory: The skeleton of science. *Management Science, 2,* 197–208.

Burlingame, G. M., & Hope, C. A. (1997). Dynamical systems theory and social psychology: The promises and pitfalls. *Psychological Inquiry, 8,* 104–110.

Byrne, D. (1998). *Complexity theory and the social sciences: An introduction.* New York: Routledge.

Cacioppo, J. T. (2002). Social neuroscience: Understanding the pieces fosters understanding the whole and vice versa. *American Psychologist, 57,* 819–831.

Cacioppo, J. T., Berntson, G. G., Sheridan, J. F., & McClintock, M. K. (2000). Multilevel integrative analyses of human behavior: Social neuroscience and the complementing nature of social and biological approaches. *Psychological Bulletin, 126,* 829–843.

Capra, F. (1996). *The web of life: A new scientific understanding of living systems.* New York: Anchor Books.

Capra, F. (2005). Complexity and life. *Theory, Culture & Society, 22,* 33–44.

Carter, J. D., Crowe, M., Carlyle, D., Frampton, C. M., Jordan, J., McIntosh, V. V. W., … & Joyce, P. R. (2012). Patient change processes in psychotherapy: Development of a new scale. *Psychotherapy Research, 22,* 115–126.

Carver, C. S., & Scheier, M. F. (1999). Themes and issues in the self-regulation of behavior. In R. S. Wyer, Jr. (Ed.), *Advances in social cognition* (Vol. 12, pp. 1–105). Mahwah, NJ: Lawrence Erlbaum Associates.

Chamberlain, L. (1998). An introduction to chaos and nonlinear dynamics. In L. Chamberlain & M. R. Butz (Eds.), *Clinical chaos: A therapist's guide to nonlinear dynamics and therapeutic change* (pp. 3–14). Philadelphia: Brunner/Mazel.

Chandler, D. (1995). Technological or media determinism. Retrieved May 6, 2011, from http://www.aber.ac.uk/media/Documents/tecdet/tdet03.html

Chao, R. (2002). Seeing the forest and seeing the trees in psychology. *American Psychologist, 57,* 1128–1129.

Checkland, P. (1981). *Systems thinking, systems practice.* New York: Wiley.

Cicchetti, D., & Toth, S. L. (2009). The past achievements and future promises of developmental psychopathology: The coming of age of a discipline. *Journal of Child Psychology and Psychiatry, 50,* 16–25.

Chu, D., Strand, R., & Fjelland, R. (2003). Theories of complexity. *Complexity, 8,* 19–30.

Clinical Sciences Enterprise Task Force (2006). Transforming the university: Final report of the Clinical Sciences Enterprise Task Force. Retrieved December 1, 2012, from http://www1.umn.edu/systemwide/strategic_positioning/tf_ahc_clinical.html

Constantino, M. J., Boswell, J. F., Bernecker, S. L., & Castonguay, L. G. (in press). Context-responsive psychotherapy integration as a framework for a unified clinical science: Conceptual and empirical considerations. *Journal of Unified Psychotherapy and Clinical Science.*

Corning, P. A. (1998). The synergism hypothesis: On the concept of synergy and its role in the evolution of complex systems. *Journal of Social and Evolutionary Systems, 21,* 133–172.

Corsini, R. J., & Wedding, D. (2008). *Current psychotherapies* (8th ed.). Belmont, CA: Thomson Brooks/Cole.

de Groot, A. D. (1989). Unifying psychology: Its preconditions. In W. J. Baker M. E. Hyland R. van Hezewijk & S. Terwee (Eds.), *Recent trends in theoretical psychology* (Vol. *II*, pp. 1–25). New York: Springer-Verlag.

Eisenberg, N., Robertson, L. C., & Sher, K. J. (2000). Introduction to the special issue: Psychology in the 21st century. *Psychological Bulletin, 126,* 803–805.

Elliott, R. (2008). A linguistic phenomenology of ways of knowing and its implications for psychotherapy research and psychotherapy integration. *Journal of Psychotherapy Integration, 18,* 40–65.

Engel, G. (1977). The need of a new model: A challenge for biomedicine. *Science, 196,* 129–136.

Engel, G. (1980). The clinical application of the biopsychosocial model. *American Journal of Psychiatry, 137,* 535–544.

Engel, G. L. (1997). From biomedical to biopsychosocial: Being scientific in the human domain. *Psychosomatics, 38,* 521–528.

Fava, G. A., & Sonino, N. (2008). The biopsychosocial model thirty years later. *Psychotherapy and Psychosomatics, 77,* 1–2

Fay, B. (1996). *Contemporary philosophy of social science: A multicultural approach.* Cambridge, MA: Blackwell.

Francois, C. (1999). Systems and cybernetics in a historical perspective. *Systems Research and Behavioral Science, 16,* 203–219.

Funch, F. (1999). Whole system quotes. Retrieved July 13, 1999, from: http://www.worldtrans.org/whole/wsquotes.html

Gabbard, G. O. (2005). Mind, brain, and personality disorders. *American Journal of Psychiatry, 162,* 648–655.

Gell-Mann, M. (1994). Complex adaptive systems. In G. A. Cowan D. Pines & D. Meltzer (Eds.), *Complexity: Metaphors, models and reality* (pp. 17–29). Reading, MA: Addison-Wesley.

Gilbert, P. (2004). Depression: A biopsychosocial, integrative, and evolutionary approach. In M. Power (Ed.), *Mood disorders: A handbook of science and practice* (pp. 99–142). West Sussex, England: John Wiley & Sons Ltd.

Gilgen, A. R. (1987). The psychological level of organization in nature and interdependencies among major psychological concepts. In A. W. Staats & L. P. Mos (Eds.), *Annals of theoretical psychology* (Vol. 5, pp. 179–209). New York: Plenum Press.

Gleick, J. (1987). *Chaos: Making a new science.* New York: Viking Press.

Glass, L., & Mackey, M. C. (1988). *From clocks to chaos: The rhythms of life.* Princeton, NJ: Princeton University Press.

Gottman, J. M. (1979). Detecting cyclicity in social interaction. *Psychological Bulletin, 86,* 338–348.

Guastello, S. (2001). Nonlinear dynamics in psychology. *Discrete Dynamics in Nature and Society, 6,* 11–29.

Haynes, S. N. (1992). *Models of causality in psychopathology: Toward synthetic dynamic nonlinear models of causality in psychopathology.* Des Moines, IA: Allyn & Bacon.

Haynes, S. N., O'Brien, W. H., Kaholokula, J. K., & Witteman, C. L. M. (2012). Concepts of causality in psychopathology: Applications in clinical assessment. *Journal of Unified Psychotherapy and Clinical Science, 1,* 87–103.

Henriques, G. R. (2003). The tree of knowledge system and the theoretical unification of psychology. *Review of General Psychology, 7,* 150–182.

Henriques, G. R. (2004). Psychology defined. *Journal of Clinical Psychology, 60,* 1207–1221.

Henriques, G. (2011). *A new unified theory of psychology.* New York: Springer Verlag.

Henriques, G., & Stout, J. (2012). A unified approach to conceptualizing people in psychotherapy. *Journal of Unified Psychotherapy and Clinical Science, 1,* 37–60.

Heylighen, F., & Joslyn, C. (2001). Cybernetics and second-order cybernetics. In R. A. Meyers (Ed.), *Encyclopedia of Physical Science & Technology,* (Vol. 4, 3rd ed., pp. 144–170). New York: Academic Press.

Higginbotham, N., Briceno-Leon, R., & Johnson, N. (Eds.). (2003). *Applying health social science: Best practice in the developing world.* London: Zed Books.

Holland, J. H. (1995). *Emergence: From chaos to order.* Reading, MA: Addison-Wesley.

James, W. (1992). Pragmatism: A new name for some old ways of thinking. In D. Olin (Ed.), *William James: Pragmatism, in focus* (pp. 13–142). New York: Routledge. (Original work published 1907).

Joslyn, C. (1992). The nature of cybernetic systems. In F. Heylighen C. Joslyn & V. Turchin (Eds.), *Principia Cybernetica Web* (Principia Cybernetica, Brussels). Retrieved September 16, 1999, from http://pespmc1.vub.ac.be/CYBSNAT.html

Kagan, J. (2012). *Psychology's ghosts: The crisis in the profession and the way back.* New Haven, CT: Yale University Press.

Kauffman, S. (1995). *At home in the universe: The search for the laws of self-organisation and complexity.* London: Penguin Books.

Kautz, R. (2011). *Chaos: The science of predictable random motion.* New York: Oxford University Press.

Kendler, H. H. (1987). A good divorce is better than a bad marriage. In A. W. Staats & L. P. Mos (Eds.), *Annals of theoretical psychology* (Vol. 5, pp. 55–89). New York: Plenum Press.

Kendler, H. H. (2002). Romantic versus realistic views of psychology. *American Psychologist, 57,* 1125–1126.

Kendler, K. S. (2005). Toward a philosophical structure for psychiatry. *American Journal of Psychiatry, 162,* 433–440.

Kenny, V. (2009). "There's nothing like the real thing". Revisiting the need for a third-order cybernetics. *Constructivist Foundations, 4,* 100–111.

Kessel, F., & Rosenfield, P. L. (2008). Toward transdisciplinary research: Historical and contemporary perspectives. *American Journal of Preventive Medicine, 35*(2S), S225–S234.

Kessel, F. S., Rosenfield, P. L., & Anderson, N. B. (Eds.). (2003). *Expanding the boundaries of health and social science: Case studies in interdisciplinary innovation.* New York: Oxford University Press.

Kiel, L. D., & Elliott, E. (Eds.). (1996). *Chaos theory in the social sciences: Foundations and applications.* Ann Arbor, MI: The University of Michigan Press.

Kiesler, D. J. (1999). *Beyond the disease model of mental disorders.* Westport, CT: Praeger.

Klein, J. T. (2008). Evaluation of transdisciplinary and interdisciplinary research: A literature review. *American Journal of Preventive Medicine, 35*(2S), S116–S123.

Koch, S. (1981). The nature and limits of psychological knowledge: Lessons of a century qua "science." *American Psychologist, 36,* 257–269.

Kossman, M. R., & Bullrich, S. (1997). Systematic chaos: Self-organizing systems and the process of change. In F. Masterpasqua & P. A. Perna (Eds.), *The psychological meaning of chaos: Translating theory into practice* (pp. 199–224). Washington, DC: American Psychological Association.

Krippner, S., Ruttenber, A. J., Engelman, S. R., & Granger, D. L. (1985). Toward the application of general systems theory in humanistic psychology. *Systems Research, 2,* 105–115.

Kuhn, T. S. (1970). *The structure of scientific revolutions* (2nd ed.). Chicago: University of Chicago Press.

L'Abate, L. (Ed.). (2012). *Paradigms in theory construction* New York: Springer.

Leischow, S. J., Best, A., Trochim, W. M., Clark, P. I., Gallagher, R. S., Marcus, S. E., & Matthews, E. (2008). Systems thinking to improve the public's health. *American Journal of Preventive Medicine, 35*(2S), S196–S203.

Levin, S. A. (2003). Complex adaptive systems: Exploring the known, the unknown and the unknowable. *Bulletin (New Series) of the American Mathematical Society, 40,* 3–19.

Levitt, H. M., & Williams, D. C. (2010). Facilitating client change: Principles based upon the experience of eminent psychotherapists. *Psychotherapy Research, 20,* 337–352.

Lorenz, E. N. (1972). *Predictability: Does the flap of a butterfly's wings in Brazil set off a Tornado in Texas?* Paper presented at the 1972 meeting of the American Association for the Advancement of Science, Washington, DC.

Lukowitsky, M. R., & Pincus, A. L. (2011). The pantheoretical nature of mental representations and their ability to predict interpersonal adjustment in a nonclinical sample. *Psychoanalytic Psychology, 28,* 48–74.

Mabry, P. L., Olster, D. H., Morgan, G. D., & Abrams, D. B. (2008). Interdisciplinarity and systems science to improve population health: A view from the NIH Office of Behavioral and Social Sciences Research. *American Journal of Preventive Medicine, 35*(2S), S211–S224. Magnusson, 1995

Magnavita, J. J. (2005). *Personality-guided relational therapy: A unified approach.* Washington, DC: American Psychological Association

Magnavita, J. J. (2008). Toward unification of clinical science: The next wave in the evolution of psychotherapy? *Journal of Psychotherapy Integration,*

Magnavita, J. J. (2012). Mapping the clinical landscape with psychotherapedia™: The unified psychotherapy project. *Journal of Unified Psychotherapy and Clinical Science, 1,* 21–36.

Magnusson, D. (1995). Individual development: A holistic, integrated model. In P. Moen, G. H. Elder, Jr., & K. Luscher (Eds.), *Examining lives in context: Perspectives on the ecology of human development* (pp. 19–60). Washington, DC: American Psychological Assocation.

Magnusson, D., & Torestad, B. (1993). A holistic view of personality: A model revisited. *Annual review of psychology, 44,* 427–454.

Mahoney, M. J. (1991). *Human change processes: The scientific foundations of psychotherapy.* New York: Basic Books.

Mahoney, M. J. (2003). *Constructive psychotherapy: A practical guide.* New York: Guilford.

Mahoney, M. J., & Moes, A. J. (1997). Complexity and psychotherapy: Promising and practical issues. In F. Masterpasqua & P. A. Perna (Eds.), *The psychological meaning of chaos: Translating theory into practice* (pp. 177–198). Washington, DC: American Psychological Association.

Malanson, G. P. (1999). Considering complexity. *Annals of the Association of American Geographers, 89,* 746–753. Retrieved July 14, 2011, from www.u.arizona.edu/~conniew1/696 m/malanson%201996.pdf

Marquis, A. (in press). Methodological considerations of studying a unified approach to psychotherapy: Integral methodological pluralism. *Journal of Unified Psychotherapy and Clinical Science.*

Maturana, H., & Varela, F. (1980). Autopoiesis and cognition: The realization of the living. In R. S. Cohen & M. W. Wartofsky (Eds.), *Boston studies in the philosophy of science V. 42.* Dordrecht, Holland: Reidel.

Mayer, J. D. (2004). How does psychotherapy influence personality? A theoretical integration. *Journal of Clinical Psychology, 60,* 1291–1315.

McClellan, J. E., & Dorn, H. (2006). *Science and technology in world history: An introduction* (2nd ed.). Baltimore: Johns Hopkins University Press.

Mebratu, D. (2001). The knowledge dimension of the sustainability challenge. *International Journal of Economic Development, 3,* 1–21. Retrieved August 16, 2012, from http://spaef.com/articleArchives.php?journal=IJED

Melchert, T. P. (2011). *Foundations of professional psychology: The end of theoretical orientations and the emergence of the biopsychosocial approach.* Waltham, MA: Elsevier.

Melchert, T. P. (2013). Beyond theoretical orientations: The emergence of a unified scientific framework in professional psychology. *Professional Psychology: Research and Practice, 44,* 11–19.

Meyer, K. A. (2005). Common metaphors and their impact on distance education: What they tell us and what they hide. *Teachers College Record, 107,* 1601–1625.

Miller, J. G. (1978). *Living systems.* New York: McGraw-Hill.

Miller, J. H., & Page, S. E. (2007). *Complex adaptive systems: An introduction to computational models of social life.* Princeton, NJ: Princeton University Press.

Miller, R. B. (1992). Introduction to the philosophy of clinical psychology. In R. B. Miller (Ed.), *The restoration of dialogue: Readings in the philosophy of clinical psychology* (pp. 1–27). Washington, DC: American Psychological Association.

Millon, T. (2000). Toward a new model of integrative psychotherapy: Psychosynergy. *Journal of Psychotherapy Integration, 10,* 37–53.

Millon, T., & Grossman, S. D. (2012). Personalized psychotherapy: The unification of customization of trait-oriented treatments. *Journal of Unified Psychotherapy and Clinical Science, 1,* 61–86.

Miranda, R., & Andersen, S. M. (2010). The social psychology of transference. In J. P. Tangney & J. E. Maddux (Eds.), *Social foundations of clinical psychology* (pp. 476–498). New York: Guilford.

Morowitz, H. J., & Singer, J. L. (Eds.). (1995). *The mind, the brain, and complex adaptive systems.* Reading, MA: Addison-Wesley.

Nicolis, G., & Prigogine, I. (1977). *Self-organization in non-equilibrium systems: From dissipative structures to order through fluctuations.* New York: Wiley.

Norcross, J. C. (2005). A primer on psychotherapy integration. In J. C. Norcross & M. R. Goldfried (Eds.), *Handbook of psychotherapy integration* (2nd ed., pp. 3–23). New York: Oxford University Press.

Norman, G. J., Cacioppo, J. T., & Berntson, G. G. (2010). Social neuroscience. In L. Nadel (Ed.), *Wiley Interdisciplinary Reviews: Cognitive Science, 1,* 60–68.

Nowotny, H. (2005). The increase of complexity and its reduction: Emergent interfaces between the natural sciences, humanities and social sciences. *Theory, Society & Culture, 22,* 15–31.

Office of Behavioral and Social Sciences Research (2007). *The contributions of behavioral and social sciences research to improving the health of the nation: A prospectus for the future.* Bethesda, MD: NIH. Retrieved December 11, 2011, from http://obssr.od.nih.gov/pdf/OBSSR_Prospectus.pdf

Ostreng, W. (2007). Reductionism versus holism–Contrasting approaches? In W. Ostreng (Ed.), *Consilience. Interdisciplinary communications 2005/2006* (pp. 11–14). Oslo, Norway: Centre for Advanced Study. Retrieved May 1, 2012, from http://www.cas.uio.no/Publications/Seminar/Consilience.pdf

Perna, P. A., & Masterpasqua, F. (1997). Introduction: The history, meanings, and implications of chaos and complexity. In F. Masterpasqua & P. A. Perna (Eds.), *The psychological meaning of chaos: Translating theory into practice* (pp. 1–19). Washington DC: American Psychological Association.

Pincus, A. L. (2010). Introduction to the special series on integrating personality, psychopathology, and psychotherapy using interpersonal assessment. *Journal of Personality Assessment, 92,* 467–470.

Polkinghorne, D. (1983). *Methodology for the human sciences: Systems of inquiry.* Albany, NY: SUNY Press.

Pouvreau, D., & Drack, M. (2007). On the history of Ludwig von Bertalanffy's "general systemology", and on its relationship to cybernetics. *International Journal of General Systems, 36,* 281–337.

Pumain, D. (Ed.). (2006). *Hierarchy in natural and social sciences.* Durtrecht, Netherlands: Springer.

Reis, H. T. (2007). Steps toward the ripening of relationship science. *Personal Relationships, 14,* 1–23.

Reis, H. T., Collins, W. A., & Berscheid, E. (2000). The relationship context of human behavior and development. *Psychological Bulletin, 126,* 844–872.

Rosenfield, P. C. (1992). The potential of transdisciplinary research for sustaining and extending linkages between health and social science. *Social Science Medicine, 35,* 1343–1357.

Royce, J. R. (1987). A strategy for developing unifying theory in psychology. In A. W. Staats & L. P. Mos (Eds.), *Annals of theoretical psychology* (Vol. 5, pp. 275–285). New York: Plenum Press.

Rychlak, J. F. (1976). The multiple meanings of dialectic. In J. F. Rychlak (Ed.), *Dialectic: Humanistic rationale for behavior and development* (pp. 1–17). Basel, Switzerland: S. Karger AG.

Rychlak, J. F. (1992). Foreword. In R. B. Miller (Ed.), *The restoration of dialogue: Readings in the philosophy of clinical psychology* (pp. xv–xvi). Washington, DC: American Psychological Association.

Ryff, C. D., & Singer, B. (1998). The contours of positive human health. *Psychological Inquiry, 9,* 1–28.

Ryff, C. D., & Singer, B. H. (2000). Biopsychosocial challenges of the new millennium. *Psychotherapy and Psychosomatics, 69,* 170–177.

Ryff, C. D., & Singer, B. H. (2006). Best news yet for the six-factor model of well-being. *Social Science Research, 35*, 1103–1119.

Schore, A. N. (1994). *Affect regulation and the origin of the self: A neurobiology of emotional development.* Hillsdale, NJ: Lawrence Erlbaum Associates.

Schore, A. N. (2003a). *Affect regulation and the repair of the self.* New York: Norton.

Schore, A. N. (2003b). *Affect dysregulation and disorders of the self.* New York: Norton.

Schore, A. N. (2012). *The science of the art of psychotherapy.* New York: Norton.

Senge, P. M. (1990). *The fifth discipline: The art and practice of the learning organization.* New York: Doubleday.

Shahar, G., Anchin, J. C., Gottdiener, W. H., Levy, K. N., & Mor, N. (2012). An editorial statement. *Journal of Psychotherapy Integration, 22*, 1–4.

Simon, H. A. (1962). The architecture of complexity. *Proceedings of the American Philosophical Society, 106*, 467–482.

Singer, J. A. (2005). *Personality and psychotherapy: Treating the whole person.* New York: Guilford.

Slife, B. D., & Williams, R. N. (1995). *What's behind the research? Discovering hidden assumptions in the behavioral sciences.* Thousand Oaks, CA: Sage.

Smith, L. B., & Thelen, E. (2003). Development as a dynamic system. *Trends in Cognitive Sciences, 7*, 343–348.

Spinhoven, P., Giesen-Bloo, J., van Dyck, R., Kooiman, C. G., & Arntz, A. (2007). The therapeutic alliance in schema-focused therapy and transference-focused psychotherapy for borderline personality disorder. *Journal of Consulting and Clinical Psychology, 75*, 104–115.

Staats, A. W. (1987). Unified positivism: Philosophy for the revolution to unity. In A. W. Staats & L. P. Mos (Eds.), *Annals of theoretical psychology* (Vol. 5, pp. 11–54). New York: Plenum Press.

Staats, A. W. (1991). *Unified positivism and unification psychology: Fad or new field? American Psychologist, 46*, 899–912.

Staats, A. W. (1999). Unifying psychology requires new infrastructure, theory, method, and a research agenda. *Review of General Psychology, 3*, 3–13.

Stebly, L. (1998). Faculty perspectives on teaching with digital images. In H. Besser & R. Yamashita (Eds.), *The cost of digital image distribution: The social and economic implications of the production, distribution, and usage of image data (A report to the Andrew W. Mellon Foundation).* Berkeley, CA: UCB School of Information Management & Systems. Retrieved January 10, 2013, from http://besser.tsoa.nyu.edu/howard/imaging/1998mellon/finalreport/6-focus.html

Sternberg, R. J. (Ed.). (2004). *Unity in psychology: Possibility or pipedream?* Washington, DC: American Psychological Association.

Sternberg, R. J., & Grigorenko, E. L. (2001). *Unified psychology. American Psychologist, 56*, 1069–1079.

Stokols, D. (2006). Toward a science of transdisciplinary action research. *American Journal of Community Psychology, 38*, 63–77.

Stokols, D., Hall, K. L., Taylor, B. K., & Moser, R. P. (2008). The science of team science: Overview of the field and introduction to the supplement. *American Journal of Preventive Medicine, 35*(2S), S77–S89.

Strack, S. (2005). Measuring normal personality the Millon way. In S. Strack (Ed.), *Handbook of personology and psychopathology* (pp. 372–389). New York: Wiley.

Stricker, G., & Gold, J. (2011). Integrative approaches to psychotherapy. In S. B. Messer & A. S. Gurman (Eds.), *Essential psychotherapies: Theory and practice* (pp. 426–459). New York: Guilford.

Teachman, B. A., Drabick, D. A. G., Hershenberg, R., Vivian, D., Wolfe, B. E., & Goldfried, M. R. (2012). Bridging the gap between clinical research and clinical practice: Introduction to the special section. *Psychotherapy, 49,* 97–100.

Thelen, E., & Smith, L. B. (2006). Dynamic systems theories. In W. Damon & R. L. Lerner (Eds.), *Handbook of child psychology: Theoretical models of human development* (Vol. 1, 6th ed., pp. 258–312). New York: Wiley.

Tschacher, W., Junghan, U. M., & Pfammatter, M. (in press). Towards a taxonomy of common factors in psychotherapy—Results of an expert survey. *Clinical Psychology & Psychotherapy.*

Umpleby, S. (1990). The science of cybernetics and the cybernetics of science. *Cybernetics and Systems, 21,* 109–121.

Vallacher, R. R., & Nowak, A. (1999). The dynamics of self-regulation. In R. S. Wyer, Jr. (Ed.), *Advances in social cognition* (Vol. 12, pp. 241–259). Mahwah, NJ: Lawrence Erlbaum Associates.

Vallacher, R. R., & Nowak, A. (2007). Dynamical social psychology: Finding order in the flow of human experience. In A. W. Kruglanski & E. T. Higgins (Eds.), *Social psychology: Handbook of basic principles* (2nd ed., pp. 734–758). New York: Guilford.

Viney, W. (1989). The cyclops and the twelve-eyed toad: William James and the unity–disunity problem in psychology. *American Psychologist, 44,* 1261–1265.

von Bertalanffy, L. (1968). *General system theory: Foundations, development, applications.* New York: Brazziler.

Wallis, S. E. (2010). Toward a science of metatheory. *Integral Review, 6,* 73–120. Retrieved January 2, 2013, from http://integral-review.org/back_issues/backissue12_ Vol6No3/metatheory-issue_index.asp.

Wampold, B. E. (2001). *The great psychotherapy debate: Models, methods, and findings.* Mahwah, NJ: Lawrence Erlbaum Associates.

Watzlawick, P., Beavin, J. H., & Jackson, D. D. (1967). *Pragmatics of human communication: A study of interactional patterns, pathologies, and paradoxes.* New York: Norton.

Werndl, C. (2009). What are the new implications of chaos for unpredictability? *The British Journal for the Philosophy of Science, 60,* 195–220.

Wertheimer, M. (1988). Obstacles to the integration of competing theories in psychology. *Philosophical Psychology, 1,* 131–137.

Wikipedia (2010). Holism. Retrieved August 3, 2010, from http://en.wikipedia.org/wiki/Holism

Wolfe, B. E. (2008). Toward a unified conceptual framework of psychotherapy. *Journal of Psychotherapy Integration, 18,* 292–300.

Woolfolk, R. L., & Richardson, F. C. (2008). Philosophy and psychotherapy. *Journal of Psychotherapy Integration, 18,* 25–39.

Yanchar, S. C., & Slife, B. D. (1997). Pursuing unity in a fragmented psychology: Problems and prospects. *Review of General Psychology, 1,* 235–255.

Yela, M. (1987). Toward a unified psychological science: The meaning of behavior. In A. W. Staats & L. P. Mos (Eds.), *Annals of theoretical psychology* (Vol. 5, pp. 241–274). New York: Plenum Press.

Zucker, R. A. (2006). Alcohol use and the alcohol use disorders: A developmental-biopsychosocial formulation covering the life course. In D. Cicchetti & D. J. Cohen (Eds.), *Developmental psychopathology: Risk, disorder, and adaptation* (Vol. 3, 2nd ed., pp. 620–656). New York: Wiley.

Chapter 2

THE PERSONALITY SYSTEM

All mental health and behavioral treatment is, at its best, personality-guided (Millon, 1999; Magnavita, 2010). In this chapter we explain why treatment is enhanced when an understanding of the personality system and how it operates is at our fingertips. Old conceptions of personality as a static, immutable, or fixed structure have given way to a more contemporary notion of personality as an organic and holistic entity. Our personality is a system—not a static structure. Developing an understanding of the operation of the personality system provides essential insight into our most fundamental human processes.

In this chapter we provide a description of the holistic map of the human personality system that we use to orient our unifying approach to psychotherapy. This is followed by a discussion of the fundamental relationship between the personality system and stress, coping, adaptation, and maladaptation. The linkage between the transactional theory of stress (e.g., Lazarus & Folkman, 1984) and the cognitive–motivational–relational theory of coping (e.g., Lazarus, 1993) serves as the framework guiding this discussion. We bring to bear different lenses tied to different levels of the personality system to illuminate some key ways in which the latter strongly influences components of the human stress process and its outcomes. In conjunction with the previous and the following chapter, the present chapter helps lay ground for Part II of this book, which offers the reader a more nuanced understanding of the four levels of the personality system and implications for understanding and approaching treatment of psychological disorders and relational disturbances from a unified perspective.

CONCEPTUALIZING AND MAPPING THE HUMAN PERSONALITY SYSTEM

Our approach to unified psychotherapy has been strongly influenced by the personality-guided conceptions of psychopathology and psychotherapy developed by Theodore Millon (1999). His work has been seminal in drawing attention to the perspective that psychopathology, ranging from specific symptom constellations to long-standing personality disorders and relational disturbances, stems fundamentally from the structure and functioning of a client's personality—his or her "lifelong style of relating, coping, behaving, thinking, and feeling" (Millon, 1996, p. 15). Millon and Grossman (2012) eloquently depict the intrinsic biopsychosocial unity of the person:

> whether we work with "part functions" that focus on behaviors, or cognitions, or unconscious processes, or biological defects, and the like, or whether we address contextual systems which focus on the larger environment, the family, or the group, or the socio-economic and political conditions of life, the crossover point, the place that links parts to contexts is the person. The individual is the intersecting medium that brings them together. Persons, however, are more than crossover mediums. They are the only organically integrated system in the psychological domain, inherently created from birth as naturally unified entities, rather than experience-derived gestalts constructed via cognitive attribution. Moreover, it is persons who lie at the heart of the psychotherapeutic experience, the substantive beings that give meaning and coherence to symptoms and traits—be they behaviors, affects, or mechanisms—as well as those beings, those singular entities, that give life and expression to family interactions and social processes. (pp. 64–65)

The whole person is thus central to Millon's conception of personality, and it is heartening to find that in contemporary personality science and its clinical applications, interest in the whole person is burgeoning. In this regard, a state-of-the art special issue of the *Journal of Personality* focused on personality psychology and psychotherapy warrants particular mention. In his introduction, Singer (in press) indicates that the diverse collection of work presented "taken as a whole makes a compelling case for an integrative understanding of the whole person (rather than a set of symptoms) in the course of psychotherapy." Moreover, paralleling an important theme of this volume's first chapter and Mechert's (2011, 2013) forward-looking analyses, Singer (in press) observes that in personality science "the older therapeutic orientations of cognitive, behavioral, psychodynamic, humanistic, biological, and so on are breaking down and being replaced by a more integrated and less partisan vision of the person." In his studied review of the National Institute of Mental Health (NIMH) 2012 budget, he also observed the recurrent emphasis on translational research, the purpose of which is to translate findings from basic scientific research into applications within the applied clinical realm, and in this regard—consistent with the trend toward unification—Singer (in press) indicates that close reading of NIMH's objectives for the future of translational research highlights its interdisciplinary foundation. In this light, he shares his

> sense that the true aspiration of translational mental health research is (or at least should be) the re-integration of discrete processes, as studied by interdisciplinary teams, into a larger vision of interrelated biological and behavioral systems in a sociocultural context. In other words, its ultimate goal is to rediscover the person through the consolidated efforts of personality psychology and clinical science.

Notably, the findings of another scholar in the area of personality science dovetail with the holistic, "whole-person" themes voiced by Singer. In the context of discussing contemporary approaches to studying and analyzing personality, Cervone (2005) points out: "An encouraging sign for personality science is that at the level of meta-theory there is much consensus. It reflects developments in the sciences at large (Kauffman, 1995, Taylor, 2001, Waldrop, 1992). Numerous writers view personality as a complex dynamical system (Fraley & Brumbaugh 2004, Nowak & Vallacher, 1998, Read & Miller, 2002, Shoda et al., 2002)" (p. 432). Still others who have recently articulated explicitly systemic frameworks for understanding and studying personality include Block (2002), Carver and Scheier (2002), Cloninger (2004), Kuhl (2000), Mayer (2004, 2005), and Peck (2007).

Of course, conceptualizing human personality in holistic, systemic terms is far from new. Andras Angyal (1941) presaged the contemporary era's metatheoretical systemic conceptions of personality some 70 years ago, while other earlier conceptualizations of personality reflecting a distinctly systemic perspective include those by Murphy (1947), Murray (1959), Allport (1961a, 1961b), Smelser and Smelser (1963), and Miller (1978). The point we highlight is that, within the field of personality science, a view of human personality as a complex dynamical system remains as vital and viable as ever (cf. Cervone & Mischel, 2002).

Personality Systematics—The Four Levels of the Personality System

In sync with these views, we view personality as a complex system that is expressed in and shaped by the total human ecosystem at multiple levels, from the microsystem (mind/brain) to the macrosystem (families, culture, environment). Personality is an emergent phenomenon, arising from the enormously complex network of interwoven biopsychosocial structures and processes that constitute and contextualize human being-in-the-world. We have used the term *personality systematics* to character-ize this metatheoretical model of personality; fundamentally holistic in nature, it offers a significant step toward unifying psychotherapy and the clinical sciences. Personality systematics seeks to pull together and organize within a coherent framework the vast sea of structures and processes that interactively constitute, influence, and color human per-sonality, functioning, and experience, and entails the study of the inter-relationships among all the domains composing the personality system. Personality is not something that resides within the person, but rather is viewed in terms of nested levels of embedded structures that range from the microlevel to the macrolevel, paralleling Urie Bronfenbrenner's (1979) description of the interconnected domains of human ecology as "a set of nested structures, each inside the next, like a set of Russian dolls" (p. 3). Psychology has been slow to take up Bronfenbrenner's ideas—surprising to us, but perhaps our focus on the individual has been so myopic that we lost sight of the whole; it is worth reading Bronfenbrenner's (1979) original text, as there is much to distill that is beyond the scope of this volume. In sync with Bronfenbrenner's conceptual scheme, the various levels of the human personality system are hierarchical in that microlevel processes are increasingly subsumed by higher-level processes. These levels are comprised of various domain systems that themselves are (sub)systems of interrelated structures and feedback processes. Discussed in greater detail in the next section, the four levels of the personality system are as follows (see Figure 2.1).

Level I: Intrapsychic—Biological

This level includes motivation, the affective–cognitive–defensive matrix, and the neurobiological substrate or nanosystem of the individual from which this matrix is an emergent phenomenon. Characteristic of nonlin-ear systems, perturbations of any components of the motivational, affec-tive, cognitive, and/or defensive subsystems will alter the organization of the matrix. The domains of this matrix include hereditary predisposition, temperament, and integrity of neurobiological systems, and internalized cognitive and relational schematic representations. Relative to this matrix, our concerns include the integrity of the system to adapt to environmental challenge as it seeks to accomplish its aims, goals, and strivings without

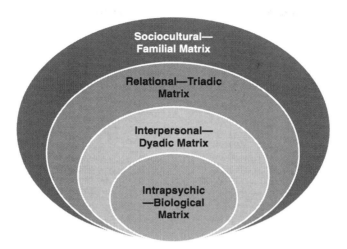

FIGURE 2.1   *Levels of the human personality system.*

becoming impaired or symptomatic. Thus, we are concerned with the capacity of the defensive structure to regulate affect, the suitability of cognitive and relational schema, and the maintenance of self-cohesion as the individual pursues his or her goals and strivings and navigates the demands and opportunities of the human condition.

Level II: Interpersonal—Dyadic

This level encompasses the processes that occur in interpersonal or dyadic configurations created when two individuals are in relationship. These include the verbal and nonverbal aspects and forms of communicative processes, the attachment system shaped and encoded by early maternal–infant experience, and the impact of trauma in disrupting these structures and processes. At this level of the personality system's organization, we are concerned with interpersonal processes primarily as they are enacted in current relationships, expected relationships (i.e., as enacted in transference and countertransference), and their patterning based on their origins in past relationships. Much therapeutic action is concerned with using tools of pattern recognition to map and then restructure these encoded schematic representations and relational scripts. Attachment experiences, internalized schemas of self and other, and interpersonal expectations strongly influence these dyadic patterns, which are also shaped and reinforced by family interactions at Level III. As development unfolds, internalized relational–schematic encodings from Level I and type of attachment are transformed into the capacity for intimacy/closeness, which are a hallmark of differentiation and integration of this dyadic matrix as it is embedded in family, social, and cultural structures. Self–other functioning that appropriately regulates intimacy/closeness and dependency–autonomy polarities enables the individual to have satisfying intimate attachments throughout the lifespan—a bequest of human evolution.

Level III: Relational—Triadic

This level includes relational configurations of two or more (2 + n) and is particularly concerned with structure, function, and processes that occur in unstable dyadic configurations that transmit anxiety to a third person in an effort to provide stabilization for the dyad. A common example is that of a highly conflicted marital dyad in which one of the couple's children is enlisted to absorb the anxiety and thus stabilize the couple. The lower the level of either or both spouse's intrapsychic differentiation (Level I) in emotional capacity (i.e., the capacity to experience, appropriately label, and express different feelings), and the lower the boundary definition between self and other, the more prone toward triangulation (Bowen, 1976). These triadic configurations, which are expressed in a variety of forms (Guerin, Fogarty, Fay, & Kautto, 1996), are ubiquitous in dysfunctional family systems and can often be seen generationally represented.

Level IV: Sociocultural—Familial

This level, also termed the mesosystem, includes the sociopolitical system, family system, and the individual personality system, and their triadic interrelationships. The domains represented in this total ecological matrix include the mutual influence of structure and organization among the social and cultural system, the family, and the individual. Evolutionary psychology provides a valuable perspective in this matrix in that it contributes to understanding how the mind shapes culture and culture shapes the mind. In essence, culture carries codes that Dawkins (1982) referred to as *memes*, which are similar to the genetic code carried biologically, but in this case the codes are carried socioculturally. The family transmits the cultural codes through child-rearing practices, which are also heavily influenced by the attachment experiences of the caregivers and multigenerational transmission processes.

THE PERSONALITY SYSTEM IN STRESS, COPING, AND ADAPTATION

The multilevel and interwoven biopsychosocial structures and processes captured by personality systematics are essential to understanding the development and emergence of psychological disorder, but insufficient for a comprehensive understanding of the etiology and course of a given client's disorder and in formulating treatment strategies and interventions. Critical as well is an understanding of the stress process as an essential multicomponent influence on human adaptation and maladaptation; it is within the context of the dynamic stress process that the operation of the human personality system in all its strengths and weaknesses becomes most clear.

Fundamentals of the Stress Process

Hans Selye (1936) coined the term *stress* and anchored its fundamental modern meanings in 1936 within the context of his work as an endocrinologist. Although Selye's definition of stress underwent several modifications over time (Puglisi-Allegra, 1999), the basic conception that stress is the body's response to environmental demands endures. Integrating prior work by Cannon (1929) on the fight-or-flight response, Selye formulated the General Adaptation Syndrome, according to which the body responds to a threatening environmental event with a three-stage physiological response: alarm, resistance, and exhaustion. As Selye's understanding of stress evolved, he incorporated the important role of psychological processes in the assessment of and reaction to stress, captured in his deceptively straightforward assertion: "It is not what happens to you that matters, but how you take it" (cited by Everly, 2005, p. 366).

Embedded in this assertion are the three principal domains of the stress process: sources of stress, stress mediators, and manifestations of stress (Pearlin, 1989; Pearlin, Menaghan, Lieberman, & Mullan, 1981). The *sources of stress*, characteristically referred to as stressors, entail the external environmental challenges, threats, and demands that impinge upon an individual, although it is important to note that transitions over the course of the human life cycle can also operate as stressors (Pearlin, 2010); these developmental processes invariably incorporate environmental elements but also encompass adjustmental demands inherent to the evolution of a human life. *Stress mediators* encompass biological, psychological, relational, and sociocultural factors, resources, and processes that influence an individual's reaction to stressors and hence the latter's impact on the individual. Mediated by these interacting factors, the actual effects of stressors on an individual are characteristically denoted by the term *stress*, which customarily involves the noxious physiological and psychological reactions triggered in reaction to the external demands, challenges, and threats. Pearlin et al.'s (1981) concept of *manifestations of stress* usefully expands this concept to include not only the internal impacts of stressors but also overt expressions of these negative internal effects.

The Stress Process in Motion: Transactional Theory of Stress and Cognitive–Motivational–Relational Theory of Coping

While the distinction among sources of stress, stress mediators, and manifestations of stress is useful in identifying critical components of the stress process, a biopsychosocial systems perspective underscores that in real time these components spin out over time and are intricately intertwined through feedback loops. This perspective is fundamental to Lazarus and Folkman's (1984) transactional stress theory, "the most influential psychological stress model of the last decades" (Vollrath, 2001, p. 336), and the evolution of this theory in the form of Lazarus's cognitive–motivational–relational theory (CMRT) of coping. Lazarus (2000) explicitly encouraged the study and understanding of these processes from a systemic perspective in view of the intricately textured, multi-domained, and holistic way of thinking that it encourages (cf. Lazarus, 1991); thus, commenting favorably on directions researchers were pursuing in the study of coping, he underscored that "they are examining psychological events more closely (micro-analytically), in depth (relevant to levels of unconsciousness and defense), longitudinally, and more holistically as people cope with stress (as process), think (appraise and construct relational meanings), want, feel, and act in their struggle to advance their interests and adapt. More than in the past, these researchers are also increasingly attending to individual differences (both intra- and interindividual)" (pp. 672–673).

The synthesis of transactional stress theory and CMRT conveys the holistic biopsychosocial nature of the stress process and points to the utility of personality systematics for capturing and guiding clinical intervention into these multiple processes. Central to Lazarus and Folkman's formulations are the concepts of *appraisal* and *relational meaning*; the conceptual chord connecting these concepts is that neither the person nor the environment alone creates stress, but rather, stress is the product of a dynamic interrelationship—the *transaction*—between these two dynamic domains of phenomena. Appraisal is the critical process that mediates this transaction.

In primary appraisal, relative to an environmental event or circumstance, an individual constructs a relational meaning, which embodies his or her subjective interpretation of the relevance and significance of that external situation in terms of the degree of harm or benefit it poses to his or her beliefs and valued personal goals (Lazaarus, 1993; Ntoumanis, Edmunds, & Duda, 2009). An individual's network of personal strivings (Singer, 2005) may encompass immediate, short-term, and long-term goals, may vary along dimensions (e.g., rational/irrational), and may be hierarchically nested, but whatever their content and configurations, collectively they are essential to giving human life its directionality (Anchin, 2003, 2008).

A relational meaning contains not only cognitive content reflecting one's interpretive appraisal of the person–environment relationship, but it is also experienced as an emotion. To the extent that a situation or event is appraised as harmful, dangerous, or threatening to one's goals and integrally related well-being, the individual will experience principally negative emotion(s)—of which stress is but one subset (Lazarus, 1993)—thereby demarcating the external event functionally as a stressor. Appraising an environmental event as beneficial to one's goal strivings and well-being is characterstically accompanied by positive emotionality, and hence functionally does not constitute a stressor. Lazarus (1991) succinctly conveyed the manner in which relational meaning encapsulates this dynamic transaction between an individual's environment, goals and beliefs, appraisal, and emotion: "relational meaning...centers on the significance of what is happening for personal well-being. It depends on how the environmental conditions are conjoined with a person's beliefs and goals.... We can understand [an] emotional response in terms of how what is happening is construed by the person from the standpoint of personal interest and adaptation" (pp. 39–40).

In instances when the relational meaning an individual constructs reflects an appraisal that a situation poses a threat to well-being and concomitantly experiences negative emotionality, secondary appraisal ensues. In this process, an individual evaluates his or her options and resources for coping with the stressor. "Once a person has appraised a transaction as stressful, coping processes are brought into play to manage the troubled person-environment relationship (Lazarus, 1990a; Lazarus & Folkman, 1984)" (Vollrath, 2001, p. 336). Lazarus (1991) defined coping as "cognitive and behavioral efforts to manage specific external or internal demands (and conflicts between them) that are appraised as taxing or exceeding the resources of the person" (p. 112); coping is thus a regulatory process (Crockett, Iturbide, Torres Stone, McGinley, Raffaelli, & Carlo, 2007). Considering the robust evidence of "a relationship between coping and [healthy] psychological outcomes" (Folkman, 2011, p. 458), the importance of closely addressing a patient's coping processes, vis-à-vis the acute and/or chronic stressors that have been instrumental in their distress and pursuit of treatment, cannot be overstated.

Two forms of coping have occupied center stage in both transactional stress theory and CMRT. Both may be considered approach/engagement strategies in that they entail different facets of essentially moving toward and addressing head-on the stressor at hand. Problem-centered coping seeks to regulate the situation triggering the stress, while emotion-centered coping is focused on regulating the subjectively experienced aversive emotions. These two forms of coping are not mutually exclusive, and in fact may be complementary, each facilitating the other (Snyder, 1999). By the same token, different kinds of stressful events seem to warrant more of one than the other approach. As Snyder (1999) points out, under circumstances in which the stressful situation can be changed for the better and personal control can be exercised, problem-centered coping seems most appropriate, whereas emotion-focused coping seems especially warranted when the stressful situation itself is not amenable to change. However, whichever set or mixture of strategies one employs, as changes in the stressful situation and one's emotional reactions evolve as a function of implementing coping processes, these situational and/ or emotional alterations operate as feedback and lead to initiation of a new round of appraisals. Ultimately, "[i]n terms of the adaptive consequences of stress, coping strategies are more important than the duration and frequency of actual stress episodes. These coping processes influence the person's subsequent appraisal and hence the kind and intensity of the stress reaction" (Vollrath, 2001, p. 336).

While problem-centered and emotion-centered coping are both approach strategies, individuals may alternatively engage in avoidance/disengagement strategies (Connor-Smith & Flachsbart, 2007; Fortier, DiLillo, Messman-Moore, Peugh, DeNardi, & Gaffey, 2009; Kim & Duda, 2003)—in essence, moving away from and disengaging with the stressor (e.g., through substance use, behavioral withdrawal, or psychological defenses). As Roth and Cohen (1986) pointed out, the use of approach/ engagement strategies does not definitively exclude the use of avoidance/ disengagement in the course of coping with a stressful event: "The two basic orientations toward threatening information, approach and avoidance, can vary in primacy across time for an individual, and both modes of coping with stress may be present at any particular time, as when certain aspects of the threatening material are approached, and others are avoided" (p. 815). A mixture of approach and avoidance coping strategies is not surprising, particularly if the time frame is opened up and there ensues a process of stress proliferation (Pearlin, 2010), whereby a primary stressor (e.g., involuntary job loss) gives rise to secondary stressors (e.g., economic strain; family conflict), thereby confronting the individual with multiple coping demands. Moreover, approach and avoidance strategies each carry benefits and costs (see, e.g., Roth & Cohen, 1986, Table 1), depending on such factors as the nature and complexity of the stressor, the time point in the stress process when a given strategy is used, and personality factors specific to the individual. Bearing in mind these considerations, Roth and Cohen (1986)

> outline an "ideal" case of coping with stress, an example of how in the best of all possible worlds the coping process might operate at maximum effectiveness.... In this ideal case, both modes of coping with stress would be operative, with the benefits of each realized and the costs of each minimized. Thus, adaptive

coping efforts would be mobilized and maintained, and there would be a gradual assimilation and resolution of threat or trauma. Although there would be psychological retreats from threatening material, these would not be so consistent or complete as to be costly, and although there would undoubtedly be a significant amount of distress experienced in response to the threat or trauma, this would be time limited due to a successful working-through process. (p. 818)

An important development in the realm of stress and coping research over the past two decades that must be added to this equation, and containing significant therapeutic implications, is the role played by positive emotion in the coping process. Folkman (2011; cf. Folkman & Moskowitz, 2000) indicates that evidence continues to accrue that positive emotions can co-occur with negative emotions during stress episodes, that they exert an independent effect on adaptational outcomes, and that individuals can find positive meanings and perceive personal growth as a consequence of their stress. The concept of resilience has emerged as central within this context, and in this regard, "researchers are turning their attention to *actual coping processes* that sustain positive well-being, promote recovery, and provide opportunity for growth" (p. 457, emphasis in original). Toward this end, Folkman has identified "meaning-focused coping," in which individuals attempt to draw "something good from something bad" (p. 457), as a third form of approach-oriented coping alongside problem-oriented and emotion-oriented coping. Central to meaning-focused coping is drawing on "values, goals, beliefs, and commitments," which can increase positive emotion and motivate individuals to engage in and maintain their coping efforts.

The Role of the Personality System in Mediating Stress

Linking a dynamic transactional/CMRT model of fundamental processes operative in stress and coping to a biopsychosocial understanding of the multilevel, multidomain structure and functioning of the human personality system optimizes the clinical utility of both domains of knowledge. An integrated transactional stress/CMRT model keys the therapist into the dynamic person–environment relationship and in particular the nature and powerful role of appraisal and coping processes vis-à-vis stressful life events in influencing the directionality of the patient's course along a continuum from healthy adaptation and well-being to psychopathology and distress. Synergistically, understanding the biological, psychological, and sociocultural levels of the patient's personality system sheds light on his or her unique individual differences in shaping and navigating this ongoing transaction, carrying highly textured implications for understanding the patient's problems in living and formulating therapeutic interventions.

Millon's (1996; Millon & Grossman, 2012) characterization of the personality system as the equivalent of the immune system provides a valuable metaphor for grasping this profound role exerted by the personality system in mediating stress. The immune system is the body's inherent capacity, through distinct biological structures and processes, to protect itself from destructive biological agents (e.g., bacteria, viruses, carcinogens) in the physical environment that can lead to illness and disease. When the immune system is robust, the individual "will counteract the usual range of infectious microbes with ease, whereas those with weakened immunosuppressive capacities are vulnerable, fail to handle these 'intrusions,' and quickly succumb" (Millon, 1996, p. 9). In the same vein,

> it is…the patient's personality pattern—that is, coping skills and adaptive flexibilities—that determines whether or not the person masters or succumbs to his or her psychosocial environment. Just as physical ill health is likely to be less a matter of some alien virus than it is a dysfunction in the body's capacity to deal with infectious agents, so too is psychological ill health likely to be less a product of some intrusive psychic strain than it is a dysfunction in the personality's capacity to cope with life's difficulties. Viewed this way the structure and characteristics of personality become the foundation for the individual's capacity to function in a mentally healthy or ill way. (Millon, 1996, p. 10)

Individuals who develop psychological disorders are those whose personality, conceived as a multilayered and dynamical biopsychosocial system, contains deficiencies that negatively impact their capacities to adaptively appraise and effectively cope with life's threats, challenges, and vicissitudes (see Kiesler, 1999, p. 102). These deficiencies in the personality system, whether characterized as dysfunctions, vulnerabilities, deficits, or liabilities, eventuate in interpretations of stressful events and/ or modes of coping that are maladaptive, rigid, and self-perpetuating—and thus inevitably distressogenic. Several different lenses illustrate more specifically how various levels of the patient's biopsychosocial personality matrix can impact the stress process.

The Diathesis-Stress Model. The central role of deficiencies in the personality system in predisposing an individual toward maladaptive reactions to stressors and in turn the emergence of clinical psychopathology is integral to the diathesis-stress model. Originally offered as an explanation for the development of schizophrenia (Meehl, 1962; Rosenthal, 1970; Zubin &

Spring, 1977), over ensuing years the diathesis-stress model has evolved as pertinent to understanding the etiology of psychopathology more generally (Paris, 1999). A diathesis is a vulnerability or predisposition toward developing a disorder and can, as Kiesler (1999) pointed out, be inborn or acquired. An inborn diathesis is genetically based and literally embodied in inherent dysfunction in the individual's neurophysiological system, while an acquired diathesis is environmentally imposed, due "'to the influence of traumas, specific diseases, perinatal complications, family experiences, adolescent peer interactions, and other life events that either enhance or inhibit the development of subsequent disorder' (Zubin & Spring, 1977, p. 109)" (Kiesler, 1999, p. 175).

The model provides an explanation for how an individual can have a particular threshold of biological and/or psychological vulnerability that, when impinged on by a certain level of acute or chronic stress, can result in an "outbreak" of psychological disorder (Monroe & Simons, 1991). Whether genetically and/or environmentally created, a diathesis can exist at the neurobiological, intrapsychic, dyadic, triadic, and/or sociocultural–familial levels of the human personality system; its existence carries significant implications not only for understanding and treating a current episode of psychological disorder, but also for psychotherapeutic work aimed at remediating the vulnerability in the service of reducing the risk of future episodes of disorder as new stressors are inevitably introduced over the life course.

Personality Traits: The Big-Five Personality Factors. A significant linkage between personality and the stress process has received robust support from studies examining relationships between the latter and the Big Five Personality Factors (Widiger & Costa, 2013). The Big Five, consensually viewed as the most comprehensive taxonomy of factors characterizing the structure of human personality, represents an approach to the study of personality that views personality structure as organized in terms of traits (see Millon & Grossman, 2012 and Wiggins, 2003 for additional examples of trait models of personality structure). Paraphrasing Haslam (2007), a trait (a) is a relatively enduring disposition (or tendency) to think, feel, or behave in a particular patterned and consistent way across situations and time, (b) has a sizeable inherited genetic component, and (c) is a way that people differ from one another, such that, when compared, different individuals will have different degrees of the same trait (hence the characterization of trait approaches as capturing "individual differences").

Table 2.1 contains a listing of each of the Big Five factors and defining characteristics of normal high and normal low adaptive variants, and maladaptively high and maladaptively low variants, of each factor.

Literature summarized by Connor-Smith and Flachsbart (2007), DeLongis and Holtzman (2005), Vollrath (2001), and Lecic-Tosevski, Vukovic, and Stepanovic (2011) found that the Big Five factors exert an

TABLE 2.1 *The Big Five Personality Factors*

Trait	Examples of Adaptive Variants		Examples of Maladaptive Variants	
	Normal High	Normal Low	Maladaptively High	Maladaptively Low
Neuroticism (versus Emotional Stability)	Worrisome, vigilant, pessimistic, resentful, embarrassed, self-indulgent, vulnerable	Relaxed, even-tempered, not easily discouraged, self-assured, restrained, resilient	Fearful, anxious, depressed, uncertain of self, rageful, unable to resist impulses, unstable, helpless	Fearless, oblivious to signs of threat, overly optimistic, unrealistic, shameless, overly restrained
Extraversion (versus Introversion)	Affectionate, warm, sociable, outgoing, assertive, energetic, adventurous, high-spirited, joyful	Formal, reserved, independent, passive, slow-paced, cautious, sober, serious	Intense attachments, attention-seeking, dominant, authoritarian, pushy, frantic, reckless, melodramatic	Distant, cold, isolated, resigned, lethargic, dull, listless, anhedonic
Openness (versus Closedness)	Imaginative, aesthetic interests, unconventional, expressive, self-aware, creative, curious, open/flexible values	Practical, realistic, constricted, blunted, predictable, pragmatic, traditional values	Eccentric, weird, unrealistic, lives in fantasy, bizarre interests, out of place, intense, radical values	Concrete, disinterested, alexithymic, stuck in routine, mechanized, close-minded, rigid, moralistically intolerant and dogmatic re: values

Agreeableness (versus Antagonism)	Trusting, honest, giving, generous, cooperative, obedient, humble, unassuming, empathic, sympathetic, gentle	Cautious, skeptical, Cunning, shrewd, frugal, critical, contrary, confident, self-assured, strong, tough	Gullible, guileless, self-sacrificial, yielding, docile, meek, self-denigrating, self-effacing, overly soft-hearted	Cynical, suspicious, deceptive, dishonest, manipulative, exploitative, combative, aggressive, pretentious, arrogant, callous, ruthless
Conscientiousness (versus Undependability)	Efficient, resourceful, organized, dependable, reliable, responsible, purposeful, diligent, self-disciplined, reflective	Casual, disorganized, easy-going, capricious, carefree, leisurely, quick to make decisions	Perfectionistic, preoccupied with organization, rigidly principled, workaholic, single-mindedly determined, ruminative, indecisive	Lax, disinclined, careless, sloppy, irresponsible, undependable, immoral, aimless, desultory, negligent, hasty, rash

Adapted from Widiger, 2011, Figure 1; Widiger & Presnall, in press; and Widiger, 2006.

impact on virtually every component of the stress process, including the likelihood that stressful events will occur, selection and shaping of stressful situations, the ways in which stressful situations are construed and appraised, the coping strategies that individuals choose to employ, and these strategies' effectiveness or outcomes.

In translating this finding into clinical implications, it is essential to recognize that personality traits are not literally structures in an individual's personality, not something one "has." Rather, traits are *patterned regularities* in what they think, feel, strive for, and enact that are learned, experienced, and expressed within the context of particular types of situations, and these thoughts, feelings, goals, and actions are themselves dynamic, fluid processes that interweave and unfold over given segments of time (cf. Cervone, 2005, pp. 428–429). Thus, while research valuably indicates that personality characteristics indeed influence a person's appraisal of and coping with stressful events, it does not tell us *how* these characteristics actually operate in real time in specific contexts. Thus, in the doing of psychotherapy, it is useful although not sufficient to know that a patient's personality system is characterized by, for example, a certain degree of neuroticism that influences his or her appraisal of a stressor or approach to coping and its specific mechanisms. It is essential, as well, to know *how* his or her level of neuroticism plays out in appraisal and coping processes—for example, by virtue of his or her neuroticism, the idiosyncratic content of the subjective meaning he or she ascribes to a stressful event. This perspective translates personality traits, which are otherwise depicted in terms that misleadingly suggest static qualities (e.g., the patient has a particular level of neuroticism or agreeableness), into a dynamical systems perspective that incorporates the importance of context (see, e.g., Lee-Baggley, Preece, & Delongis, 2005) and it is entirely consistent with the process conception at the heart of an integrated transactional stress theory/CMRT model. Fay (1996) offered a recommendation and observation that can be extrapolated to this process conception of trait theories of personality and their idiographic application to a given patient's appraisal and coping processes:

> *Think processurally, not substantively (that is, think in terms of verbs, not nouns). Include time as a fundamental element in all social entities. See movement—transformation, evolution, change—everywhere.* Much social thought reifies activities and processes, turning them into things with fixed identities: "the" self or "this society or culture are treated as objects with definitive boundaries and essential structure....But social and psychological entities are activities, not things. Consequently, they are better described by means of verbs rather than nouns. We talk of human beings as if they were

entities like stones, and not continuous processes of activity—
forgetting that "being" is a gerund, and that it refers to an
ongoing process. (p. 242)

As a dynamical system situated in real time, personality is a process,
and as such, regularities in thought, feeling, motivation, and behavior in
relation to life's stressors spin out in sequential, concurrent, and interactive fashion; trait profiles capture these patterns in a manner akin to still
photographs, but in the practice of psychotherapy, it is essential for the
therapist and patient to also "see" the latter's traits in motion as he or
she enacts and experiences their systemically entwined components in
the very real day-to-day contexts of his or her life.

Social Support. Taylor and Sherman (2004) define social support as
"the perception or experience that one is loved and cared for by others,
esteemed and valued, and part of a social network of mutual assistance
and obligations (Wills, 1991)" (p. 308). Within the context of coping with
stressors, Thoits (2010) amplifies the instrumental dimension of social
support implicit in this definition, indicating that social support refers
to "emotional, informational, or practical assistance from significant
others, such as family members, friends, or coworkers; support actually may be received from others or simply perceived to be available
when needed" (p. S46). Empirical evidence strongly supports that social
support has beneficial effects on psychological and physical health
(DeLongis & Holtzman, 2005), and still more to the point in the present context, "[s]ocial support consistently reduces psychological distress, such as depression and anxiety, during times of stress, and it
promotes psychological adjustment to chronically stressful conditions, including coronary artery disease (Holahan, Moos, Holahan, &
Brennen, 1997), diabetes, HIV infection (Turner-Cobb et al., 2002), cancer
(Stone, Mezzacappa, Donatone, & Gonder, 1999), rheumatoid arthritis
(Goodenow, Reisine, & Grady, 1990), and many more disorders" (Taylor
& Sherman, 2004, p. 308).

The impact of social support on an individual's stress process and outcomes speaks to the importance of the dyadic–interpersonal, relational–
triadic, and sociocultural–familial levels of the personality system in
adaptation to stressors. In the face of stressful events, the utilization of
social support as a valuable component of coping can potentially draw
from any of these social–interpersonal levels, ranging for example from
the patient's spouse or partner, friends, siblings, and work colleagues to
formal support groups (for individuals sharing a specific acute or chronic
stressor, for example the death of a loved one or alcoholism, respectively), spiritual and religious institutions, and indeed even the internet
(Bauer, Wolf, Haug, & Kordy, 2011; Kim, Sherman, & Taylor; 2008; Suvak,
Taft, Goodman, & Dutton, 2013; Taylor & Sherman, 2004). By the same

token, Thiots (2010) offered this critical caveat: "Lower status, disadvantaged group members (women, unmarriedpersons, working class and poor individuals) generally have lower levels of [social-support] coping resources (Thiots, 1995; Turner & Marino, 1994; Turner & Roszell, 1994), which means that they are doubly at risk of developing ill health and mental health problems: Acute and chronic stressors are concentrated in the very groups that are deficient in these stress-buffering assets" (p. S47). Thus, with any given patient the existence of social support resources cannot be assumed. Rather, their potential presence in the patient's life needs to be collaboratively determined, their selective use actively encouraged to the extent available, and when not available, proactively sought out by the patient in the context of authentic therapist support.

Strengths and Resources. To be complete, a discussion of the human personality system and its integrality to stress, coping, and psychological health and disorder must reference client strengths and resources. As pointed out by Strack (2005),

> Until recently, students of clinical psychiatry, psychology, social work, and nursing were trained to see the pathology in their patients but not necessarily what is normal or healthy.... Among recent changes is a greater willingness to consider the normality and health of psychiatric patients in addition to their pathology—to understand the whole person, not just the presenting problems. In the twenty-first century, comprehending psychopathology is not just a matter of discerning symptoms, syndromes, and diagnoses; it is also grasping the biopsychosocial context of the individual, including his or her strengths and abilities (APA, 2000; Millon, 1996; Sabshin, 2005; Sperry, 2003). (p. 372)

Recognizing the importance of strengths and resources in the human personality is part and parcel of the dialectical nature of a holistic, unifying perspective. Indeed, Fosha (2004) puts forth the concept of "dialectical common factors [that represent] integration at the level of the therapist's stance vis-à-vis the patient and the clinical material" (p. 83); among the eight such factors she proposes is "[f]ocus on health and the patient's resourcefulness versus focus on pathology and the patient's disturbance" (p. 83).

Amid the patient's vulnerabilities and dysfunctions, strengths and resources entail zones and pockets of health in biological, psychological, and/or sociocultural levels of the patient's personality system, and in our experience their identification and harnessing is invaluable to the therapeutic process and to treatment outcome (see, e.g., Anchin, 2003,

2005, 2006). It is worth noting that Wright and Lopez (2005) recommend that the assessment of strengths and resources be explicitly integrated into the process of clinical assessment; encouraging "a four-front approach to assessment" (p. 37), they assert: "Professionals must give serious attention to (a) deficiencies and undermining characteristics of the person; (b) strengths and assets of the person; (c) lacks and destructive factors in the environment; and (d) resources and opportunities in the environment" (p. 37).

The ever-growing literature on human strengths and their constructive contributions to processes of appraisal and coping is solidly anchored in empirical research and replete with applications to clinical practice. Snyder and Lopez (2005), Linley and Joseph (2004), and Bertolino, Kiener, and Patterson (2009) provide a rich compendium of discussions of these positive personality characteristics and their integration into the psychotherapeutic endeavor; a brief sampling of some of the attributes and resources discussed in these volumes imparts the flavor of their potency for contributing to a truly holistic appreciation of the human personality system: optimism, hope, wisdom, humility, compassion, gratitude, love, spirituality, collaborativeness, toughness, creativity, and humor. A unifying approach to psychotherapy not only addresses dysfunctions and vulnerabilities, but also actively seeks to harness and build a patient's assets and strengths (cf. Seligman, 2005).

Coda: The Importance of Shifting Perspectives and Viewing Subsystems Operating at the Four Levels of the Personality System

One of the challenges of unified psychotherapy is the ability to shift perspectives while maintaining a holistic perspective. There is a tendency when unchecked to favor a particular perspective and try to fit the clinical data into our schema, which will be discussed in Chapter 10 in the section on clinical decision making. This attributional bias is something natural for psychotherapists. We want to confirm our biases—and therefore must continually check ourselves by shifting perspectives and trying to understand other ways of explaining what is being revealed in the clinical setting. This is especially important when working with challenging clinical presentations that are not responsive to first-line, evidence-based approaches. This shifting of perspectives allows us to broaden our perspective and consider changing approaches or offering another modality when the treatment process is stuck. For example, a clinician treating a patient from a primarily intrapsychic orientation might shift perspectives to consider including a spouse or partner, thereby changing the frame and opening directions for dyadic-level interventions still appropriate to the goals of treatment. Conducting unified psychotherapy from the perspective of personality systematics requires flexibility and the capacity to hold multiple and sometimes contradictory perspectives (Magnavita, 2010).

SUMMARY

Unified psychotherapy is fundamentally personality guided. The holistic, biopsychosocial map of the human personality system that we use to orient our approach to treatment identifies four levels of thoroughly interconnected phenomena: the intrapsychic–biological level, the interpersonal–dyadic level, the relational–triadic level, and the sociocultural–familial level. Personality systematics are necessary but not sufficient for a comprehensive understanding of the etiology and course of a given client's disorder and in formulating treatment strategies and interventions. Critical as well is an understanding of the stress process, as mapped by the synthesis of transactional stress theory and the CMRT model. The human personality system is akin to the immune system in influencing the muticomponent stress process and its outcomes. The diathesis-stress model, personality traits, social support, and an individual's strengths and resources illustrate four key pathways through which the personality system impacts adaptation—maladaptation vis-à-vis acute and chronic stressful life events.

REFERENCES

Allport, G. W. (1961a). The open system in personality theory. *Journal of Abnormal and Social Psychology, 61*, 301–310.

Allport, G. W. (1961b). *Pattern and growth in personality.* New York: Holt, Rinehart & Winston.

Anchin, J. C. (2003). Cybernetic systems, existential phenomenology, and solution-focused narrative: Therapeutic transformation of negative affective states through integratively oriented brief psychotherapy. *Journal of Psychotherapy Integration, 13*, 334–442.

Anchin, J. C. (2005, May). Using a nonlinear dynamical biopsychosocial systems paradigm to individually tailor the process of psychotherapy. In J. J. Magnavita & J. C. Anchin (Co-chairs), *Unified psychotherapy: Implications for differential treatment strategies and interventions.* Symposium presented at the 21st Annual Conference of the Society for the Exploration of Psychotherapy Integration, Toronto, Ontario, Canada.

Anchin, J. C. (2006). A hermeneutically informed approach to psychotherapy integration. In G. Stricker & J. Gold (Eds.), *A casebook of psychotherapy integration* (pp. 261–280). Washington, DC: American Psychological Association.

Anchin, J. C. (2008). Pursuing a unifying paradigm for psychotherapy: Tasks, dialectical considerations, and biopsychosocial systems metatheory. *Journal of Psychotherapy Integration, 18*, 310–349.

Angyal, A. (1941). *Foundations for a science of personality.* London: Oxford University Press.

Bauer, S., Wolf, M., Haug, S., & Kordy, H. (2011). The effectiveness of internet chat groups in relapse prevention after inpatient psychotherapy. *Psychotherapy Research, 21*, 219–226.

Bertolino, B., Kiener, M., & Patterson, R. (2009). *The therapist's notebook on strengths and solution-based therapies.* New York: Routledge.

Block, J. (2002). *Personality as an affect-processing system: Toward an integrative theory.* Mahwah, NJ: Lawrence Eralbaum Associates.

Bowen, M. (1976). Theory in the practice of family therapy. In P. J. Guerin, Jr. (Ed.), *Family therapy: Theory and practice* (pp. 42–90). New York: Gardner Press.

Bronfenbrenner, U. (1979). *The ecology of human development: Experiments by nature and design.* Cambridge, MA: Harvard University Press.

Cannon, W. B. (1929). The wisdom of the body. *Physiological Review, 9*, 399–431.

Carver, C. S., & Scheier, M. F. (2002). Control processes and self-organization as complementary principles underlying behavior. *Personality and Social Psychology Review, 4*, 304–315.

Cervone, D. (2005). Personality architecture: With-person structures and processes. *Annual Review of Psychology, 56*, 423–452.

Cervone, D., & Mischel, W. (2002). Personality science. In D. Cervone & W. Mischel (Eds.), *Advances in personality science* (pp. 1–26). New York: Guilford.

Cloninger, C. R. (2004). *Feeling good: The science of well-being.* New York: Oxford University Press.

Connor-Smith, J. K., & Celeste Flachsbart, C. (2007). Relations between personality and coping: A meta-analysis. *Journal of Personality and Social Psychology, 93*, 1080–1107.

Crockett, L. J., Iturbide, M. I., Torres Stone, R. A., McGinley, M., Raffaelli, M., & Carlo, G. (2007). Acculturative stress, social support, and coping: Relations to psychological adjustment among Mexican American college students. *Cultural Diversity & Ethnic Minority Psychology, 13*, 347–355.

Dawkins, R. (1982). *The extended phenotype.* Oxford, UK: Oxford University Press.

DeLongis, A., & Holtzman, S. (2005). Coping in context: The role of stress, social support, and personality in coping. *Journal of Personality, 73*, 1633–1656.

Everly, G. S. (2005). Personality-based assessment of posttraumatic stress disorder. In S. Strack (Ed.), *Handbook of personology and psychopathology* (pp. 364–371). Hoboken, NJ: Wiley.

Fay, B. (1996). *Contemporary philosophy of social science: A multicultural approach.* Cambridge, MA: Blackwell.

Folkman, S. (2011). Stress, health, and coping: Synthesis, commentary, and future. In S. Folkman (Ed.), *The Oxford handbook of stress, health, and coping* (pp. 453–462). New York: Oxford University Press.

Folkman, S., & Moskowitz, J. T. (2000). Positive affect and the other side of coping. *American Psychologist, 55*, 647–654.

Fortier, M. A., DiLillo, D., Messman-Moore, T. L., Peugh, J., DeNardi, K. A., & Gaffey, K. J. (2009). Severity of child sexual abuse and revictimization: The mediating role of coping and trauma symptoms. *Psychology of Women Quarterly, 33*, 308–320.

Fosha, D. (2004). Brief integrative therapy comes of age: A commentary. *Journal of Psychotherapy Integration, 14*, 66–92.

Guerin, P. J., Fogarty, T. F., Fay, L. F., & Kautto, J. G. (1996). *Working with relational triangles: The one-two-three of psychotherapy*. New York: Guilford.

Haslam, N. (2007). *Introduction to personality and intelligence*. Thousand Oaks, CA: Sage Publications.

Kiesler, D. J. (1999). *Beyond the disease model of mental disorders*. Westport, CN: Praeger.

Kim, M. S., & Duda, J. L. (2003). The coping process: Cognitive appraisals of stress, coping strategies, and coping effectiveness. *The Sport Psychologist, 17*, 406–425.

Kim, H. S., Sherman, D. K., & Taylor, S. E. (2008). Culture and social support. *American Psychologist, 63*, 518–526.

Kuhl, J. (2000). A functional-design approach to motivation and volition: The dynamics of personality systems interactions. In M. Boekaerts P. R. Pintrich & M. Zeidner (Eds.), *Self-regulation: Directions and challenges for future research* (pp. 111–169). San Diego: Academic Press.

Lazarus, R. S. (1991). *Emotion and adaptation*. New York: Oxford University Press.

Lazarus, R. S. (1993). From psychological stress to the emotions: A history of changing outlooks. *Annual Review of Psychology, 44*, 1–21.

Lazarus, R. S. (2000). Toward better research on stress and coping. *American Psychologist, 55*, 665–673.

Lazarus, R. S., & Folkman, S. (1984). *Stress, appraisal, and coping*. New York: Springer Publishing.

Lecic-Tosevski, D., Vukovic, O., & Stepanovic, J. (2011). Stress and personality. *Psychiatriki, 22*, 290–297.

Lee-Baggley, D., Preece, M., & Delongis, A. (2005). Coping with interpersonal stress: Role of big five traits. *Journal of Personality, 73*, 1141–1180.

Linley, P. A., & Joseph, S. (Eds.). (2004). *Positive psychology in practice*. Hoboken, NJ: Wiley.

Magnavita, J. J. (2010). Methods, components, and strategies of unified treatment: Using evidence and personality systematics to enhance outcome. In J. J. Magnavita (Ed.), *Evidence-based treatment of personality dysfunction: Principles, methods, and processes* (pp. 253–285). Washington, DC: American Psychological Association.

Mayer, J. D. (2004). How does psychotherapy influence personality? A theoretical integration. *Journal of Clinical Psychology, 60*, 1291–1315.

Mayer, J. D. (2005). A tale of two visions: Can a new view of personality help integrate psychology? *American Psychologist, 60*, 294–307.

Meehl, P. E. (1962). Schizotaxia, schizotypy, schizophrenia. *American Psychologist, 17*, 827–838.

Melchert, T. P. (2011). *Foundations of professional psychology: The end of theoretical orientations and the emergence of the biopsychosocial approach*. Waltham, MA: Elsevier.

Melchert, T. P. (2013). Beyond theoretical orientations: The emergence of a unified scientific framework in professional psychology. *Professional Psychology: Research and Practice, 44*, 11–19.

Miller, J. G. (1978). *Living systems*. New York: McGraw-Hill.

Millon, T., with Davis R. D. (1996). *Disorders of personality: Toward DSM-IV and beyond* (2nd ed.). New York: Wiley.

Millon, T., with Grossman, S., Meager, S., Millon, C., & Everly, G. (1999). *Personality-guided therapy*. Hoboken, NJ: Wiley.

Millon, T., & Grossman, S. D. (2012). Personalized psychotherapy: The unification and customization of trait-oriented treatments. *Journal of Unified Psychotherapy and Clinical Science, 1*, 61–86.

Monroe, S. M., & Simons, A. D. (1991). Diathesis-stress theories in the context of life stress research. *Psychological Bulletin, 110,* 406–425.

Murphy, G. (1947). *Personality: A biosocial approach to origins and structure.* New York: Harper & Brothers.

Murray, H. A. (1959). Preparations for the scaffold of a comprehensive system. In S. Koch (Ed.), *Psychology: A study of a science* (Vol. 3, pp. 7–54). New York: McGraw-Hill.

Ntoumanis, N., Edmunds, J., & Duda, J. L. (2009). Understanding the coping process from a self-determination theory perspective. *British Journal of Health Psychology, 14,* 249–260.

Paris, J. (1999). A diathesis-stress model of personality disorders. *Psychiatric Annals, 29,* 692–697.

Pearlin, L. I. (1989). The sociological study of stress. *Journal of Health and Social Behavior, 30,* 241–256.

Pearlin, L. I. (2010). The life course and the stress process: Some conceptual comparisons. *The Journals of Gerontology Series B: Psychological Sciences and Social Sciences, 65B,* 207–215.

Pearlin, L. I., Menaghan, E. G., Lieberman, M. A., & Mullan, J. T. (1981). The stress process. *Journal of Health and Social Behavior, 22,* 337–356.

Peck, S. C. (2007). TEMPEST in a gallimaufry: Applying multilevel systems theory to person-in-context research. *Journal of Personality, 75,* 1127–1156.

Puglisi-Allegra, A. (1999). Stress and adaption: A psychobiological interpretation of Selye's concepts. In C. L. Bolis & J. Licinio (Eds.), *Stress and adaptation: From Selye's concept to application of modern formulations.* Geneva, Switzerland: World Health Organization.

Rosenthal, D. (1970). *Genetic theory and abnormal behavior.* New York: McGraw-Hill.

Roth, S., & Cohen, L. J. (1986). Approach, avoidance, and coping with stress. *The American Psychologist, 41,* 813–819.

Seligman, M. E. P. (2005). Positive psychology, positive prevention, and positive therapy. In C. R. Snyder & S. J. Lopez (Eds.), *Handbook of positive psychology* (pp. 3–9). New York: Oxford University Press.

Selye, H. (1936). A syndrome produced by diverse nocuous agents. *Nature, 138,* 32.

Singer, J. A. (2005). *Personality and psychotherapy: Treating the whole person.* New York: Guilford.

Singer, J. A. (in press). Lost in translation? Finding the person in the emerging paradigm of clinical science: Introduction to a special issue on personality psychology and psychotherapy. *Journal of Personality.*

Smelser, N. J., & Smelser, W. T. (1963). *Personality and social systems.* New York: Wiley.

Snyder, C. R. (Ed.). (1999). *Coping: The psychology of what works.* New York: Oxford University Press.

Snyder, C. R., & Lopez, S. J. (Eds.). (2005). *Handbook of positive psychology.* New York: Oxford University Press.

Strack, S. (2005). Measuring normal personality the Millon way. In S. Strack (Ed.), *Handbook of personology and psychopathology* (pp. 372–389). New York: Wiley.

Suvak, M. K., Taft, C. T., Goodman, L. A., & Dutton, M. A. (2013). Dimensions of functional social support and depressive symptoms: A longitudinal investigation of women seeking help for intimate partner violence. *Journal of Consulting and Clinical Psychology, 81,* 455–466.

Taylor, S. E., & Sherman, D. K. (2004). Positive psychology and health psychology: A fruitful liaison. In P. A. Linley & S. Joseph (Eds.), *Positive psychology in practice* (pp. 305–319). Hoboken, NJ: Wiley.

Thoits, P. A. (2010). Stress and health: Major findings and policy implications. *Journal of Health and Social Behavior, 51(S)*, S41–S53.

Vollrath, M. (2001). Personality and stress. *Scandanavian Journal of Psychology, 42*, 335–347.

Widiger, T.A. (2006). *Five-factor model rating form*. Retrieved July 9, 2013, from http://www.uky.edu/~widiger

Widiger, T. A. (2011). Integrating normal and abnormal personality structure: A proposal for DSM-V. *Journal of Personality Disorders, 25,* 338–363.

Widiger, T. A., & Costa, P. T. Jr. (Eds.). (2013). *Personality disorders and the five-factor model of personality* (3rd ed.). Washington, DC: American Psychological Association.

Widiger, T. A., & Presnall, J. R. (in press). Clinical application of the five-factor model. *Journal of Personality*.

Wiggins, J. S. (2003). *Paradigms of personality assessment*. New York: Guilford.

Wright, B. A., & Lopez, S. J. (2005). Widening the diagnostic focus: A case for including human strengths and environmental resources. In C. R. Snyder & S. J. Lopez (Eds.), *Handbook of positive psychology* (pp. 26–44). New York: Oxford University Press.

Zubin, J., & Spring, B. J. (1977). Vulnerability: A new view of schizophrenia. *Journal of Abnormal Psychology, 86,* 103–126.

Chapter 3

THE RELATIONAL MATRIX: FUNDAMENTAL PRINCIPLES AND PROCESSES

The conception of the human personality system presented in the previous chapter essentially partitions the biopsychosocial system into four domains of interactive structures and processes. In sync with metatheory serving unifying functions delineated in Chapter 1, this conception of personality is intended to capture and interrelate all the major domains and composite subsystems that we have come to learn about in over a century of clinical science and depict in the biopsychosocial model (Engel, 1980). In this respect, there remains one further component to round out this picture, and this is the ubiquitous influence of social–interpersonal processes at every level of human development, functioning, and change. In this chapter we seek to impart an understanding of this ubiquity through the framework of the *relational matrix* and point to its importance in developing, studying, and applying a unifying paradigm for psychotherapy and clinical science. At the end of the 20th century, Berscheid (1999) described the "greening of relational science" to signify the birth of this new and rapidly expanding body of knowledge (Magnavita, 2000). There have been a number of divergent advancements in relational science that represent various branches of the relational tree, which include: "(a) the intersubjectivity of the dyadic relationship, (b) the development of triadic theory, (c) the centrality of relationships in women's development, (d) the therapeutic alliance, and (e) a new model of relational diagnosis and treatment" (Magnavita, 2000, p. 999). Each of these branches, however, share a common belief in the centrality of the relational matrix.

THE RELATIONAL MATRIX: DEFINING COMPONENTS AND HISTORICAL CONTEXT

The *relational matrix* is a framework developed by Stephen Mitchell (1988) that captures a seemingly irrefutable truth of the human condition: From beginning to end, we are soaked in and suffused by the world of others. In developing the relational-matrix conception, Mitchell effectively crystallized the radical transformation taking place in recent decades in psychoanalytic theory and practice, and his formulation continues as a striking realization of the provocative observation offered some 40 years ago by Guntrip (1971): "Today the question to ask is not so much 'What did Freud say?' but 'What has Freud's work led on to?' It is all that Freud started that becomes increasingly important" (p. 5). Relational psychoanalysis continues as arguably the most significant development that Freud's work has indeed "led on to." Although a number of relational psychoanalytic approaches have evolved (e.g., Frank, 1999, 2002; Ghent, 1992; Greenberg & Cheselka, 1995; Wachtel, 2008), all converge on the fundamental assumption that the human being is intrinsically relational in nature—hardwired to connect with others and to possess capacities necessary for navigating the omnipresent complexities of the social world. From the moment of conception, through fetal development, then birth, and over the entire life course thereafter, human beings are embedded in social relationships—biologically and psychologically, internally and externally, developmentally and contemporaneously.

Unification-related meanings and implications contained within the relational matrix become apparent when this formulation is juxtaposed with traditional psychoanalytic theory. Greenberg and Mitchell (1983) exquisitely detailed relationalism's radical departure from traditional psychoanalytic postulates in their classic volume *Object Relations in Psychoanalytic Theory*. As summarized elsewhere (Anchin, 2002), Greenberg and Mitchell (1983) characterized the traditional Freudian view as a drive/structural model built on the classical metapsychology of biologically rooted sexual and aggressive drives, the governing id–ego–superego psychic apparatus, and the view of conflict as entailing drive–defense constellations: "The main point to grasp about the drive/structural model is its focus on a self-contained individual .... It is a one-person or one-body psychology, 'a biologically closed system seeking to discharge energy in order to maintain homeostasis' or equilibrium (Aron, 1990, p. 466)" (Messer & Warren, 1995, pp. 73–74). In this classical psychoanalytic view, the intrapsychic life of the individual and the vicissitudes of drives housed therein are the domain of singular importance.

In sharp contrast, the relational psychoanalytic perspective views "relations with others, not drives, [as] the basic stuff of mental life" (Mitchell, 1988, p. 2). The foundations of this axiom lie in Sullivanian-rooted interpersonal psychoanalysis, British object relations theory, and self-psychologies rooted in Kohutian theory. As discussed elsewhere (Anchin, 2002), Aron (1996) credited Mitchell (e.g., 1988) with having made the vital connective observation that "these diverse schools ... tended, each in its own way, to be critical of Freudian drive theory and alternatively to emphasize the centrality of relationships between people, real and imagined, internal and external" (p. 33). Certainly each of these schools differentially conceptualized the precise composition, motivational dynamics, and psychological and interpersonal effects of these internal and external relational configurations. Nevertheless, drawing on their fundamentally shared postulate that the social–interpersonal pervades every level of human existence, Mitchell forged the relational-matrix concept as a synthesizing framework for understanding the complexities of human development and functioning as a way to "transcend the unfortunate tendency to dichotomize concepts like interpersonal relations and 'object' relations, or the interpersonal and the intrapsychic, as if a focus on either side necessarily implies a denial or de-emphasis of the other. *The most useful way to view psychological reality is as operating within a relational matrix which encompasses both intrapsychic and interpersonal realms* [.....that] create, interpenetrate, and transform each other in a subtle and complex manner" (Mitchell, 1988, p. 9, italics in original).

The relational matrix's holistic fusion of the intrapsychic and the interpersonal is rooted in and germinates out of recognition of the human organism's intrinsically dualistic nature. We quote at length Greenberg and Mitchell's (1983) sensitive portrayal of this most fundamental dualism that characterizes the human experience and out of which virtually all elements of relational thinking—and its unifying implications—are cultivated:

> The human condition embraces a fundamental paradox. On the one hand, man lives an individual existence. Each person is born, is caught in time, and dies. Each individual has his own idiosyncratic experience of life, woven out of his constitutional equipment and potential and out of the serendipity of his fate. Each of us lives in his own subjective world, pursuing personal pleasures and private fantasies, constructing a lifeline which, when his time is over, will vanish. On the other hand, people live necessarily and unavoidably within a human community. The human infant cannot survive without parental care. Much

of the process of child development is constituted by internalization of interaction with others. Although there may have been feral children, living briefly outside a human community, their status as fully human is questionable; there are no feral men or women. The most reclusive hermit thinks in language learned from others, experiences the world in categories influenced by early social relations. The human community and culture transcend the individual life span; in some sense, the community creates the individual life, giving it substance and meaning. Man is an essentially individual animal; man is an essentially social animal. (p. 400)

This dualism reflects the root dialectic between self and other (Anchin, 2002, 2005), iterating at ever-higher levels of complexity, powering the human journey over the course of life. Our consciousness and capacities to be self-aware and to self-reflect adaptively enable us to become highly individualized in focus, vividly experiencing ourselves as distinctly separate beings. Yet we cannot escape our embeddedness in an interpersonal nexus: "The fish is in the water, and the water is in the fish" (A. Miller, 1958).

Another advancement in relational theory has been achieved by J. Miller (1976) and Jordan (1997), who believed that traditional psychodynamic models of treatment focusing on individual personality structure and the reification of the "self" tended to over- pathologize women, minorities, and marginalized groups. J. Miller and Jordan developed a relational/cultural model, which emphasized "mutual empathy and mutual empowerment" (Jordan, 2000, p. 1007). Their work emphasizes the importance of understanding "patterns of connections and disconnections" (p. 1007). Jordan emphasizes how "people grow through and toward relationships throughout the life span" (p. 1007).

UNPACKING THE RELATIONAL MATRIX

Consistent with a major theme of this volume—that analysis and synthesis are both vital for comprehensive understanding of a phenomenon—we engage here in some dissection of the relational matrix, undertaken against the backdrop of the immediately preceding synthetic portrait. The wealth of dynamically interconnected structures and processes that comprise the relational matrix at first glance renders any attempt at analysis daunting, but the constrains of time and space serve as convenient moderators. As such, we limit ourselves here to first very briefly highlighting in general terms a number of key findings that have emerged from multiple lines of theory and research into the relational context of human being and becoming. This is followed by a selective focus on the two cardinal defining components of the relational matrix, which play a prominent role in conceptually and clinically informing our unifying perspective and treatment approach.

Pervasiveness of the Relational Matrix

The powerful multidirectional influences of interpersonal relationships, contexts, and variables on human behavior and development serve as a major point of convergence for theorists, researchers, and clinicians alike (Anchin, 2012). The sizeable bodies of literature associated with each of these sets of findings are such that elaborating each could constitute a handbook in its own right; for those interested in developing more in-depth understanding, we heartily encourage reflecting on implications of each of these findings for one's own distinct areas of clinical work and study and to use the representative sampling of citations as springboards into the literature. Among key findings reflecting the pervasive influence of the relational matrix are the following:

- Social interactions, relationships, and groups have been cited as critical to human evolution (Bailey, 2000; Berscheid, 1999; Jordan, 2000; Reis, Collins, & Berscheid, 2000)

- Humans possess innate social response systems (Beaulieu & Bugental, 2007; Berscheid, 1999; Bowlby, 1969/1982; Reis, Collins, & Berscheid, 2000)

- Starting at birth and continuing over the course of the entire life cycle, development and functioning of the human brain and its neurochemistry are influenced by processes and dynamics of interpersonal attachment (Cozolino, 2006; Grawe, 2007; Lipton & Fosha, 2011; Schore, 2012; Siegel, 2012)

- Powerful reciprocal influence processes transpire among social relationships, culture, biology, cognition, and emotion (Berntson & Cacioppo, 2006; Cacioppo, 2002; Cacioppo, Berntson, Sheridan, & McClintock, 2000; Cacioppo & Decety, 2011)

- The evolution of self and identity across the life span is inseparably tied to the nature of one's interpersonal experiences (McAdams & Cox, 2010; Morf & Mischel, 2012; Stern, 1985)

- Vicissitudes of attachment and connectedness to others over the course of human development play a fundamental role in mental health and well-being and in the development, onset, and maintenance of psychological disorders (Connors, 2011; Hawkley & Cacioppo, 2010; Liotti, 2011; Kiesler, 1996; Norman, Cacioppo, & Berntson, 2010; Rogoff, 2003; Ryff & Singer, 1998; Segrin, 2001; Shonkoff & Phillips, 2000)

- Relational processes are integral to effective psychotherapeutic interventions (Anchin & Kiesler, 1982; American Psychological Association [APA], 2006; Castonguay & Beutler, 2005; Goldfried & Davila, 2005; Lambert & Simon, 2008; Norcross, 2011)

At every level of the biopsychosocial system, the influence of the relational matrix on development, functioning, and change is ubiquitous. Indeed, the pervasive relationalism in which biopsychosocial structures and processes are awash may well be the ultimate unifying principle of personality, psychopathology, and psychotherapy (Magnavita, 2006).

Specific Components of the Relational Matrix: Self and Relatedness

Mitchell (1988) provided a clear framework for a more focused analysis of the relational matrix through crystallizing, within the context of the thoroughgoing interaction between the intrapsychic and interpersonal realms, that "[t]he mind operates with motivations concerning self-regulation as well as regulation of the interpersonal field" (p. 9). Forging and maintaining an individual self and establishing and maintaining relationships with others are the yin and yang of the relational matrix. Here we briefly describe three well-established lines of theory and research that convergently illustrate the centrality of these two realms of dynamic phenomena in personality and its development, psychopathology, and psychotherapy.

Relatedness and Self-Definition

For Blatt and his colleagues (e.g., Blatt, 2008; Blatt & Blass, 1992; Blatt & Shahar, 2005), normal personality development entails a complex dialectic over the course of the life cycle between, on the one hand, relatedness, and on the other hand, self-definition (also characterized elsewhere as individuality [Guisinger & Blatt, 1994] and self-sufficiency [Blatt & Levy, 2007]):

Personality development is the result of the complex transaction of two fundamental developmental lines: the development of increasingly mature, reciprocal, and satisfying interpersonal relationships, and the development of a consolidated, realistic, essentially positive, increasingly integrated self-definition or identity. These two developmental lines normally evolve throughout the life cycle in a complex dialectical process. The development of an increasingly differentiated, integrated, and mature sense of self is contingent upon establishing satisfying interpersonal experiences and, conversely, the development of increasingly mature and satisfying interpersonal relationships depends on the development of more mature self-definition and identity. In normal personality development, these two developmental processes evolve in an interactive, reciprocally balanced, mutually facilitating fashion from birth through senescence (Blatt, 1990; Blatt & Schichman, 1983). (Blatt & Blass, 1992, pp. 399–400)

Blatt and Blass (1992) integrated this conception with Erik Erikson's epigenetic model of psychosocial development to create a reformulation of the latter that makes explicit how the dialectical interplay between the relatedness–self-definition polarity is expressed over the nine stages defined by Erikson's life-cycle model (see Figure 3.1).

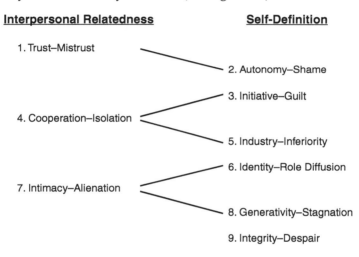

Interpersonal Relatedness   **Self-Definition**

1. Trust–Mistrust

                                    2. Autonomy–Shame

                                    3. Initiative–Guilt

4. Cooperation–Isolation

                                    5. Industry–Inferiority

                                    6. Identity–Role Diffusion

7. Intimacy–Alienation

                                    8. Generativity–Stagnation

                                    9. Integrity–Despair

FIGURE 3.1 *The dialectical interaction of interpersonal relatedness and self-definition implicit in Erikson's psychosocial model.* From Blatt (1990, p. 304). Copyright 1990 by University of Chicago Press. Reprinted with permission.

This polarity has also been applied to the understanding of different forms of psychopathology, conceptualized "as an overemphasis and exaggeration of one of these developmental lines (relatedness or self-definition) at the expense of the development of the other line [thereby defining] two distinctly different configurations of psychopathology, each containing several types of disordered behavior that range from relatively severe to relatively mild" (Blatt & Levy, 2007, p. 115). Depression and implications for therapeutic intervention have been a particular focus of this work (e.g., Blatt, 1995; Corveleyn, Luyten, & Blatt, 2005).

Agency and Communion

As discussed by Pincus, Lukowitsky, and Wright (2010), the interpersonal tradition in clinical science and psychotherapy, rooted in Sullivan's (1953a, 1953b, 1954, 1956, 1962, 1964) seminal interpersonal theory of psychiatry, has a 60-year history that has witnessed increasing integration of theoretical perspectives, sophistication in measurement methodologies, and scope of application.

As discussed elsewhere (Anchin & Pincus, 2010), among fundamental contemporary assumptions of the interpersonal tradition is that *agency* and *communion*, core domains of human existence, provide an integrative metastructure for conceptualizing interpersonal situations and their internal representations (Wiggins, 2003). *Agency* refers to the condition of being a differentiated individual, and it is manifested in strivings for power and mastery that can protect and enhance one's differentiation. Agency speaks to the fact that the construct of self occupies a central position in the interpersonal tradition (Anchin & Pincus, 2010; Kiesler, 1982, 1996), originating in Sullivan's conception of the self-system as a psychological structure and process that develops out of—and contains symbolic contents based on—interactions and experiences with others. *Communion* refers to the condition of being part of a larger social entity, and it is manifested in strivings for intimacy, union, and solidarity with the larger entity.

Pincus et al. (2010) elaborate these conceptions, pointing out that the metaconcepts of agency and communion form a superordinate structure, referred to as the *interpersonal circle* (IPC; Leary, 1957) or *interpersonal circumplex* (Wiggins, 1996), which can be used to derive descriptive and explanatory concepts of personality, mental health, and psychopathology at different levels of specificity (see Figure 3.2). At the broadest and most interdisciplinary level, agency and communion encompass the fundamental interpersonal motives, strivings, and values of human relations (Horowitz, 2004). Thus, when seeking to understand essential motivations in interpersonal situations, one may consider both the agentic and communal nature of the individual's personal strivings or current concerns (e.g., to be in control, to be close to others) and the specific behaviors enacted to achieve those goals. At a sharper level of resolution, the IPC provides conceptual coordinates for describing and measuring interpersonal traits and behaviors (Locke, 2006, 2011). Agentic and communal traits imply enduring patterns of perceiving, thinking, feeling, and behaving that describe an individual's relational tendencies aggregated across time, place, and relationships (Anchin & Pincus, 2010; Pincus et al., 2010).

Although detailed elaboration is beyond the scope of the present volume, it is important to note that, in conjunction with additional constructs and principles associated with the interpersonal tradition, the agency and communion metaframework (Wiggins, 1991) has been applied with breadth and depth to clinical science and psychotherapy, including "the integrative study of personality (e.g., Wiggins & Broughton, 1985; Wright, Pincus, Conroy, & Elliot, 2009), personality assessment (e.g., Pincus & Gurtman, 2003), psychotherapy (e.g., Anchin & Pincus, in press; Pincus & Cain, 2008), symptom syndromes (e.g., Barrett & Barber, 2007;

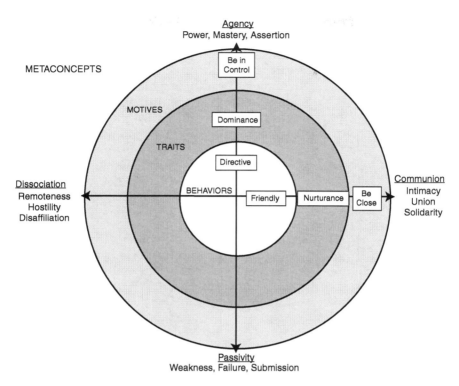

FIGURE 3.2   *Agency and communion: Metaconcepts for the integration of interpersonal motives, traits, and behaviors.* Adapted from Pincus et al. (2010, p. 529). Copyright by Guilford Press. Reprinted with permission.

Hopwood, Clarke, & Perez, 2007; Horowitz, 2004), personality disorders (e.g., Benjamin, 1996; Horowitz & Wilson, 2005; Pincus, 2005a, 2005b), and health psychology and behavioral medicine (e.g., Gallo, Smith, & Cox, 200; Lackner & Gurtman, 2004, 2005)" (Pincus et al., 2010, p. 524).

Attachment, Separation, and Exploration

Emanating fundamentally from John Bowlby's (1944, 1951) research on infant and child development originating nearly 70 years ago, his ensuing formulations (e.g., Bowlby, 1969/1982, 1973, 1980, 1988) and critical advancements by Mary Ainsworth and her student Mary Main, the impact of attachment theory on conceptualizations of personality, psychopathology, psychological health, and psychotherapy over the past several decades has been nothing short of explosive (e.g., Cassidy & Shaver, 2008; Costello, in press; Fosha, 2000; Hughes, 2007; Slade & Aber, 1992). Because conceptions directly associated with this perspective are brought into play later in this volume, here we limit ourselves to highlighting the central thrust of attachment theory in order to convey its distinct parallels to Blatt and colleagues' conceptions and to those in the interpersonal tradition that center on life's perpetual dance between connection to and apartness from others. Attachment theory's variation on this tune posits that evolution has hard-wired into the human being several behavioral systems designed to optimize survival and the individual's adaptation to life; chief among these are the attachment system and the exploratory system (Ainsworth, Blehar, Waters, & Wall, 1978; Bowlby, 1969/1982). In attachment theory, these two systems are interlocking and complementary in their operation (Elliot & Reis, 2003; Green & Campbell, 2000).

"Attachment, as both phenomenon and construct, refers to the fundamental human need to form close affectional bonds" (Fosha, 2000, p. 33). Bowlby (1969/1982) made the compelling case that the human attachment system is an innate, adaptive product of evolution, "'selected' during the early evolution of the human species because it made survival more likely; children in the proximity of the mother are less vulnerable to predators. Thus, the child's attachment to the mother is part of an 'archaic heritage' whose function is species survival" (Greenberg & Mitchell, 1983, p. 185). The attachment system is thus fundamentally protective in purpose, "active from the earliest moments of infancy" (Blatt & Blass, 1992). Through the affectional bonds that develop between child and mother via the reciprocal interaction of the former's attachment behavioral system and the latter's innate caretaking behavioral system (Bowlby, 1969/1982), the child develops feelings of safety, comfort, and security. Crucially, as well, over time "the attachment relationship becomes represented and internalized: The individual forms an *internal working model of relationships* in which the self is represented in dynamic relation to a specific caregiving other" (Fosha, 2000, p. 39). With recurrent positive, secure attachment experiences, the child develops

> an internal working model that represents "an unconscious belief system into which early experiences are integrated and that, under favorable conditions, reflects *the individual's confidence in the significant other's availability, understanding and responsiveness*" (Fonagy et al., 1995 p. 234, italics added). In such an internal working model, one that characterizes secure attachment, the other is represented as responsive and reliable and the self as worthy of being protected and responded to. (Fosha, 2000, p. 39)

The powerful matrix of human attachment is thus fundamentally relational in its structure and process, as well as vital to the process of developing a psychological (cognitive–affective) representation of self. It is integrally tied, too, to the operation of the exploratory system, "whose primary purpose is to promote learning about the environment (Ainsworth et al., 1978)" (Fosha, 2000, p. 34). Indeed, as explained by Slade and Aber (1992) and Elliot and Reis (2003), exploring the environment—which concurrently entails separating from the caregiver—is the most common activity of the infant and toddler when not engaged with the caregiver, but at the same time exploration exposes the child to risk. Perceiving danger activates the attachment system, prompting the child's return to the caregiver for protection, but with feelings of security thereby reinstilled, the child again separates and ventures back out into the environment to continue exploration. This process entails a dialectical cycling between attachment and separation/exploration, reflecting the dynamic, complementary balance between these two innate systems. "In Ainsworth et al.'s (1978) words, the infant uses the caregiver as a 'secure base from which to explore' (p. 22)" (Elliot & Reis, 2003, p. 317).

In promoting learning about the environment, the exploratory system and the separation predicating its activation would also appear to be implicated in the individuals' development of a sense of self *as* a distinct self. Thus, as Mahoney (1991, p. 167) pointed out, even within the first 18 months of life the child's activities are focused on not only emotional attachment, but also self-regulation and his or her own agency or competence. This line of thinking also seems implicit in Elliot and Reis's (2003) formulation as to how the attachment and exploratory systems may interact during adulthood, and in particular, their conception of the nature of the exploratory system in adults. The latter springboard from the link made by Ainsworth between the exploratory system and White's (1959) concept of effectance motivation "defined … as the desire for effective, competent interactions with the environment, … [an] innate, organismic propensity that impels the individual to investigate, manipulate, and master the environment" (Elliot & Reis, 2003, p. 318). They point out that White conceived of effectance motivation as operative throughout life, over time differentiating into such more complex motives as the need to be competent in one's actions and integrally related motivations to achieve. Notably, all of these interrelated motives and desires—to explore, to experience effectiveness and competency in dealing with the environment, to achieve—are individualistic in nature. They are also highly concordant with the interpersonal tradition's metaconstruct of agency and the importance it ascribes to self-differentiation and the individual's strivings for mastery. Thus, the attachment and exploratory systems function innately and hand-in-hand in promoting both connectedness to others and development of a differentiated individual able to operate competently and effectively within the environment.

Although Blatt and his colleagues, the interpersonal tradition, and attachment theory utilize different terminology, these perspectives coalesce in the view that, at the most overarching level, human development and functioning over the life course entail a continuous dialectical interplay between, on the one hand, the self and its multiple structures and processes, and on the other hand, relatedness to others. At any given moment in time, and during any given stage in one's life, an individual's focus on one domain may predominate over the other, but this is a matter of degree. We return to Mitchell (1988) for a definitive statement of this relativity in the sphere of self and others:

> We are concerned with both the creation and maintenance of a relatively stable, coherent sense of self out of the continual ebb and flow of perception and affect, and the creation and mainte- nance of dependable, sustaining connections with others, both in actuality and as internal presences. The dialectic between self-definition and connection with others is complex and intricate, with one or the other sometimes being more promi- nent. Self-regulatory and field-regulatory processes sometimes enhance each other and sometimes are at odds with each other, forming the basis for powerful conflicts. The intrapsychic and the interpersonal are continually interpenetrating realms, each with its own set of processes, mechanisms, and concerns. (p. 35)

THE BIOPSYCHOSOCIAL SYSTEM IS GROUNDED IN THE RELATIONAL MATRIX

The two domains of self and relatedness transcend any specific theo- retical school of thought, capturing a fundamental duality in the human condition—in some respects, the dual nuclei that permeate and reverber- ate through human *being*. In this respect, like the biopsychosocial model and systems theory, the relational matrix is metatheoretical. In our view, the biopsychosocial system is grounded in the relational matrix (Anchin, 2012; Anchin & Magnavita, 2006; Magnavita, 2012).

A conceptual-visual metaphor is helpful in explicating this idea (Figure 3.3). Just as DNA can be viewed as a ladder, with the base pairs serving as the rungs and the sugar-phosphate backbone serving as the support- ing sides of the ladder, the biopsychosocial system, as noted in Chapter 1, can similarly be mapped as a ladder, with the intrapsychic–biological, dyadic–interpersonal, triadic–relational, and sociocultural–familial levels composing the rungs, and self and relatedness operating as the support- ing sides. Whatever "rung" we focus on, self and interpersonal processes are integral to the action. Thus, whether we move up or down the ladder, and whether we narrow the lens in a reductionistic way by homing in on the action occurring along any one of the rungs or open the lens and move toward a more holistic view by focusing on the interconnectedness of the

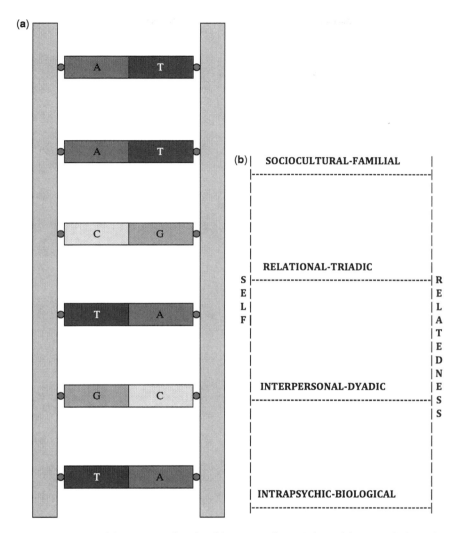

FIGURE 3.3 *(a) DNA molecule; (b) Biopsychosocial model grounded in the relational matrix.*

action occurring between two or more rungs, considerations involving both the self and relatedness are always integral to the action.

Over the course of the four chapters composing the next section, we focus more sharply on each of the rungs composing the biopsychosocial ladder. Though not always labeled explicitly, the continuous dynamic interplay among structures, mechanisms, and processes associated with the self and those associated with being in relationships with others is always implicit.

SUMMARY

Humans are essentially relational beings whose personality systems are shaped and formed by our connections and interactions with others, beginning with our earliest attachments. The relational matrix is a unifying construct, which advances our understanding of our need for *agency* (separateness) and *communion* (connection to others). There is no escaping the ubiquity or our relational nature. The dialectic between intrapsychic and interpersonal processes is critical to our understanding of human nature, and treatment of maladaptive behavior and psychopathology. At each level of the personality system the relational encodings operate as a guide to our behavior and interpersonal–social interactions. The relational matrix encompasses the four domains of the personality system, which can be conceptualized as a ladder of hierarchical structures. These structures, similar to DNA, are the rungs of the biopsychosocial model embedded in this relational matrix and from which our self-other functions emanate.

REFERENCES

Ainsworth, M. D. S., Blehar, M. C., Waters, E., & Wall, S. (1978). *Patterns of attachment: A psychological study of the strange situation*: Hillsdale, NJ: Lawrence Erlbaum Associates.

American Psychological Association Presidential Task Force on Evidence-Based Practice (2006). Evidence-based practice in psychology. *American Psychologist, 61,* 271–285.

Anchin, J. C. (2002). Relational psychoanalytic enactments and psychotherapy integration: Dualities, dialectics, and directions: Comment on Frank (2002). *Journal of Psychotherapy Integration, 12,* 302–346.

Anchin, J. C. (2005). Introduction to the special section on philosophy and psychotherapy integration and to the inaugural focus on moral philosophy. *Journal of Psychotherapy Integration, 15,* 284–298.

Anchin, J. C. (2012). Prologue to unified psychotherapy and clinical science. *Journal of Unified Psychotherapy and Clinical Science, 1,* 1–20.

Anchin, J. C., & Kiesler, D. J. (Eds.). (1982). *Handbook of interpersonal psychotherapy.* New York: Pergamon.

Anchin, J. C., & Magnavita, J. J. (2006). The nature of unified clinical science: Implications for psychotherapeutic theory, practice, training, and research. *Psychotherapy Bulletin, 41*(2), 26–36.

Anchin, J. C., & Pincus, A. L. (2010). Evidence-based interpersonal psychotherapy with personality disorders: Theory, components, and strategies. In J. J. Magnavita (Ed.), *Evidence-based treatment of personality dysfunction: Principles, methods, and processes* (pp. 113–166). Washington, DC: American Psychological Association.

Aron, L. (1996). *A meeting of minds: Mutuality in psychoanalysis.* Hillsdale, NJ: Analytic Press.

Bailey, K. G. (2000). Evolution, kinship, and psychotherapy: Promoting psychological health through human relationships. In P. Gilbert & K. G. Bailey (Eds.), *Genes on the couch: Explorations in evolutionary psychotherapy* (pp. 42–67). Philadelphia: Taylor & Francis.

Beaulieu, D. A., & Bugental, D. B. (2007). An evolutionary approach to socialization. In J. E. Grusec & P. D. Hastings (Eds.), *Handbook of socialization: Theory and research* (pp. 71–95). New York: Guilford Press.

Berntson, G. G., & Cacioppo, J. T. (2006). Reciprocal determinism. In N. J. Salkind (Ed.), *Encyclopedia of human development*. (Vol. 3, pp. 1066–1068). Thousand Oaks, CA: Sage Press.

Berscheid, E. (1999). The greening of relationship science. *American Psychologist, 54,* 260–266.

Blatt, S. J. (1990). Interpersonal relatedness and self-definition: Two personality configurations and their implications for psychopathology and psychotherapy. In J. L. Singer (Ed.), *Repression and dissociation: Implications for personality theory, psychopathology & health* (pp. 299–335). Chicago: University of Chicago Press.

Blatt, S. J. (1995). The destructiveness of perfectionism: Implications for the treatment of depression. *American Psychologist, 50,* 1003–1020.

Blatt, S. J. (2008). *Polarities of experience: Relatedness and self-definition in personality development, psychopathology, and the therapeutic process.* Washington, DC: American Psychological Association.

Blatt, S. J., & Blass, R. B. (1992). Relatedness and self-definition: Two primary dimensions in personality development, psychopathology, and psychotherapy. In J. Barron, M. Eagle & D. Wolitsky (Eds.), *The interface between psychoanalysis and psychology* (pp. 399–428). Washington, DC: American Psychological Association.

Blatt, S. J., & Levy, K. N. (2007). Attachment theory, psychoanalysis, personality development, and psychopathology. *Psychoanalytic Inquiry, 23,* 102–150.

Blatt, S. J., & Shahar, G. (2005). A dialectic model of personality development and psychopathology: Recent contributions to understanding and treating depression. In J. Corveleyn, P. Luyten & S. J. Blatt (Eds.), *The theory and treatment of depression: Towards a dynamic interactionism model* (pp. 137–162). Mahwah, NJ: Lawrence Erlbaum Associates.

Blatt, S. J., & Shichman, S. (1983). Two primary configurations of psychopathology. *Psychoanalysis and Contemporary Thought, 6,* 187–254.

Bowlby, J. (1944). Forty-four juvenile thieves: Their characters and home-life. *International Journal of Psychoanalysis, 25,* 19–52; 107–127.

Bowlby, J. (1951). Maternal care and mental health (WHO Monograph No. 2). Geneva, Switzerland: World Health Organization.

Bowlby, J. (1969/1982). *Attachment and loss: Vol. 1. Attachment* (2nd ed.). New York: Basic Books.

Bowlby, J. (1973). *Attachment and loss: Vol. 2. Separation.* New York: Basic Books.

Bowlby, J. (1980). *Attachment and loss: Vol. 3. Loss.* New York: Basic Books.

Bowlby, J. (1988). *A secure base: Parent-child attachment and healthy human development.* New York: Basic Books.

Cacioppo, J. T. (2002). Social neuroscience: Understanding the pieces fosters understanding the whole and vice versa. *American Psychologist, 57,* 819–831.

Cacioppo, J. T., Berntson, G. G., Sheridan, J. F., & McClintock, M. K. (2000). Multilevel integrative analyses of human behavior: Social neuroscience and the complementing nature of social and biological approaches. *Psychological Bulletin, 126,* 829–843.

Cacioppo, J. T., & Decety, J. (2011). Social neuroscience: Challenges and opportunities in the study of complex behavior. *Annals of the New York Academy of Sciences, 1224*, 162–173.

Cassidy, J., & Shaver, P. R. (Eds.) (2008). *Handbook of attachment: Theory, research, and clinical applications* (2nd ed.). New York: Guilford.

Castonguay, L. G., & Beutler, L. E. (Eds.) (2005). *Principles of therapeutic change that work*. New York: Oxford University Press.

Costello, P. C. (in press). *Attachment-based psychotherapy: Helping patients develop adaptive capacities*. Washington, DC: American Psychological Association.

Connors, M. E. (2011). Attachment theory: A "secure base" for psychotherapy integration. *Journal of Psychotherapy Integration, 21*, 348–362.

Corveleyn, J., Luyten, P., & Blatt, S. J. (Eds.) (2005). *The theory and treatment of depression: Towards a dynamic interactionism model*. Mahwah, NJ: Lawrence Erlbaum Associates.

Cozolino, L. (2006). *The neuroscience of human relationships: Attachment and the developing social brain*. New York: Norton.

Elliot, A. J., & Reis, H. T. (2003). Attachment and exploration in adulthood. *Journal of Personality and Social Psychology, 85*, 317–331.

Engel, G. L. (1980). The clinical application of the biopsychosocial model. *American Journal of Psychiatry, 137*, 535–544.

Fosha, D. (2000). *The transforming power of affect: A model of accelerated change*. New York: Basic Books.

Frank, K. A. (1999). *Psychoanalytic participation: Action, interaction, and integration*. Hillsdale, NJ: Analytic Press.

Frank, K. A. (2002). The "ins and outs" of enactment: A relational bridge for psychotherapy integration. *Journal of Psychotherapy Integration, 12*, 267–286.

Ghent, E. (1992). Foreword. In N. J. Skolnick & S. C. Warshaw (Eds.), *Relational perspectives in psychoanalysis* (pp. xiii–xxii). Hillsdale, NJ: Analytic Press.

Goldfried, M. R., & Davila, J. (2005). The role of relationship and technique in therapeutic change. *Psychotherapy: Theory, Research, Practice, Training, 42*, 421–430.

Grawe, K. (2007). *Neuropsychotherapy: How the neurosciences inform effective psychotherapy*. New York: Psychology Press.

Green, J. D., & Campbell, W. (2000). Attachment and exploration in adults: Chronic and contextual accessibility. *Personality and Social Psychology Bulletin, 26*, 452–461.

Greenberg, J., & Cheselka, O. (1995). Relational approaches to psychoanalytic psychotherapy. In A. S. Gurman & S. B. Messer (Eds.), *Essential psychotherapies* (pp. 55–84). New York: Guilford.

Greenberg, J., & Mitchell, S. A. (1983). *Object relations in psychoanalytic theory*. Cambridge, MA: Harvard University Press.

Guisinger, S., & Blatt, S. J. (1994). Individuality and relatedness: Evolution of a fundamental dialectic. *American Psychologist, 49*, 104–111.

Guntrip, H. (1971). *Psychoanalytic theory, therapy, and the self*. New York: Basic Books.

Hawkley, L. C., & Cacioppo, J. T. (2010). Loneliness matters: A theoretical and empirical review of consequences and mechanisms. *Annals of Behavioral Medicine, 40*, 218–227.

Horowitz, L. M. (2004). *Interpersonal foundations of psychopathology*. Washington, DC: American Psychological Association.

Hughes, D. (2007). *Attachment-focused family therapy*. New York: Norton.

Jordan, J. V. (Ed.) (1997). *Women's growth in diversity*. New York: Guilford.

Jordan, J. V. (2000). The role of mutual empathy in relational/cultural therapy. *Journal of Clinical Psychology/In Session: Psychotherapy in Practice, 56*, 1005–1016.

Kiesler, D. J. (1982). Interpersonal theory for personality and psychotherapy. In J. C. Anchin & D. J. Kiesler (Eds.), *Handbook of interpersonal psychotherapy* (pp. 3–24). New York: Pergamon.

Kiesler, D. J. (1996). *Contemporary interpersonal theory and research: Personality, psychopathology, and psychotherapy.* New York: Wiley.

Lambert, M. J., & Simon, W. (2008). The therapeutic relationship: Central and essential in psychotherapy outcome. In S. F. Hick & T. Bien (Eds.), *Mindfulness and the therapeutic relationship* (pp. 19–34). New York: Guilford.

Leary, T. (1957). *Interpersonal diagnosis of personality.* New York: Ronald.

Liotti, G. (2011). Attachment disorganization and the controlling strategies: An illustration of the contributions of attachment theory to developmental psychopathology and to psychotherapy integration. *Journal of Psychotherapy Integration, 21,* 232–252.

Lipton, B., & Fosha, D. (2011). Attachment as a transformative process in AEDP: Opertionalizing the intersection of attachment theory and affective neuroscience. *Journal of Psychotherapy Integration, 21,* 253–279.

Locke, K. D. (2006). Interpersonal circumplex measures. In S. Strack (Ed.), *Differentiating normal and abnormal personality* (2nd ed., pp. 383–400). New York: Springer.

Locke, K. D. (2011). Circumplex measures of interpersonal constructs. In L. M. Horowitz & S. Strack (Eds.), *Handbook of interpersonal psychology* (pp. 313–324). Hoboken, NJ: Wiley.

Magnavita, J. J. (2000). Introduction: The growth of relational therapy. *Journal of Clinical Psychology/In Session 56*(8), 999–1004.

Magnavita, J. J. (2006). In search of the unifying principles of psychotherapy: Conceptual, empirical, and clinical convergence. *American Psychologist, 61,* 882–892.

Magnavita, J. J. (2012). Mapping the clinical landscape with psychotherapedia ™: The unified psychotherapy project. *Journal of Unified Psychotherapy and Clinical Science, 1,* 21–36.

Mahoney, M. J. (1991). *Human change processes: The scientific foundations of psychotherapy.* New York: Basic Books.

McAdams, D. P., & Cox, K. S. (2010). Self and identity across the life span. In R. M. Lerner, M. E. Lamb & A. M. Freund (Eds.), *Handbook of life-span developmental psychology* (Vol. 2, pp. 158–207). Hoboken, NJ: Wiley.

Messer, S. B., & Warren, C. S. (1995). *Models of brief psychodynamic therapy.* New York: Guilford.

Miller, A. (1958, August). The shadows of the gods: A critical review of the American theater. *Harper's Magazine, 217,* 35–43. Retrieved March 14, 2013, from http://harpers.org/archive/1958/08/the-shadows-of-the-gods/

Miller, J. B. (1976). *Toward a new psychology of women.* Boston: Beacon Press.

Mitchell, S. A. (1988). *Relational concepts in psychoanalysis.* Cambridge, MA: Harvard University Press.

Morf, C. C., & Mischel, W. (2012). The self as a psycho-social dynamic processing system: Toward a converging science of selfhood. In M. R. Leary & J. P. Tangney (Eds.), *Handbook of self and identity* (2nd ed., pp. 21–49). New York: Guilford.

Norcross, J. C. (2011). (Ed.) *Psychotherapy relationships that work: Evidence-based responsiveness* (2nd ed.). New York: Oxford University Press.

Norman, G. J., Cacioppo, J. T., & Berntson, G. G. (2010). Social neuroscience. In L. Nadel (Ed.), *Wiley interdisciplinary reviews: Cognitive science, 1,* 60–68.

Pincus, A. L., Lukowitsky, M. R., & Wright, A. G. C. (2010). The interpersonal nexus of personality and psychopathology. In T. Millon, R. F. Krueger & E. Simonsen (Eds.), *Contemporary directions in psychopathology: Scientific foundations for the DSM-V and ICD-11* (pp. 523–552). New York: Guilford.

Reis, H. T., Collins, W. A., & Berscheid, E. (2000). The relationship context of human behavior and development. *Psychological Bulletin, 126,* 844–872.

Rogoff, B. (2003). *The cultural nature of human development.* New York: Oxford University Press.

Ryff, C. D., & Singer, B. (1998). The contours of positive mental health. *Psychological Inquiry, 9,* 1–28.

Schore, A. N. (2012). *The science of the art of psychotherapy.* New York: Norton.

Segrin, C. (2001). *Interpersonal processes in psychological disorders.* New York: Guilford.

Shonkoff, J. P., & Phillips, D. A. (Eds.) (2000). *From neurons to neighborhoods: The science of early childhood development.* Washington, DC: National Academy Press.

Siegel, D. J. (2012). *Pocket guide to interpersonal neurobiology: An integrative handbook of the mind.* New York: Norton.

Slade, A., & Aber, J. L. (1992). Attachments, drives, and development: Conflicts and convergences in theory. In J. Barron, M. Eagle & D. Wolitsky (Eds.), *The interface between psychoanalysis and psychology* (pp. 154–185). Washington, DC: American Psychological Association.

Stern, D. (1985). *The interpersonal world of the infant.* New York: Basic Books.

Sullivan, H. S. (1953a). *Conceptions of modern psychiatry.* New York: Norton.

Sullivan, H. S. (1953b). *The interpersonal theory of psychiatry.* New York: Norton.

Sullivan, H. S. (1954). *The psychiatric interview.* New York: Norton.

Sullivan, H. S. (1956). *Clinical studies in psychiatry.* New York: Norton.

Sullivan, H. S. (1962). *Schizophrenia as a human process.* New York: Norton.

Sullivan, H. S. (1964). *The fusion of psychiatry and social sciences.* New York: Norton.

Wachtel, P. L. (2008). *Relational theory and the practice of psychotherapy.* New York: Guilford.

White, R. W. (1959). Motivation reconsidered: The concept of competence. *Psychological Review, 66,* 297–333.

Wiggins, J. S. (1991). Agency and communion as conceptual coordinates for the understanding and measurement of interpersonal behavior. In D. Cicchetti & W. M. Grove (Eds.), *Thinking clearly about psychology: Essays in honor of Paul E. Meehl. Vol 2. Personality and psychopathology* (pp. 89–113). Minneapolis: University of Minnesota Press.

Wiggins, J. S. (1996). An informal history of the interpersonal circumplex tradition. *Journal of Personality Assessment, 66,* 217–233.

Wiggins, J. S. (2003). *Paradigms of personality assessment.* New York: Guilford.

Part II

UNIFIED PSYCHOTHERAPEUTICS

In this part we provide a presentation of the four levels of the patient's *total ecological system* (TES), briefly described in the previous part. Other clinical theorists have developed similar systems, such as the "supraparadigmatic integrative model" offered by Opazo (1997), who identified "six fundamental causal paradigms: biological, environmental/behavioral, cognitive, affective, the unconscious, and systems view" (p. 26), with the self giving a "sense of connectedness and wholeness to these causal paradigms" (p. 26). We, too, utilize these components but seek to organize them in a more parsimonious fashion. Of course no clinician, no matter how knowledgeable and well trained, can identify the influence of every variable at every level of the TES. Given the enormous amount of information with which we are faced as clinicians, it can in fact sometimes seem like we're looking for a needle in a haystack. The pattern recognition tools that have been developed and that are presented here make orienting our clinical work less overwhelming and advance our conceptual understanding of clinical treatment.

For each of the four domain levels of the TES, the distinct pattern recognition tool deployed entails the use of a triangular configuration to identify key subsystems composing the level at hand and to depict subsystem interactions. "The triangle is one of the most persistent metaphors in developmental, cultural, and social psychology" (Zittoun, Gillespie, Cornish, & Psaltis, 2007, p. 208). Features of the triangle indeed render it a highly suitable geometric, visual representation of structure and process in the human personality system, encompassing "three irreducible elements...and theori[zing] the relationships between these elements, represented as the sides of the triangle" (Zittoun et al., 2007, p. 209). Each of these elements can be understood to be in a constant state of fluctuation, but they nevertheless converge and reciprocally interact to form dynamic patterns that can be discerned by the trained clinician and researcher.

We believe that the four levels of the TES—*intrapsychic–biological* (Level I), *interpersonal–dyadic* (Level II), *relational–triadic* (Level III), and *sociocultural–familial* (Level IV)—and the distinct triangle representing each level provide crisp conceptual tools that fit together in a useful way for clinicians. Within each chapter of this part we pursue both analytic and synthetic objectives, unpacking the important subsystems constituting each level's triangular configuration and delineating the nature of these subsystems' interactions, respectively. We remind the reader that, while we are artificially dividing the TES in a manner that accords with theoretical, clinical, and empirical findings from over a century of clinical science (Anchin & Magnavita, 2006), in real time the personality system is embedded in the TES in a thoroughly holistic and integrated way. In this respect, we also suggest that in a certain sense we are dealing with fractals—self-replication at various levels. For example, the attachment system is experienced dyadically in an infant–maternal dyad, but as development proceeds the dyad's recurrent processes are encoded at an intrapsychic level in the form of relational schema, and in turn recapitulated in our intimate relationships—dyadically as well as triadically. In a similar vein, as we shall see when we reach the fourth level (sociocultural and familial), over time family systems collectively shape culture and cultural conditions reciprocally shape family structures and processes, part of humankind's evolutionary journey.

In addition to explicating the four levels of the TES and their primary subsystems, we extract from the discussion of each level several key principles of treatment. These principles are general guidelines for how to clinically proceed when working with phenomena pertaining to a given domain and subsystems constituting that domain. Principles may be differentiated from techniques, which entail more specific interventions for targeting specific forms and facets of clinical dysfunction and psychopathology, and serve as the primary emphasis of Part III.

Chapter 4

THE MIND/BRAIN

This chapter, on the *Level I intrapsychic–biological* component of the total ecological system (TES), focuses on the *mind/brain*, the fundamental domain level of psychology represented by the individual personality system or self—"the most basic psychological structure—the molecule of dynamic therapy" (Pinsof, 1995). We use the term mind/brain to reflect the contemporary understanding that the mind and the brain are inseparable; simply put, "What we call 'mind' can be understood as the activity of the brain (Andreasen, 1997)" (Gabbard, 2000). The notion that mind and brain can be split, that "minds [are] separate, isolated entities residing in heads" (Mahoney, 2005, pp. 338–339), is a vestige of Cartesian mind–body dualism rendered defunct by modern-day neuroscience. Thus, "[w]hile the two constructs [of mind and brain] represent domains that have their own languages and can be separated for purposes of discussion, they are always integrated" (Gabbard, 2000, p. 117).

Crucially, this is not to state that the brain and the mind are one and the same. As succinctly stated by Andreasen (1997), "mental phenomena arise from the brain" (p. 1586). The mind is thus an emergent property of the brain, though in the bigger picture encouraged by holism, it is more accurately characterizable as an emergent property from the brain and *its* interactions with structures and processes at other levels of the TES. For example, the sociocultural domain affects the regulation of emotions (Von Scheve & Von Luede, 2005), and these regulatory processes act through the brain (Franks & Smith, 1999), such that the mind (and in this illustrative case, its emotional content and related parameters, for example its intensity) is better understood as an emergent property of a complex system consisting of domains of nested, interacting structures that include but go beyond the brain—a concept well captured by Bateson's (1972) notion of "steps to an ecology of mind." Be that as it may, the mind and its subjectively experienced phenomena (e.g., cognitions and emotions, thoughts and feelings) are not identical to the neurophysiological structures and processes in which they are anchored, but their existence requires the operation of those neurophysiological mechanisms. As further reflection of the nonisomorphism of brain and mind, there is the compelling fact that the mind and its subjectively experienced contents reciprocally influence the brain (Andreasen, 1997; Gabbard, 2000; Linden, 2006; Schwartz & Begley, 2002)—the very foundation for the compelling discovery that integral to psychotherapy's effects and effectiveness is its alteration of the brain's physical architecture (Cozolino, 2010).

THE FOUNDATION—ESSENTIAL NEUROBIOLOGICAL COMPONENTS

We are strong supporters of the trend to use neuroscientific findings as one pillar for grounding unified psychotherapy in clinical science and as a component domain of a biopsychosocial-systems metatheoretical foundation for guiding treatment (Grigsby & Stevens, 2000; Grawe, 2007; Cozolino, 2010; Siegel, 1999). Unified psychotherapeutics requires a basic understanding of the brain's structure and how it functions in order to recognize the important neurobiological subsystems underpinning the functioning of the mind and shaping the relational matrix. Although it is not necessary to have an advanced degree in neuroscience, a basic familiarity with neuroscientific findings will enhance clinicians' ability to make a comprehensive assessment of all the systems implicated in the psychopathological expression of the patient's dysfunctional systems. In the following sections, we review what we believe to be the most important neurobiological component subsystems and structures to provide familiarization with basic neurobiological concepts. We strongly believe that advancing our knowledge with the most current research about the neurobiological brain systems is crucial to the advanced practice that is required of unified psychotherapeutics.

BASIC BRAIN STRUCTURE AND FUNCTIONS

In spite of the massive amount of information accumulated about the structure and functions of the neural networks, the brain still remains a mystery. The brain is an extraordinary organ with over 100 billion neurons and over a trillion synapses or connections among these neurons.

The human brain is structured in such a way that appears similar to a closed version of the fist with one's thumb inside; the closed fingers represent the forebrain and the thin outer shell the cerebral cortex, and the thumb is representative of the midbrain, which includes the limbic system. This system is mainly concerned with emotional processes and memory and houses a very important circuit activated during trauma and implicated in many forms of psychopathology. In the present analogy, one's wrist represents the brain stem (basil ganglia), responsible for basic physiological functions such as breathing, temperature regulation, and eating. The brain, which is divided into these three structures, roughly follows evolutionary lines, with each of the three parts developing on top of the others. The reptilian brain (brainstem) was the first to develop, followed by the mammalian brain, that is, the neocortex or midbrain, and then the cerebral cortex, which is responsible for higher-level functioning and consciousness, the latest evolutionary region. This division has been described as the "triune brain" (MacLean, 1990); however, while useful, this depiction is somewhat of a simplification (Panksepp, 1998).

The brain consists of two cerebral hemispheres connected by the corpus callosum, which consists of high-density fibers allowing each hempisphere to communicate with the other. If the corpus callosum is severed, each half of the brain operates on its own without the ability to coordinate functions. The brain is not fully symmetrical and each hemisphere does not share all tasks equally (Geschwind, 1979). Depending on handedness (right-handed people tend to have left-dominate hemispheres), most peoples' left hemisphere is primarily concerned with verbal ability and the nondominant or right hemisphere primarily with nonverbal ability. This specialization is known as lateralization, with each hemisphere responsible for the functions on the opposite or contralateral side of the body. More recent conceptions of the brain emphasize the high level of interconnectivity of neural structures, which work in close concert. Viewed from the outside, deep crevasses (fissures) divide the cerebral cortices into four regions, termed lobes, each of which has specialized functions: the *frontal* (front of brain behind your forehead), *parietal* (midsection), *temporal* (bottom section), and *occipital* (back brain) (see Figure 4.1). Although these regions have different functions, there are many overlaps and interconnections among various regions. The frontal lobes are central to our ability to organize, strategize, plan, and execute sequences of behavior known as executive functions. The parietal lobe is concerned mainly with our tactile experiences. The temporal lobe is primarily concerned with language, speech, and hearing. Broca's and Wernicke's areas are specific sections of this brain region (Damasio, 1999).

The brain is composed of neurons and grey matter. A single neuron may have between 1,000 and 10,000 synapses. "This degree of interconnectedness is the basis for the practically unlimited number of possible communication patterns among the neurons. The communication or

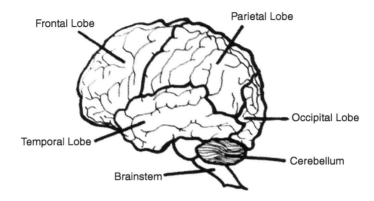

FIGURE 4.1   *Regions of the brain.*

neural activation patterns are the basis of our experience and behavior" (Grawe, 2007, p. 42). Neurons have three basic structures: the soma or cell body; dendrites, which are hair-like structures that emanate from the cell body; and elongated portions called axons (Magnavita, 2012). Nerve impulses are carried by electrical impulses along the axon of the neuron. When they reach the synaptic cleft, neurotransmitters are activated or inhibited in an "all-or-nothing" firing of the connected neurons, which are organized into complex neural structures and circuits. Synapses are the gaps between two neurons where more than 100 different neurotransmitters may be released in a complex exchange. Neurotransmitters have been implicated in a variety of mental disorders. Most psychotropic medications target one or more neurotransmitters by either blocking uptake in the synaptic gap or stimulating their release.

Neurotransmitter Action. An important neurotransmitter, *dopamine,* controls levels of arousal in various parts of the brain. In those with severely depleted dopamine levels it may be impossible to control voluntary movements, such as seen in Parkinson's disease. Overly high dopamine levels are implicated in schizophrenia. Another neurotransmitter, *serotonin,* is associated with mood regulation, sleep, and appetite. High levels are associated with serenity and optimism, and low levels seem to have a profound effect on anxiety. *Acetylcholine* controls activity in the brain related to attention, learning, and memory. Those with Alzheimer's disease typically have low levels of acetylcholine. *Noradrenaline* is an excitatory neurotransmitter that induces arousal and heightens mood, and is central in the activation of the stress-response syndrome preparing us for fight-or-flight reactions. *Glutamate* is an excitatory neurotransmitter vital for forging neuronal connections, which are the basis of learning and long-term memory. *Enkephalins* and *endorphins* are endogenous opiates, which modulate pain, reduce stress, and create a sense of well-being.

There have been attempts to develop rudimentary theories of personality based on the features of various neurotransmitters, most notably by Depue (1996), Cloninger (1986), and Siever and Davis (1991). They may provide some guidance for pharmacological intervention but at this point are limited in their usefulness. These are basically factor models, which correlate various neurobiological predispositions with dimension of personality. It is hypothesized that there may be a genetic predisposition to certain neurotransmitter systems, which may underlie temperament. The pharmacological treatment of mental illness has outpaced the use of psychotherapy in North America. Grawe (2007) wrote: "The use of pharmacotherapy alone—in the absence of the professional and competent structuring of the treated patient's life experience—is not justifiable from a neuroscientific perspective" (p. 6). He believes that neurotransmitters influence

> the activation threshold of problematic thought, emotion, action, and reaction potentials, but such pharmacological alterations could not result in the emergence of new memory traces. To create new memory content, which can then change subsequent experience and behavior, the person needs to take in new sensory experiences that change old memory content. (p. 5)

Hebb's (1949) law—"neurons that fire together wire together"—remains an important guiding principle, highlighting the necessity of exercising neuronal connections for learning. Psychotherapy rewires the brain by exercising new neuronal connections and stimulating neurogenesis. Trauma can have the opposite effect and stimulate apoptosis or cell death.

The Limbic System—LHPA Axis

The limbic system is a highly complex neural circuit strongly indicated in the development of many psychological disturbances (Davidson, Jackson, & Kalin, 2000; Herman, Ostrander, Mueller, & Figueiredo, 2005), and it has become a central focus of clinicians and affective scientists (Arizmendi, in press; Panksepp, 1998; Panksepp & Biven, 2012). This system is a ring of structures located underneath the cerebral cortex and connected by a ring of neural pathways (Corr, 2006; Sapolsky, 2004). Initially observed by Paul Broca, the limbic system was later described by Papez (1937) as the "emotional circuit" or "Papez circuit" of the brain. Later, MacLean (1952) formally introduced the term *limbic system* and created a more articulated map of this complex neurobiological circuit. This highly interconnected set of brain structures responsible for our emotional functioning, motivation, and long-term memory includes the amygdala, hippocampus, anterior thalamic nuclei, septum, fornix, and limbic cortex.

Among other functions, this circuit rapidly processes vital information about danger from our environment before our cerebral cortical functions can come to a decision about what kind of action should be taken. There are more neural pathways leading up to the cerebral cortices than the ones that connect downward to the limbic system, which explains why it is often difficult to extinguish the associations made during the high states of emotional arousal present in traumatic situations. Learning that takes place during limbic hyperarousal is highly impactful, occurs very quickly, and can be enduring. The hypothalamic-pituitary-adrenal (HPA) axis responds to stress with increased release of cortisol. "Chronic stress is not at all healthy, and certainly not for the hippocampus, which is damaged by this high cortisol level to such a degree that the volume shrinks measurably" (Grawe, 2007, p. 19).

Neuroscientific findings reveal important information about various structures within the limbic system. The hippocampus is a structure in the middle of the brain related to memory and is used to rapidly recognize potentially dangerous situations. A connected structure, the amygdala is responsible for rapid emotional processing. Thus, when the hippocampus, using cognitive schema or templates, recognizes a familiar pattern in which there exists a potential threat based on previous experiences, the amygdala immediately activates a number of major neurobiological systems that mobilize the HPA axis, preparing us for rapid *flight-fight-freeze* reactions (Corr, 2006). Most important for our purposes is the central position of the limbic-hypothalamic-pituitary-adrenal (LHPA) axis (see Figure 4.2) in the development of trauma and in the use of unified psychotherapeutics to return the neural structures to a state of optimal balance.

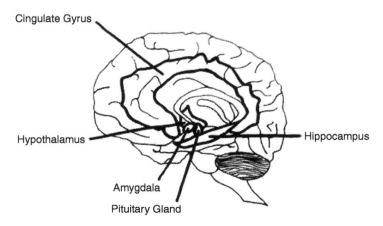

FIGURE 4.2   *Limbic-hypothalamic-pituitary-adrenal axis.*

One of the evolutionary advantages of the LHPA axis is that it pro-vides a deeply encoded memory of previously experienced, potentially dangerous situations that need to be rapidly avoided or responded to in order to maximize chances for survival. With this rapid perception of and response to threat, the highly attuned limbic system thereby provides an evolutionary advantage. Unfortunately, this system does not readily turn off as it does with other species, such as the zebra, in many traumatic situations (Sapolsky, 2004). Animals have a much greater ability to wash out the neuroendorcrine effects of trauma and return to homeostasis. Because of our high level of relational interconnectedness, humans, as well as some other primates, can be traumatized by psychological, social, and cultural factors not present in other species. Individuals with a his-tory of traumatic experiences, which include neglect as well as physical, sexual, and emotional abuse, may become stuck in a state of limbic hyper-arousal. In many cases, this hyperarousal results in a variety of second-ary psychological disturbances including anxiety, affective, depressive, and personality disorders, as well as an array of relational disturbances. The effect of states of limbic hyperarousal from trauma may also become a pathway for the expression of neurobiological vulnerabilities, or diathe-sis-stress point, in a variety of disorders including schizophrenia (Read, Perry, Moskowitz, & Connolly, 2001), eating disorders, bipolar disorder, and others.

Read et al. (2001) offer a *traumagenic neurodevelopmental* model that is consistent with our findings and clinical experience. Traumatic experi-ences early in the course of development can activate some neurobiologi-cal sensitivity. Often what the clinician sees in practice are the secondary and tertiary effects of either severe acute trauma or chronic trauma, be it neglect or emotional abuse. Traumatic experiences alter brain structures and may be a pathway to a variety of clinical conditions. A growing lit-erature documents effects across a spectrum of neurobiological functions among maltreated and physically abused children (Skowron et al., 2011).

An understanding and appreciation of the role played by the limbic system in the development and maintenance of psychological disorders can be useful. Grawe (2007) explained:

> A traumatic event is an extremely potent fear stimulus that triggers an immediate, very strong reaction in the amyg-dala, which then leads to the sort of conditioning of visual, acoustic, and other sensory cues associated with the trauma that later become very difficult to extinguish. These memory traces become engraved in the amygdala and can subse-quently be easily triggered in full strength by corresponding sounds, smells, or images—without such exposure leading to extinction. Based on the discussions on fear and anxiety...,

we already know that the anxiety reaction in the amygdala generally cannot be extinguished but, at best, can only be inhibited. Individuals who develop PTSD [posttraumatic stress disorder] are distinct from others because they do not develop this inhibition. (p. 144)

There is accumulating evidence that impairment in the HPA axis is implicated in most forms of psychopathology. The extensive comorbidities evident in clinical practice and supported empirically make "one point crystal clear: Traumatizing events—that is, life experiences that cause uncontrollable stress—play a central role in the development of mental disorders, including disorders other than PTSD" (Grawe, 2007, p. 147).

Explaining the neurobiological foundations and contribution of a hypersensitive limbic system offers a nonpathologizing way for patients to understand why it is often so difficult to overcome the impact of trauma. This is also useful in that it may allow the individual to develop a level of compassion for him- or herself. We must remember that one of the aspects of being a victim of trauma is that there may be a belief that one was responsible for causing the traumatic experience. We will see later that these dysfunctional beliefs are a central part of the trauma network that needs to be restructured in order for the individual to attain a healthier level of functioning.

Clinicians need to be exquisitely attuned to the physiological concomitants of limbic system hyperarousal. Hyperarousal may be readily observable in heightened states of conscious anxiety, or it may appear as other variants such as fatigue, exhaustion, or hypoarousal. Generally speaking, chronic states of limbic hyperarousal will eventually weaken both the psychological and physical immune systems. There are many consequences of these chronic states, but the important point is assessing whether the limbic system is in a state of hyperarousal and the unique pathway this has taken for each individual. When an individual experiences chronic levels of stress, this can lead to what McEwen and Seeman (2003) term *allostatic loading*. Allostasis refers to an organism's ability to maintain stability in normal functioning in the face of one or more environmental stressors through adaptive physiological changes, which includes activation of the limbic system and production of such stress hormones as cortisol and adrenalin. However, over time, conditions of frequent and/or chronic stress can lead to allostatic loading—the cumulative price paid by the body and brain, in the form of "wear and tear" (Kapczinski et al., 2008, p. 676), a consequence of having to recurrently adapt to various psychosocial challenges and adverse environments. Malta (2012), for example, cites "evidence of long-term alterations in neuroendocrine systems in PTSD" (p. 242). More generally, chronic overreaction of bodily systems that are involved in responding to recurrent or chronic environmental stressors can have deleterious effects that result in chronic stress-related somatic illnesses and psychiatric disorders. Notably, patients with stress-related and anxiety disorders represent a significant proportion of patients seeking medical care (Gevirtz, 2007).

Understanding the concept of allostatic loading provides clinicians with a very useful framework with which to understand and attempt to identify contributory factors resulting in current psychopathological adaptations. The allostatic load usually is expressed in the most vulnerable part of the system, even though the whole system may be affected. For example, in the case of two identical twins with a genetic predisposition for schizophrenia, which is thought to have a strong heritability, one twin might, under conditions of chronic stress, activate the genetic loading whereas the other twin who has not been subjected to the same stress might never show clinical manifestation of the disorder. Allostatic load may impact an individual who has a more fragile personality structure than someone with more robust adaptive strategies and resilience.

The Central Nervous System (CNS) and Autonomic Nervous System (ANS)

The *central nervous system* (CNS) includes the spinal cord, and the brain, and the autonomic nervous system (ANS), which interacts with the environment and carries out the commands of the CNS. The ANS is made up of two branches—the *sympathetic* and *parasympathetic* branches—which play a central role in anxiety disorders. Both branches are responsible for regulating internal processes in the body (Corr, 2006). The sympathetic branch is primarily concerned with activating the *fight-flight response* in times of emergency or threat, during which the activity of the parasympathetic nervous system is inhibited in the form of a *freeze response* until the threat passes. During activation of the sympathetic branch there is increased heart rate and blood flow to the muscles. This system was primarily designed to respond to imminent threat, and then when the threat is no longer present to return to homeostasis. The parasympathetic branch is concerned with rest and digestion. When the parasympathetic nervous system dominates, blood is diverted from muscles and is used to assist the digestive process.

Vagal Tone and Heart Rate Variability

There is ever-increasing emphasis on the importance of the mind–body connection (e.g., Schore, 2012; Solomon & Siegel, 2003). One important line of research uses heart rate variability (HRV) as a biomarker of physical and psychological health. Stephen Porges (2011) has developed a polyvagal theory of neuroception using HRV as a distinctly measurable physiological marker. HRV represents the variation in heart rate accompanying breathing (Lehrer, 2007). When we inhale our heart rate increases, and it decreases when we breathe out; the difference is an indication of HRV. The heart affects the brain and the brain the heart, and thus this reciprocally interacting system strongly influences emotional reactions. Porges uses this theory to explain stress vulnerability and how we perceive danger—a process he refers to as *neuroception*. When we perceive danger, our ANS is activated, which lowers our social engagement system, in turn reducing social relatedness. In this conceptualization he identifies two vagal pathways, one that is myelinated, and the other—an earlier evolutionary adaptation—unmyelinated. These vagal nerves are connected to various body organs and thus influence many systems. The primary vagus nerve is inhibitory and keeps the heart rate from getting out of control and overreacting (Grawe, 2007). This primary myelinated vagal nerve exerts an inhibitory effect on the sympathetic nervous system and thus keeps the heart rate from spiraling out of control by acting as a brake, which when released allows the sympathetic nervous system to respond. The unmyelinated vagal nerve serves a different function and is responsible for feigning death and cardiac shut down. The vagal tone or respiratory sinus arrthymia (RSA), which is an indication of flexibility, can be measured by measuring HRV. When HRV is high there tends to be enhanced emotional and physical functioning. The coordination of the sympathetic and parasympathetic nervous systems and their level of arousal is seen in the capacity of the vagal nerve (regulates heart rate in order to match physiological response to environmental demands) to flexibly respond to the demands of a situation. This flexibility in HRV is associated with emotional regulation, behavioral responsiveness, and flexible response to situational demands.

Clinicians who do not have medical training need to familiarize themselves with the basic medical disorders that present as psychological disturbance. Barbara Schildkrout's (2011) volume, *Unmasking Psychological Symptoms: How Therapists Can Learn to Recognize the Psychological Presentation of Medical Disorders*, is a useful book that familiarizes the reader with characteristics of physical disorders that may present in psychological practice.

The Neuroendocrine System

The endocrine system has a strong influence on emotional and behavioral states and reactions. It is among primary contributors to allostatic loading, which in turn can be involved in the etiology of many somatic disorders; for example, chronic fatigue syndrome, fibromyalgia, irritable bowel syndrome, and migraine headaches. When the CNS experiences stress, it alerts the endocrine system, which through glands and neurons secretes hormones into the blood; these hormones in turn target certain cells that contain specific receptors for specific hormones. Organs whose function is to release hormones are called endocrine glands. Other organs such as the stomach, intestine, and heart also release hormones, although this is not their primary function. Most hormones are released in bursts rather continuously. The importance of the endocrine system is due to the effect that chronic activation has on the body and emotional response systems (Corr, 2006).

Epigenetics: Environmental Influences on Gene Expression

Over the past two decades there has been increasing understanding of the process of epigenetics. Essentially, experience may influence gene expression without altering the information within the gene (Nestler, 2011). "The term [epigenetics] refers to a complex system of molecular machinery that carries out experience-driven (i.e., learning-driven) modifications of gene expression without mutating the genes themselves" (Ecker, Ticic, & Hulley, 2012, p. 36). The interaction of environment and genes can occur over the life span. There is accruing research demonstrating a relationship between early deprivation and telomeres length, which are related to chromosomal stability. Telomere length shrinks under conditions of adversity and represents an important biomarker of chronic allostatic loading in both children and adults (Drury, Theally, Gleason, Smyke, De Vivo, Wong, Fox, Zeanah, & Nelson, 2011).

Epigenetics also appears to be relevant to the important distinction between common and unique family environments (Kiesler, 1999) and their differential contributions to the development of personality and psychopathology:

> The *common-shared* family environment denotes the common settings and experiences, the shared advantages and disadvantages, that siblings experience growing up as members of the same family….In contrast, the *unique-unshared* family environment denotes the environmental experiences (both subjective and objective) that are different from child to child in a given family. These consist of often subtle differences or changes in settings, social experiences, family circumstances, and parent–child and sibling–sibling interactions. The notion of unique family environment recognizes the fact that different children in the same family often experience substantially different environmental events. (p. 111)

Of particular importance in the present context, evidence from research in behavioral genetics indicates that unique unshared family–environmental factors are far more crucial than common-shared family factors in the development of personality and psychopathology (Kiesler, 1999).

Research cited by Gabbard (2000) suggests that this relationship may be due in part to the impact of the unique-unshared family environment on a child's gene expression over the course of his or her development within the family. Moreover, different children from the same family encounter different social environments (e.g., specific peers, teachers, and settings) as they develop, which in turn may also influence their respective gene expression as well as personality and levels of adjustment and maladjustment (see, e.g., Champagne, 2010, 2012; Champagne & Curley, 2011; Rutten & Mill, 2009). Such considerations can be valuable for clinicians in understanding and communicating to others why, for example, one son or daughter becomes a cocaine addict yet other siblings do not succumb to substances and are more resilient (Nestler, 2011).

Clinical Implications of Understanding the Basic Neurobiological Substrate

Educating patients about their psychological or personality system and the neurobiological basis of these processes is often an essential strategy of unified treatment that can empower the patient system. Enhancing awareness about basic physiological states and their related somatic and physiological concomitants is essential. Some patients are not aware of the chronic state of anxiety in which they live and others find progressive increases in anxiety to be almost more than they can bear. As we shall see, anxiety regulation is both an adaptive function and one that is susceptible to dysregulation from the impact of trauma and other occurrences that are neurobiologically driven and encoded and psychologically induced. Gabbard (2000) provided another unifying insight associated with neurobiological understanding, shedding light on specifically epigenetic mechanisms that may contribute to psychotherapy's effectiveness: "If psychotherapy is regarded as a form of learning, then the learning process that occurs in psychotherapy may produce alterations of gene expression and thereby alter the strength of synaptic connections" (Gabbard, 2000, p. 117).

From the standpoint of distinct interventions, there are also many technological advances that offer clinicians an array of inexpensive tools that can be used to assist specifically in resetting the limbic system. Most helpful are biofeedback devices that offer a direct experience of feedback about physiological arousal. These include galvanic skin response (GSR) feedback, muscle tension sensors, and thermal temperature sensors, which allow for a rapid assessment of arousal and provide different measures to discern what can effectively bring down states of arousal (Wickramasekera, Davies, & Davies, 1996). HRV biofeedback is a fairly new development applying the technology from cardiology to stress management, and has proven especially useful for balancing the autonomic nervous system and increasing parasympathetic tone (Chamberlin, 2011).

Work using HRV, as discussed above in the context of polyvagal theory, has been pioneered by Stephen Porges (1995). His theory of neuroception suggests that the vagal pathway can be rebalanced using biofeedback. Electroencephalogram (EEG) technology has also advanced to the point where it is very affordable to purchase research-grade and easy-to-use EEG technology to map and alter brain states. Thermal monitors, which are very inexpensive, provide another easy-to-use tool that patients can use to monitor and learn how to alter their states of coherence. It is likely that these and other neurobiological measures and tools will be incorporated on a regular basis into the practice of unified psychotherapeutics.

Some Neurobiologically Based Principles

- Be alert and note possible states and causes of allostatic loading.
- Carefully assess each patient for limbic system status.
- Always seek to create an environment where the patient feels as safe as possible.
- When appropriate use a limbic probe to test the integrity of the system.
- Vigilantly monitor physiological reactivity, making certain never to increase limbic arousal to the point of overwhelming or flooding the patient.
- Attempt to map the optimal level of arousal needed for learning.
- Use anxiety-reducing techniques in patients who have a high level of limbic arousal.
- Use anxiety-enhancing techniques for those who are ego-syntonic and not aware of emotional experience.

OVERVIEW OF INTRAPSYCHIC MATRIX AND COMPONENTS

"As living organisms, all individuals can be described biologically or bio-psychologically (e.g., as being at a particular level of maturation) and psycho-biologically (e.g., as complex systems with cognitive, affective, motivational, and behavioral characteristics)" (Orlinsky, 2009, p. 334). The *intrapsychic–biological level* of our metatheoretical framework bears equivalencies to Orlinsky's psycho-biological description, and is depicted using the *intrapsychic–biological triangle* (Figure 4.3)—a basic schematic of how this level of the personality system operates at the psychological level of the mind. We refer to this triangular configuration as the *intrapsychic*

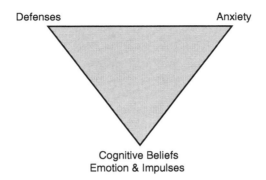

Defenses   Anxiety

Cognitive Beliefs
Emotion & Impulses

FIGURE 4.3   *Intrapsychic–biological matrix.*

matrix. At the base of the triangle, usually out of conscious awareness, are both *cognitive beliefs* that are encoded neurobiologically in the memory network and interrelated partially or nonmetabolized affect/emotion (i.e., not experienced or processed and reorganized in a narrative). Anxiety is contained in the upper right-hand corner of the triangle, while defenses are located in the triangle's upper left-hand corner.

In order to fully appreciate the pattern recognition potential of all the triangular matrices presented in this volume, one needs to have an overview of all of them because they are intertwined components of the TES. While a number of other clinical theorists have outlined various biopsychosocial organizations, we believe that the framework presented in this volume brings together well-worn constructs that have immense clinical utility, very useful for guiding clinical process regardless of one's favored therapeutic approach.

Essentially, when an individual encounters certain situations or relationships (depicted at the *interpersonal–dyadic level* [II] in the next chapter), the unconscious schematic representation (thoughts and beliefs and resulting feelings about self and others) is activated, and because these have not been metabolized, anxiety ensues. These internal, unconscious relational schemata are robust and guide our relationships (Hassin, Uleman, & Bargh, 2005). Thus, as *anxiety* intensifies, *defenses* are called into action to defend against excessive anxiety and nonmetabolized affect in an attempt to contain or repress the painful feelings being activated. An example illustrates how this intrapsychic matrix operates. An individual who was encoded to believe that he was "stupid" based on responses he received from his father whenever he attempted something new and did not do it perfectly decided to pursue his education. After starting a course, he became increasingly anxious with each class and assignment but without an awareness or understanding of what was generating the anxiety. He was "unable" to complete his assignments and dropped out of school. In this simple example, we can see that as he approached the time when he would be evaluated, his unconscious anxiety was mobilized and the internal belief that "I am stupid" activated. Instead of risking having his self-related belief "confirmed" by doing poorly on his assignment, he utilized a number of defenses to mitigate the anxiety, most notably *avoidance, rationalization*, and *withdrawal*. This pattern is common in all forms of psychopathology—that is, activation of the feeling and negative schema, increased anxiety, and then utilization of defenses to keep the system in equilibrium at the cost of creating "vicious cycles" or self-defeating patterns of behavior. Since new learning cannot take place, the old neural network is again reinforced, leading to more cycles of self-sabotage. Thus, repeating of learned behavioral repertories reinforces neural networks and defensive adaptations. A closer look at the important component subsystems of this intrapsychic matrix follows.

COGNITIVE–AFFECTIVE–DEFENSIVE PROCESSES

Cognition and affect are embedded in a number of neural circuits and regions of the brain, and most researchers feel it is impossible to separate emotional processes from thoughts (Opazo, 1997). At the level of the individual self, cognition and affect are interactive elements of the intrapsychic system, and these in turn interact with psychological defenses. We will begin by isolating the important affective, cognitive, and defensive elements of these domains of the intrapsychic system, which are essential to treatment and imperative to understand.

Affective Components

The affect system, responsible for our emotional responses, is a central organizing psychological structure and serves as an attractor state in the personality system (Block, 2002; Magnavita, 2006). "Emotion manifests across physiological, cognitive, behavioral, social and cultural systems; thus it is no surprise that specialists in each domain have constructed definitions, measures, and theories of function as they relate to that specific domain" (Mayne & Ramsey, 2001, p. 2). The centrality of emotion in human adaptation has been evident in the modern era since the publication of Darwin's (1972/1998) seminal treatise, *The Expression of the Emotions in Man and Animals*, considered the beginning of the field of affective science. In-depth understanding of affective components and processes is essential to a unified approach to psychotherapy, and while imparting the vast complexities of this system is beyond the scope of this volume, we present here some of the key basics.

Emotion has held a central position in psychotherapy and continues to be a central concept in understanding psychopathology. Emotions have a bioregulatory function and, evolving over millennia, serve to maximize adaptation to our environment (Damasio, 1999). Emotional disturbance is one of the hallmarks of most forms of human psychopathology. In most psychological disturbances the emotional system is over- or underregulated, resulting in a wide spectrum of maladaptive states and behavioral repertoires. Scientists now view emotional expression as a safeguard for survival, as well as an important component for enriching our experience and quality of life. The face, an exquisitely designed communicative network of about 53 facial muscles, plays a central role in expressing emotion (Ekman & Rosenberg, 2005). Human relationships are guided by the capacity for rapid recognition and processing of emotional states communicated through complex facial expressions (Ekman & Davidson, 1994). Affective responses are natural elements of our interactions from birth, and serve to prime and shape the attachment system, touched on in Chapter 3 and discussed in greater depth in the context of the next chapter's focus on dyadic processes. The study of emotion and the practice of psychotherapeutic methods that facilitate emotional development have always been central to psychotherapy but are becoming even more compelling to clinicians of all theoretical orientations.

Basic Emotion. There is evidence that across cultures there are up to 10 primary emotions with many secondary blends. Parrott (2001) proposes six basic emotions: love, joy, surprise, anger, fear, and sadness. The recognition, identification, and expression of emotion has been termed emotional intelligence (Salovey & Mayer, 1990) and popularized by Goleman (1995). There are a number of clinical theorists and researchers who believe that emotional experience in relationship to an attuned other is transformative (Fosha, 2000, 2005; Greenberg & Paivio, 1997; Schore, 2003). Our distillation of this literature suggests that whenever possible the therapist should facilitate and encourage the experiencing of core emotion. Experiencing core emotion and learning to label and express these feelings is an essential element of intimate relationships. Those individuals with a greater capacity for emotional experience and differentiation are less prone to psychological disorders.

Affect Phobia. As infants develop they internalize and encode their caretakers' socialization about the expression of their emotion. Healthy emotional development allows for full emotional expression and capacity to experience emotion at a high level. When an individual is taught through traumatic experiences of invalidation (Linehan, 1993) that their emotions are unacceptable or overwhelming, they may develop an affect phobia (McCullough, 2003). This is a very useful concept both for clinicians and patients in that it explains why it is difficult to resolve issues that are in the past. Instead of facing them squarely and processing one's thoughts and feelings, painful feelings are avoided and thus often remain symptomatic. Again, it is clinically advisable to focus the patient on his or her avoided emotion but always within the framework of a collaborative and culturally sensitive relationship. In this vein, we also encourage the therapist, when possible, to verbally reflect back the emotion the patient is demonstrating in his or her facial expressions, particularly to the extent the patient is unaware of his or her emotional states. Reflected emotion is a powerful form of "locating" the patient in an attuned way and generally deepens his or her emotional experiences. Emotional processing is an essential aspect of unified psychotherapy, and based on our research and experience, should be included in all therapeutic approaches.

Anxiety. Anxiety is a physiological state that is associated with autonomic nervous system arousal, leading to a variety of changes in the neurobiological and cognitive–affective–defensive system. Most individuals characteristically describe anxiety with the following physiological features: increased heart rate, cardiac palpitations, tightness in the chest, dry mouth, flushing or blushing, light-headedness, sweating, urinary urgency, and in some individuals a need to defecate often associated with a history of irritable bowel syndrome. The surge of adrenaline, as we have discussed, prepares the individual for flight or fight. Other components often include a state of foreboding and hypervigilance, which when severe can lead to a state of psychological fragmentation.

Anxiety is a physiologically experienced sense that the individual is in danger either physically or psychologically (Block, 2002), and this may be beneficial to the organism if it is appropriately modulated and moves one to action. As nonmetabolized emotion is activated, anxiety (upper right-hand corner of the triangle in Figure 4.3) is mobilized. Fear and anxiety are often confused but important to differentiate despite considerable overlap. As we have discussed, fear is a core emotion that results from imminent danger. We can differentiate anxiety in that there is no clear or imminent danger, or the danger may be social or psychological, activated by internal beliefs. Anxiety signals that an adaptive reaction is warranted to escape danger or to avoid risk-taking that might have dire results.

Pathways of Anxiety. Clinicians should observe the pathways of anxiety that are evident in the clinical situation and also inferred from history. The following pathways, having differing clinical implications, have been observed by Davanloo (1980): (a) striated muscle pathway—lower back, neck, shoulders, and across the chest; (b) smooth muscle pathway—autonomic nervous system expression in the gastrointestinal tract, the pulmonary system, and migraine headaches; (c) cognitive–perceptual pathway—cognitive and perceptual distortion when ego-system is flooded; and (d) personality–defense system pathway—increased ego-syntonicity of character defenses (Magnavita, 2005). Observing the channel of anxiety informs treatment. Patients who primarily channel anxiety to the striated muscles are, generally speaking, good candidates for brief treatment (Magnavita, 1997), and those who channel their anxiety to the smooth muscles or cognitive–perceptual system are likely to require more systematic cognitive restructuring before they are able to handle too much anxiety.

Cognitive Components

The cognitive system is another major, interactive domain of the intrapsychic system that is an essential domain of unified psychotherapy. "The way people process data about themselves and others is influenced by their beliefs and the other components of their cognitive organization" (Beck & Freeman, 1990, p. 30). Humans are continually processing information at the conscious and nonconscious level. The interplay between emotion and cognition is apparent in the fact that emotionally arousing experiences are more likely to be remembered (Siegel, 1999). It is for this reason that trauma experienced by children is so deeply etched into neural networks and from a treatment perspective difficult to restructure. Rooted in our neurobiology, the ways in which we process and store information based on our interpersonal experiences shape our core beliefs and schematic representations of self and other. Internal beliefs form the core of our relational schema. Cognitive learning is enhanced and laid down in the neuronal networks with the assistance of emotion, which serves as an attractor state.

Beliefs. Beliefs are internalized messages that are encoded throughout the developmental process and form the building blocks of one's self-identity and relationships. A belief is a way of organizing information from one's environment and may be positively or negatively valenced. For example, if one's spouse is slamming the door, one may assume accurately or falsely that he or she is angry. A belief is a small byte of information such as "I am inept," "I am not athletic," "I don't perform well on tests," "I am clumsy," or " I am unattractive." Patients are continually communicating beliefs about themselves, which needs to be decoded and organized by the psychotherapist. Often the patient is not conscious of dsyfunctional self-related beliefs, which need to be brought to awareness if they are to be changed. Beliefs tend to be organized into schema, which are part of the operating system of the personality.

Schema. Schema, a concept first articulated by George Kelly (1955) with the term "personal constructs," are templates of associated beliefs that in part operate as pattern recognition tools that guide one's organization and processing of information, including the interpretation of and meaning given to events, including the actions of others. Young (1990) offered the concept of early maladaptive schema (EMS) to refer to constellations of stable and deeply held assumptions about the self and others that create expectancies about the world. These EMSs are very common in individuals with personality dysfunction as well as in most patients with any type of trauma history. Schema represent an interconnected set of core beliefs about oneself and about others based on relational experiences. These are major guiding templates for living that can vary along such dimensions as breadth, rigidity or flexibility, valence, and permeability–impermeability, and they play a prominent role in influencing one's goals, emotional states, and transactions with the world. Characteristically schema are not crystallized in the patient's consciousness, but they are often quite obvious to the trained clinician. Illustrations of core maladaptive self-relational schema include "I am unlovable," "I am not safe," "I am bad," "I don't deserve to live," "I am weak," "I am insignificant," "I am not good enough," "I am unworthy," and "I am abandoned." Examples of core maladaptive other schema include: Other people "will hurt me," "cannot be trusted," "are better than me," "will disappoint me," "will abandon me," and "will take advantage of me." These core schema are encoded developmentally so that the clinician can have some sense of when they developed based on their structure. These represent a collection of experiences that are organized through the perspective of the maturity of the cognitive apparatus at that developmental time. For example, very young children tend to perceive things as "good" or "bad," while older adolescents may view their experiences through a more sophisticated cognitive and perceptual apparatus and perceive that they are "not good enough" or "unworthy."

Defensive Functioning

An understanding of the nature and characteristics of defensive functioning is a valuable asset for any clinician or anyone who seeks to understand human behavior. Many defenses have been empirically validated (Cramer, 2000) and a basic knowledge of these and their developmental onset is useful (Vaillant, 1992). Defenses are mechanisms that are used through the course of development and are automatically triggered when the individual perceives a threat. Defenses serve to protect the individual but can also stand in the way of resolving conflict, establishing and maintaining intimacy, and perceiving the world accurately. The process of understanding defenses is akin to listening to a symphony—the entirety of the ebb and flow and rhythms of defenses must be discerned. Listening to an individual instrument in a symphony misses the point. Blackman (2004) has done an excellent job of cataloging the defenses reported in the literature in his volume, *101 Defenses: How the Mind Shields Itself,* which we highly recommend.

Defenses can be organized in four basic categories: (a) psychotic, (b) immature (primitive), (c) neurotic, and (d) mature. At the lowest level on the continuum are psychotic defenses, which massively distort reality, incapacitate reality testing, and suggest a very low level of adaptive functioning and/or capacity. Immature or primitive defenses may look self-destructive but are generally considered the best adaptive solution available to a patient. These include projection, acting out, blocking, introjection, splitting, idealization, and projective identification, to name a few. Neurotic defenses are the most abundant and easiest to modify because they are generally less relied upon and rigid. They may include repression, displacement, isolation of affect, detachment, avoidance, and compartmentalization. Mature defenses represent the best adaptive possibilities and adaptation to life and include humor, suppression, anticipation, and sublimation.

It is important to carefully catalogue the patient's defensive constellation, which can be done by observing and experiencing them in relationship with the patient and by asking him or her to describe events that are disturbing and have the patient describe his or her reactions.

The Nature and Impact of Relational Trauma

In order to bridge the gap to the next chapter on interpersonal–dyadic processes we should preview the notion that the component domains described in this chapter are highly susceptible and shaped by relational and other types of trauma. We will be widening our observational lens as we proceed to the next chapter, incorporating another level of the relational matrix responsible for encoding the schematic representations of self and others. However, before turning to this next chapter, we present here a number of key implicational principles of treatment based on our above discussion of components and processes of the intrapsychic-biological matrix.

Principles of Treatment

Affective Principles

Converging research and clinical observation demonstrate the importance of identifying and unpacking the patient's emotions (including their meanings), and understanding the extent to which he or she effectively regulates particular emotions.

- Affective states are fundamentally *experienced* by the patient, and as such strive to empathically grasp what a given state of emotion *feels* like for the patient.
- Inherent within affective states are important meanings pertaining to the patient's valued goals and the extent to which the

patient's movement toward achievement of his or her goals is being advanced or impeded.

- Too much or too rapid activation of emotion can overwhelm the psychic system of the patient and should be vigilantly monitored.

- The clinician should closely monitor emotional response and level of affective activation. An important goal is to continually strive to enhance emotional tolerance.

- Emotional experience should be carefully titrated based on the integrity of the intrapsychic system.

Anxiety Regulation Principles

The regulation of anxiety is a central therapeutic activity of the clinician (Valliant & McCullough, 1997). Many advances have been made in this regard in terms of understanding and treating anxiety disorder.

- Emphasize the ubiquitous nature of anxiety and explain its value as a signaling system to alert us to danger.

- Carefully assess the level of anxiety and make careful note of the optimal threshold or range of anxiety that is necessary for functioning and the point at which it paralyzes the intrapsychic and behavioral response system.

- In the service of facilitating the patient's coping, use anxiety-reducing methods such as relaxation training, biofeedback, neurofeedback, yoga, mindfulness, mediation, and training in self-soothing. Also consider psychopharmacological approaches when the anxiety cannot be managed with psychological approaches.

Cognitive Principles

- Do not assume the patient is consciously aware of his or her schematically rooted beliefs about self and others.

- The patient's schema of self and of others are most accurately conceptualized as cognitive–affective in nature, and therefore be mindful that when affect is activated, core beliefs are more accessible.

- Pay close attention to the manner in which core beliefs about self and others influence the patient's appraisal of (e.g., meanings given to) current stressors.

- Be attuned to healthy and constructive beliefs (e.g., about self, others, the world) held by the patient.

Trauma Principles at the Intrapsychic–Biological Level

- Assess for trauma and be alert for a history of hidden forms of trauma such as emotional abuse, neglect, and reversal of the parent–child relationship (Bacciagaluppi, 2012).
- Offer exposure-based trauma treatment or EMDR as a first-line treatment when a clear history of trauma presents.
- Explain how the stress-response system, including the HPA axis, works and do so in language calibrated to that of the individual. Use this language to normalize adaptive responses that have become stuck or gone awry.

Defensive Principles

- The clinician should identify preferred defenses that the patient uses and then make note of how defenses shift when under increased stress. The defense constellation should be catalogued. This is one of the major operations that allows the clinician to develop a highly reliable hologram of the individual's adaptive capacities.
- With patients who are ego-syntonic, more focal defensive work should be considered as a way to achieve enhanced access to the emotional system.
- Explain to the patient(s) how defenses are a *vital part of our adaptive capacity* and survival system. Emphasize that defenses at one time were developmentally the best adaptive solution possible but that they can lose their adaptive value as we mature.

SUMMARY

In this chapter we have described the intrapsychic-biological level of the TES as comprised of a number of interconnected subsystems representing the structure and organization of the "mind/brain" (Bucci, 1997; Schore, 2001). This level can be conceptualized as the individual personality system, which does not exist in isolation but rather is constantly being shaped and reorganized by interrelationships with and influences from the other component domain levels and subsystems of the TES. Essential processes that occur within the individual at the intrapsychic–biological level are based on the integrity of brain structures and include microlevel processes such as neurotransmitter action and limbic system functioning. Psychological components of the internal operating system, which organizes the individual's functioning, are reciprocally interactive and include affective experiences and processes (e.g., emotional regulation), schematic representations (internalized thoughts and beliefs about self and others), and defensive operations. Key principles for guiding clinical work given intrapsychic–biological subsystems can be specified.

REFERENCES

Anchin, J. C., & Magnavita, J. J. (2006). The nature of unified clinical science: Implications for psychotherapeutic theory, practice, training, and research. *Psychotherapy Bulletin, 41*(2), 26–36.

Andreasen, N. C. (1997). Linking mind and brain in the study of mental illnesses: A project for a scientific psychopathology. *Science, 275*, 1586–1593.

Arizmendi, T. (in press). Stress and HPA axis responsivity: Mediating factors and implications for treatment. *Journal of Unified Psychotherapy and Clinical Science.*

Bacciagaluppi, M. (2012). *Paradigms in psychoanalysis: An integration.* London: Karnac Books Ltd.

Bateson, G. (1972). *Steps to an ecology of mind: Collected essays in anthropology, psychiatry, evolution and epistemology.* Chicago, IL: University of Chicago Press.

Beck, A. T., Freeman, A., & Associates. (1990). *Cognitive therapy of personality disorders.* New York: Guilford Press.

Blackman, J. S. (2004). *101 defenses: How the mind shields itself.* New York: Brunner-Routledge.

Block, J. (2002). *Personality as an affect-processing system: Toward an integrative theory.* Mahwah, NJ: Lawrence Eralbaum Associates.

Bucci, W. (1997). *Psychoanalysis and cognitive science: A multiple code theory.* New York: Guilford.

Chamberlin, D. E. (2011). Physiological psychotherapy: Opening the trauma window™ on high achievers. *Biofeedback, 39*, 21–26.

Champagne, F. A. (2010). Epigenetic influence of social experiences across the life span. *Developmental Psychobiology, 52*, 299–311.

Champagne, F. A. (2012). Interplay between social experiences and the genome: Epigenetic consequences for behavior. *Advances in Genetics, 77*, 33–57.

Champagne, F. A., & Curley, J. P. (2011). Epigenetic influence of the social environment. In A. Petronis & J. Mill (Eds.), *Brain, behavior and epigenetics* (pp. 185–208). Berlin: Springer-Verlag.

Cloninger, C. R. (1986). A unified biosocial theory of personality and its role in the development of anxiety states. *Psychiatry Developments, 3*, 167–226.

Corr, P. J. (2006). *Understanding biological psychology.* Malden, MA: Blackwell.

Cozolino, L. (2010). *The neuroscience of psychotherapy: Healing the social brain* (2nd ed.). New York: Norton.

Cramer, P. (2000). Defense mechanisms in psychology today: Further processes for adaptation. *American Psychologist, 55*, 637–646.

Damasio, A. (1999). *The feeling of what happens: Body and emotion in the making of consciousness.* New York: Harcourt Brace & Company.

Darwin, C. R. (1998). *The expression of the emotions in man and animal* (3rd ed.). New York: Oxford University Press. (Original work published 1872).

Davanloo, H. (Ed.). (1980). *Short-term dynamic psychotherapy.* New York: Jason Aaronson Press.

Davidson, R. J., Jackson, D. C., & Kalin, N. H. (2000). Emotion, plasticity, context and regulation: Perspectives from affective neuroscience. *Psychological Bulletin, 126,* 890–906.

Depue, R. A. (1996). A neurobiological framework for the structure of personality and emotion: Implications for personality disorders. In J. Clarkin & M. Lenzenweger (Eds.), *Major theories of personality disorder* (pp. 347–390). New York: Guilford.

Drury, S. S., Theally, K., Gleason, M. M., Smyke, A. T., De Vivo, I., Wong, J. Y. Y., Fox, N. A., Zeanah, C. H., & Nelson, C. A. (2011). Telomere length and early severe social deprivation: Linking early adversity and cellular aging. *Molecular Psychiatry, 17,* 719–727.

Ecker, B., Ticic, R., & Hulley, L. (2012). *Unlocking the emotional brain: Eliminating symptoms at their roots using memory reconsolidation.* New York: Routledge.

Ekman, P., & Davidson, R. J. (Eds.). (1994). *The nature of emotions: Fundamental questions.* New York: Oxford Press.

Ekman, P., & Rosenberg, E. L. (Eds.). (2005) *What the face reveals: Basic and applied studies of spontaneous expression using the facial action coding system (FACS)* (2nd ed.). New York: Oxford University Press.

Fosha, D. (2000). *The transforming power of affect: A model for accelerated change.* New York: Basic Books.

Fosha, D. (2005). Emotion, true self, true other, core state: Toward a clinical theory of affective change process. *Psychoanalytic Review, 92,* 513–552.

Fran, D. D., & Smith, T. S. (Eds.). (1999). *Mind, brain and society: Toward a neurosociology of emotion.* Stamford, CT: JAI Press.

Gabbard, G. (2000). A neurobiologically informed perspective on psychotherapy. *British Journal of Psychiatry, 177,* 117–122.

Geschwind, N. (1979). Specializations of the human brain. *Scientific American, 241,* 180–199.

Gevirtz, R. N. (2007). Psychophysiological perspectives on stress-related and anxiety disorders. In P. M. Lehrer, R. L. Woolfolk & W. E. Sime (Eds.), *Principles and practice of stress management* (3rd ed., pp. 209–226). New York: Guilford.

Goleman, D. (1995). *Emotional intelligence.* New York: Bantam Books.

Grawe, K. (2007). *Neuropsychotherapy: How the neurosciences inform effective psychotherapy.* New York: Psychology Press.

Greenberg, L. S., & Paivio, S. C. (1997). *Working with emotion in psychotherapy.* New York: Guilford Press.

Grigsby, J., & Stevens, D. (2000). *The neurodynamics of personality.* New York: Guilford.

Hassin, R. R., Uleman, J. S., & Bargh, J. A. (Eds.). (2005). *The new unconscious.* New York: Oxford University Press.

Hebb, D. O. (1949). *The organization of behavior: A neuropsychological theory.* New York: Wiley.

Herman, J., Ostrander, M., Mueller, N., & Figueiredo, H. (2005). Limbic system mechanisms of stress regulation: Hypothalamo-pituitary-adrenocortical axis. *Progress in Neuropsychopharmacology and Biological Psychiatry, 29,* 1201–1213.

Kapczinski, F., Vieta, E., Andreazza, A. C., Frey, B. N., Gomes, F. A., Tramontina, J., Kauer-Sant'Anna, M., Grassi-Oliveira, R., & Post, R. M. (2008). Allostatic load in bipolar disorder: Implications for pathophysiology and treatment. *Neuroscience and Biobehavioral Reviews, 32,* 675–692.

Kelly, G. (1955). *The psychology of personal constructs.* New York: Norton.

Kiesler, D. J. (1999). *Beyond the disease model of mental disorders*. Westport, CN: Praeger.

Lehrer, P. M. (2007). Biofeedback training to increase heart rate variability. In P. M. Lehrer, R. L. Woolfolk & W. E. Sime (Eds.), *Principles and practice of stress management* (3rd ed., pp. 227–248). New York: Guilford.

Linden, D. E. (2006). How psychotherapy changes the brain—The contribution of functional neuroimaging. *Molecular Psychiatry, 11*, 528–538.

Linehan, M. M. (1993). *Cognitive-behavioral treatment of borderline personality disorder*. New York: Guilford.

MacLean, P. D. (1952). Some psychiatric implications of physiological studies on frontotemporal portion of limbic system (visceral brain). *Electroencephalography and Clinical Neurophysiology, 4*, 407–418.

MacLean, P. D. (1990). *The triune brain in evolution: Role in paleocerebral functions*. New York: Plenum Press.

Magnavita, J. J. (1997). *Restructuring personality disorders: A short-term dynamic approach*. New York: Guilford.

Magnavita, J. J. (2005). *Personality-guided relational therapy: A unified approach*. Washington, DC: American Psychological Association.

Magnavita, J. J. (2006). The centrality of emotion in unifying and accelerating psychotherapy. *Journal of Clinical Psychology, 62*, 585–596.

Magnavita, J. J. (2012). *Theories of personality*. San Diego, CA: Bridgepoint Education, Inc.

Mahoney, M. J. (2005). Suffering, philosophy, and psychotherapy. *Journal of Psychotherapy Integration, 15*, 337–352.

Malta, L. S. (2012). Allostasis: The emperor of all (trauma-related) maladies. *Clinical Psychology: Science and Practice, 19*, 241–259.

Mayne, T. J., & Ramsey, J. (2001). The structure of emotion: A nonlinear dynamic systems approach. In T. J. Mayne & G. A. Bonanno (Eds.), *Emotions: Current issues and future perspectives* (pp. 1–37). New York: Guilford.

McCullough, L. (2003). *Treating affect phobia: A manual for short-term dynamic psychotherapy*. New York: Guilford.

McEwen, B. S., & Seeman, T. (2003). Stress and affect: Applicability of the concepts of allostasis and allostatic loading. In R. J. Davidson, K. R. Scherer & H. H. Goldsmith (Eds.), *Handbook of affective sciences* (pp. 1117–1137). New York: Oxford University Press.

Nestler, E. J. (2011). Neuroscience: Hidden switches in the mind. *Scientific American, 305*, 77–83.

Opazo, R. (1997). In the hurricane's eye: A supraparadigmatic integrative model. *Journal of Psychotherapy Integration, 7*, 17–54.

Orlinsky, D. E. (2009). The "generic model of psychotherapy" after 25 years: Evolution of a research-based metatheory. *Journal of Psychotherapy Integration, 19*, 319–339.

Panksepp, J. (1998). *Affective neuroscience: The foundations of human and animal emotions*. New York: Oxford Press.

Panksepp, J., & Biven, L. (2012). *The archaeology of mind: Neuroevolutionary origins of human emotion*. New York: Norton.

Papez, J. W. (1937). A proposed mechanism of emotion. *Archives of Neuropsychiatry, 38*, 725–743.

Parrott, W. (2001). *Emotion in social psychology*. Philadelphia, PA: Psychology Press.

Pinsof, W. M. (1995). *Integrative problem-centered therapy: A synthesis of family, individual, and biological therapies*. New York: Basic Books.

Porges, S. W. (1995). Orienting in a defensive world: Mammalian modifications of our evolutionary heritage. A polyvagal theory. *Psychophysiology, 32*, 301–318.

Porges, S. W. (2011). *The polyvagal theory: Neurophysiological foundations of emotions, attachment, communication, and self-regulation.* New York: Norton.

Read, J., Perry, B. D., Moskowitz, A., & Connolly, J. (2001). The contributions of early traumatic events to schizophrenia in some patients: A traumagenic neurodevelopmental model. *Psychiatry, 64*, 319–345.

Rutten, B. P. F., & Mill, J. (2009). Epigenetic mediation of environmental influences in major psychotic disorders. *Schizophrenia Bulletin, 35*, 1045–1056.

Salovey, P., & Mayer, J. D. (1990). Emotional intelligence. *Imagination, Cognition, and Personality, 9*, 185–211.

Sapolsky, R. (2004). *Why Zebras don't get ulcers* (3rd ed.). New York: Holt.

Schildkrout, B. (2011). *Unmasking psychological symptoms: How therapists can learn to recognize the psychological presentations of medical disorders.* Hoboken, NJ: Wiley.

Schwartz, J. M., & Begley, S. (2002). *The mind and the brain: Neuroplasticity and the power of mental force.* New York: Regan Books/Harper Collins.

Schore, A. N. (2001). Minds in the making: Attachment, the self-organizing brain, and developmentally oriented psychoanalytic psychotherapy. *British Journal of Psychotherapy, 17*, 299–328.

Schore, A. N. (2003). *Affect dysregulation and disorders of the self.* New York: Norton.

Schore, A. N. (2012). *The science of the art of psychotherapy.* New York: Norton.

Siegel, D. J. (1999). *The developing mind: Toward a neurobiology of interpersonal experience.* New York: Guilford Press.

Siever, L. J., & Davis, K. L. (1991). A psychobiological perspective on the personality disorders. *American Journal of Psychiatry, 148*, 1647–1658.

Skowron, E. A., Loken, E., Gatzke-Kopp, L. M., Cipriano-Essel, E. A., Woehrle, P. L., Van Epps, J. J., Gowda, A., & Ammerman, R. T. (2011). Mapping cardiac physiology, parenting, and dyadic processes in maltreating mother-child dyads. *Journal of Family Psychology, 25*, 663–674.

Solomon, M. F. & Siegel, D. J. (Eds.). (2003). *Healing trauma: Attachment, mind, body and brain.* New York: Norton.

Vaillant, G. E. (Ed.). (1992). *Ego mechanisms of defense: A guide for clinicians and researchers.* Washington, DC: American Psychiatric Association.

Valliant McCullough, L. (1997). *Changing character: Short-term anxiety regulating psychotherapy for restructuring defenses, affects, and attachments.* New York: Basic Books.

Von Scheve, C., & Von Luede, R. (2005). Emotion and social structures: Towards an interdisciplinary approach. *Journal for the Theory of Social Behaviour, 35*, 303–328.

Wickramasekera, I., Davies, T. E., & Davies, S. M. (1996). Applied psychophysiology: A bridge between the biomedical model and the biopsychosocial model in family medicine. *Professional Psychology: Research and Practice, 27*, 221–233.

Young, J. E. (1990). *Cognitive therapy for personality disorders: A schema-focused approach.* Sarasota, FL: Professional Resource Exchange, Inc.

Zittoun, T., Gillespie, A., Cornish, F., & Psaltis, C. (2007). The metaphor of the triangle in theories of human development. *Human Development, 50*, 208–229.

Chapter 5

SELF–OTHER DYADS

In this chapter we widen our observational lens to examine the interpersonal–dyadic level of the total ecological system (TES). This level encompasses the structures and processes of the basic interpersonal molecule—*self–other dyads*. The dyad is the smallest and arguably the most crucial unit of our social systems. There is no chance of surviving or of thriving without at least one dyad—the infant would perish without a care-giving other. Within the discipline itself, ever since William James's (1890) *Principles of Psychology*, "psychologists have long been interested in the interpersonal nature of the self and the potential for past relationships to manifest in present ones" (Anderson & Przybylinski, 2012, p. 370). In the specific field of psychotherapy, most treatment occurs in a dyadic framework, and therefore the dyad holds a privileged place in psychotherapeutics. Indeed, dyadic healing has a long and rich tradition across cultures, beginning with recorded history (Frank & Frank, 1991). Considered in this context, the robust finding that the therapeutic relationship accounts for more of the benefit of psychotherapy than specific techniques (Wampold, 2001) is all the more telling. We note, too, that even when clinically working in larger relational configurations (e.g., family or group therapy), dyadic processes are operative (e.g., Becker-Weidman, 2010; Yalom & Leszcz, 2005).

In the ensuing pages of this chapter, we synthesize two key constructs—the *interpersonal pattern* and the *interpersonal–dyadic triangle*—to establish an organizing framework for elucidating key structures, mechanisms, and processes essential to unified understanding and clinical intervention into dysfunctional and distressogenic self–other dyadic functioning. Each of these constructs themselves organizes a vast array of phenomena, and when joined together, they provide the clinician with a powerful set of conceptual tools for navigating with the patient toward meaningful therapeutic understanding and change.

INTERPERSONAL PATTERNS

The interpersonal pattern is the basic unit of analysis when working at the dyadic level, and is broadly definable as the recurrent and more or less lawful interrelationships among an individual's overt (verbal and nonverbal) and covert (intrapsychic–biological) processes in relation to a specific other's verbal and nonverbal behavior in particular settings and contexts (Anchin, 1982, 2002; Anchin & Pincus, 2010). Kiesler's (1996) valuable distinction between individualistic versus transactional perspectives on interpersonal behavior sharpens this definition:

> ... in an *individualistic sense,* interpersonal behavior refers to a person's actions in the presence of other humans—the behavior of an individual directed toward one or more interactants. In a *transactional sense,* interpersonal behavior refers to two people's conjoint behaviors during their interactions with each other— what person A and person B do reciprocally to and with each other during their transactions. (p. 7)

Kiesler (1992) maintained that both of these perspectives have a place in studying interpersonal behavior in dyads.

Through this lens, it is valid and useful to distinguish between individualistic and transactional perspectives on a person's interpersonal patterns. Consistent with the centrality of the relational matrix, this distinction preserves the root dialectic between persons as individuals and as social creatures while encompassing the intrinsic complexity that inescapably derives from the interpenetration of these two levels. Thus, at one level, a specific interpersonal pattern is an individualistic expression of a person's intrapsychic–biological and overt–interpersonal processes, which interdigitatively exert significant influence in motivating, structuring, regulating, and creating particular forms of interpersonal (self–other) connectedness and experience. However, while at an individualistic level Person A thus enacts and experiences multilevel, multidomain patterning in relation to a given other, an interpersonal pattern becomes a full-fledged transactional phenomenon only to the extent that Person B is intrapsychically–biologically and interpersonally engaged in direct exchange with Person A, responding, acting, and subjectively experiencing in ways reciprocally linked with Person A's responses, actions, and experiences—the vis-à-vis that is the spawning ground of intersubjectivity (Stolorow & Atwood, 1992). Once this individualistic–transactional level distinction is made, in the course of clinical work on interpersonal patterns it becomes valid and useful to elucidate both the individualistic and the transactional structure of an interpersonal pattern, its individualistic and transactional functions, and the individualistic and transactional consequences that are engendered. Each of these dimensions of an interpersonal pattern contains significant data that complements the other dimensions (Anchin, 2002).

It is also useful to note that the interpersonal pattern is a mid-level concept; as elaborated elsewhere (Anchin, 1982, 2002), it is situated between two other important conceptual levels, underlied by the concept of *interaction sequences* and overarched by the concept of *interpersonal styles*.

Interaction Sequences

An interaction sequence refers to the live, ongoing process of overt behavioral exchange that spins out in real time between Persons A and B in a specific setting over a finite duration of time. This dynamic process of overt exchange is simultaneously bound in complex ways to ongoing intrapsychic–biological processes on the part of each interactant. Thus, two individuals come together in a particular setting and over a time-bound period say things to one another, simultaneously enacting an array of nonverbal behaviors that contribute in an implicit way to the definition and experiencing of their relationship at that time. Concurrent and interacting with the flow of overt events, each person continuously engages in a rapidly firing, complex, more or less organized array of intrapsychic–biological processes vis-à-vis the other. As part of this internal mix, both interactants are pursuing a set of goals, each at varying degrees of awareness that range from thoroughgoing consciousness to thoroughgoing unconsciousness. To illustrate, two individuals may agree to get together for lunch, each seeking to satisfy his or her hunger needs. At the same time, they may share the nested goals of catching up on what has been happening in their respective lives over recent weeks, experiencing through that process the satisfaction of close connectedness and at still another level the validation of a valued view of self. As their interaction plays out, these goals, operating in a matrix of other intrapsychic–biological and overt processes, influence perception and interpretation of the overt acts, their nature and course, and the personal and relational experiences, meanings, and other consequences Person A and Person B each derives.

Moving from interaction sequences to interpersonal patterns is a shift toward a more inferential level. Whereas an interaction sequence entails a time-bound series of concrete behavioral exchanges that have interconnected intrapsychic–biological concomitants, an interpersonal pattern represents a regularity among these overt and covert processes that may be extracted from this and other sequences (Anchin, 1982). This patterning may be identified both at an individualistic level and at a trans-actional level.

Interpersonal Styles

The concept of an interpersonal style is a level of abstraction above that of the interpersonal pattern. It encompasses the notion that across the range of specific interpersonal patterns that an individual characteristically enacts with others over the course of time in his or her day-to-day interaction sequences, there is a central theme or thread running through many of these patterns. For example, in the following descriptions of antago-nistic–harmful and cooperative–helpful interpersonal styles, the notion of an interpersonal style as encompassing a constellation of related but distinctive patterns becomes vividly evident if each of the defining items is viewed as descriptive of patterns:

> **Antagnostic–Harmful.** This person is frequently discourteous, often seems to ignore others' feelings, and is quick to take what he wants. He often complains and quarrels, tends to dispute others' statements, and finds it easy to tell others off. He prefers to resist cooperation, to refuse requests from others, and readily obstructs others' activities. He seems eager to provoke others, and to annoy and insult them. He impresses others as being irritable, oppositional, and rude. (Kiesler, 1996, p. 17)

> **Cooperative–Helpful.** This person tries hard to be thoughtful of others and is careful to respect others' rights. He cooperates easily and is ready to do his part. He can be expected to speak softly and tactfully, finds it easy to remain patient with irrita-tions, works to smooth over disagreements, and is difficult to rile. He seeks to comfort others, seems eager to accede to their requests, and is quick to offer help. He impresses others as being courteous, pleasant, and supportive. (Kiesler, 1996, p. 18)

Consistent with these definitions, two distinct interpersonal patterns enacted by an antagonistic–harmful individual in dyadic interactions include being quarrelsome and disputational, while in other situations enacting some mixture of provocative, annoying, and insulting behav-ior. While these respective patterns would give the respective interaction sequences in which they are embedded a different look, they are tied together by the antagnonistic–harmful stylistic theme. In the same way, an individual who is chiefly cooperative–helpful may display a pattern of cooperativeness when working on a task with a coworker, enact another pattern of offering comfort to a person who is experiencing distress, and still a third pattern of equanimity in the face of another's annoyance.

Each of these specific patterns, then, reflects a general interpersonal style. Moreover, since interpersonal patterns incorporate intrapsychic components, it is important to note that, while an interpersonal style seems to be defined principally by reference to overt behavior, the notion of generality inherent to the "style" concept suggests that we can also talk about central themes running through the range of an individual's specific construals of self and other, affective states, and motivations.

Interpersonal style is thus a unifying concept, enabling one to pull together and summarize the various interpersonal patterns an individual enacts with others under the roof of a single interpersonal label. Moreover, this conception of an interpersonal style, in incorporating the idea that there is a general character to an individual's interpersonal–dyadic behavior, coincides with Carson's (1969) classic work in which he defines "style" as "a discernible tendency to enact sets [of interpersonal behavior] falling preponderantly, although often subtly, within a particular range of the interpersonal behavior circle" ([p. 142]; see Chapter 3, Figure 3.2).

The interpersonal style, interpersonal pattern, and interaction sequence concepts thus provide complementary perspectives on the day-to-day interpersonal–intrapsychic processes that are an integral part of a human life. The interpersonal style, as a summary label, is a useful conceptual short-hand device for capturing the central theme running through the range of more concrete, specific, interpersonal patterns that an individual plays out from day to day. An interpersonal pattern encompasses the recurrent, more or less lawful relationships among an individual's ongoing overt and covert processes in relation to others' actions and reactions in particular settings and contexts. However, these regularities are embedded within and therefore emerge through detailed examination of the live, ongoing verbal and nonverbal behavioral exchange process that flows out over a finite time period between two individuals during an interaction sequence.

Essential Considerations When Addressing Interpersonal Patterns

As the discussion above suggests, the interpersonal pattern is a complex unit of interrelated phenomena. Here we dissect in greater detail its essential composition, highlighting structures and processes that are essential to consider when pursuing both an analytic and a synthetic understanding of a patient's interpersonal patterns in the clinical setting.

The Attachment System

The attachment system, discussed in Chapter 3 in the context of unpacking the relational matrix, is the anchoring consideration in work on the patient's maladaptive interpersonal patterns. It is a biologically hardwired motivational system that, from the moment of birth onward, impels the human being to seek contact with others—and as such, the attachment system operates as the infrastructural foundation of all interpersonal relationships and the building block of larger relational constellations. The early attachment system is one of the building blocks of personality, as well as an influence in the structuralization of the brain. There are critical periods in development during which, if certain neural networks are not stimulated, *apoptosis* or cell death may occur in a process known as neural pruning. In contrast, if appropriate stimulation is experienced then a process of neurogenesis occurs and the brain builds neurocircuitry that will allow for further growth and development. Extreme emotional deprivation in infancy can result in a failure to thrive syndrome through an epigenetic process (Gudsnuk & Champagne, 2011).

The Centrality of Emotion. As eloquently detailed by Fosha (2000), in concentrating on ways in which the quality of the bond between a child and his or her caregiver influences a child's development, attachment theory and research have brought to the fore the fundamentality of affect in the attachment process. From infancy forward, the child needs a caregiving other in order to experience *feelings of safety*, the *allaying of fear* triggered by perceived environmental danger, and *diminishment of anxiety* activated by perceiving the mother as inaccessible or insufficiently responsive. Affective experience is integral to attachment processes not only during the early years of childhood, but over the entire life course: "Many of the most intense emotions arise during the formation, the maintenance, the disruption and the renewal of attachment relationships.... Because such emotions are usually a reflection of the state of a person's affectional bonds, the psychology and psychopathology of emotion is found to be in large part the psychology and psychopathology of affectional bonds. (Bowlby, 1980, p. 60)" (cited in Fosha, 2000, p. 33). Thus, as discussed elsewhere (Anchin, 2003), an emotional state—in addition to its subjectively felt dimension—contains vital information about the extent to which one's aims and goals are being advanced or impeded, and in the context of any given significant relationship, this includes the degree of stability characterizing the attachment bond. *Emotions can thus be partially understood as barometers of what is happening in one's significant relationships.* Crucially, this includes, but is not limited to, the quality and status of attachment bonds.

Internal Working Models, Schemas, and Scripts. The centrality of emotions in attachment processes is also reflected in the internal working models one develops in the context of specific attachment experiences. Constructs containing components and meanings more or less equivalent to internal working models include cognitive–affective self–other schemas (Anchin & Pincus, 2010), internalized relational patterns (Frank, 2002), role relationship models (Horowitz, 1988, 1991), important persons and their internalized representations (Benjamin, 1996), interpersonal schemas (Reeve, Inck, & Safran, 1993; Safran & Segal, 1990), and the relational self (Andersen & Chen, 2002). Focusing specifically on internal working models, Slade and Aber point out that these models "are not static but *dynamic 'working'* models" (p. 161, emphasis added) entailing representations of self in relation to the other extracted from recurrent experiences in attachment relationships. The model of the other centers on his or her dependability for responding to self's attachment needs, and integrally related communications of fear and anxiety, through providing the protection and closeness that engender feelings of safety, comfort, and security; the model of self focuses especially on both self's degree of power or powerlessness to gain safety and security from the other and on self's worthiness and lovability (Gerson, 2010; Slade & Aber, 1992). Fosha (2000) provided an example that prototypically captures the critical role of emotions in internal working models: "The repeated experience of crying followed by being soothed 'leads to the expectation that distress will be met by reassurance and comforting' (Fonagy et al., 1995, pp. 234–235); note the nod to affect: 'Integrated with, and perhaps integrating, … these expectations are the emotional experiences associated with these interactions' (Fonagy et al., 1995, pp. 234–235)" (p. 39).

It is important, as well, to take explicit note of the expectancy component of internal working models, a point to which we will return. As Gerson (2010) pointed out, in addition to containing a model of other and of self, internal working models contain "scripts for expected interactions" (pp. 101–102). Slade and Aber (1992) elaborated this expectancy component and its significant implications for future relationships: "[Internal working models] not only 'represent' the nature of past interactional experience, but they also permit the forecasting of future experience and become the prototype for the formation of future relationships" (p. 161).

Research demonstrates that early internal working models indeed persist into adulthood and contribute to explaining adult behavior in relationships (Singer, 2005, p. 135), but as life advances, degrees of change in an individual's internal working models are also expectable. As Mahoney (1991) points out, "[l]ife span development involves the ongoing construction and reconstruction of these working models, reflecting a dynamic and generative tension between continuity (familiarity) and change (novelty)" (p. 168). By the same token, in line with needs for self-cohesion and predictability in the world, one's internal working models, through circular self-perpetuating processes, likely impose constraints on the degree of change that naturalistically occurs: "Private (and predominantly unconscious) models of self, others, and the world become increasingly firm (resistant to change) with the confirmation of experience, and such confirmation tends to accelerate as the infant, child, adolescent, and adult become more active and effective participants in selecting and creating their own environments" (Mahoney, 1991, p. 168).

Features of Maladaptive and Secure Attachment. Still, "even if much remains to be done concerning the *degree* of continuity in attachment orientation over the course of the life cycle, there is no question that orientation toward attachment is a major variable in a host of adult behaviors, including most particularly the management of intimate relationships, especially in times of stress" (Gerson, 2010, p. 105, emphasis added). In this respect, patterned after the four forms of problematic attachment that have been identified in children—anxious, avoidant, insecure, and disorganized (see Magnavita, 2005)—Florsheim, Henry, and Benjamin (1996) provided a useful taxonomy of maladaptive adult attachment styles (see Table 5.1). These different forms and features of attachment pathology may be usefully and instructively contrasted with characteristics associated with secure attachment:

> [Overall], the combination of laboratory findings, longitudinal, and self-report studies suggest that, relative to their insecurely attached peers, children, adolescents, and adults who feel secure in their intimate relationships:
>
> 1. Exhibit earlier, greater flexibility and resilience in their engagements with their worlds
> 2. Exhibit and experience themselves as more competent in a variety of realms
> 3. Are more likely to engage in exploratory behavior and to remain behaviorally organized in the face of novelty and stress
> 4. Are more sought out and popular among peers
> 5. Report higher self-esteem
> 6. Are more capable of establishing and maintaining secure and satisfying relationships with others
> 7. Are at less risk of developing major psychological disorders
> 8. Are more likely to express their feelings directly, to seek comfort when they are distressed, and to offer comfort to their distressed companions (Mahoney, 1991, cited in Magnavita, 2005, p. 86)

TABLE 5.1 *Forms and Features of Dysfunctional Adult Attachment Styles*

- *Preoccupied attachment.* An individual with an underlying feeling of unworthiness looks to valued others for acceptance (Bartholomew & Horowitz, 1991).
- *Dismissive attachment style.* An individual with a basically "positive" view of him- or herself and a negative view of others who avoids the vulnerability of intimacy by assuming an independent stance (Bartholomew & Horowitz, 1991; Main & Goldwyn, 1985).
- *Fearful–avoidant attachment style.* An individual with a negative view of him- or herself and others who avoids involvement to reduce the chance of perceived rejection and attack (Bartholomew & Horowitz, 1991).
- *Compulsive care-seeking attachment style.* An individual compulsively seeks to confirm that there is access to a responsive attachment figure and feels ill-equipped to care for oneself (Bowlby, 1977; West & Sheldon, 1988).
- *Angry–withdrawn attachment style.* An individual who displays anger and is defensive to the response or unavailability of another (West & Sheldon, 1988).
- *Obsessive–compulsive attachment style.* An individual who rigidly adheres to how things should be, putting work and being productive ahead of relationships (Pilkonis, 1988).
- *Interpersonal insensitive attachment style.* An individual who is not influenced by or is oblivious to the effect his or her actions have on others (Pilkonis, 1988).

Adapted by Magnavita (2005, pp. 151–152) from Florsheim et al. (1996, pp. 84–85).

Impact of Attachment on Stress, Early Neuroendocrine–Immune Development, and Adult Health. Bearing in mind that, through a biopsychosocial systems lens, the relationship between health status and the nature of social–interpersonal functioning is a two-way street, it is important to be aware of the critical role of attachment's impact on the early development of biological structures and processes that shape health over the life span. Johnson, Riley, Granger, and Riis (2013) reviewed scientific evidence demonstrating the strong association between "early life 'toxic stress'" (p. 320) and certain physical and mental health problems in adulthood. Defining toxic stress as "the extreme, frequent, or extended activation of the stress response, without the buffering response of a supportive adult" (p. 320), they indicated that "[r]isk factors for toxic stress in childhood include neglect and abuse, extreme poverty, family violence, substance abuse, and parental mental health problems" (p. 320) and underscored that "toxic stress is defined by the absence of supportive caregiving" (p. 320). Their review delineates the manner in which early life toxic stress exerts influence on developmental and health outcomes specifically through its adverse impacts on the "neuroendocrine–immune (NEI) network"

(p. 320)—that is, the brain, endocrine, and immune systems and their interactions. Pointing to the vital interconnections among quality of attachment, intensity of the stress response, early developmental impact on biology, and adult health outcomes, a major implication of their report is "ensuring that every child has a stable source of adult nurturance [which] can foster resilience to a number of common disease outcomes in adulthood by transforming toxic stress into 'tolerable' stress" (p. 324).

Psychotherapeutic Implications of Attachment Styles. There is clinical significance to recognizing adult attachment style—how the patient dyadically seeks, avoids, or oscillates in establishing and maintaining intimacy and closeness—and utility in using attachment-guided interventions and relational processes in treatment (Diener & Monroe, 2011; Levy, Ellison, Scott, & Bernecker, 2011). We offer the following specific suggestions:

1. Conduct a developmental history to see whether a determination can be made about the patient's likely attachment style.

2. Gather as much information as possible about the personality system and attachment style of significant early attachment figures.

3. Determine the type and style of attachment that the patient has with current figures in his or her life.

4. Examine and take note of the attachment experience that the patient elicits and expresses in the therapeutic relationship.

5. Notice the attachment style evident in dyadic and triadic relationships. (Magnavita, 2005a, p. 152)

Intimacy

Fundamentally rooted in the attachment system, issues associated with intimacy are of inestimable importance in understanding and clinically addressing an individual's interpersonal patterns. Intimacy is the ability to achieve and maintain emotional closeness with others (McLemore & Hart, 1982). As discussed in Chapter 3, the striving for intimacy, captured in the interpersonal tradition by the term communion, is a basic human motive and its achievement and maintenance is a key direction of healthy personality development.

Theory and research by Ryff and her colleagues' (1989; Ryff & Singer, 1998, 2006) identified positive relationships with others as one among six dimensions of psychological well-being, and she includes the capacity for intimacy among the central defining features of this dimension. Intimacy theory (Reis & Gable, 2003) "identifies several qualities that are central to feeling close and connected to others: revealing central aspects of the self (especially emotions) to partners through words, deeds, and nonverbal behavior; perceiving that partners are responsive to the self and the self's needs; and feeling understood, validated, and cared for" (p. 147). In an ongoing relationship imbued with intimacy, these self-disclosive processes, perceptions of responsiveness by the other, and feelings of being understood, validated, and cared for are over time reciprocal and intersubjectively experienced. Intimacy is thus a relational process as well as a relational state. In this regard, Tronick's (2007) observations suggest the manner in which the shared experience of emotional intimacy and meanings that derive therefrom can enhance the growth of both partners:

> A particularly effective way of growing and expanding complexity occurs when two or more individuals convey and apprehend (i.e., take hold of) meanings from each other to create a dyadic state of consciousness. This dyadic state contains more information than either individual's state of consciousness alone, and when individuals co-create a dyadic state they can appropriate meanings from it [i]nto their own state of consciousness and increase its complexity. (pp. 3–4)

In spite of its many positive functional and experiential benefits, emotional intimacy is not for everyone—whether by choice or otherwise. Whether by virtue of such factors as genetic wiring, deficiencies in social learning, enduring psychological pain stemming from trauma at any point in one's life, developmental dysynchrony, or recurring interpersonal and/or intrapersonal conflict, achieving and/or maintaining intimacy is, for many individuals and dyads, a domain of struggle and strife. Indeed, difficulties with intimacy are distinctly instantiated in psychopathology. Research undertaken through the lens of the interpersonal tradition demonstrates that problems in affiliation and communion with others operate as central dimensions in the majority of personality disorders, and they are strongly implicated in symptom syndromes as well (Anchin & Pincus, 2010; Pincus et al., 2010; Pincus & Wright, 2010). Of course, problems in the realm of intimacy are among fundamental issues in distressed couples (Bradley & Johnson, 2005; Gerson, 2010; Karpel, 1994).

Autonomy

As discussed in Chapter 3, establishing and maintaining close interpersonal relationships is one pole of the relational matrix, while forging and maintaining an individual self operates as its dialectical counterpart. Autonomy is integral to the latter process. Though terminology differs, Blatt's self-definition pole, the interpersonal tradition's metaconstruct of agency, and attachment theory's exploratory system cite capacities for autonomy as among optimal characteristics. Ryff's (1989; Ryff & Singer, 1998, 2006) model of psychological well-being includes autonomy among its six dimensions and indicates that an individual whose functioning reflects an optimal level of this feature "is self-determining and independent; able to resist social pressures; regulates behavior from within; [and] evaluates self by personal standards" (Ruini & Fava, 2004, p. 376). Brown and Ryan (2004, p. 106) cited research indicating that people across a variety of cultures endorsed autonomy as a primary need and source of satisfaction, and meeting autonomy needs on a day-to-day basis has been shown to be associated with emotional well-being (Reis, Sheldon, Gable, Roscoe, & Ryan, 2000).

Brown and Ryan (2004) placed healthy self-regulation at the heart of autonomous functioning, and discussed the manner in which autonomous regulation "can be facilitated both from without—through social supports—and from within, through the receptive attention and awareness to present experience that defines mindfulness" (p. 119). In this context, it is interesting to note that in his special issue—alluded to in Chapter 2—centered on current research in personality psychology, its relationship to psychotherapy, and the overarching theme of a holistic perspective on the person in clinical science, J. Singer (in press) observed that a common theme in all of the contributors' articles is acknowledgment of the central role of social attachment *and self-regulation* in individual personality. He defined the latter as "the capacity to manage one's biological needs, address temperamental and emotional concerns, and to engage in goal pursuits" (p. 3).

Although by definition autonomy is individualistic in nature, its very existence as a need, motive, trait, and process draws meaning through its juxtaposition as "figure" against the "ground" of social connectedness. As visually reflected in circumplex models of interpersonal behavior (Figure 3.2; see also Benjamin, 1996; Kiesler, 1996; Locke, 2011), autonomy and its deficiencies are an integral dimension of how one navigates the social world. This is underscored by the theme of dependence characteristic of functioning when an individual's level of autonomy is impaired. As Ryff describes (cited in Ruini & Fava, 2004), in such cases "the subject is overconcerned with the expectations and evaluation of others; relies on judgment of others to make important decisions; [and] conforms to social pressures to think or act in certain ways" (p. 376). In treatment, patients whose interpersonal patterns include problems in the realm of dependence can be partially understood as struggling with issues associated with autonomy. However, as Bornstein (2005) incisively pointed out, "in the process of fostering autonomy in dependent patients, many clinicians inadvertently go too far and move the patient toward inflexible independence. Healthy dependency (i.e., a blend of autonomy and connectedness coupled with situation-appropriate help and support seeking) should be the ultimate goal of clinical work with dependent patients (Bornstein & Languirand, 2003)" (p. 87).

Reciprocal Influence Processes and Interpersonal Complementarity

Central to understanding the dynamics and mechanisms of interpersonal patterns is the assumption that, during an ongoing interaction, interpersonal behaviors create reciprocal influences on the interactants (Anchin & Pincus, 2010). To illustrate, consider an interaction sequence between a dependent individual (Person A) and a nurturing individual (Person B). If we break into an ongoing interaction sequence between these two individuals, A's dependent request (e.g., for advice) exerts an immediate influence on B. The latter's momentary internal responses (e.g., cognitively, the thought "I know what he should do"; affectively, feelings of liking; motivationally, the desire to help) and overt response (providing the requested advice) are directly influenced by A's behavior. However, the influence process does not flow in this singular, linear direction at each step in the interaction sequence. Rather, by virtue of *feedback*, B's response immediately acts back on A to produce a new array of responses on A's part, both internally (e.g., the thought, "That's a good idea"; a feeling of relief; and a feeling of satisfaction that his need has been met) and overtly (e.g., nodding his head as a nonverbal expression of agreement with B's advice). In turn, A's affirmative head-nodding response acts back once again to elicit a new constellation of covert and overt reaction by B, and so forth. The tendency to designate one interactant's (e.g., A's) behavior as the "cause" and the other's (B's) behavior as the "effect" reflects an arbitrary punctuation imposed on the naturally occurring process of interpersonal communication and transaction. As crisply stated by Danziger (1976), "two individuals in interaction are simultaneously the causes and effects of each other's behavior" (p. 184). Reciprocity and circularity are indeed hallmarks of ongoing interpersonal transaction (Kiesler, Bernstein, & Anchin, 1976; Kiesler, 1982a, 1996; Pincus et al., 2010)—this holds whether the dyadic interaction is between, for example, a parent and child, two siblings, a husband and wife, a teacher and student, two friends, or a patient and psychotherapist.

A significant corollary of the centrality of reciprocal influence processes in ongoing transactions is that interpersonal patterns functionally operate as field-regulatory pulls (Pincus, 2005), in that each interactant is enacting patterns—characteristically more unconsciously than not—designed to elicit and evoke from the other a restricted class of responses. The most fundamental interpersonal pattern is referred to as *interpersonal complementarity* (Anchin & Pincus, 2010; Carson, 1969; Kiesler, 1983, 1996; Pincus & Wright, 2010), which "occurs when there is a match between the field-regulatory goals of each person. That is, reciprocal patterns of activity evolve in which the agentic and communal motives of both persons are fulfilled in the interpersonal situation, leading to stability and likely recurrence of the pattern (Horowitz et al., 2006)" (Pincus et al., 2010, p. 539). In the example provided previously between dependent Person A and nurturant Person B, we see the process of interpersonal complementarity in action.

As Sadler, Ethier, and Woody (2010, p. 124) point out, the predominant framework for studying interpersonal complementarity has been the interpersonal circle or circumplex. The interpersonal circle represented in Figure 3.2 is one variant of this framework (see Kiesler, 1983; Benjamin, 1996), and using the figure for mapping purposes, complementarity is defined by reciprocity on the vertical dimension of Agency (e.g., dominance pulls for submission, while submission pulls for dominance) and correspondence on the horizontal dimension of Communion (friendliness pulls for friendliness, while disaffiliation pulls for disaffiliation). Extending this principle to the illustrative interaction sequence above, A's interpersonal pattern of friendly submission (i.e., dependence) pulls for B's pattern of friendly dominance (nurturance) and vice versa; each individual's interpersonal behavior is constrained or controlled in a more or less predictable way by the behavior received from the other (Carson, 1969, p. 145).

Sadler et al. (2010) provided a review of empirical evidence regarding interpersonal complementarity; while clearly much research remains to be conducted relative to, for example, different types of dyadic pairings, varying time periods within the same dyad, and within different contexts, overall there is distinct support for the "probabilistic predictions" (Pincus et al., 2010, p. 540) as to the reciprocal interpersonal pulls exerted by behavior falling along both the agentic and communal dimensions. Thus, as suggested by Pincus et al. (2010), "complementarity is most helpful if considered a common baseline for the field-regulatory pulls and invitations of interpersonal behavior. If used in this way, chronic deviations from complementary reciprocal patterns may be indicative of pathological functioning" (p. 540), a perspective to be elaborated shortly.

The Interpersonal Transaction Cycle and Rigidity—Flexibility

These various considerations informing the understanding of interpersonal patterns are pulled together in a conceptually consistent and clinically useful way in Kiesler's (1986a, 1988, 1991, 1996; Wagner, Kiesler, & Schmidt, 1995) *interpersonal transaction cycle*, a dynamic, circular process model of adaptive and maladaptive interpersonal functioning (see Figure 5.1). Conceptions concordant with this circular model include

Wachtel's (e.g., Gold & Wachtel, 1993) cyclical psychodynamics conception, Carson's (1982) self-fulfilling expectancy model, Safran's (Safran & Segal, 1990) cognitive–interpersonal cycle, Andrews's (1991) self-confirmation model, and Strupp and Binder's (1984; cf. H. Levenson, 1995) cyclical maladaptive pattern.

Starting with Person A in the upper left-hand corner and moving clockwise, interactions among A's intrapsychic processes—for example, agentic and communal motives, self–other schema, and associated expectancies and emotions—produce congruent, overt interpersonal behavior enacted vis-à-vis Person B. This behavior functionally operates as an "invitation" intended to evoke from the latter the desired, complementary response, covertly registered by B in the form of a restricted range of direct feelings, action tendencies, attributions about A, and/or fantasies. In the interpersonal tradition, these internal engagements and reactions evoked by an individual's interpersonal behavior are termed *impact messages* (Kiesler, 1982, 1988, 1996; Anchin & Pincus, 2010), B's subjective experiencing of the pulls for the complementary response exerted by A's verbal and nonverbal behavior. When, in the next step in this rapid

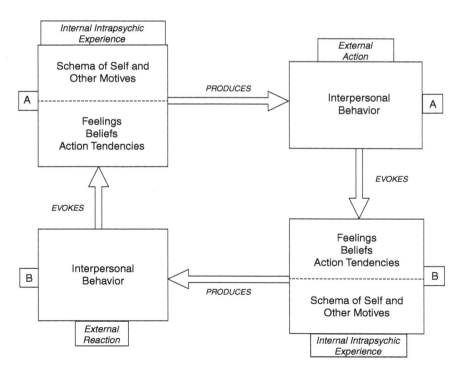

FIGURE 5.1   *Interpersonal transaction cycle.* Adapted from Kiesler (1986b).

process, B overtly enacts the complementary response, this satisfies A's agentic and communal motives, confirms A's schema of self and other, activates particular associated emotions, and reinforces A's interpersonal style. This descriptive analysis is in essence a slow-motion depiction of a moment in time in the interaction between A and B, reductively and usefully segmenting the recurrent intrapsychic and overt components of a given interpersonal pattern and style enacted by A, and the components of the two-step process operative on B's part when providing the complementary response. However, in real time the interpersonal transaction cycle is "an ongoing transactional chain of events" (Pincus et al., 2010, p. 540), with A and B reciprocally enacting their respective interpersonal styles, which includes enactment of their respective constellation of agentic and communal motives, self-other schemas, expectancies, affective state, and so forth. In real-time, then, the interpersonal field is co-regulated.

The interpersonal transaction cycle also provides a framework for understanding and explaining interpersonal–dyadic pathology. Among hallmarks of maladaptive interpersonal patterns are rigidity and/or extremeness in the individual's subsuming interpersonal style and thus in the relational patterns enacted with others (see Pincus et al., 2010, pp. 532–539 for additional important parameters that define interpersonal dysfunction). In the case of a "maladaptive transaction cycle" (Kiesler, 1996, pp. 141–143), A's overt interpersonal rigidity is reciprocally tied to equally rigid agentic and communal motives, self–other schema, expectancies, and affectivity; in essence, A is *locked into* the satisfaction of his particular agentic and communal motivations, confirmation of his self–other schema and emotional state(s), and expectancies. At an early stage in his relationship with B or others, this may not be problematic, in that the initial process of complementarity that plays out between A and B may be satisfying and confirming for both partners. However, over the course of time and successive interactions, A's rigidity takes its toll and, for both members of the dyad, painful consequences ensue. By virtue of A's interpersonal rigidity, B may feel increasingly "pushed around" (Kiesler, 1996, p. 143) and controlled by A; essentially, A is consistently and rigidly pulling for responses that complement his own interpersonal behavior, but is insufficiently reciprocating with responses complementary to B's behavior, a state of affairs that speaks to a lack of mutuality in the relationship. For B, this renders his internal experience toward A—including the recurrent impact messages he experiences— aversive. While B may nevertheless continue, over time, to provide A with the latter's desired complementary responses, this unwittingly reinforces A's interpersonal dysfunctionality by continuing to satisfy his skewed agentic and communal motives, verify his rigid cognitive– affective self–other schemas and expectancies, and enable his consistent overt-behavioral rigidity. Moreover, B's reciprocal overt responses may become laced with hostile, rejecting, and/or "mixed-message" communicative elements that create painful psychological and emotional states for A. Indeed, at some point B may leave the relationship entirely.

Thus, just as rigidity and extremeness are among hallmarks of interpersonal pathology, flexibility is among the definitive characteristics of healthy and adaptive interpersonal–dyadic relating. Persons, whatever their degree of adjustment, do tend to develop particular interpersonal stances with which they are most familiar and comfortable. However, the more adaptive individual is less wedded to a narrow and constricted interpersonal style and set of interpersonal patterns, instead being capable of shifting his or her style within and across interactions in ways that are attuned to and appropriate to the situation and specific interpersonal "other" at hand. This capacity for a broader range of styles of interacting is reciprocally tied to greater differentiation and flexibility in the intrapsychic domain. Thus, though having preferred levels of agency and communion vis-à-vis others, the more adaptive individual is capable of agentic and communal variability, has a broader range of and greater flexibility in his or her working models of self and others, including tolerance for a greater range and intensity of emotions within the interpersonal sphere, and can adjust and attune his or her expectancies to the realities of the present interpersonal situation and partner. By implication, the flexible individual is less dependent on acquiring a delimited range of responses from his or her interpersonal partners. Greater mutuality in interactions and relationships can thus take place. The individual is freer to meet his or her own needs and to recognize, comprehend, and meet the agentic and communal needs of his or her dyadic partner(s), and consequently a greater give-and-take characterizes his or her significant relationships.

THE INTERPERSONAL–DYADIC MATRIX: COMPONENTS AND INTERRELATIONSHIPS

Using the central concept of the interpersonal pattern as a context, we have highlighted key structures, processes, and dynamics informing and operating in adaptive and maladaptive dyadic relationships. The interpersonal–dyadic matrix (see Figure 5.2) provides a useful pattern recognition tool for interrelating and applying this knowledge in the treatment setting, facilitating the therapist's and patient's collaborative efforts to identify and understand significant material pertaining to and links between the latter's past, expected, and current relationships, and to pursue durable therapeutic change relative to these domains of interpersonal phenomena.

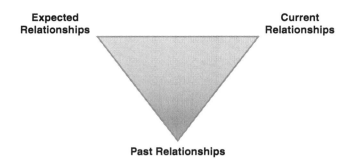

Expected
Relationships

Current
Relationships

Past Relationships

FIGURE 5.2   *Interpersonal–dyadic matrix.*

Past Relationships

Located at the bottom of the triangle, the patient's *past relationships* encompass all early and later-life relational experiences, along with other salient life experiences, that influence (a) how the patient has learned to relate to others in ways that maintain security and self-esteem and to avoid or decrease anxiety, and (b), more broadly, how he or she navigates the interpersonal and sociocultural world both in times of stress and otherwise. The patient's internal working models (internalized self–other schemas) and their integrally related motivational and affective components are enduring representations and manifestations of this frequently complex formative history, neurobiologically encoded and operating as templates that guide enactment of interpersonal patterns and such critical underlying processes as selectively perceiving, organizing, processing, interpreting, and assigning and experiencing cognitive and emotional meanings vis-à-vis interpersonal and other environmental situations and events (Anchin, 2002, 2006).

Emphasis on discussing the individual's infancy, early childhood, and later developmental experiences has been placed on the importance of the patient's attachment experiences in shaping the latter's internal working models, his or her schemas and scripts. However, in understanding the impact of the patient's history on these critical cognitive–affective structures and processes, we also wish to attune the reader to the possibility of previous trauma, relational or otherwise, as another critical stream of influence. Major advances have been made in the understanding and classification of various types of trauma, and it is essential to be knowledgeable about these and their developmental effects. Some people experience significant life-altering events that occur in natural disasters, assaults, accidents, and unexpected loss. Other types of trauma are more developmentally ongoing and insidious in their effects, as in cases of chronic neglect. Neborsky and Solomon (2001) provided a conception that has enormous conceptual and clinical utility, arranging trauma on a continuum from "small-t" to "big-T"; we have added neglect to this typology, believing that it deserves its own category by virtue of its insidiousness and, though often unrecognized, its distinct dysfunctional effects. Big-T are those events which involve physical harm and threat to life and safety and small-t are lesser events, which are often chronic relational or society injuries. In virtually every case in the following types of trauma, the source is explicitly interpersonal, and in those instances when it is not, the probability nevertheless seems high that important interpersonal contexts in the patient's life were negatively affected:

1. RELATING: (a) Faulty attunement by either or both caregivers, (b) Faulty empathy by either or both caregivers
2. PARENTING: (a) Faulty application of boundaries by caregivers, (b) Favoritism; sibling rivalry, (c) Defective affect regulation
3. EXPLOITATIVE: (a) Sexual abuse, (b) Physical abuse, (c) Power: children as pawns or scapegoats, (d) Triangulation
4. ENVIRONMENAL: (a) Death of a parent or sibling, (b) Injury of person or body part, (c) Divorce, (d) Poverty, (e) Natural disasters, (f) Social discrimination: sex, race, culture
5. NEGLECT: A failure to provide for the physical, social, psychological, educational or emotional needs of a child (Neborsky & Solomon, 2001, p. 163)

In assessing previous trauma and its impact on the patient, it is also important to take into consideration the patient's of resilience. People exposed to the same "traumatic" event may not experience the same disturbance. However, to the extent that trauma has induced psychological and emotional damage, these effects are embedded in the patient's neurobiologically rooted cognitive–affective schema and thereby carried forward into his or her present-day relational functioning, operating as nodes of vulnerability that can be activated by current interpersonal triggers, experienced subjectively, and manifested in social–behavioral ways.

Expected Relationships

In the upper left-hand corner of the triangle are the patient's *expected relationships*. The expected relationship depicts the manner in which interpersonal expectancies, a fundamental component of the patient's internalized schema, infuse the process of forming a new relationship. The powerful influence of expectancies on the trajectory of new relationships in the present has been a keen focus of both clinical theorists and researchers. For example, in his classic chapter on self-fulfilling prophecy and maladaptive behavior, Carson (1982) maintained that

> by far the most important cause of persistently maladaptive behavior is the tendency of the interpersonal environment to confirm the expectancies mediating its enactment. In simplest terms, if a client expects the world to be a hostile place, he or she will tend to behave in a manner that conforms to that expectation, and will thereby induce others, sooner or later, to enact behaviors confirming the "reality" of the original expectancy. The other side of the coin is that such a client will tend to have minimal corrective experience of the type that suggests that *some* people in the world are *not* necessarily hostile.... (p. 71)

Expressing a coalescent view from a research perspective, Reis and Collins (2004) point out "existing evidence indicates a substantial degree of continuity between early experiences and diverse relationships during childhood, adolescence, and adulthood" (p. 235) and they posit as among explanatory factors "that early relationships are key sources of expectations about social relationships. These 'residues' of early relationships have been found repeatedly to be related to the characteristics of later relationships in childhood, adolescence, and adulthood (Roisman, Madsen Henninghausen, Stroufe, & Collins, 2001)" (p. 236).

The expected relationship encapsulates the process of what psychodynamically oriented therapists term *transference* (see, e.g., Levenson, 2004). In this process, the patient unconsciously transfers onto the therapist certain schemas of self and others, including embedded expectancies, emotions, and motivations, that have been developed on the basis of relational experiences with previous significant others, and the patient overtly plays these out through in-session enactment of his or her intimately related maladaptive interpersonal patterns. Transference thus essentially entails the patient enacting, with the therapist, the same maladaptive transaction cycles he or she engages in with others. In this respect, transference is a robust phenomenon in the patient's relationships outside of treatment as well. Andersen and her colleagues (see, e.g., Andersen & Chen, 2002; Andersen & Przybylinski, 2012; Andersen, Reznik, & Glassman, 2005) have artfully demonstrated the ubiquity and operative mechanisms of transference in everyday life through research guided by an elegant social–cognitive model of transference, which accords considerably with the definition above. Although their studies have used nonclinical samples in nonclinical settings, the mechanisms identified have clear implications for the therapeutic context (see Andersen & Przybylinski, 2012), particularly given the modern-day recognition that the therapist, no less than the patient, is an external, real person (K. Frank, 2002)—and thus, despite certain unique features, the patient–therapist relationship is itself a very real one indeed (Anchin, 2002). Based on their findings, Andersen et al. (2005) cited four main conclusions of particular pertinence to understanding and clinically working with the expected-relationships component of the interpersonal–dyadic triangle:

1. Significant-other representations are activated automatically in transference.

2. Affect arises relatively automatically in transference when the significant-other representation is activated.

3. The relational self ("that is, the particular sense of self usually experienced when with this other" [Andersen & Przybylinski, 2012, p. 371]) is activated relatively automatically when the significant-other representation is activated.

4. Some self-regulatory processes in the relational self are evoked in response to "threat" (e.g., negative cues) in transference and may be automatic (p. 423).

When the patient is engaging in transference, the therapist not only directly witnesses the dysfunctional interpersonal patterns that the patient enacts with others, but also experiences the complementary impact messages including, over time, their cumulative aversiveness, that others register when interacting with the patient. Impact messages are the equivalent of the relational psychoanalytic concept of *countertransference* (Anchin, 2002, 2008), and more specifically, what Kiesler (2001) characterized as objective, as compared to subjective, countertransference. Depicting the former as "the complementary response being pulled for so expertly and tenaciously by clients during their sessions," he underscored that objective countertransference is the "generalizable pattern of emotional impact and interpersonal reaction experienced by both significant others and the therapist" (pp. 1055–1056). In contrast, paralleling the meaning of countertransference in classic psychoanalytic thinking, subjective countertransference refers to "the defensive and irrational reactions and feelings a therapist experiences with a particular client that represent residual effects of the therapist's own unresolved conflicts and anxieties" (p. 1057), or as captured by Gelso and Hayes (2007), "the therapist's internal and external reactions that are shaped by the therapist's past or present emotional conflicts and vulnerabilities" (p. 130). Objective and subjective countertransference are both clearly significant, but in the present context of the expected-relationship corner of the interpersonal–dyadic matrix, we use the term countertransference in its objective form.

When the patient and therapist are jointly engaged in transference–countertransference processes, including the therapist's countertransference fueling her *overt* reactions toward the patient, the patient's maladaptive interpersonal transaction cycle is in full swing. This process impedes forging and/or maintaining the therapeutic alliance, that is, the positive, collaborative relationship between patient and therapist robustly demonstrated as bearing a distinct relationship to therapy outcome (Castonguay & Beutler, 2006; Horvath, Del Re, Fluckiger, & Symonds, 2011). Yet, to the extent that the patient's problems in living include significant, recurrent interpersonal dysfunction, in-session enactments of the patient's maladaptive transaction cycles and the challenges they pose to the therapeutic alliance are virtually inevitable (Anchin & Pincus, 2010; Magnavita, 2010; Muran, Eubanks-Carter, & Safran, 2010). "The therapist cannot *not* be hooked or sucked in by the client because the client is more adept, more expert in his distinctive rigid, and extreme game of interpersonal encounter" (Kieser, 1982, p. 281). The upside of this process, however, is that, as a trained participant–observer (Anchin & Pincus, 2010; Levenson, 2004; Sullivan, 1953), the therapist has opportunities to experience and observe first-hand covert and overt processes comprising the patient's maladaptive transaction cycles. The charged configuration of problematic expectancies, feelings, and motivations tied to the patient's disordered schemas of self and of others, along with the field-regulatory behavioral expressions and interpersonal impacts of these intrapsychic processes, thus become directly accessible to the patient–therapist dyad for purposes of close exploration, understanding, and therapeutic intervention and change efforts.

Effectively navigating and turning to therapeutic advantage the patient's in-session enactments of his or her rigidly adhered-to maladaptive interpersonal patterns encompasses a number of interrelated tools. These include:

- Recognizing and effectively managing countertransference/ impact messages (see Gordon, 1998; Hayes, Gelso, & Hummel, 2011; Wolf, Goldfried, & Muran, 2013)

- Feeding back impact messages in therapeutic ways (see Anchin & Pincus, 2010; Kiesler, 1988) and facilitating the patient's processing of this feedback (see Clairborn, Goodyear, & Horner, 2002)

- Engaging the patient in therapeutic metacommunication (literally, communication about communication) in the form of collaborative examination of problematic processes transpiring in the treatment relationship in the service of advancing the patient's awareness and understanding of his or her maladaptive transaction cycle(s) (see Anchin & Pincus, 2010; Kiesler, 1988, 1996; Levenson, 2004; Safran & Muran, 2000; Safran, Muran, & Eubanks-Carter, 2011)

Cultivating these tools and a sensitivity to parameters that guide their usage provides the clinician with a powerful armamentarium for working therapeutically with the patient, in vivo, on the maladaptive, self-defeating patterns that plague his or her dyadic relationships. Illustrations of these clinical processes in action may be found in Anchin and Pincus (2010, pp. 129–135), Wolf et al. (2013), Kiesler (1988), Levenson (2004, pp. 267–274), and Safran and Muran (2000). It is also important to note here that, akin to Alexander and French's (1946) seminal concept of the corrective emotional experience, engaging the patient in metacommunication in and of itself provides the latter with a healthy, and therefore reparative, interpersonal experience differing from the pathogenic relational experiences likely encountered during earlier developmental years and/or self-perpetuatingly induced by the patient in current relationships. Patient–therapist metacommunication about their in-session relational processes thereby provides the patient with both the *"new experiences* and *new understandings"* (Levenson, 2004, p. 258) pivotal to interpersonal change.

Current Relationships

The patient's *current relationships,* located in the upper right-hand corner of the interpersonal–dyadic triangle, encompass his or her dyadic relationships with present-day significant others, for example spouse, partner, friends, work colleagues, boss, siblings, and other individuals with whom the patient has meaningful relationships. These are the day-to-day dyadic relationships in which the patient enacts his or her maladaptive and adaptive interpersonal transaction cycles, principal interpersonal contexts that influence his or her levels of distress and well-being. Though the realities and parameters of human variability (see, e.g., Wright, 2011; Pincus & Wright, 2010) are such that realistically the patient does not engage all dyadic partners, in all interactions, in maladaptive transaction cycles, evidence for their distinct recurrence is likely to emerge over time as the patient reports his or her between-session interpersonal experiences and their costly consequences.

As when working with in-session enactments of maladaptive transaction cycles, the overarching goal when focusing on their manifestation in current relationships is fostering awareness, understanding, and adaptive changes in dysfunctional self–other processes. In the course of extra-session work it is also valuable to identify positive interpersonal experiences and relationships, past and present, as well as strengths and healthy psychosocial capacities—potent resources that expedite therapeutic change.

Collaborating with the patient in this work is tantamount to joining with him or her in the self-reflective loop described by Yalom (1975) in interpersonally oriented group psychotherapy: "If the powerful curative factor of interpersonal learning is to be set into motion, the group must recognize, examine, and understand process. It must examine itself, it must study its own transactions, it must transcend pure experience and apply itself to the integration of that experience" (p. 122). In the same way, to understand and modify his or her maladaptive transaction cycles in current relationships, the patient must be actively engaged in the self-reflective loop vis-à-vis specific relationships and interactions integral to his day-to-day life. It is crucial, as well, that the patient's growing awareness and understanding of overt and covert components of his maladaptive interpersonal patterns be translated into actual changes in his or her functioning and experiencing in current relationships. These adaptive change processes can be actively promoted in several ways. These include encouraging the patient to bring to bear, in specific problematic interpersonal situations, relevant new learning about his or her dysfunctional self–other processes; incorporating "structured skill intervention strategies" (Sperry, 2003, p. 28; e.g., emotional regulation training) to address specific skill deficits; and assigning collaboratively fashioned between-session homework in which the patient actively attempts more adaptive covert and/or overt processes and actions. A clinical illustration of selected methods involved in targeting a maladaptive interpersonal pattern enacted in a significant extratherapy relationship may be found in Anchin and Pincus (2010, pp. 141–149).

Integrating Psychotherapeutic Work on Past, Current, and Expected Relationships

The interpersonal–dyadic triangle is a powerful recognition tool that orients the clinical process when working with self–other dysfunctionality, vivifying the interconnections between past, expected, and current relationships and the clinical desirability of integrating work in all three spheres. Shuttling among and connecting the yield that derives from applying these different lenses to specific interpersonal patterns and their components maximize opportunities for fostering therapeutic insight, cultivating more adaptive and flexible interpersonal transactional processes, and enhancing the probabilities of durable change. For example, identifying a recurrently problematic interpersonal pattern in the patient's current relationships (e.g., excessive dependence) sensitizes the therapist to its in-session occurrence, including countertransferential markers, in turn facilitating management of the latter and metacommunication with the patient as he or she attempts to play this pattern out in the therapy relationship. Furthermore, examining self–other understandings developed in relation to the therapist for their pertinence to current extra-session relationships is vital to fostering generalization of specific insights and their change implications to the client's naturalistic environment—for example, the patient learning that she automatically expects that the therapist will provide advice and the impact this creates, that she carries this same expectation into her relationship with close friends, and that an alternative is to generate, test out, and develop trust in her own solutions to problems. In a reciprocal manner, linking a maladaptive interpersonal pattern in the client's extratherapy relationships to its enactment in session enables the client to examine this pattern in a safe environment and to develop vivid, in vivo understanding of its composition, meanings, and interpersonal impact (Levenson, 2004).

As illustrated elsewhere, both current relationships (see Anchin, 2006) and the transference relationship with the therapist (see Anchin & Pincus, 2010, pp. 135–141) can also serve as springboards, as warranted by the context of the work, for shifting focus to the past-relationships component of the interpersonal–dyadic triangle in pursuit of identifying and understanding historical bases and underpinnings of the patient's maladaptive interpersonal patterns—for example, faulty attachment experiences; trauma(s); and/or other formative relational experiences within the family of origin, with peers (e.g., during adolescence), or with later significant others (e.g., a highly painful divorce). In addition to drawing these important connections between past and present interpersonal problems, past relationships can themselves be a focus of therapeutic work. In this regard, while the specific events constituting earlier pathogenic relational experiences cannot be changed, their psychological and emotional meanings and consequences can be (Anchin, 2003, 2006), with liberating, mutative effects on the patient's agentic and communal self–other processes in present-day relationships (see Anchin, 2003 and 2006 for specific case examples; cf. Sandler, 2007). In these instances the therapist and patient are collaboratively reworking the patient's memories, and thus the intrapsychic and interpersonal levels of change are inseparably tied to changes at the substrative neurobiological levels in which affectively charged memories are stored and from which they emerge (see, e.g., Cozolino, 2010; Schore, 2012).

A BRIEF WORD ON MARITAL/COUPLE DYADS

A holistic, unified understanding of the personality system necessitates understanding the patient's adaptive and maladaptive processes in significant dyadic relationships. In cases where a couple relationship is part of the patient's life, this in turn points to the importance of having some grasp of this special and unique dyad. By couple relationship we mean a significant, long-term romantic relationship with a singular partner with whom the patient lives, prototypically the patient's spouse, but alternatively this may involve a romantic partner of the opposite or same sex with whom he or she is unmarried and cohabitating. Of course, in cases when a distressed couple presents for treatment, this dyadic relationship is itself the primary focus of understanding and intervention. Content areas discussed above—for example, attachment, intimacy, autonomy, and reciprocal influence processes—are equally pertinent to marital/couple relationships, but they also take on special features by virtue of the long-term and romantic nature of the couple relationship; moreover, there are particular considerations unique to couple relationships. In Chapter 7 we detail these common, special, and unique factors within the context of discussing the sociocultural–familial matrix.

SUMMARY

Knowing what to pay attention to and what is less relevant is one of the most important skills psychotherapists possess. Attention is the scalpel of the psychotherapist (Siegel, 2012). When the illuminating light of attention is not on central issues, time is lost and suffering continues. In this vein, the present chapter has focused on structures, processes, and mechanisms central to understanding and clinically treating dysfunction in the interpersonal–dyadic level of the human personality system. To guide this discussion, two key constructs—the *interpersonal pattern* and the *interpersonal–dyadic triangle*—have been presented, unpacked, and synthesized. We differentiated interpersonal patterns from interaction sequences and interpersonal styles, noting that these concepts provide complementary perspectives on interpersonal–intrapsychic processes enacted in dyadic relationships. We then detailed five considerations essential to analytic and synthetic understanding of a patient's interpersonal patterns in the clinical setting: the attachment system, intimacy, autonomy, reciprocal influence processes (underscoring interpersonal complementarity), and the interpersonal transaction cycle, including the importance of the rigidity–flexibility dimension relative to maladaptive and adaptive interpersonal patterns. Subsequently, we turned to delineating components of the interpersonal–dyadic matrix, a powerful pattern-recognition tool for interrelating and clinically applying evolving knowledge about the patient's interpersonal patterns. The triangular configuration of this matrix is composed of past relationships, expected relationships, and current relationships. We emphasized significant elements and clinical implications of each of these relational domains, as well as the importance of integrating therapeutic work across all three spheres. We concluded with a brief word on marital/couple relationships, reserving the elaboration of this special and unique interpersonal–dyadic system for Chapter 7.

REFERENCES

Alexander, F., & French, T. M. (1946). *Psychoanalytic therapy*. New York: Ronald.

Anchin, J. C. (1982). Sequence, pattern, and style: Implications and treatment implications of some interpersonal concept. In J. C. Anchin & D. J. Kiesler (Eds.), *Handbook of interpersonal psychotherapy* (pp. 95–131). New York: Pergamon.

Anchin, J. C. (2002). Relational psychoanalytic enactments and psychotherapy integration: Dualities, dialectics, and directions: Comment on frank (2002). *Journal of Psychotherapy Integration, 12,* 302–346.

Anchin, J. C. (2003). Cybernetic systems, existential phenomenology, and solution-focused narrative: Therapeutic transformation of negative affective states through integratively oriented brief psychotherapy. *Journal of Psychotherapy Integration, 13,* 334–442.

Anchin, J. C. (2006). A hermeneutically informed approach to psychotherapy integration. In G. Stricker & J. Gold (Eds.), *A casebook of psychotherapy integration* (pp. 261–280). Washington, DC: American Psychological Association.

Anchin, J. C. (2008). Pursuing a unifying paradigm for psychotherapy: Tasks, dialectical considerations, and biopsychosocial systems metatheory. *Journal of Psychotherapy Integration, 18,* 310–349.

Anchin, J. C., & Pincus, A. L. (2010). Evidence-based interpersonal psychotherapy with personality disorders: Theory, components, and strategies. In J. J. Magnavita (Eds.), *Evidence-based treatment of personality dysfunction: Principles, methods, and processes* (pp. 113–166). Washington, DC: American Psychological Association.

Andersen, S. M., & Chen, S. (2002). The relational self: An interpersonal social-cognitive theory. *Psychological Review, 109,* 619–645.

Anderson, S. M., & Przybylinski, E. (2012). Experiments on transference in relations: Implications for treatment. *Psychotherapy, 49,* 370–383.

Anderson, S. M., Reznik, I., & Glassman, N. S. (2005). The unconscious relational self. In R. R. Hassin, J. S. Uleman & J. A. Bargh (Eds.), *The new unconscious* (pp. 421–481). New York: Oxford University Press.

Andrews, J. D. W. (1991). *The active self in psychotherapy*. Boston: Allyn & Bacon.

Becker-Weidman, A. (2010). *Dyadic developmental psychotherapy: Essential practices & methods*. Lanham, MD: Jason Aronson.

Benjamin, L. S. (1996). *Interpersonal diagnosis and treatment of personality disorders* (2nd ed.). New York: Guilford.

Bornstein, R. F. (2005). The dependent patient: Diagnosis, assessment, and treatment. *Professional Psychology: Research and Practice, 36,* 82–89.

Bowlby, J. (1977). The making and breaking of affectional bonds. I. Aetiology and psychopathology in the light of attachment theory. *British Journal of Psychiatry, 130,* 201–210.

Bradley, B., & Johnson, S. M. (2005). Emotionally focused couples therapy: An integrative contemporary approach. In M. Haraway (Ed.), *Handbook of couples therapy*. New York: Wiley.

Brown, K. W., & Ryan, R. M. (2004). Fostering healthy self-regulation from within and without: A self-determination theory perspective. In P. A. Linley & S. Joseph (Eds.), *Positive psychology in practice* (pp. 105–124). Hoboken, NJ: Wiley.

Carson, R. C. (1969). *Interaction concepts of personality*. Chicago, IL: Aldine.

Carson, R. C. (1982). Self-fulfilling prophecy, maladaptive behavior, and psychotherapy. In J. C. Anchin & D. J. Kiesler (Eds.). *Handbook of interpersonal psychotherapy* (pp. 64–77). New York: Pergamon.

Castonguay, L. G., & Beutler, L. E. (Eds.). (2006). *Principles of therapeutic change that work.* New York: Oxford University Press.

Clairborn, C. D., Goodyear, R. K., & Horner, P. A. (2002). Feedback. In J. C. Norcross (Ed.), *Psychotherapy relationships that work: Therapist contributions and responsiveness to patients* (pp. 217–233). New York, NY: Oxford University Press.

Cozolino, L. (2010). *The neuroscience of psychotherapy: Healing the social brain* (2nd ed.). New York: Norton.

Danziger, K. (1976). *Interpersonal communication.* New York: Pergamon.

Diener, M. J., & Monroe, J. M. (2011). The relationship between adult attachment style and therapeutic alliance in individual psychotherapy: A meta-analytic review. *Psychotherapy, 48,* 237–248.

Florsheim, P., Henry, W. P., & Benjamin, L. S. (1996). Integrating individual and interpersonal approaches to diagnosis: The structural analysis of social behavior and attachment theory. In F. W. Kaslow (Ed.), *Handbook of relational diagnosis and dysfunctional family patterns* (pp. 81–101). New York: Wiley

Fosha, D. (2000). *The transforming power of affect: A model for accelerated change.* New York: Basic Books.

Frank, J. D., & Frank, J. B. (1991). *Persuasion and healing: A comparative study of psychotherapy* (3rd ed.). Baltimore: The Johns Hopkins University Press.

Frank, K. A. (2002). The "ins and outs" of enactment: A relational bridge for psychotherapy integration. *Journal of Psychotherapy Integration, 12,* 267–286.

Gelso, C. J., & Hayes, J. A. (2007). *Countertransference and the therapist's inner experience: Perils and possibilities.* Mahwah, NJ: Lawrence Erlbaum Associates.

Gerson, M. J. (2010). *The embedded self: An integrative psychodynamic and systemic perspective on couples and family therapy* (2nd ed.). New York: Routledge.

Gold, J. R., & Wachtel, P. L. (1993). Cyclical psychodynamics. In G. Stricker & J. R. Gold (Eds.), *Comprehensive handbook of psychotherapy integration* (pp. 59–72). New York: Plenum.

Gordon, R. M. (1998). Handling transference and countertransference issues with the difficult patient. *The Independent Practitioner, 18*(3), 147–149.

Gudsnuk, K. M., & Champagne, F. A. (2011). Epigenetic effects of early developmental experiences. *Clinical Perinatology, 38,* 703–717.

Hayes, J. A., Gelso, C. J., & Hummel, A. M. (2011). Managing countertransference. In J. C. Norcross (Ed.), *Psychotherapy relationships that work: Evidence-based responsiveness* (2nd ed., pp. 239–258). New York: Oxford University Press.

Horowitz, M. J. (1988). *Introduction to psychodynamics.* New York: Basic Books.

Horowitz, M. J. (1991). States, schemas, and control: General theories for psychotherapy integration. *Journal of Psychotherapy Integration, 1,* 85–102.

Horvath, A. O., Del Re, A. C., Fluckiger, C., & Symonds, D. (2011). Alliance in individual psychotherapy. In J. C. Norcross (Ed.), *Psychotherapy relationships that work: Evidence-based responsiveness* (2nd ed., pp. 25–69). New York: Oxford University Press.

James, W. (1890). *The principles of psychology* (Vol I & II). New York: Holt.

Johnson, S. B., Riley, A. W., Granger, D. A., & Riis, J. (2013). The science of early life toxic stress for pediatric practice and advocacy. *Pediatrics, 131,* 310–327.

Karpel, M. A. (1994). *Evaluating couples: A handbook for practitioners.* New York: Norton.

Kiesler, D. J. (1982a). Interpersonal theory for personality and psychotherapy. In J. C. Anchin & D. J. Kiesler (Eds.), *Handbook of interpersonal psychotherapy* (pp. 3–24). New York: Pergamon.

Kiesler, D. J. (1982b). Confronting the client–therapist relationship in psychotherapy. In J. C. Anchin & D. J. Kiesler (Eds.), *Handbook of interpersonal psychotherapy* (pp. 274–295). New York, NY: Pergamon.

Kiesler, D. J. (1983). The 1982 interpersonal circle: A taxonomy for complementarity in human transactions. *Psychological Review, 90*, 185–214.

Kiesler, D. J. (1986a). The 1982 interpersonal circle: An analysis of DSM-III personality disorders. In T. Millon & G. L. Klerman (Eds.), *Contemporary directions in psychopathology: Toward the DSM-IV* (pp. 571–597). New York: Guilford.

Kiesler, D. J. (1986b). Interpersonal methods of diagnosis and treatment. In R. Michaels & J. Cavenar (Eds.), *Psychiatry* (vol. 1, no. 4). Philadelphia: Lippincott.

Kiesler, D. J. (1988). *Therapeutic metacommunication: Therapist impact disclosure as feedback in psychotherapy.* Palo Alto, CA: Consulting Psychologists Press.

Kiesler, D. J. (1991). Interpersonal methods of assessment and diagnosis. In C. R. Snyder & D. R. Forsyth (Eds.), *Handbook of social and clinical psychology: The health perspective* (pp. 438–468). New York: Pergamon.

Kiesler, D. J. (1992). Interpersonal circle inventories: Pantheoretical applications to psychotherapy research and practice. *Journal of Psychotherapy Integration, 2*, 77–99.

Kiesler, D. J. (1996). *Contemporary interpersonal theory and research: Personality, psychopathology, and psychotherapy.* New York: Wiley.

Kiesler, D. J. (2001). Therapist countertransference: In search of common themes and empirical referents. *Journal of Clinical Psycholology, 57*, 1053–63.

Kiesler, D. J., Bernstein, A. J., & Anchin, J. C. (1976). *Interpersonal communication, relationship, and the behavior therapies.* Richmond: Virginia Commonwealth University.

Levenson, H. (1995). *Time-limited dynamic psychotherapy.* New York: Basic Books.

Levenson, H. (2004). Time-limited dynamic psychotherapy. In J. J. Magnavita (Ed.), *Handbook of personality disorders: Theory and practice* (pp. 254–279). New York: Wiley.

Levy, K. N., Ellison, W. D., Scott, L. N., & Bernecker, S. L. (2011). Attachment style. *Journal of Clinical Psychology: In Session, 67*, 193–203.

Locke, K. D. (2011). Circumplex measures of interpersonal constructs. In L. M. Horowitz & S. Strack (Ed.), *Handbook of interpersonal psychology: Theory, research, assessment and therapeutic interventions* (pp. 313–324). Hoboken, NJ: Wiley.

Magnavita, J. J. (2005). *Personality-guided relational therapy: A unified approach.* Washington, DC: American Psychological Association.

Magnavita, J. J. (2010). Methods, components, and strategies of unified treatment: Using evidence and personality systematics to enhance outcome. In J. J. Magnavita (Ed.), *Evidence-based treatment of personality dysfunction: Principles, methods, and processes* (pp. 253–285). Washington, DC: American Psychological Association.

Mahoney, M. J. (1991). *Human change processes: The scientific foundations of psychotherapy.* New York: Basic Books.

McLemore, C. W., & Hart, P. P. (1982). Relational psychotherapy: The clinical facilitation of intimacy. In J. C. Anchin & D. J. Kiesler (Eds.), *Handbook of interpersonal psychotherapy* (pp. 227–247). New York: Pergamon.

Muran, J. C., Eubanks-Carter, C., & Safran, J. D. (2010). A relational approach to the treatment of personality dysfunction. In J. J. Magnavita (Ed.), *Evidence-based treatment of personality dysfunction: Principles, methods, and processes* (pp. 167–192). Washington, DC: American Psychological Association.

Neborsky, R. J., & Solomon, M. F. (2001). Attachment bonds and intimacy: Can the primary imprint of love change? In M. F. Solomon, R. J. Neborsky, L. McCullough, M. Alpert, F. Shapiro & D. Malan (Eds.), *Short-term therapy for long-term change.* New York: Norton.

Pincus, A. L. (2005). A contemporary integrative interpersonal theory of personality disorders. In J. Clarkin & M. Lenzenweger (Eds.), *Major theories of personality disorder* (2nd ed., pp. 282–331). New York: Guilford.

Pincus, A. L., Lukowitsky, M. R., & Wright, A. G. C. (2010). The interpersonal nexus of personality and psychopathology. In T. Millon, R. F. Krueger & E. Simonsen (Eds.), *Contemporary directions in psychopathology: Scientific foundations for the DSM-V and ICD-11* (pp. 523–552). New York: Guilford.

Pincus, A. L., & Wright, A. G. C. (2010). Interpersonal diagnosis of personality. In L. M. Horowitz & S. Strack (Eds.), *Handbook of interpersonal psychology: Theory, research, assessment and therapeutic interventions* (pp. 359–382). Hoboken, NJ: Wiley.

Reeve, J., Inck, T. A., & Safran, J. (1993). Toward an integration of cognitive, interpersonal, and experiential approaches to therapy. In G. Stricker & J. R. Gold (Eds.), *Comprehensive handbook of psychotherapy integration* (pp. 113–123). New York: Plenum Press.

Reis, H. T., & Gable, S. L. (2003). Toward a positive psychology of relationships. In C. L. M. Keyes & J. Haidt (Eds.), *Flourishing: Positive psychology and the life well-lived* (pp. 129–159). Washington, DC: American Psychological Association.

Reis, H. T., & Collins, W. A. (2004). Relationships, human behavior, and psychological science. *Current Directions in Psychological Science, 13,* 233–237.

Reis, H. T., Sheldon, K. M., Gable, S. L., Roscoe, J., & Ryan, R. M. (2000). Daily well-being: The role of autonomy, competence, and relatedness. *Personality and Social Psychology Bulletin, 26,* 419–435.

Ruini, C., & Fava, G. A. (2004). Clinical applications of well-being therapy. In P. A. Linley & S. Joseph (Eds.), *Positive psychology in practice* (pp. 371–387). Hoboken, NJ: Wiley.

Ryff, C. D. (1989). Happiness is everything, or is it? explorations on the meaning of psychological well-being. *Journal of Personality and Social Psychology, 57,* 1069–1081.

Ryff, C. D., & Singer, B. (1998). The contours of positive human health. *Psychological Inquiry, 9,* 1–28.

Ryff, C. D., & Singer, B. H. (2006). Best news yet for the six-factor model of well-being. *Social Science Research, 35,* 1103–1119.

Sadler, P., Ethier, N., & Woody, E. (2010). Interpersonal complementarity. In L. M. Horowitz & S. Strack (Eds.), *Handbook of interpersonal psychology: Theory, research, assessment and therapeutic interventions* (pp. 123–142). Hoboken, NJ: Wiley.

Safran, J. D., & Muran, J. C. (2000). *Negotiating the therapeutic alliance: A relational treatment guide.* New York: Guilford.

Safran, J. D., Muran, J. C., & Eubanks-Carter, C. (2011). Repairing alliance ruptures. In J. C. Norcross (Ed.), *Psychotherapy relationships that work: Evidence-based responsiveness* (2nd ed., pp. 224–238). New York: Oxford University Press.

Safran, J. D., & Segal, Z. (1990). *Interpersonal process in cognitive therapy.* New York: Basic Books.

Sandler, S. (2007). The reunion process: A new focus in short-term dynamic psychotherapy. *Psychotherapy: Theory, Research, Practice, Training, 44,* 121–136.

Schore, A. N. (2012). *The science of the art of psychotherapy.* New York: Norton.

Siegel, D. J. (2012). *Pocket guide to interpersonal neurobiology: An integrative handbook of the mind.* New York: Norton.

Singer, J. A. (2005). *Personality and psychotherapy: Treating the whole person.* New York: Guilford.

Singer, J. A. (in press). Lost in translation? finding the person in the emerging paradigm of clinical science: Introduction to a special issue on personality psychology and psychotherapy. *Journal of Personality.*

Slade, A., & Aber, J. L. (1992). Attachments, drives, and development: Conflicts and convergences in theory. In J. Barron, M. Eagle & D. Wolitsky (Eds.), *The interface between psychoanalysis and psychology* (pp. 154–185). Washington, DC: American Psychological Association.

Sperry, L. (2003). *Handbook of diagnosis and treatment of DSM–IV–TR personality disorders* (2nd ed.). New York, NY: Brunner-Routledge.

Stolorow, R. G., & Atwood, G. E. (1992). *Contexts of being: The intersubjective foundations of psychological life.* Hillsdale, NJ: Analytic Press.

Strupp, H. H., & Binder, J. L. (1984). *Psychotherapy in a new key.* New York: Basic Books.

Sullivan, H. S. (1953). *The interpersonal theory of psychiatry.* New York: Norton.

Tronick, E. (2007). *The neurobehavioral and social-emotional development of infants and children.* New York: Norton.

Wagner, C. C., Kiesler, D. J., & Schmidt, J. A. (1995). Assessing the interpersonal transaction cycle: Convergence of action and reaction interpersonal circumplex measures. *Journal of Personality and Social Psychology, 69,* 938–949.

Wampold, B. E. (2001). *The great psychotherapy debate: Models, methods, and findings.* Mahwah, NJ: Lawrence Erlbaum Associates.

Wolf, A. W., Goldfried, M. R., & Muran, J. C. (Eds.). (2013). *Transforming negative reactions to clients: From frustration to compassion.* Washington, DC: American Psychological Association.

Wright, A. G. C. (2011). Quantitative and qualitative distinctions in personality disorder. *Journal of Personality Assessment, 93,* 370–379.

Yalom, I. (1975). *The theory and practice of group psychotherapy* (2nd ed.). New York: Basic Books.

Yalom, I., & Leszcz, M. (2005). *The theory and practice of group psychotherapy* (5th ed.). New York: Basic Books.

Chapter 6

TRIADS AND FAMILY SYSTEMS

We begin this chapter on the *Level III relational–triadic* components by expanding the dyadic configuration presented in the previous chapter with the addition of another person, which creates an important relational molecule—*a three-person* relationship. The relational–triadic level of the total ecological system (TES) presented in this chapter is a fundamental building block of larger relational systems (families, communities, cultures, etc.) explored in the following chapter, and an important part of a unified framework. The importance of a unified theory of relational systems requires an understanding of how relations operate at all the hierarchical levels. L'Abate (2003) wrote: "We cannot have a theory for individuals, a theory for couples, and a theory for families. We can have, instead, a theory of relationships where individuals remain the products and producers of significant relationships with others" (p. iv).

To place this chapter in context, psychotherapists devote considerable attention to dyads and most are broadly trained interpersonally. Triangular configurations have been developed to represent a number of psychological processes, with which most readers who are not family trained may be less familiar. Triangles are useful because they can depict processes among important interrelated components. For example, if one member of a triangle shifts his or her position by attempting to gain more autonomy, the other two members are impacted. In our unified framework, we use triadic theory to represent the matrix among three-person relational systems. These three-person relationships are common configurations, and as is often seen in clinical practice, become problematic when they are fixed in a rigid state of organization characterized by the term *triangulation*. We devote this chapter to triadic configurations, saving a more detailed presentation of family and larger systems and how they interact to mutually shape the individual personality system for the next and final chapter in this part.

WHEN A THREE-PERSON CONFIGURATION TRIANGULATES

We all have experienced the entry of a new member of our peer group who threatens our status and may create rivalry within a new three-person relationship system. A new clinician joins our practice and the dynamics with our partners are inevitably altered to some degree. A divorced woman brings a new partner into her family system, which requires accommodation among her children. In most cases, these three-some relationships are able to tolerate and metabolize the anxiety without becoming symptomatic, and each member is able to maintain a distinct relationship with the other two members. Each member of a nontriangulated threesome is able to grow and develop without impediment from the others. A healthy three-person system differs from a triangulated one in that each person in a three-person relationship can carry on a separate relationship with each of the others, whereas in a triangulated relationship the participants are not able to have separate relationships and development is often fixated. Triangulated relationships have trouble accommodating change and assimilating new information. It is a type of closed subsystem.

Triangulated relationships may be nested in one generation or they may be multigenerational. A new bride might be so tied to a dominant father that the marital dyad does not coalesce and tension ensues. When relationships become triangulated, emotional processes become stagnant; repetitive adaptive strategies that don't work are repeated, and yet the triangulated threesome seemingly remains intractably stuck. Individuation cannot progress in the members, as they are locked into one another in a kind of emotional and psychological fusion. Symptoms may worsen over time and outsiders are then often drawn into the mixture. In many cases, where children and adolescents are involved, the adolescent does not transition into more autonomous independent functioning of young adulthood, and if not remedied, these young adults may spend their lives not achieving their goals of finding a partner and establishing their own family. Many of these adolescents display what we call cliff diving in that they seem to function very well and then for no apparent reason "fall off a cliff," often withdrawing from life, school, and work. A lack of emotional differentiation in many of these young adults seems to lead to them running out of energy. They often suffer from very low emotional intelligence, which is discussed later in this chapter. An analogy is driving a car without a functioning gas gauge. The person may run out of gas in an isolated area because he or she has driven too far from a populated area. The person then sits by the side of the road and spends a great deal of time feeling overwhelmed because he or she doesn't have a gas can, no gas station is close by, and others are not open. Someone must come to the rescue—often parents trained to "hop to." Often these individuals, who lack differentiation, may show up for the first time in clinical practice in their 40s or 50s when their parents are aging or one has died. They often present with severe depression and anxiety related to unresolved issues and developmental dysynchrony (i.e., while their peers have progressed and matured, they have not experienced the learning generated by life experiences). An example is an attractive professional woman in her mid-40s, who focused on her career and never had a romantic relationship because she was "waiting for the right man." Now distressed and in a panic, she has come to the realization that she "might not get married and have a family." Further evidence showed she was highly enmeshed in a triangulated relationship with her aging parents who still controlled many aspects of her life. Her development had not resulted in advancing her emotional differentiation or maturity. Her level of self–other differentiation remained low.

Murray Bowen (1976) introduced his triadic theory to family therapy and clinical science, as well as a number of other important theoretical constructs important to our understanding of unified psychotherapy. Family psychology was the first branch of psychology to embrace a system model almost from its inception, and Bowenian theory constituted an important contribution to this family movement (Bray & Stanton, 2009; Magnavita, 2012). Indeed, as pointed out in Chapter 1, just as system theory was critical to forging the biopsychosocial model, system theory also provided the family psychology movement with a conceptual framework for its transformational shift in focus from the dyad to the triad—arguably a paradigm shift for the field of psychotherapeutics (Magnavita, 2012).

As we have said, triads are relational molecules of three people and a basic element of our relational system. "It is important to remember that the essence of a triangle is to lower anxiety in the individual and tension in the twosome by shifting to the discussion of the third person" (Guerin et al., 1996, p. 49). Freud recognized the importance and power of triadic relationships when he posited that the Oedipal relationship—*father–mother–child triangle*—was fundamental in shaping character, or what we refer to as the personality system. However, Freud did not have the benefit of system theory when he articulated his metapsychology. It would take a confluence of scientific advances and theoretical breakthroughs to elucidate our understanding of how relational systems greater than two (2+) operate. Infants enter the world in both dyadic—with mother—and multiple triadic configurations with parents and significant others. Although the function of the dyad became increasingly apparent as Bowlby and others articulated this essential relational unit, the operation of triads was not so obvious. Yet triadic relationships are common, and expectations that speak to the importance of the triad begin before we are born and they may be influenced by generational patterns. Guerin et al. (1996) described this process:

> At the very beginning of your life, as soon as your conception became known, either your father, your mother, or both may have experienced you as an intruder. The fact of your existence may have overjoyed your father and presented a threat to your mother's career, making your father too eager for your arrival and your mother too anxious. Even before your conception, not-so-subtle pressure from your maternal grandmother may have led the campaign for your existence. At your birth, whatever genetic map was on your face was probably the stimulus for all kinds of loyalty-driven distinctions by well-meaning relatives. "He looks just like George's mother," says George's mother's sister. (p. 1)

Triads also have an important evolutionary basis. Due to the long gestation period and length of development for our offspring, a triad was basic to survival. The mother could not devote her time to taking care of and protecting her child without at least one other adult to ensure the survival of the maternal–infant dyad until the infant became self-sufficient.

Bowen (1976) believed that relational triangles are the basic building blocks of any relational system, including marriages and families, and introduced the concept of the triangle into family therapy. Within a treatment context, these triads are at times obvious and at other times not readily recognizable, and they are often multigenerational. Their dynamics are linked to those of the dyad, which, as noted in the previous chapter, oscillates between intimacy and autonomy or distance; there is an ongoing quest for comfortable relational space that ebbs and flows in our intimate relationships: "cycles of closeness and distance appear ... in all dyadic relationships—parent and child, brother and sister, husband and wife, even friend and friend. These behavioral cycles are reactions to internal anxiety: separation anxiety compelling attempts at closeness, incorporation anxiety driving distance" (Guerin et al., 1996, p. 11). As we shall discuss later in this volume, these cycles become amplified or polarized in some forms of psychopathological adaptations such as seen in various personality dysfunctions and relational disturbances. The important point is that these are inherent components of a relational system, which to some degree or another are always in flux. In the course of oscillations within dyads, the latter can become increasingly unstable, especially those highly conflicted with elevated levels of anxiety, and it is this instability that results in triadic relationships (Guerin et al., 1996); triads are formed when the anxiety in a dyad cannot be tolerated and this anxiety is transmitted to a third person to stabilize the dyad, forming a fixed triad. A three-person relationship, which is *triangulated*, is one in which the emotional attractors create a rigid structure that cannot flexibly respond to the demands of development and life cycle changes.

Discussing triangulation, Fogarty (1973–1978) wrote:

> While two persons may shorten or lengthen the space between them, at no time is there change in the overall area of the triangle. Increased closeness between any two family members results in increased distance from the third member. Movement of persons along the lines of the triangle is reactive, often unaware, and without the free use of self-control. The triangle is a closed system with the sum of the distance between the three members remaining fixed. (p. 42)

In extreme cases of triangulation, none of the three members of this configuration can differentiate, as they are locked in an intense emotional relationship. The ultimate fear is annihilation if any of them differentiate, which may have been an important earlier adapted emotional system to ensure survival.

One of the main functions of triangular relationships is to establish defense (Guerin et al., 1996). In this respect, early family system theorists discovered that the pathway of anxiety in a system is relational and that triangulated relationships are often rooted in past developmental and generational processes that have led to a low level of differentiation in the members of the dyad (e.g., Minuchin, 1974). This lack of differentiation within the dyad can be viewed as a *dyadic diathesis* to the extent that it disposes the dyad toward engaging in processes of triangulation. Essentially, triangular relationships occur when there is too much nonmetabolized anxiety associated with this low level of differentiation within the dyadic relationship, which in turn seeks homeostasis by engaging and transmitting the anxiety to a third—usually emotionally vulnerable—person. Steinglass (1978) described how a dyadic configuration moves to the triadic: "Although two-person systems may exhibit relative stability during periods of calm, at times of stress a two-person system is highly unstable, and the tendency of such a dyad is to attempt to involve or incorporate a third person, thereby establishing a triangle" (p. 332). The third person in a fixed triad is characteristically the one that becomes symptomatic, which serves as a diversion from the conflict and distress in the dysfunctional dyad.

OVERVIEW OF THE TRIADIC MATRIX AND COMPONENTS

The *relational–triadic* Level III can also be depicted using a triangular configuration as we have depicted at Levels I and II (see Figure 6.1). We refer to this Level III matrix as *triadic*. At the top of the triangle, on each side are individuals in a relationship, and at the bottom of the triangle is a third person caught in the emotional vortex of the dyad. Fogarty (1975) described a triangulated relationship as a threesome with a rubber band around them, which limits their mobility and keeps them locked into an inflexible relationship with one another. To keep the rubber band from dropping to the floor or snapping, Fogarty believed that each member needed to keep their focus on the other two. A threesome and a triadic relationship differ in the degree of rigidity. Threesomes are more flexible and not fixed relational molecules that come together and apart as required by relational demands and context; triangulated relationships are fixed and rigid.

There are essential constructs that will assist in understanding the nature of relational triangles. Murray Bowen introduced into family therapy the foundational construct of *differentiation*, of which there are two interrelated types. We note in this context that, broadly speaking, the aim of unified psychotherapeutics is to increase differentiation and integration of component parts.

The Concept and Process of Differentiation

Differentiation is a dynamic developmental process that occurs throughout the life time and family life cycle, as well as generationally. Complex systems necessarily become more complicated as they evolve and require more integration among the various units. The orthogenetic principle offered by Werner (1948) is important to understanding complex relational systems. This principle states: "development . . . proceeds from a state of

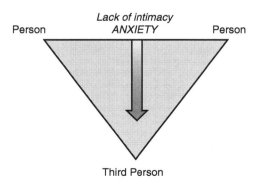

FIGURE 6.1   *Relational–triadic matrix.*

relative globality and lack of differentiation to a state of increasing differentiation, articulation, and hierarchic integration" (Werner, 1957, p. 126). Essentially, development becomes increasingly complex and differentiated at each successive stage of development. Siegel (2012) adopts this concept as a guiding principle of interpersonal neurobiology. He writes:

> ...integration is the fundamental mechanism of health and well-being. Integration is the linkage of differentiated parts of a system. Differentiation means that subsets of a collection of elements—water molecules in a cloud, functions of the mind, regions of the brain, people in a family—are able to become unique or specialized in their individuality. Linkage means that subsets interact with one another. (p. 16-1)

Bowen introduced the concept of *differentiation* and its opposite, *fusion*; both of which are important to our understanding of dyadic and triadic processes. There are basically two aspects of differentiation, which are related: *emotional differentiation* and *self-differentiation*. It is again helpful to draw attention to the concept of intimacy, discussed in the previous chapter. The person with an undifferentiated individual personality system—and who is thus at heightened risk to seek triangulation with others—has a low capacity for intimacy. In this respect, a lack of differentiation is a diathesis, a deficiency, at the intrapsychic level that, through its negative impact on intimacy, disposes the individual toward relational problems. Intimacy is highly important to dyadic and family relationships: "It is the necessary, albeit not sufficient, ingredient for human survival. Intimacy is the basic interpersonal variable necessary for the maintenance and prolongation of close relationships, both inside and outside the family, as in friendships" (L'Abate, 1986, p. 227). The individual who cannot recognize his or her feelings and share them with others, which are processes that allow for empathy and bonding, will struggle to have intimacy. We discussed the intrapsychic matrix in Chapter 4 and the relationship among anxiety, defense, and emotion–cognition. Emotional differentiation operates in part in this matrix, but it is also central to dyadic and triadic and larger system processes and is therefore central to our understanding. *Self–other* differentiation refers to dyadic or interpersonal processes where two or more individuals are capable of both autonomous functioning and intimacy. These individuals are unlikely to seek fused relationships dyadically or triadically, becoming fixed-triangulated relational configurations.

Emotional Differentiation

Emotional differentiation refers to the increasingly complex capacity to experience emotion as opposed to defenses or anxiety. Emotional differentiation can be depicted at Level I in the individual's capacity for emotional experience without undue activation of anxiety and subsequent defenses. An emotionally differentiated person is fluid and responsive, using defenses adaptively. In popular terms, we refer to this capacity as *emotional intelligence* (Goleman, 1995). A high level of emotional differentiation includes the capacity to experience the range of emotions without becoming symptomatic by channeling them into anxiety or by excessive use of defensive responding. Emotional differentiation and capacity for emotional experience is essential for maintaining intimate relationships. Emotional differentiation is an aspect of self-differentiation.

Emotional Intelligence as a Marker of Level of Differentiation

The concept of emotional intelligence offered to psychological science by Peter Salovey and Jack Mayer was a breakthrough conceptual development that gained much popular attention through the work of Daniel Goleman (1995). Salovey and Mayer (1990) defined emotional intelligence as the "ability to monitor one's own and others' feelings, to discriminate among them, and to use this information to guide one's thinking and action" (Grewal & Salovey, 2005, p. 333). They went on to categorize these skill sets in the following way: (a) *Perceiving emotions in others*—what is he or she feeling?; (b) *Using emotion to facilitate thought*—what could I do to resolve a challenge or conflict?; (c) *Understanding emotions*—being able to describe what I am feeling; and (d) *Managing emotions*—the ability to regulate and keep emotion from becoming too reactive (Mayer & Salovey, 1997).

William James (1890) recognized that the conscious experience of anxiety is a prelude to the emergence of recognized emotions. If the emotion is not recognized and the anxiety is sustained, this can operate as the equivalent of "flipping a circuit breaker to 'on' in an electrical system: Now there is a conduit for emotional energy to move back and forth among the people in the triangle" (Guerin et al., 1996, p. 93). Emotional differentiation is a basic function of self–other differentiation.

Self–Other Differentiation

Self–other differentiation refers to the capacity to remain separate in relationship with others, without losing one's sense of self. Bowen referred to this capacity to relate authentically without becoming *fused* as a state of self–other differentiation. Bowen depicted differentiation and fusion on a spectrum. We find these concepts to serve as very useful guides for clinical practice (see Box 6.1). Individuals who are differentiated do not rely excessively on defenses when in intimate relationships and are not prone to triangulation. Self-differentiation requires a consolidated and mature individual personality system that does rely on projection in relation to others. Many psychotherapists have experienced the force

---

Box 6.1 Clinical Tool

Self–other differentiation continuum

Fused functioning	Autonomous functioning
Undifferentiated emotionally	Differentiated emotionally
Excessively projects internal world on others	Understands others as separate
Has a limited theory of mind	Has insight into how others feel and think

---

of triangulation, which is manifest in couples with personality disorders that tend to rely on projection as a defense (Lachkar, 2004). In these situations there is a strong force that may result in countertransference phenomena being aroused—not infrequently a distinct indicator that either or both members of the couple are attempting to triangulate the therapist.

The lower the level of emotional differentiation in an individual the more likely that person is to seek fusion with another person; in essence, this is the diathesis of a low level of differentiation in action. We can refer to "developmental levels of personality organization" (McWilliams, 2011, p. 43) on a structural continuum (neurotic—borderline—psychotic; see Magnavita & Carlson, 2003, p. 280, figure 1; McWilliams, 2011, chap. 3) and note that individuals with borderline personality structures are more likely to seek to fuse with others, yet they then often become terrified, resulting in oscillating patterns of, on the one hand, closeness, and on the other hand, aversive behaviors, which in a self-defeating manner encourage distancing and abandonment by others.

Anxiety Pathways in Triadic Configurations

Triangulated relationships are essentially anxiety-regulating systems, which seek to stabilize two-person systems. Several common pathways are regularly seen in clinical settings and are important to articulate.

Anxiety Flowing to a Vulnerable Child

A commonly observed pathway of anxiety seen in clinical practice occurs when anxiety in a dyad is channeled to a child. In these cases, children become symptomatic as a result of absorbing nonmetabolized dyadic anxiety. Families may select those with physical or psychological impairment or on the basis of birth order or physical or emotional resemblance to a figure from another generation with whom there is unresolved emotional conflict. Bowen believed that when a child is triangulated at some level the rest of the family conspires to focus on this individual in order to balance the energy in the family system. Whatever the precise mechanisms at play in selecting the child to be triangulated, it is important to note that the distress and impairments in functioning (e.g., relative to school and peers) that may occur for the child during the course of his or her symptomatology is but one facet of the costs to the child caught in the web of triangulation. To the extent that his or her symptomatology, distress, and/or impaired functioning leaves effects on enduring structures (e.g., the child's inner working models of self and others; his or her interpersonal style), a personality-based diathesis has also been set in place within the child, placing him or her at heightened risk for subsequent disorder. This is among mechanisms through which maladaptive patterns may be transmitted from one generation to another and set in motion the eventual reconfiguration of disturbed dyadic and triadic patterns as the child and adolescent evolves into adulthood.

Anxiety Flowing to Another Adult

Dyadic anxiety can also flow to another adult. The most ubiquitous form of this relational triad occurs when a member of a couple is having an affair, which introduces the third person. These triadic configurations can be quite complicated and carefully orchestrated. At times these affairs have many features, which may seem unlikely to the uninitiated. Especially in long-term "stable" affairs there seems to be collusion among all three members of this triangulated relationship to allow the situation to continue, often for years, and can include other children to be born out of the affair. Triangulated relationships can also cross generational boundaries. A conflicted father–daughter dyad may emerge as a triangulated relationship when the daughter finds a partner and establishes a committed relationship.

Anxiety Flowing to a Nonhuman

Dyadic anxiety can also flow to a nonhuman position, such as in an addiction. Some symbolic meaning often attends the nonhuman corner of this type of triangular configuration. We often hear that an alcoholic has a primary relationship with the bottle, which in a sense then becomes the anxiety regulator for the dyad. In essence, the individual is maintaining a relationship that is more important than the relationship with the dyadic other. People often speak of their psychological disorder in this way. For example, one patient spoke of "his depression" in almost loving and personified terms. The nonhuman corner of the triangle often has attachment-related schematic representations that are unconscious. The man who relates more to his depression than his wife may be connected to a maternal figure who suffered from depression or the alcoholic man may have identified with a figure from the past. What is important is to look for patterns that can suggest treatment interventions, which identify the point of diathesis and address the underlying attachment issues.

A Common Sign of Triangulation—Failure to Launch

A common phenomenon observed by many clinical practitioners that can be better understood with triadic theory occurs when a child's normal developmental progression fails at the point where the young adult is preparing to move into independent adulthood. We call this *failure to launch,* and it usefully illustrates triadic processes. Typical in many of these cases is that the parental subsystem within the family is low in its level of differentiation and may be locked into a highly conflicted state, leading the couple to transmit their anxiety to one of their children. The other children are often spared as this one child has absorbed the negative energy, allowing the couple to remain in a kind of homeostasis. As Bowen illustrated, these triangulated relationships seem to be the result of generations of unresolved family pathology.

CASE EXAMPLE: THE COLLEGE STUDENT TRIANGULATED IN PARENTAL DYAD

The patient is a 20-year-old female who attended college and stopped going to class. She was treated for depression with both psychopharmacology and dynamic psychotherapy. She returned to school and relapsed again, reporting that she stayed in bed and didn't go to class. She lied to her parents until the school called them and said she needed to take a medical leave. The family was seen for evaluation. There were three children of a successful physician and his wife who was a homemaker. Upon history it was revealed that the parents' marriage was highly conflicted and had been troubled for decades. It also was reported that the wife was an active alcoholic who had previously been treated but was currently in an active relapse phase of her alcoholism. The husband reported that he was unable to leave his wife but hated his situation. The young woman who was the identified patient reported that she grew up with a raging alcoholic mother. The father confirmed that his wife would drive their young children around while she was intoxicated and that no

(continued)

CASE EXAMPLE *(continued)*

other parents would allow her to carpool their children because it was known that she was an alcoholic. The patient's father allowed this to continue, growing more angry and hostile over the years. The two other children seemed to have been spared and were working or going to graduate school. The patient was unable to mobilize herself and was being enabled by her father, who supported her financially. It was pointed out to the patient that her behavior was becoming ever more like a "dry drunk" version of her mother. Mother and daughter engaged in fights where they would both become emotionally dysregulated and verbally abusive to one another. The father sometimes was "in the middle" of these episodes. Their daughter would attempt work or school and then collapse for days in bed, mirroring the mother's drinking episodes. On each side of this family there were previous generations of disturbance. The father grew up with a very distant father and was responsible for taking care of his mother. The mother endured being raised by alcoholic parents. These three individuals were locked in what seemed like a death spiral, with each of them being tied to the triangulated threesome and unable to leave without experiencing what seemed like intolerable affect emerging from abandonment issues they all seemed to share at their core. In cases like these it is imperative when one treatment modality is not working to add more components to augment the treatment. In this case, after extensive individual, couples, and alcohol treatment, it was suggested that the siblings who were spared be involved to begin to help their sister detriangulate.

Dynamic Energy in the Triad

As we have described, information flows in relational systems through emotional exchanges and dynamic processes. The dynamic energy contained in extreme triadic configurations is incredibly strong, and when clinicians attempt to restructure these there may be strong reaction. Possessing even a basic knowledge of triadic structures, their function and process will be enormously helpful to clinicians who have not been exposed to these conceptual developments. According to Guerin et al. (1996), "A person emotionally trapped in a triangle is likely, by virtue of being trapped, to suffer some loss of function" (p. 31). Feeling trapped and hopeless increases anxiety and often escalates reactivity to discharge this tension. In a sense the clinician is forming a new triad by engaging parts of the system. A clinician who is pursuing a course of individual psychotherapy with a member of a triangle may experience the other members becoming extremely emotionally activated, which may result in them attempting to undermine the progress made by the patient in individual therapy. Fears of one or another member of the triangle committing suicide are often aroused when these triangles are threatened. These triadic configurations can become so fixed over time that children who are caught in their throes may never establish adult intimate partnerships and may forego more typical stages of psychosexual development. In a few cases we have treated women who have entered treatment in their 30s and 40s and said that they wanted to get married and have children but have never had a sexually intimate relationship. These individuals were often triadically locked in to aging parents who continued to undermine the process of separation and individuation.

The harm done by unaddressed triangulated relationships can be significant as the developmental fixation then leads to a developmental dysynchrony, which then must be addressed, often in terms of mobilizing pathological grief when the person starts realizing that he or she may have missed important life experiences that others in their age cohort have attained. A good clinical clue is that when there is evidence of a developmental fixation the clinician should consider that the patient is triangulated. Guerin et al. (1996) comment: "Triangles get people 'caught,' depriving them of options ensuring that their behavior will continue in the same dysfunctional rut" (p. 35).

Because fixed triads are not highly adaptive, they increase stress and become self-perpetuating, with increased emotional intensity resulting in the formation of more triangulated relational units. This often leads to increasing family disorganization and involvement of numerous agencies such as court, therapy, and school special services (Guerin et al., 1996). The important point clinically is to identify these fixed triangulated relationships and to educate the patients about the way this system limits their life satisfaction and impedes growth. Most people easily recognize these configurations when they are pointed out and explained.

General Triadic Principles and Clinical Implications

What we find useful about understanding the basic function and structure of triadic relationships is how often they are operative in a spectrum of psychological and relational disturbances. The central concept introduced in this chapter is differentiation, which has two components—emotional differentiation and self–other differentiation. Jankowski and Hooper (2012) suggest that the use of the Differentiation of Self Inventory-Revised (DSI-R) (Skowron & Schmitt, 2003) has valuable clinical utility and implications. "When the clinician sees a triangle, he or she can think that it's serving one of the following functions: stabilizing an unstable dyad, displacing dyadic conflict, or avoiding intimacy in the dyad. The structure of the triangle can be assumed to have been formed by underlying tension or anxiety" (Guerin et al., 1996, p. 56). Triadic theory helps us identify and understand the structure of certain common family patterns that might otherwise go unnoticed, and it can be used to guide their restructuring so that the involved members and the family can evolve more adaptively. In the context of a specific example, L'Abate (1986) offered a general principle for changing the disturbed family structure: "For example, the mother is overinvolved with the symptom bearer. Get her to become uninvolved and put someone else in her place—father, grandmother, and so on. That is, *we change the context by changing the pattern or configurations of relationships in the family*" (p. 84).

Additional treatment principles associated with triangulation include the following:

- Undertake individual work with the child who has been triangulated, with an eye toward not only reducing his or her symptomatology, but also toward identifying and repairing any diatheses introduced into the child's personality structure and processes (e.g., internal working model of self and others) as a consequence of the triangulation.

- In the case of the triangulating dyad, work both with the couple and the individuals who comprise the couple to foster emotional differentiation, self–other differentiation, and the development of healthy intimacy.

- Work with the couple to develop tools for healthy conflict resolution and for conjoint management and problem solving of dyadic stressors, which can not only serve as another pathway for building closeness and intimacy but also reduce the risk of the couple triangulating a third party (e.g., a child; a nonhuman "object") as a form of coping when anxiety is experienced or builds within the dyad.

- When triangulation has taken the form of an extramarital affair, the affair must be relinquished as a necessary condition for repair work to be undertaken with the couple.

- The issues within the couple that have spawned the affair are highly emotionally charged, and therefore the process of identifying and working on these issues needs to occur at a pace that both members of the couple can emotionally tolerate.

SUMMARY

Triadic theory offers a way of understanding relational configurations beyond the dyad. Individuals who are low on emotional and self–other differentiation often form dyadic relationships, which are highly conflictual with excessive anxiety. When this anxiety is unmanageable in the dyad, triangulated relationships are often formed, which are implicated in many developmental pathologies and mental disturbances. One of the common issues encountered in clinical practice are triangulated relationships, which express themselves variously in children, affairs, and nonhuman configurations such as substance abuse and so forth. Triangulated relationships are vulnerable points in family systems, which become the diathesis or point of vulnerability. When clinicians identify triangulated relationships, and recurrent patterns are recognized, it becomes easier to offer interventions. When unaddressed, triangulated relationships can attract more parties in an attempt to regulate the anxiety. Until these are restructured, development and differentiation are impeded and thus it is critical to understand the ubiquity of these in human relationships. The goal of treatment is to increase differentiation among the various components of a triangle by enhancing emotional differentiation and self–other differentiation.

REFERENCES

Bowen, M. (1976). Theory in the practice of family therapy. In P. J. Guerin, Jr. (Ed.), *Family therapy: Theory and practice* (pp. 42–90). New York: Gardner Press.

Bray, J. H., & Stanton, M. (Eds.). (2009). *The Wiley-Blackwell handbook of family psychology*. West Sussex, UK: Blackwell Publishing Ltd.

Fogarty, T. F. (1975). Triangles. *The Family, 2*, 11–20.

Fogarty, T. F. (1973–1978). Triangles. In E. G. Pendagast (Ed.), *The family: Compendium I* (pp. 41–49). Rye Brook, NY: Center for Family Learning.

Goleman, D. (1995). *Emotional intelligence*. New York: Bantam Books.

Grewal, D., & Salovey, P. (2005). Feeling smart: The science of emotional intelligence. *American Scientist, 93*, 330–339.

Guerin, P. J., Fogarty, T. F., Fay, L. F., & Kautto, J. G. (1996). *Working with relational triangles: The one-two-three of psychotherapy*. New York: Guilford.

James, W. (1890). *The principles of psychology* (Vol. I & II). New York: Holt.

Jankowski, P. J., & Hooper, L. M. (2012). Differentiation of self: A validation study of the Bowen theory construct. *Couple and Family Psychology: Research and Practice, 1*, 226–243.

L'Abate, L. (1986). *Systemic family therapy*. New York: Brunner/Mazel, Publishers.

L'Abate, L. (2003). *Family psychology: Theory building, theory testing, and psychological interventions*. Lanham, MD: University Press of American.

Lachkar, J. (2004). *The narcissistic/borderline couple: New approaches to marital therapy*. New York: Brunner-Routledge.

Magnavita, J. J. (2012). Advancing clinical science using system theory as the framework for expanding family psychology with unified psychotherapy. *Couple and Family Psychology: Research and Practice, 1*, 3–13.

Magnavita, J. J., & Carlson, T. M. (2003). Short-term restructuring psychotherapy: An integrative model for the personality disorders. *Journal of Psychotherapy Integration, 13*, 264–299.

McWilliams, N. (2011). *Psychoanalytic diagnosis: Understanding personality structure in the clinical process* (2nd ed.). New York: Guilford.

Mayer, J. D., & Salovey, P. (1997). What is emotional intelligence? In P. Salovey & D. Sluyter (Eds.), *Emotional development and emotional intelligence: Educational implications* (pp. 3–31). New York: Basic Books.

Minuchin, S. (1974). *Families and family therapy.* Cambridge, MA: Harvard University Press.

Salovey, P., & Mayer, J. D. (1990). Emotional intelligence. *Imagination, Cognition, and Personality, 9,* 185–211.

Siegel, D. J. (2012). *Pocket guide to interpersonal neurobiology: An integrative handbook of the mind.* New York: Norton.

Skowron, E. A., & Schmitt, T. A. (2003). Assessing interpersonal fusion: Reliability and validity of a new DSI fusion with others subscale. *Journal of Marital and Family Therapy, 29,* 209–222.

Steinglass, P. (1978). The conceptualization of marriage form a systems theory perspective. In T. J. Paolino & B. S. McCrady (Eds.), *Marriage and marital therapy: Psychoanalytic, behavioral and systems theory perspectives* (pp. 298–365). New York: Brunner/Mazel.

Werner, H. (1948). *Comparative psychology of mental development.* New York: International Universities Press.

Werner, H. (1957). The concept of development from a comparative and organismic point of view. In D. B. Harris (Ed.), *The concept of development* (pp. 125–148). Minneapolis: University of Minnesota Press.

Chapter 7

LARGER SYSTEMS

In this final chapter of Part II, we present an overview of the Level IV—*sociocultural–familial* matrix, also referred to as the mesosystem (Magnavita, 2005). The power of the relationship is evident at all levels of the total ecological system (TES). We began this part focusing on the microsystem, with an exploration of the components of the Level I—*intrapsychic–biological* matrix, which represents our *individual personality system* as it is organized in the mind/brain in the form of structures and processes involving, for example, motivations and goals, anxiety/affective pathways, internalized relational schemas, and defensive operations. We then expanded our focus to Level II, the *interpersonal–dyadic* matrix, suggesting that dyads are fundamental molecules of our relational system and showing how attachment and other interpersonal processes affectively bond us. We then broadened our perspective to Level III—the *relational–triadic* matrix, or what occurs in three-person relational units, the building blocks of families and larger relational systems. We discussed how these triadic configurations become problematic when they are *triangulated* or fixed.

The human personality system is expressed in one's relationships and shaped by one's family as well as larger sociocultural forces. A person's dyadic and triadic relationships expand as development progresses, forming family units, peer groups, communities, and cultural structures. Personality and behavior influence and are influenced by the family, social, and political structures we co-create over the course of generations. Mahoney (1991) centered in on the importance of the mesosystem: "Cultural evolution and the transmission of (tacit) beliefs and skills across generations have had far greater significance for human development than have genetic changes that led to the human body as we know it" (p.13). In this chapter, we examine the interplay among the individual personality system, the family system, and the sociocultural structures that not only shape who we are at any given point in time, but also account for ways in which cultural, social, and family knowledge systems are transmitted over time and across generations.

OVERVIEW OF THE SOCIOCULTURAL–FAMILIAL MATRIX AND COMPONENTS

We can depict the components of the sociocultural–familial matrix using a triangle, which shows the interrelationships among the three corners (see Figure 7.1). At the bottom of the triangle is the *individual personality system*. At the upper right corner, we place the *family system,* and at the upper left corner the *sociocultural and political system*. This configuration depicts the multiple systems of influence operative in a human life. We begin by focusing on the bottom point of the triangle, the individual personality system, emphasizing particular features within the context of this triangular matrix.

The Individual Personality System

In Chapter 4 we detailed the essential components of the individual personality system, highlighting key neurobiological and intrapsychic structures and processes. Traditionally, psychologists have conceptualized and studied personality or the "self" as a relatively distinct, self-contained

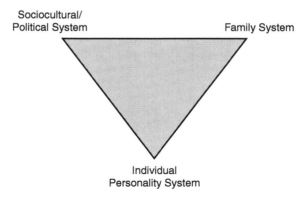

FIGURE 7.1.   *Level IV: Sociocultural–familial matrix.*

structure that is relatively stable over time. More recently, advances in relational and interpersonal neuroscience as well as in other disciplines have altered this conceptualization. Personality is now seen as an emergent phenomenon of the nested structures of the TES. When the system is stressed to the point that it can no longer maintain homeostasis, symptoms may emerge and, if not addressed in some corrective fashion, may over time become stable patterns of thinking, feelings, and acting that are more difficult to change.

Symptoms as an Emergent Phenomenon of the Personality System

What makes a particular individual symptomatic at a certain point in time? Why does an individual's personality system enter into states of dysfunction in which the individual's patterns appear to be self-defeating and self-sabotaging? Although we discuss symptom presentations and how to recognize the underlying structure and patterns in the next part of this volume, we note here that Murray Bowen, advanced for his time, offered insight, maintaining, as do we, that symptoms are an expression of the TES. Hargrove (2009) described the Bowenian perspective:

> Symptoms are not located in the person's character, but develop as an aspect of the struggle of the system to adapt to stressful conditions. It is important to maintain a consistent perspective of symptom development as being a consequence of stress in the system, not a personality characteristic of the individual who absorbs the anxiety for the system. This important principle differentiates systems thinking from individual thinking. (p. 292)

Clinicians using a unified framework nevertheless need to be able to shift perspectives to the individual personality system when necessary and yet maintain cognizance of the entire system and its influence. According to Stanton and Welsh (2012, p. 19): "The ability to shift one's perspective to analyze a situation from a different vantage point facilitates the understanding of complex systems issues and problems." Patients often present for mental health assistance individually, and the temptation for clinicians is to hold tightly to an individual perspective and not take into consideration interpersonal, familial, and societal influences. For example, a clinician who is primarily trained in cognitive-behavioral therapy (CBT) might prematurely treat a woman presenting with an anxiety disorder with an evidence-based CBT approach, when the anxiety might be better understood as a result of problematic dyadic processes with her partner. As such, from the standpoint of treatment, couples therapy may be more responsive to her distress and symptomatology than CBT. The latter might also be clinically useful, but only after the nature of the anxiety is understood and the part of the total system from which it is an emergent phenomenon is identified—a critical contextual factor that distinctly enhances understanding of sources, contents, and other facets of the patient's anxiety (see J.G. Beck, 2010).

Conceptualizing the Individual Personality System

We believe that metaphors and analogies are inherent in science and clinical practice, capturing certain processes in ways that can contribute to our work with a given patient. Metaphors can serve a very powerful explanatory function, allowing us to assimilate and encode into useful packages complicated information. In this respect, a specific metaphor that we have used over time with multiple patients entails likening the concept of personality, as a complex system, to an *operating system* that runs a computer (Magnavita, 2012). Operating systems for computers are continually being upgraded and new versions offered. A powerful computer with an antiquarian operating system will be inefficient and process information slowly, even freezing at times, requiring rebooting of the system. The computer hardware, which is distinct from the operating system, is comprised of motherboards, hard drives, and such, and can be equated to the human body, which houses our brain—our neural hardware. Our operating system, encoded from experiences in our family and larger relational matrices, is our program for how to deal with the information we receive and is comprised of such components as our attachment style, defenses, internalized beliefs, and schema about self and others. We sometimes use this analogy with patients to help them differentiate between that which can be modified through reprogramming or learning, and that which may be more related to hardware issues, which are neurobiological or physical in nature. Accordingly, after we explain the aforementioned analogy, we might say to a patient, "Your operating system is no longer adaptive. It may have been at one time but now it is antiquated and does not allow you to maximize your potential in life." We then explain that these internalized structures (beliefs, schema, ways of viewing self and others) "need to be altered to more accurately reflect what is going on in your life today." A patient suffering from a depressive episode is, in a certain manner, attempting to "reboot" his neurobiological and intrapsychic system. This operating-system metaphor has also been useful when employed to depict dyadic processes: "The operating system defines the action, the movement, the method that people use to connect within a system" (Fogarty, 1976, p. 146).

An operating system is indeed an appropriate metaphor for all levels of the personality system, and where we draw the boundaries is important yet also somewhat murky. Anchin (2003) described the embedded aspects of the individual personality system and the arbitrary nature of where boundaries are marked:

> The patient…is a system in his or her own right, constituted by simultaneously interacting subsystems, and inescapably inter-twined with other systems comprising the social environment. At a more macrolevel of analysis, each of these "individual systems" can also be viewed as subsystem components of the broader system of, e.g., the family, with multiple family systems in turn construable as respective subsystems in its own right, and the point at which a given system can be considered to be just one subsystem component of a broader system, is arbitrary; where one draws boundaries differentiating "subsystem" from "systems" is highly contingent on one's judgment relative to the analytic and/or applied purposes at hand. (p. 337)

We believe that in clinical practice the more one thinks in systemic rather than in linear terms, the more options for intervention will become available. If personality is a system with identifiable interacting compo-nents, we can decide to focus our attention on the specific domain most amenable to change at a particular time. For example, an adolescent who is having difficulty being launched from her nuclear family and whose per-sonality is not highly differentiated may benefit from being de-triangulated from her overly "other-focused" parents, who do not seem to allow emer-gence of the adolescent's self by virtue of being inordinately invested in the outcome, integrally linked to the fact that they are themselves low in their respective levels of self-differentiation. As we have discussed, one's unique individual personality system emerges in dyadic and triadic rela-tionships, which are initially embedded in one's family system. Our clini-cal processes and outcomes improve when can find a *fulcrum point* where our intervention efforts can be focused and leveraged for maximal change.

The Family System

The family system, aptly characterized by Vangelisti (2004) as "the crucible of society" (p. ix), is an essential domain of human functioning and dys-function. Incorporating the family system level is fundamental to a unified approach to formulation and treatment and requires a basic understanding of key features, structures, and processes of family systems; these concepts include but go beyond those introduced in the previous chapter. The spe-cialty of family psychology, which has been formalized into Division 43 (Society for Family Psychology) of the American Psychological Association and its recently launched journal, *Couple and Family Psychology: Research and Practice*, indeed shares much in common with our unifying framework and its emphasis on advanced system thinking. The study of families is by no means new, even though by and large the majority of those trained in mental health disciplines, with the exception of marriage and family therapists and family psychologists, receive very little training in this area. Most clinicians are well versed in models of individual psychotherapy but fewer have formally trained in couples and family methods.

During the early part of the 20th century, Ernest Burgess, considered the father of family studies (Crosbie-Burnett & Klein, 2009), taught one of the first academic courses on families at the University of Chicago and wrote a seminal paper entitled "The Family as a Unity of Interacting Personalities" (Burgess, 1926). He believed that families change and over time create new patterns of relating that result in equilibrium. This is consistent with concepts from family system theory (Crosbie-Brunett & Klein, 2009) and from personality systematics. The family system is a multigenerational configuration of related individuals who generally share lineage, although, as we will discuss, in contemporary society the nature of the family is evolving to include many other configurations. The diverse definitions and changing nature of the family led the National Institute of Mental Health to define the family as a "network of mutual commitment" (Pequegnat & Bray, 1997). The nuclear family is a smaller division of the extended family, and in clinical practice, in addition to receiving treatment as a unit unto itself, is seen in various combinations, for example, the marital/couple dyad, parent–child dyad, and in some cases members outside of the nuclear family are brought in.

According to Crosbie-Burnett and Klein (2009) there is some agreement between sociologists and psychologists about the function of families; they serve to "(a) support the physical development of members, including food, clothing, shelter, (b) educate and socialize children, (c) create an environment supportive of the sexual needs of couples, (d) care for the dependency needs of young, old, ill, and disabled family members, and (e) care for the human emotional needs for affiliation, belonging, and feeling valued" (p. 39). Regardless of what subsystem or individual unit we are focusing on in treatment, we are still operating within the family matrix, and any changes in one member will impact the others. It is critical to keep in mind that no matter what subset of a family is in our office, the shadows of the others are present as well. Therefore, we urge our readers to develop a greater knowledge base in this vital area of unified psychotherapeutics. An excellent reference in this regard is *The Wiley-Blackwell Handbook of Family Psychology* (Bray & Stanton, 2009).

Bray (2009, pp. 151–153) summarized a number of characteristics that are important to consider when working at the family level; these entail:

Family structure and composition. This includes family membership (e.g., a couple with children; a single-parent family) and structure (e.g., a first-marriage family; a cohabitating couple).

Family process. This includes how the family communicates and the functions or outcomes of these communications.

Relationship patterns. This refers to the sequence of communication patterns over time. As but one example, Gottman's research has shown that happy couples express five positive statements to each negative. On the other hand, unhappy couples express one positive to one negative statement, which creates a relational pattern of criticism, contempt, defensiveness, and stonewalling, which in turn is a strong predictor of divorce (Gottman, 1994).

Family affect. This relates to the nature of emotional expression within the family. The tone, volume, and valence of affective expression—positive (e.g., loving and nurturing) versus negative (e.g., hostile and sarcastic)—are predictive of a spectrum of psychological disturbances. Bray elaborates:

> ...the level or volume of affective tone is...important and may range from families in which there is little affect, or affect is overcontrolled, to families in which the volume of either positive or negative affect is very high. Negative affect at a high volume is usually disruptive of family life. Hence there is a widespread acceptance that negative affect is undesirable and in need of therapeutic intervention. (p. 153)

An accumulating body of empirical literature demonstrates that expressed emotions (EEs), characterized by high levels of criticism, hostility, and emotional overinvolvement, are indicators of families whose members are at risk for relapse.

Family organization. This includes the roles and explicit and implicit rules to which the family adheres. Within this category there are three critical elements: "(1) boundaries, (2) decision-making hierarchy, and (3) the distribution of labor and emotional support functions" (Bray, 2009, p. 153).

Family diversity. This refers to ethnic background, cultural influences, socioeconomic status, sexual orientation, and religious affiliation/beliefs. Bray points out that this factor interacts among, and therefore leads to important variations within and across, the previous five factors.

Tuning into and assessing these factors significantly enhances our understanding of family systems. In a certain sense, they tell us "where to look" in the effort to develop clinically meaningful knowledge about a given family. "The ability to recognize trends and patterns within systems is essential to systemic thinking" (Stanton & Welsh, 2012, p. 17). Once we become familiar with specific facets of how families function we are in a much better position to organize our treatment interventions in a focal manner. The most important aspect of a unified approach may well be "the ability to see the system" (Stanton & Welsh, 2012, p. 15). Patterns in systems emerge and reconfigure over time, so it is imperative to refrain from the seduction of static perspectives, which do not afford the opportunity to see process patterns and trends unfold.

The Changing Family Landscape

Notable revisions in the nature of American family life are transpiring (Bianchi, Raley, & Casper, 2012). Social trends suggest that the basic monolithic structure of the traditional nuclear family has significantly changed. Marriage is being delayed and cohabitation has become a popular choice in adult homes at all educational levels (Pasley & Olmstead, 2009). Although marriage remains the overwhelming choice for most people, the rate of divorce indicates that between 40% and 50% of first marriages will end in divorce. Many are postponing parenthood, and childrearing outside of marriage is becoming more common. As crystallized by Walsh (2002), "Family cultures and structures have become increasingly diverse and fluid" (p. 133). Pasley and Olmstead (2009) delineate several clinical implications deriving from these trends that are of importance for practitioners. Chief among these is that clinicians must be prepared to deal with many family forms and structures. In addition to treating traditional married heterosexual families, couple and family therapists need to cultivate skills in working with "gay and lesbian couples, cohabitating families, single-parent families, and divorced and remarried families. Each of these family forms includes complex issues and potential problems [about] which therapists should be educated and trained to treat" (p. 62). Pasley and Olmstead (2009) also emphasize the need for clinicians to develop cultural competence, which includes both knowledge of racial and cultural diversity of families and skills in delivering therapeutic interventions that are tailored to specific racial and cultural contexts and issues (Sue & Zane, 2005; cf. Hardy & Laszloffy, 1995; Hennon & Wilson, 2008; Thomas, 1998; Sherif Trask & Hamon, 2007).

Dysfunctional Family Systems

Clinicians generally do not see functional families in their practice, but rather families in various states of dysfunction. As presented in Table 7.1, there are some common patterns observed in families that provide terms—essentially, denoting points along a dimensional spectrum of family functionality—according to which we can organize the clinical data, for example, high functioning, midrange, and dysfunctional (Beavers & Hampson, 2000; Lewis, Beavers, Gossett, & Phillips, 1976). Empirical investigation may help determine which systems are likely to promote

TABLE 7.1 Clinical Tool: Spectrum of Family Functionality

High Functioning	Midrange	Dysfunctional
Flexibility in family structure & process	Some flexibility in family structure & process	Rigid/chaotic family structure
Capacity for intimacy/ closeness in members	Some capacity for intimacy/closeness	Limited capacity to trust
Flexible internal & external boundaries	Some flexibility	Extreme or diffuse boundaries
Ability to flexibly form three-person relationships	Some tendency to triangulate	Triangulated relationships predominate
Able to navigate family life-cycle transitions	Difficulty with life-cycle transitions	Gets stuck in life-cycle transitions
Ability to acculturate and maintain ethnic identity	Has trouble acculturating	Severe isolation from dominant culture
No evidence of multigenerational pathology	Some pathology	Severe multigenerational pathology
Limited personality dysfunction (PD)	Some personality dysfunction	Multiple members present with PD
Communication patterns are constructive	Mixed positive and negative communication patterns	Communication abusive, contemptuous
Affect expression accepted	Discomfort with affect expression	Hostile or Pollyannaish affect expression

various manifestations of psychopathology. Severely dysfunctional family systems are more likely to be associated with various forms of personality dysfunction and relational disturbances.

Some of the features that have been observed in dysfunctional families include:

- Impermeable or weak external boundaries that separate the family system from others.
- Poor boundaries among family members.
- Disturbed levels of communication and overreliance on primitive defenses.
- Reversal of the parent–child relationships.

- Need for family to revolve around a narcissistic parent.
- Poor emotional differentiation and regulation.
- Emotional malnourishment.
- Financial instability.
- Multigenerational transmission effects (Magnavita, 2000, p. 54).

With regard to this last feature, we underscore that a not uncommon feature of severely dysfunctional family systems is a history of *multigenerational trauma* in the form of neglect; emotional, physical, or sexual abuse; and reversal of parent–child dyadic relations. A careful assessment of generational trauma patterns is imperative. These patterns can be transferred through social learning in the form of modeling, adoption of certain parenting styles, spouse selection, or the results of untreated trauma that perpetuate disturbed attachment patterns across generations. More generally, the multigenerational transmission process is critical to our understanding of forces that shape and result in expressions of psychopathology. In dysfunctional families one frequently finds the effects "of an endless chain of influence linking the developmental experience of each generation to that of its immediate and distant ancestors" (Terkelsen, 1980, p. 43); patterns are thus re-enacted and recreated across generations. There may be certain family themes that are carried on, sometimes being lost in one generation, but then reappearing in another. We strongly recommend that clinicians be alert to deterioration in the mental health and adaptive capacity of the individuals over generations. When there is a worsening of psychopathology as generations unfold, there may be a very tragic series of events that have occurred in previous generations that have never been adequately addressed and should be identified where possible.

Additional features, commonly reported in clinical practice, that may be observed when working with patients that raise the possibility that the family system is dysfunctional include negative reactions at holidays, including increased incidence of depression; dramatically inconsistent private versus public family persona, such that the family is highly dysfunctional but looks like the "model" family to the community; family rationalizations, wherein members joke and romanticize neglect and abuse stories as if they were humorous; numerous family members with evidence of low self-esteem, such that members often underachieve despite their potential and opportunities that present themselves; and a level of chronic misery, entailing families that never seem to thrive or enjoy abundance but rather suffer (Magnavita, 2000). These are among useful features that can heighten the clinician's recognition of certain patterns reflective of dysfunctional family systems and operative as important pathways to adult psychopathology.

In providing a family history, individuals often report that they had "ideal," "normal," or "happy" childhoods and family relations. We advise the clinician to view this initial report with a degree of tentativeness because as more material emerges one might find that there are much deeper trauma nodes that have not been reported. In our experience, many patients do not report more severe experiences with family-related trauma until some trust has been established. Even when we suspect trauma, pushing too hard for disclosure may be damaging to the therapeutic alliance. A patient's tendency to have a somewhat idealized version of his or her childhood is usually not due to a desire to conceal the reality, but rather for many people who grew up in dysfunctional families this is their "normal," what they have known. In this regard, it is important to keep in mind that "perception is reality." Developing an accurate picture of a family system requires time, and this picture will continue to evolve as new information is revealed and further assessments completed.

In his Circumplex Model of Marital and Family Systems, Olson (1996) differentiated three dimensions we find useful in developing our formulation of dysfunction in family cases: (a) family cohesion, (b) family flexibility, and (c) family communication.

Family cohesion is defined *"as the emotional bonding that couples and family members have toward one another. ...* [S]ome of the specific concepts or variables that can be used to diagnose and measure the family cohesion dimensions are emotional bonding, boundaries, coalitions, time, space, friends, decision-making, interests, and recreation. ... *Cohesion focuses on how systems balance separateness versus togetherness"* (Olson & Gorall, 2003, p. 516). There are four levels of cohesion, ranging from disengaged (very low), to separated (low to moderate), to connected (moderate to high), to enmeshed (very high). A very high level of cohesion indicates excessive consensus within the family and a lack of differentiation and autonomy. At the other end of the continuum, very low cohesion reflects limited attachment and weak commitment to the family. Both of these levels, conceptualized as unbalanced, are viewed as creating difficulties for individuals and relationship development in the long run. The mid-levels on this continuum (separated and connected) indicate the experiencing and balancing of emotional closeness with independence and are viewed as optimal for family functioning.

Family flexibility "is the *amount of change in its leadership, role relationships and relationship rules.* The specific concepts include leadership (control, discipline), negotiation styles, role relationships, and relationship rules. The focus of flexibility is on how systems balance stability versus change" (Olson & Gorall, 2003, p. 519). There are four levels of flexibility, ranging from rigid (very low), to structured (low to moderate), to flexible (moderate to high), to chaotic (very high). Unbalanced family systems tend to be chaotic or rigid. Systems that have too little control are characterized by disorganization, and those with too much control exhibit repression.

Whereas family systems that function with chaotic or rigid levels of flexibility over extended time periods are problematic for individuals and family development, systems that fall within the structured to flexible range on the dimension of flexibility are conceptualized as balanced and tend to be more adaptive in response to the demands of changing roles and other challenges; as such, they are more functional over time.

Family communication is considered a facilitating dimension in that it is critical for facilitating movement (i.e., modifications and alterations) in levels of cohesion and flexibility. The ability to listen (reflected, for example, in attentiveness and empathy), to speak for oneself and not others, to self-disclose, to stay on topic, and to convey respect and regard are all indices of family communication. Olson and Gorall (2003, p. 520) reported that several investigations of communication and problem-solving skills in couples and families revealed that systems balanced on the cohesion and flexibility dimensions tend to be characterized by very good communication, whereas systems that are unbalanced on these dimensions tend to have poor communication.

The Marital/Couple Dyad

Although there is a growing trend of single-parent families, the norm remains that marital or couple dyads usually bear the responsibility for effectuating, managing, and advancing the family functions discussed above. Their levels of effectiveness and success in doing so are intimately tied to the quality of their relationship, and thus explicitly considering how the marital or couple dyad functions both within the family and as a unit unto itself is a vital dimension of assessing and evaluating dysfunctional family systems, providing information essential to treatment planning. We turn here to a discussion of this distinct dyadic relationship, noting that, while in the extended family system other dyads (e.g., aunts and uncles, grandparents) may play quite important roles, within the nuclear family the marital/couple dyad is the very hub of the system.

Nichols (1988) indicated that the marital relationship "is inherently more complex and less stable than other family relationships" (p. 5). When a couple decides to marry or make a life-long commitment they are often doing so in an attempt to differentiate from their respective family of origin. In coming together they also begin to develop a couple identity. Underscoring the uniqueness of the marital/couple dyad, Nichols (1988) pointed out:

> Marriage is the lone voluntary relationship in the family. Other family relationships—such as certain stepfamily relationships—share with marriage the possibility of being terminated by divorce, but are not entered into voluntarily in the same way that one moves into marriage. (p. 6)

The marital dyad is a central factor in many clinical presentations, as the patient's relationship with his or her partner exerts a great deal of influence on his or her functioning. Issues of differentiation are also often activated or amplified at certain transition points in the couple's development.

Dysfunctional Marital/Couple Dyads

Couple dynamics in dysfunctional systems are often characterized by hostile and otherwise negatively infused interactions and experiences (Glickauf-Hughes, 1996). Some of the following features are often evident in dysfunctional and distressed couples: pathological jealousy and possessiveness, fragile self-esteem, frequent relationship breakups (and reconciliations), hostile-dependent behavior, power struggles, intermittent loving and abusive behavior, victim–persecutor dynamics, distance–pursuer dynamics, frequent and extreme blaming, problems with boundaries and limits, and explosive fights. In couples characterized by severely dysfunctional dyadic processes, each of the partners are usually suffering from personality dysfunction, and their respective forms of dysfunction often act as attractor states vis-à-vis one another. For example, an individual with a borderline personality organization may be attracted to a narcissistic mate. This couple configuration tends to be highly conflictual and, like other pathological pairings, exerts a bionegative force on their offspring and those pulled into their system.

Dimensions of Marital/Couple Relationships

A sizeable array of factors are involved in influencing where a couple is situated at a given point during the flow of time on the spectrum that ranges from healthy, well-functioning, adaptive, and highly satisfied to pathologically disturbed, dysfunctional, maladaptive, and highly dissatisfied. As noted in Chapter 5, on the one hand many of the issues and processes—for example, attachment, intimacy, autonomy, and reciprocal influence—at play in other meaningful dyadic relationships are also operative in marital/couple dyads. On the other hand, as Nichols (1988) conveys, couple relationships are unique, and factors and processes associated with other dyadic relationships acquire special meaning by virtue of the long-term and romantic nature of the couple relationship. In the following we seek to depict principal components that render this relationship so distinct, bearing in mind the ever-present dialectic between analysis and synthesis—between the "parts" that centrally constitute the marital/couple relationship and the "whole" that emerges from interrrelationships and interactions among these parts. Moreover, while our emphasis is on the marital/couple relationship, our discussion makes clear that, in circumstances where the couple has one or more children, their processes and dynamics are inextricably intertwined with the content and processes of family life—one cannot talk about the couple without talking about the family and vice versa. We also note that our portrayal draws heavily on Mark Karpel's (1994) insightful and comprehensive discussion. Though not labeled as such, Karpel integrates individual and systemic perspectives in specifying an array of significant factors that interactively influence and shape a couple's relationship (cf. Gold, 2001). Characterizing these as "organizing forces [that] constrain and direct interactional patterns between partners and present challenges with which they must grapple" (p. 3), he provides what is in certain respects a metatheoretical framework by virtue of delineating and knitting together essential dimensions of couple relationships.

As with all dyadic relationships of significance, a couple's relationship is founded on the fundamental human need for attachment. Karpel draws analogies between the earliest infant–primary caregiver attachment relationship and the attachment formed in an adult couple relationship, pointing out for example that the latter *"inherits the legacy of attachment,* that is, not only the *universal inborn need* for attachment (which is transferred from the original care-giver to adult partner) but also the partners' *particular experiences* in their respective relationships with their original care-givers, for better or for worse" (pp. 9–10; cf. Clulow, 2000; Johnson & Whiffen, 2003). Underpinned by their mutual attachment needs and the specific vicissitudes of each partner's earlier attachment experiences represented in their respective working models, "a couple's relationship usually begins with *attraction*—with an emotional pull of some kind toward a particular person—however murky its bases may be to the participants" (Karpel, 194, p. 10). Karpel suggests that the specific attraction between partners in a given couple relationship is often a function of innate attachment needs interacting with "the unconscious recognition of something about the partner and the feeling of relating to him or her that in some way resembles the characteristics of the individual's intimate relationships with early care-givers" (p. 12). Further shaping the relationship are the partners' expectations of the relationship, some of which are virtually universal:

> to be cared for and cared about; to be special to someone; to be supported, respected, and treated fairly; to share responsibility for making the relationship work; for their partner to be relatively accessible for physical, nonsexual contact, including touching, kissing, and holding; and an active and, in most cases, monogamous sexual relationship. (p. 13)

However, because needs and longings tied to early attachment relationships are reactivated in couple relationships, these, too, will influence the expectations each partner brings to the relationship. By the same token, expectations set the stage for disappointment, characterized by Karpel as the most universal emotion in couples treatment, such that how the couple deals with this specific emotional state operates as a critical factor influencing the relationship's success or lack thereof. Parenthetically, it is interesting to note the powerful impact of expectations on both the evolution of a couple's relationship and the formation and maintenance of the therapeutic alliance.

As Karpel points out, couple relationships are also contextualized by culture, gender, and time. Culture is a highly variegated, multidimensional construct discussed in greater detail below; however, among central meanings, it encompasses the values, assumptions, and beliefs, and the specific behaviors and practices that derive from those cognitive–affective contents and processes that are shared in common by a given ethnocultural group and that distinguishes them from other ethnocultural groups (Carpenter-Song, Norquest Schwallie, & Longhofer, 2007; Culture Matters, n.d.; Hennon & Wilson, 2008; Lopez & Guarnaccia, 2005). In Western industrial countries, both traditional and changing values and assumptions impinge on couple relationships. Expectations of the freedom to choose one's romantic partner rather than having this arranged and of sexual monogamy are among enduring traditional Western values and assumptions, while "the growing emphasis on *individual* development and fulfillment as a counterweight to the traditional emphasis on marital and family togetherness" (Karpel, 1994, p. 16) may well represent the most prominent change in Western culture that, continuing on through the first quarter of the 21st century, continues to influence couple relationships. By the same token, the surge of interest in multiculturalism has brought to the fore that a given couple's values and assumptions may be *inter*cultural (Hennon & Wilson, 2008), a mixture of those tied to both Western culture and those that may have been indigenous to their respective family-of-origin and other institutions in which they have been and may continue to be involved. Trends in couple relationships also suggest that *differences* in cultural background are on the rise (see Fincham & Beach, 2010), providing a potential source of relational enrichment—but also of conflict and discord.

In heterosexual couples, inescapable gender-based biological differences operate as another contextualizing set of factors, and these differences are themselves strongly interwoven with sociocultural factors that strongly shape what it means to be male or female. Karpel (1994) identified four areas, each encompassing a complex array of considerations, in which gender's organizing influence on a couple's relationship is most evident: "differences in socialization, differences in legal and economic status and power, differences involving childbirth and parenting, and differences in sexuality" (p. 18). Tied to these areas but sufficiently salient to warrant being separated out, we can add gender differences in pathways that link the marital relationship to physiological mechanisms operative in physical health outcomes (Kiecolt-Glaser & Newton, 2001). Specifically, differences are evident in women's self-representations (more interdependent and relational than men's), traits (more characterized by the other-focused trait of communion, in contrast to the stronger presence of the self-focused trait of agency in men), and marital roles (reflected, e.g., in women's greater involvement in domestic chores); these differences render women "more responsive than men, psychologically and physiologically, to the emotional tone of marital relationships (Cross & Madson, 1997b; Helgeson, 1994)" (p. 474). This heightened responsiveness in turn increases married women's vulnerability—directly through effects on biological systems (e.g., the cardiovascular, endocrine, immune, neurosensory, and neurophysiological systems) and indirectly through greater risk of depression and compromised health habits—to physiological impairments and problematic physical health outcomes. And, through the circularity of bidirectional influence processes, physical health outcomes likely feed back to affect the nature and quality of the marital relationship (Burman & Margolin, 1992).

In conjunction with culture and gender, time serves as another contextualizing force influencing couple relationships. In the case of married couples with children, time's powerful impact operates particularly through the developmental tasks and challenges posed by specific stages of the family life cycle. Carter and McGoldrick (2005) described six successive stages through which families progress:

1. Leaving home: Single young adults
2. The joining of families through marriage: The new couple
3. Families with young children
4. Families with adolescents
5. Launching children and moving on
6. Families in later life (p. 2)

Characteristically, and quite accurately, life cycle frameworks view the transition from one stage to the next as invariably associated with varying degrees of stress and disruption (Karpel, 1994; Magnavita, 2005; Walsh, 2003); as such, to the extent that coping processes are inadequate or dysfunctional, a given transition can also become the breeding ground for the emergence of individual, marital, and/or family distress and symptomatology.

However, as Gerson (2010) insightfully points out, "families, and family members, don't just pass through stages; for a time they live there" (p. 131). Thus, while a family and its members over time may successfully negotiate the transition between any two given stages, periods of stability within a given stage may also be interspersed with new challenges associated with that stage's distinct developmental tasks, reigniting individual, couple, and/or family stress processes. To illustrate, Carter and McGoldrick (2005) indicated that among developmental tasks of the stage of families with adolescents is "shifting of parent/child relationships to permit [the] adolescent to move in and out of [the] system" (p. 2). This shift may proceed with relative smoothness provided the adolescent is moving in and out of the system to get together with same-sex peers. However, perturbation in the positive tenor of this individual, couple, and family process may be introduced if, starting during the summer before her junior year in high school, the adolescent's movement out of the system steadily increases in frequency and duration by virtue of starting and developing her first romantic relationship with a partner of the opposite sex. This change may spark disruptions in the more or less steady state of interpersonal patterning that up to this point has been transpiring between the adolescent and her parents. Impairments in the couple relationship may also ensue to the extent that there is parental disagreement and/or conflict about the normativeness of their child's change and in how to respond to her increasing autonomy and desire for emotional connection outside the family. In this illustration, then, even though the family is still in the stage of "families of adolescents," a new iteration of the developmental task of "shifting of parent/child relationships to permit [the] adolescent to move in and out of [the] system" has presented itself, a potential stressor at individual, couple, and family levels depending on how all parties to the situation appraise and conjointly negotiate this shared developmental challenge and how they individually and jointly cope with its intrapersonal effects.

This example also provides a context for illustrating that a set of skills and capacities important to a couple's—as well as an individual's and family's—effective navigation of life cycle stages, events, and transitions is the capacity for effectively negotiating the dialectic between order and disorder, between stability and change (Karpel, 1994). Falicov (1988) nicely crystallized this point specifically in relation to transitional periods, while also generalizing more broadly to the *multiple* developmental challenges of the life cycle:

> The fundamental human struggle to preserve the old while striving to produce or adapt to the new is nowhere more vividly experienced than during life cycle transitions. An interactional or systems approach to human development calls for a dialectical integration of the tendency toward continuity and the tendency toward change (Gollin, 1981; Hultsch & Pemons, 1979; Urban, 1978). … For a family to be both *flexible and stable*…

the tendencies toward change and discontinuity need to occur *simultaneously* with the tendencies toward continuity and stability (Melitto, 1985). What is needed for healthy adaptation and/or coping with life cycle or other developmental challenges is an integration or synthesis of two types of processes, so that a sense of continuity, identity, and stability can be maintained while new behavioral patterns are evolving. (p. 41)

Maintaining stability while also supporting change, both within the family as a unit *and* within their relationship (Karpel, 1994), requires that the couple, within the motivating, supportive, and sustaining context of their affectional bond, be able to draw—at different times and in different combinations—upon a blend of different skills and capacities. These include, but are certainly not limited to, processes of acceptance, love, and respect (Gottman, 1994; Harvey, Pauwels, & Zickmund, 2005); communication (e.g., Kelly, Fincham, & Beach, 2003); empathy (Walsh, 2003); individual self-regulation and coping (Papp & Witt, 2010); problem solving (e.g., Jacobson & Margolin, 1979); conflict resolution and compromise (Nichols, 2005); dyadic coping (e.g., Bodenmann, 2005, 2007, 2010; Bodenmann & Randall, 2012; Revenson, Kayser, & Bodenmann, 2005); and emotional and relational positivity (Fincham & Beach, 2010; Fincham, Stanley, & Beach, 2007). For the family life cycle to unfold more successfully than not, the partners composing the marital dyad must be at the helm, functioning as co-conductors managing and orchestrating the ongoing dialectical dance between stability and change.

In addition to the forces of attachment, attraction, and expectations, and the contextual factors of culture, gender, and time, Karpel (1994) identified eight key challenges that further organize and shape the development of the couple relationship: commitment, the dialectic of autonomy and attachment, fairness and trust, sexuality, communication, the "unconscious matrix" of the relationship, its wider relational context, and the importance of vitality.

Nichols (2005) defined commitment as "how and to what extent the partners value the marital [or couple] relationship and their intentions pertaining to its maintenance and continuation" (p. 35). As Karpel (1994) points out, some degree of commitment is essential if the partners are to experience psychological safety and stability. Moreover, "commitment plays an especially important role in the preservation of the relationship when stress and conflict are high and gratifications are low. At these times, commitment is the clamp that can hold a damaged relationship together until stress is reduced and emotional repairs made" (p. 30).

The dialectic between autonomy and attachment speaks to the distinction between "I," a separate individual self in one's own right, and "We," the special and unique unity interactively and intersubjectively created and experienced when the "I" and the "You" merge (cf. Fergus & Reid, 2001). As Karpel (1994) points out, this is an oscillating process: "Partners in a healthy couple relationship move in and out of these states throughout their hour-to-hour, day-to-day existence. This smooth shifting between the states of 'I' and 'We' may go unrecognized by partners but it represents a significant developmental accomplishment" (p. 31). Problems can arise when either or both of the partners tends in the direction of excessive distance and separation by virtue of the predominance of "I" or, due to overemphasis on the "We," in the direction of undifferentiatedness, fusion, and/or clinging dependence. Healthy oscillation in the dialectic between autonomy and attachment is responsive to context (see McNulty & Fincham, 2012; Fincham & Beach, 2010) and enhanced by acceptance of and respect for each partner's *internally* oscillating needs for separateness and connection.

Over the lifetime of a couple's relationship, the partners must also deal with issues of fairness and trust—what Karpel (1994) poignantly characterizes as "the ethics of intimacy" (p. 33). Fairness is inevitably a challenge because three sets of interests exist in the relationship: those of each partner and those of the relationship. A mutual sense of fairness evolves and is maintained to the extent that these three sets of interests are equitably met—not in the sense of the exact accounting that might be found in the numbers in a ledger, but rather in ways that over time enable both partners to feel comfortable with the balance between "give and take." When the sense of fairness is damaged, repair, for example, meaningful apology and forgiveness, is necessary (Fincham, 2009; Fincham, Beach, & Davila, 2004; Fincham, Stanley, & Beach, 2007). Feelings of trust are intimately bound up with fairness: "Beyond their individual capacities for trust... the development of trust in any particular relationship depends on the *trustworthiness*, that is, the action, of the partner. Is the partner dependable? Reliable? Fair? Does he or she keep his or her word? Trust may not be everything in a relationship but, without it, there can be little else" (p. 36).

Sexuality also powerfully shapes the couple relationship. "Longings for sexual satisfaction are central to most couple relationships; they derive from physiological needs, cultural expectations, and needs for attachment, intimacy, and passionate vitality in a relationship. The power of these longings makes the quality of a couple's sexual relationship and the quality of their relationship as a whole inseparable" (Karpel, 1994, p. 38). The strong association between a couple's sexual satisfaction and relationship satisfaction is consistently borne out by research (e.g., Byers, 2005; Litzinger & Gordon, 2005), and indeed, couples who engage in more frequent and satisfying sex are more likely to stay together than couples who experience less frequent and less satisfying sex (Sprecher & Cate, 2004). The wide array of factors that can introduce complications and difficulties into a couple's sexual relationship can originate from biological, individual, or systemic sources (see Harvey, Wenzel, & Sprecher, 2004; Karpel, 1994, chapter 15), and if not effectively addressed by the couple, can contribute significantly to eroding relational satisfaction, stability, and longevity.

Marital satisfaction hinges on a host of factors and processes (see, e.g., Bradbury, Fincham, & Beach, 2000; Fincham & Beach, 2010; Sternberg & Hojiat, 1997; Twenge, Campbell, & Foster, 2003), and while sexual satisfaction is among them, so, too, is effective communication (Kelly et al., 2003; Litzinger & Gordon, 2005; Olson & Gorall, 2003). Karpel (1994) highlighted three important functions served by communication in couple relationships: from the standpoint of intimacy and closeness, it is an essential vehicle for achieving emotional connectedness; from a practical perspective, it is instrumental in enabling couples to conjointly steer their relationship in reflected-upon, purposive directions through dialogue, discussion, and decision making; and from an ethical standpoint, it is a mechanism through which partners can renegotiate particular terms of their "contract," their customary patterns of give-and-take, in the service of maintaining "the balance of fairness in the relationship" (p. 41). By the same token, as McLemore and Hart (1982) wisely point out, "communication is not a panacea" (p. 230). This sobering reality is no doubt due in part to embedded complexities that infuse communication processes and thereby influence their intent, perceived meanings, and impacts. For example, it is important to bear in mind distinctions between the "report" (linguistic, denotative) and "relationship" (emotional, connotative) levels of communication (Kiesler, 1982, 1996); that while during any given interaction the communications flowing back and forth may be more positively or negatively valenced, the impact of any such communication may be subtly influenced by the more recent *ratio* between positive and negative communication in the couple's interactions (Kelly et al., 2003; Fincham & Beach, 2010); and that communication is both verbal and nonverbal (Jones & LeBaron, 2002; Manusov & Patterson, 2006), and therefore the degree of congruence or incongruence between these two channels will also exert influence (Boland & Follingstad, 1987; Duke & Nowicki, 1982; Le Roux, 2002; Zimmer, 1983). Context and still other moderating factors further influence the meanings and effects of communication between partners. On the basis of their review of empirical literature on couple communication, Kelly et al. (2003) concluded, "there is no simple formula for functional communication in couples. The link between communication and satisfaction is likely to vary according to contextual stressors, developmental transitions, gender, and the temporal period over which satisfaction is being predicted" (p. 743).

Communication and the patterns of couple relating of which they are a part may also be colored and shaped to varying degrees by "the unconscious matrix of the relationship" (Karpel, 1994). This encompasses schemas, including images or representations (Karpel, 1994, p. 48), of self and/or of others developed in the context of earlier attachment relationships that play some determinative role in the couple's relational dynamics: "The vicissitudes of these early attachments shape the 'relational profile' of each partner—his or her characteristic ways of forming close emotional attachments with another person. The fit between the partners' relational profiles forms the 'unconscious matrix' of the relationship and organizes interactional patterns between them" (p. 49). When recurrent problems or trauma (small or big "t") in early attachment have been encountered, these images or representations of self or of the early caregiver(s) are likely to contain toxic elements, and under certain activating conditions are projected into the couple relationship with one's partner, introducing distressogenic distortions and processes into the relationship. Couched in terms discussed above, this is tantamount to an individual playing out a particular maladaptive interpersonal transaction cycle—a transference—with his or her partner within the context of the interpersonal–dyadic triangle. This dysfunctional interactional loop may be all the more entrenched and recurrent to the extent that *each* partner's relational schemas contain toxic images or representations that are complementary to and hence intersect with those of their partner, resulting in a recurring, co-scripted loop painful to both, yet seemingly unbreakable. In terms used earlier, it is as if the partners' respective maladaptive schemas operate as attractors, each self-defeatingly, yet irresistibly, pulling one toward the other. However, whether one partner's transference predominates or the couple is locked into a *mutual* transference, Karpel (1994) eloquently described the challenge facing the couple:

> The challenge…is to be able to separate then-and-there from here-and-now, to be able to see beyond the most extreme and destructive projections in order to see at least some of the reality of the actual partner. This means trying to separate what is going on *within* the self from what is going on *within* the partner and *between* the two of them. … Distinguishing then from now, and within from between involves an effort to differentiate oneself from past and present relational contexts (Bowen, 1978), to contain distressing affect instead of simply discharging it at one's partner and to listen sympathetically to the partner's description of his or her own experience instead of insisting deafly on one's own. It requires an ability to look at one's own possible contributions to relationship difficulties as well as an effort to meet the distortions of the partner with, ideally, both love and some confidence and firmness about the ways in which they do not fit one's own experience, feelings, and behavior. It is a subtle but immensely important process

that occurs for some couples through some form of therapy and for others through the accretion of years, or even decades, of "life lessons" in the relationship; for still others, it never occurs because the power of the distortions finally overwhelms the resources that might have corrected them. (pp. 53–54)

Even when its components and effects are less dysfunctional than described above, the unconscious matrix of the relationship is operative insofar as each member of the couple's self–other schemas, if only in their foundations, bear some coloring from attachment experiences in their respective family-of-origin—underscoring the inevitability of intergenerational components in couple relationships (see Weeks & Treat, 2001).

While the unconscious matrix of the relationship reflects the influence of internalized relationships from the past, couples must deal with the existential fact that their relationship exists within the context of a wider network of present-day relationships as well—for example, with parents, siblings, friends, neighbors, and coworkers (Karpel, 1994). These significant others can serve as resources or as threats:

Family, friends, and others can provide safety and stability, a sense of belonging, and concrete and emotional support in times of stress. They can dilute the pressure to have needs met within the couple relationship.

However, they may also impinge on the couple's privacy, limit their ability to take control over their lives, foster conflict, and damage trust within the relationship. (p. 44)

A central issue is the nature and dynamicism of the boundary that the couple co-creates around their relationship. Karpel (1994) cites Minuchin's (1974) axiom that the couple's challenge is to "develop boundaries that are firm but flexible ... that preserve the integrity and uniqueness of the couple relationship while fostering satisfying relationships with family and friends. Both partners engage in an ongoing effort to balance what they owe to their partners and to others (as well as to themselves), so that no one is seriously and permanently 'short-changed'" (p. 44).

Amid the vicissitudes of the couple's relationship as it temporally unfolds, the partners are also challenged to maintain a sense of vitality (Karpel, 1994). In a relationship characterized by vitality, the partners experience zest, verve, and life. In Karpel's (1994) words, "There is some kind of 'juice' or 'pizzazz.'. ... [A] relationship with vitality also suggests the experience of fun, of 'bright moments,' of enjoyment. This implies some degree of *spontaneity*. ... one [also] senses that an awareness of the *specificity* of the partner has been preserved. ... that each partner knows exactly who the other is with all of his or her peculiarities, and 'gets off' on at least some of them" (pp. 46–47). Karpel also makes the excellent point that with vitality comes resilience—there is a strength to the connection that reduces the couple's vulnerability to internal and external threats and that "functions as a relational resource, facilitating joint coping and therefore making it more likely that the relationship will endure" (p. 47). When, over the long haul, vitality goes awry, the relationship may become suffused by apathy, lifelessness, and indifference:

> The most common pathological pattern involving vitality is the relationship in which the partners interact in an automatic way, in which there is little passion, intensity, or spontaneity between them and little sense that they know and appreciate the idiosyncrasy of the other. The challenge for couples is to preserve this quality of vitality beyond the honeymoon phase of the relationship, to preserve passion, connection, and spontaneity, and to hopefully at least occasionally "have a hoot." (p. 47)

Resilience and Flourishing in Couples and Families

Just as strengths, assets, and positive characteristics have, as discussed in Chapter 2, become increasingly incorporated into the examination and understanding of the individual personality system within the context of stress, coping, and psychological health and disorder, the study and conceptualization of couples and families reflects increasing interest in the nature and effects of resources and strengths that these interpersonal systems can bring to dealing with life's challenges and adversities. As in the case of the individual, the concept of resilience is key. For example, defining the latter as "the ability to withstand and rebound from disruptive life challenges" (p. 1), Walsh (2003) has presented an elegant research-informed "family resilience meta-framework" (p. 16) that provides a conceptual roadmap for guiding intervention with families confronted by stress associated both with "predictable, normative" (p. 4) stages and transitions in the family life cycle, for example the birth of the first child, and with "unexpected or untimely events, such as the death of a young parent" (p. 4). Walsh makes clear that "the concept of family resilience entails more than managing stressful conditions, shouldering a burden, or surviving an ordeal. It involves the potential for personal and relational transformation and growth that can be forged out of adversity (Boss, 2001)" (p. 3). She combines ecological and developmental perspectives—that is, "multiple, recursive influences involving individual, families, and larger social systems" (p. 3) and the "timing [of a crisis event] in

TABLE 7.2 Key Processes in Family Resilience

Belief Systems

1. Make Meaning of Adversity

   - View resilience as relationally based vs. "rugged individual"
   - Normalize, contextualize adversity and distress
   - Sense of coherence: crisis as a meaningful, comprehensible, manageable challenge
   - Causal/explanatory attributions: How could this happen? What can be done?

2. Positive Outlook

   - Hope, optimistic bias: confidence in overcoming odds
   - Courage and en-*courage*-ment; affirm strengths and focus on potential
   - Active initiative and perseverance (Can-do spirit)
   - Master the possible; accept what can't be changed

3. Transcendence and Spirituality

   - Larger values, purpose
   - Spirituality: faith, congregational support, healing rituals
   - Inspiration: envision new possibilities; creative expression; social action
   - Transformation: learning, change, and growth from adversity

Organizational Patterns

4. Flexibility

   - Open to change: rebound, reorganize, adopt to fit new challenges
   - Stability through disruption: continuity, dependability, follow-through
   - Strong authoritative leadership: nurturance, protection, guidance
     - Varied family forms: cooperative parenting/caregiving teams
     - Couple/Co-parent relationship: equal partners

5. Connectedness

   - Mutual support, collaboration, and commitment
   - Respect individual needs, differences, and boundaries
   - Seek reconnection, reconciliation of wounded relationships

6. Social and Economic Resources

   - Mobilize kin, social and community networks; seek models and mentors
   - Build financial security; balance work/family strains

Communication/Problem solving

7. Clarity

   - Clear, consistent messages (words and actions)
   - Clarify ambiguous information; truth seeking/truth speaking

(continued)

TABLE 7.2 (Continued)

8. Open Emotional Expression

- Share range of feelings (joy and pain, hopes and fears)
- Mutual empathy; tolerance for differences
- Take responsibiliy for own feelings, behavior; avoid blaming
- Pleasurable interacions; humor

9. Collaborative Problem solving

- Creative brainstroming; resourcefulness; seize opportunities
- Shared decision making; conflict resolution: negotiation, fairness, reciprocity
- Focus on goals; take concrete steps; build on success; learn from failure
- Proactive stance: prevent problems; avert crises; prepare for future challenges

From Walsh (2003, p. 7). Copyright 2003 by John Wiley & Sons. Reprinted with permission.

individual and family life-cycle passages" (p. 4)—to forge a multisystemic approach, presented in Table 7.2, for identifying and targeting "key family processes that can reduce stress and vulnerability in high-risk situations, foster healing and growth out of crisis, and empower families to overcome prolonged adversity" (p. 6).

Fincham and Beach (2010) also point out and commend the growing literature on the study of resilience in couples and families, but they place this concept within a broader context, arguing for the need to develop a positive relationship science in which the construct of *"relationship flourishing"* (p. 5, emphasis added) is central. In this context, they reflect on the study of family resilience, noting the strengths of this framework but maintaining that still more is possible and desirable:

> In this literature, stress and crisis are not viewed as inherently negative but rather as containing opportunities for fostering healing and growth (H. L. McCubbin & McCubbin, 1988; M. A. McCubbin & McCubbin, 1996; Walsh, 2003) as well as the potential for less-favorable outcomes. This is indeed valuable insofar as it goes, but it does not go far enough. Specifically, strengths are not examined as an end in themselves, as integral to the realization of a flourishing relationship. Instead, the positive tends to be valued because of its potential to buffer the negative or to facilitate recovery from a crisis.

> This is no doubt valuable, but it would be a logical error to assume that what buffers the negative or facilitates recovery, or both, is the same as that which initiates or promotes health and flourishing. (p. 9)

The study of resilience, along with such other processes as social support and affectional expression, secure attachment, and transformative processes (Fincham et al., 2007), are thus viewed as foundations for developing a positive relationship science, but—explicitly noting that benefits can accrue to clinical intervention—Fincham and Beach (2010) advance the enticing perspective that "without understanding of optimal relationship functioning, flourishing, our understanding of marriage and family will remain incomplete" (p. 19). More broadly, they view positive relationship science both as "a necessary fourth pillar of positive psychology" (p. 18), alongside the existing three pillars of "'positive experiences and positive individual traits, and the institutions that facilitate their development' (Duckworth, Steen, & Seligman, 2005, p. 630)" (p. 17), and as offering a rich domain for cross-disciplinary scholarship.

The Sociocultural System

The social level of the biopsychosocial model not only includes the dyadic, couple, and family system levels of human being and experience, but also the highly complex level of sociocultural systems and their ingrainedness in "neighborhoods, villages, and social networks" (Lopez & Guarnaccia, 2005, p. 21) as well as in society more broadly. Earlier we characterized culture as the values, assumptions, and beliefs, and the specific behaviors and practices that derive therefrom, that are shared in common by a given ethnocultural group and that distinguishes that group from other ethnocultural groups. Bearing in mind that categories are fluid, membership in a cultural group can be defined in terms that are, for example, nationalistic (e.g., American, Russian, French), ethnic (e.g., Hispanic or Latino, Asian American), racial (e.g., African American, White, Asian), social (e.g., gay, lesbian, bisexual, transgender, heterosexual), or religious (e.g., Muslim, Jewish, Christian; Lee & Farrell, 2006). Intimately tied to a group's values, beliefs, assumptions, behaviors, and practices, components of culture include—as expressions or manifestations of these clusters of covert and overt processes—traditions, language, customs, symbols, and the arts (Aranda & Knight, 1997; Lee & Farrell, 2006). It is, in essence, "a group's way of life" (Aranda & Knight, 1997, p. 342).

Moreover, as valuably explained by Lopez and Guarnaccia (2005), culture is not a static phenomenon, but rather an ongoing, dynamic process. Culture "lives" in neighborhoods (e.g., Rosenstein, 2009), families (e.g., Bennett, Wolin, & McAvity, 1988; Hennon & Wilson, 2008), couples (e.g., Framo, 1976; Hsu, 2001), and in the heads of individuals (Hong, Morris, Chiu, & Benet-Martinez, 2000), powerfully affecting structures, processes, and functioning at each of these levels, but the actions of these systems also act back on and influence the nature of culture, and thus the latter changes—although at rates difficult to discern with precision—by virtue of reciprocal effects; it both shapes and is "a product of group values, norms, and experiences, as well as of individual innovations and life histories" (Lopez & Guarnaccia, 2005, p. 21). Benet-Martinez and Oishi (2008) nicely captured this important point:

> although many studies have established that cultural forces influence the expression of personality (i.e., culture→personality effects; Benet-Martinez & Karakitapoglu-Aygun, 2003), almost no attention has been given to the processes by which personality may in turn influence culture (personality→culture effects). Evidence from recent studies shows that our personalities shape the cultural contexts in which we live by influencing both micro- (e.g., personal spaces, music preferences, content and style of personal web pages; Gosling, Ko, Mannarelli, & Morris, 2002; Rentfrow & Gosling, 2003; Vazire & Gosling, 2004) and macro- (e.g., political orientation, social activism; Jost, Glaser, Kruglanski, & Sulloway, 2003) cultural elements. (p. 559)

Culture evolved and increased in complexity as cortical regions; in the brain developed and allowed *Homo sapiens* to become the dominant species on earth. Henriques (2011), within the context of his far-reaching Tree of Knowledge System metatheory that seeks to describe and explain "the [hierarchical] evolution of complexity" (Henriques, 2003, p. 155)—that is, from matter to life, from life to mind, and from mind to culture—has offered the intriguing postulate that the evolution of culture in *Homo sapiens* is rooted in the evolution of language. The latter is a tremendously complex and powerful tool, which developed through natural selection and gave others direct access to one's thoughts and intentions. Linked to other concepts and propostions, Henriques argues that, as a consequence, effectively navigating the social world—entailing effectiveness in exerting influence and attaining acceptance—necessitated that human beings develop the capacity to justify and legitimize to others their thoughts, feelings, actions, and intentions; in this context, Henriques maintains that culture (e.g., religion) evolved as "large-scale justification systems providing the rules and patterns for acceptable behaviors" (Henriques, 2004, p. 1217).

The evolutional—and enduring—importance of larger groups may also be tied to the attachment system and its importance to individual development, as explained by Perry (2009):

> For the vast majority of the last 200,000 years, humans have lived in hunter-gatherer clans in the natural world. The size of our living groups was small—40 to 60 people. These multigenerational, multifamily groups were the main source of safety from the dangers of the world. Our survival depended upon

the ability to communicate, bond, share, and receive from other members of our family and clan. Without others, the individual could not survive in the natural world. Then, and today, the presence of familiar people projecting the social-emotional cues of acceptance, compassion, caring, and safety calms the stress response of the individual: "You are one of us, you are welcome, you are safe." This powerful positive effect of healthy relational interactions on the individual—mediated by the relational and stress-response neural systems—is at the core of relationally based protective mechanisms that help us survive and thrive following trauma and loss. Individuals who have few positive relational interactions (e.g., a child without a healthy family/clan) during or after trauma have a much more difficult time decreasing the trauma-induced activation of the stress response systems and therefore will be much more likely to have ongoing symptoms (i.e., there will be more prolonged and intense activation of the stress response systems and, hence, a "use-dependent" alteration in these systems). This capacity to benefit from relational interactions is, in turn, derived from our individual developmental experiences. (p. 246)

In this vein, it is conceivable that cultural institutions evolved to provide its members with not only valuable large-scale justification systems, but also, on an ever-expanding scale, with innumerable opportunities to meet their hard-wired needs for attachment bonding, experiencing mutuality and connection, and, integrally related, the safety and security essential to life-span growth and development (Anchin, 2008).

Be that as it may, culture is the purview of humankind, and at the broadest level "it comprises accumulated learning, prescriptions, and proscriptions" (Bacciagaluppi, 2012, p. 216) that operate as "the nongenetic blueprint for living that is passed from one generation to the next" (Prince, cited in Kiesler, 1999, p. 129). As Csikszentmihalyi (1993) astutely points out, culture is pragmatically imperative, but from the standpoint of the ethnocentrism that it can breed, not without its dangers:

By now, to be human we need the instructions transmitted through culture almost as much as we need genetic instructions. How else would we talk, read, count, and think? The genes cannot teach these skills; we must learn them from women and men who speak our language, from the knowledge stored in books and other symbols systems. But in the process of teaching us how to be human, culture begins to make its claims. Just as genes use the body as a vehicle for their own

reproduction, a culture also tends to use individuals as vehi-
cles for its own survival and growth. In order to ensure this
end, it must convince us of its superiority. (p. 71)

Mapped onto the sociocultural–familial matrix in Figure 7.1, the
power of sociocultural blueprints is vividly illustrated in Hennon and
Wilson's (2008) comparative analysis of family life in 17 countries around
the globe. Facets of family structuring and functioning differentially
affected by sociocultural context include parenting styles and practices,
couple-formation and marital dynamics, perspectives on aging and
approaches to caregiving vis-à-vis elderly family members, sexual practices, household division of labor, views on and extent of cohabitation
and single parenting, attitudes toward marital dissolution, the value of
children, gender-linked differences in education, employment, and leisure, and the nature of characteristic stressors on and coping processes
within families.

However, as Haworth-Hoeppner (2000) points out, it is misleading to
view culture as purely deterministic, that is, as a unitary force that exerts
causal influence independent of the social contexts in which it operates.
Rather, as well illustrated by her study of the conditions under which eating disorders arise, family mediates the influence of culture. Consistent
with the configuration of influence processes represented in the sociocultural–familial matrix shown in Figure 7.1, her conceptual summarization
captures the manner in which cultural values operate through the family nexus to influence the individual personality system: "cultural ideas
about weight [e.g., the value American culture places on female thinness]
are mediated by interactions that take place in the family [e.g., weight is
among the main themes of family discourse] and that are linked to the
construction of body image [i.e., weight thus becomes central to self-iden-
tity]" (p. 224). Indeed, it is difficult to imagine culture operating other than
through meditational structures and processes. As Benet-Martínez and
Oishi (2008) point out, "Culture is *transmitted through* language, media messages, cultural practices and institutions, values and artifacts, and through
the modeling of behavior (Cohen, 1996; Markus & Kitayama, 1994)" (p. 542,
emphasis added). The family is among major structures through which these
transmissional mechanisms operate, but certainly other social groups—for
example, those associated with peers, the neighborhood, religion, the work
place, or leisure-time activities—function as additional contexts that transmit, through their dialogical contents and interactional processes, cultural
and/or subcultural values, practices, and traditions.

Through meditational transmission by social groups and social
processes, culture becomes encoded in the mind/brain of the individual and in turn shapes personality as well. A sampling of personality structures and processes that show culture-specific effects include

affect (e.g, the desirability/undesirability and verbal labeling of certain emotional states; see Benet-Martinez & Oishi, 2008; cf. von Scheve & von Luede, 2005), bases of self-esteem (Hewitt, 2005), internalized gender role expectations (Sue, 2005), the nature and sources of well-being (Benet-Martinez & Karakitapoglu-Aygune, 2003; Diener & Suh, 2000; Tov & Diener, 2007), perceived control over the ability to achieve desired outcomes and avoid undesired ones (Thompson, 2005), formation of self-identity (Cote & Levine, 2002), and styles of thinking (e.g., holistic and dialectic versus analytic; see Benet-Martinez & Oishi, 2008). By the same token, in the same way that families and other social groups *mediate* culture, thereby rendering its effects probabilistic rather than deterministic (Benet-Martinez & Oishi, 2008), individuals play some role in moderating the extent to which and how culture exerts influence. In this regard, Haworth-Hoeppner (2000, p. 213) cites Swidler's (1986) useful characterization of culture as "a 'tool kit' or repertoire from which actors select differing pieces for constructing lines of action." An example provided by Swidler (1986) places this conception in an experience-near context, providing a nuanced view of the complexities of interaction between, on the one hand, cultural influence and, on the other hand, agency on the part of actors:

> While...cultures provide a "tool kit" of resources from which people can construct diverse strategies of action, to construct such a strategy means selecting certain cultural elements (both such tacit culture as attitudes and styles and, sometimes, such explicit cultural materials as rituals and beliefs) and investing them with particular meanings in concrete life circumstances. An example might by young adults who become more church-going when they marry and have children, and who then, in turn, find themselves with re-awakened religious feelings. In such cases culture cannot be said to have "caused" the choices people make, in the sense that both the cultural elements and the life strategy are, in effect, chosen simultaneously. Indeed, the meanings of particular cultural elements depend, in part, on the strategy of action in which they are embedded (so, for example, religious ritual may have special meaning as part of a family's weekly routine). Nonetheless, culture has an effect in that the ability to put together such a strategy depends on the available set of cultural resources. Furthermore, as certain cultural resources become more central in a given life, and become more fully invested with meaning, they anchor the strategies of action people have developed. (p. 281)

Given culture's pervasive effects on the structuralization, processes, functioning, and experience of interpersonal and individual personality systems (cf. Hamamura, 2012; Markus & Kitayama, 1991), it is not surprising that comprehensive understanding of psychopathology must incorporate the role of cultural factors. Based on his comprehensive review of factors empirically associated with different dimensions of psychopathology, Kiesler (1999) drew the following conclusions, which have been consistently supported by subsequent work (see, e.g., Canino & Alegría, 2008; Draguns & Tanaka-Matsumi, 2003; Eshun & Gurung, 2009; Kleinman, 2004; Lopez & Guarnaccia, 2005; Loue & Sajatovic, 2008; Paris, 2004):

> cultural factors can have complex relationships with development and onset of mental disorders. They can serve as formative, predisposing stressors, or causal factors. Accordingly, they can influence which disorders are to develop, the forms they take, and their courses. They can create stress for an individual subsequently triggering onset of mental disorder (Al-Issa, 1982; Sue & Sue, 1987). They can serve as both risk and protective moderator factors in regard to maladjustment. (p. 130)

Kiesler (1999) also reported the findings of an American Psychological Society (1996) task force review of empirical literature pertaining to stressful events. Four factors were consistently found to heighten vulnerability for mental disorders, all directly or indirectly implicating sociocultural factors: low socioeconomic status, family instability, gender, and minority ethnic status.

Recognition of culture's powerful role in the expression and experience of psychopathology is reflected in the American Psychological Association's (2006) treatment guideline stating that "psychological services are most likely to be effective when they are responsive to the patient's specific problems, strengths, personality, *sociocultural context*, and preferences (Norcross, 2002)" (emphasis added, p. 278). Available research supports the importance of modifying treatment in ways that explicitly adapt to a patient's cultural values and beliefs; based on their review of the literature, Smith, Domenech Rodriguez, and Bernal (2011) concluded that "culturally adapted mental health therapies are moderately superior to those that do not explicitly incorporate cultural considerations" (p. 328). As pointed out by these scholars, there is an additional consideration underscoring the cruciality of integrating cultural sensitivity and competence into one's therapeutic practices: "recognizing and aligning with client culture is not only best practice, it is ethical practice (APA, 2002; Bernal, Jimenez-Chafey, & Domenech Rodriguez, 2009; Smith, 2010)" (p. 316).

Integral to integrating cultural knowledge, responsiveness, and adaptiveness into one's clinical methods and processes is the concept and practice of ethnocultural empathy. Other terms have been used to characterize empathy for persons from cultures different from one's own, including "cultural empathy (Ivey, Ivey, & Simek-Downing, 1987; Ridley & Lingle, 1996), empathetic multicultural awareness (Junn, Morton, & Yee, 1995), cultural role taking (Scott & Borodovsky, 1990), ethnic perspective taking (Quintana, Ybarra, Gonzalez-Doupe, & Baessa, 2000), and ethnotherapeutic empathy (Parson, 1993)" (Wang, Davidson, Yakushko, Bielstein Savoy, Tan, & Bleier, 2003, p. 222). Matters of terminology aside, Rasoal, Eklund, and Hansen (2011) sensitively captured the essence of this ability, defining it as "feeling, understanding, and caring about what someone from another culture feels, understands, and cares about" (p. 8, emphasis in original), and specified still more precisely what this therapeutically-influential process (see, e.g., Chang and Yoon, 2011) entails by drawing the "parallel...to feel[ing], understand[ing] or car[ing] about what someone from another generation feels, understands or cares about" (p. 8). However, while cognitive and affective experiential processes are critically necessary to grasping the other's world, these alone are not sufficient to making a meaningful therapeutic difference. This genuinely caring attunement must also be communicated (Ridley & Lingle, 1996; Wang et al., 2003). As succinctly pointed out by Chung and Bemak (2002), "to be effective with culturally diverse clients, it is critical that the counselor displays and demonstrates cultural empathy" (p. 158), which occurs through both words and actions (Wang et al., 2003).

Summarizing Chung and Bemak (2002), Miller (2012) presented 10 valuable guidelines to facilitate developing and communicating cultural empathy with a given client:

1. Being genuinely interested in the culture

2. Having some awareness of the client's culture

3. Appreciating cultural differences in the client

4. Including culture as a part of treatment

5. Understanding the dynamics of family and community

6. Including indigenous healing components in treatment

7. Knowing the history of the client's cultural group (including sociopolitical)

8. Knowing adjustments that had to be made psychologically in a move to another culture

9. Being sensitive to ongoing discrimination experienced by the client

10. Focusing on empowering the client (p. 199)

Carr and West (2013) present a very recent case study that exquisitely demonstrates many of these guidelines in action, including their seamless integration into therapeutic intervention and relationship processes.

The Political System

A discussion of the significance of sociocultural systems relative to families, couples, individuals, psychopathology, and psychotherapy would be incomplete without taking note of the importance of the political system. Scott and Mcloughlin (2012) define political systems as "the formal and informal political processes by which decisions are made concerning the use, production and distribution of resources in any given society" (p. 2). These processes are carried out through the extremely complex interrelationships between two fundamental components: (a) government, composed of institutions (e.g., in the United States, at the federal level, the Presidency, Senate, House of Representatives, and Supreme Court), and (b) the citizenry that make up society. Public policy and law operate at the interface of government and society, and to no small extent shape and are shaped by sociocultural and subcultural values, norms, and practices. Present-day controversies relative to policies and laws concerning abortion, gun control, health care, intellectual property rights, and the definition of marriage powerfully illustrate the interwovenness of politics and culture. The political system plays a significant role in effecting change at all levels of the TES, a point to which we will return in Chapter 9.

SUMMARY

Larger systems shape and mutually interact with smaller systems in an inexorable process. These larger systems, representing the TES, are conceptualized and visually represented by the sociocultural–familial matrix. Centering on the dynamic interplay between the individual personality system, the family system, and the sociocultural/political system, deconstruction of the latter two systems highlights their key structures, processes, and influence. An understanding of the complexity of these interacting system domains affords clinicians the opportunity to track process and address faulty structures that engender relational disturbances and the emergence of symptomatic expressions. These processes occur over generations, as families and social systems encode their members with unique imprints to be carried forth as each family progresses through the family life cycle and the circle of life continues.

REFERENCES

American Psychological Association Presidential Task Force on Evidence-Based Practice. (2006). Evidence-based practice in psychology. *American Psychologist, 61,* 271–285.

American Psychological Society. (1996, February 1). Human Capital Initiative (HCI). Report No. 3, *APS observer* (special issue): Washington, DC: Author.

Anchin, J. C. (2003). Cybernetic systems, existential phenomenology, and solution-focused narrative: Therapeutic transformation of negative affective states through integratively oriented brief psychotherapy. *Journal of Psychotherapy Integration, 13,* 334–442.

Anchin, J. C. (2008). The critical role of the dialectic in viable metatheory: A commentary on Henriques' tree of knowledge system for integrating human knowledge. *Theory and Psychology, 18,* 801–816.

Aranda, M. P., & Knight, B. G. (1997). The influence of ethnicity and culture on the caregiver stress and coping process: A sociocultural review and analysis. *The Gerontologist, 37,* 342–354.

Bacciagaluppi, M. (2012). *Paradigms in psychoanalysis: An integration.* London: Karnac Books Ltd.

Beavers, R., & Hampson, R. B. (2000). The Beavers systems model of family functioning. *Journal of Family Therapy, 22,* 128–143.

Beck, J. G. (Ed.). (2010). *Interpersonal processes in the anxiety disorders: Implications for understanding psychopathology and treatment.* Washington, DC: American Psychological Association.

Benet-Martinez, V., & Karakitapoglu-Aygun, Z. (2003). The interplay of cultural syndromes and personality in predicting life satisfaction: Comparing Asisan Americans and European Americans. *Journal of Cross-Cultural Psychology, 34,* 38–60

Benet-Martinez, V., & Oishi, S. (2008). Culture and personality. In O. P. John, R. W. Robins, & L. A. Pervin (Eds.), *Handbook of personality: Theory and research* (3rd ed., pp. 542–567). New York: Guilford.

Bennett, L. A., Wolin, S. J., & McAvity, K. J. (1988). Family identity, ritual, and myth: A cultural perspective on life cycle transitions. In C. J. Falicov (Ed.), *Family transition: Continuity and change over the life cycle* (pp. 211–234). New York: Guilford.

Bianchi, S. M., Raley, S. B., & Casper, L. M. (2012). Changing American families in the 21st century. In P. Noller & G. C. Karantzas (Eds.), *The Wiley-Blackwell handbook of couples and family relationships.* New York: Wiley-Blackwell.

Bodenmann, G. (2005). Dyadic coping and its significance for marital functioning. In T. Revenson, K. Kayser, & G. Bodenmann (Eds.), *Couples coping with stress: Emerging perspectives on dyadic coping* (pp. 33–50). Washington, DC: American Psychological Association.

Bodenmann, G. (2007). Dyadic coping and the 3-phase method in working with couples. In L. VandeCreek (Ed.), *Innovations in clinical practice: Focus on group and family therapy* (pp. 235–252). Sarasota, FL: Professional Resources Press.

Bodenmann, G. (2010). New themes in couple therapy: The role of stress, coping and social support. In K. Hahlweg, M. Grawe & D. H. Baucom (Eds.), *Enhancing couples: The shape of couple therapy to come* (pp. 142–156). Cambridge, MA: Hogrefe.

Bodenmann, G., & Randall, A. K. (2012). Common factors in the enhancement of dyadic coping. *Behavior Therapy, 43,* 88–98.

Boland, J. P., & Follingstad, D. R. (1987). The relationship between communication and marital satisfaction: A review. *Journal of Sex & Marital Therapy, 13,* 286–313.

Bradbury, T. N., Fincham, F. D., & Beach, S. R. H. (2000). Research on the nature and determinants of marital satisfaction: A decade in review. *Journal of Marriage and the Family, 62,* 964–980.

Bray, J. H. (2009). Couple and family assessment. In J. H. Bray & M. Stanton (Eds.). *The Wiley-Blackwell handbook of family psychology* (pp.151–164). West Sussex, UK: Wiley.

Bray, J. H., & Stanton, M. (Eds.) (2009). *The Wiley-Blackwell handbook of family psychology.* West Sussex, UK: Wiley.

Burgess, E. W. (1926). The family as a unity of interacting personalities. *Family, 7,* 3–9.

Burman, B., & Margolin, G. (1992). Analysis of the association between marital relationships and health problems: An interactional perspective. *Psychological Bulletin, 112,* 39–63.

Byers, E. S. (2005). Relationship satisfaction and sexual satisfaction: A longitudinal study of individuals in long-term relationships. *The Journal of Sex Research, 4,* 113–118.

Canino, G., & Alegría, M. (2008). Psychiatric diagnosis—Is it universal or relative to culture? *Journal of child psychology and psychiatry, 49,* 237–250.

Carpenter-Song, E. A., Nordquest Schwallie, M., & Longhofer, J. (2007). Using care with culture. In S. Loue & M. Sajatovic (Eds.), *Diversity issues in the diagnosis, treatment, and research of mood disorders* (pp. 3–16). New York: Oxford University Press.

Carr, E. R., & West, L. M. (2013). Inside the therapy room: A case study for treating African American men from a multicultural/feminist perspective. *Journal of Psychotherapy Integration, 23,* 120–133.

Carter, B., & McGoldrick, M. (2005). Overview: The expanded family life cycle. In B. Carter & M. McGoldrick (Eds.), *The expanded family life cycle: Individual, family, and social perspectives* (3rd ed., 1–26). Boston: Allyn & Bacon.

Chang, D. F., & Yoon, P. (2011). Ethnic minority clients' perceptions of the significance of race in cross-racial therapy relationships. *Psychotherapy Research, 21,* 567–582.

Chung, R. C.-Y., & Bemak, F. (2002). The relationship of culture and empathy in cross-cultural counseling. *Journal of Counseling and Development, 80,* 154–159.

Clulow, C. (Ed.) (2000). *Adult attachment and couple psychotherapy: The "secure base" in practice and research.* Philadelphia, PA: Routledge.

Cote, J. E., & Levine, C. G. (2002). *Identity formation, agency, and culture: A social psychological synthesis.* Mahwah, NJ: Lawrence Erlbaum Associates.

Crosbie-Burnett, M., & Klein, D. M. (2009). The fascinating story of family theories. In J. H. Bray & M. Stanton (Eds.). *The Wiley-Blackwell handbook of family psychology* (pp. 37–52). West Sussex, UK: Wiley.

Csikszentmihalyi, M. (1993). *The evolving self: A psychology for the third millennium.* New York: Harper Collins Publishers.

Culture Matters. (n.d.). Retrieved March 12, 2013, from http://wws.peacecorps.gov/wws/publications/culture/

Diener, E., & Suh, E. M. (Eds.) (2000). *Culture and subjective well-being.* Cambridge, MA: MIT Press.

Draguns, J. G., & Tanaka-Matsumi, J. (2003). Assessment of psychopathology across and within cultures: Issues and findings. *Behaviour research and therapy, 41,* 755–776.

Duke, M. P., & Nowicki, S., Jr. (1982). A social learning theory analysis of interactional theory concepts and a multidimensional model of human interaction constellations. In J. C. Anchin & D. J. Kiesler (Eds.), *Handbook of interpersonal psychotherapy* (pp. 78–94). New York: Pergamon.

Eshun, S., & Gurung, R. A. R. (Eds.) (2009). *Culture and mental health: Sociocultural influences, theory, and practice.* Malden, MA: Wiley-Blackwell.

Falicov, C. J. (1988). Family sociology and family therapy contributions to the family development framework: A comparative analysis and thoughts on future trends. In C. J. Falicov (Ed.), *Family transitions: Continuity and change over the life cycle* (pp. 3–51). New York: Guilford.

Fergus, K. D., & Reid, D. W. (2001). The couple's mutual identity and reflexivity: A systemic-constructivist approach to the integration of persons and systems. *Journal of Psychotherapy Integration, 11,* 305–410.

Fincham, F. D. (2009). Forgiveness: Integral to a science of close relationships? M. Mikulincer & P. Shaver (Eds.), *Prosocial motives, emotions, and behavior: The better angels of our nature* (pp. 347–365). Washington, DC: APA Books.

Fincham, F. D., & Beach, S. R. H. (2010). Marriage in the new millennium: A decade in review. *Journal of Marriage and Family, 72,* 630–649

Fincham, F. D., Beach, S. R., & Davila, J. (2004). Forgiveness and conflict resolution in marriage. *Journal of Family Psychology, 18,* 72–81.

Fincham, F. D., Stanley, S., & Beach, S. R. H. (2007). Transformative processes in marriage: An analysis of emerging trends. *Journal of Marriage and the Family, 69,* 275–292.

Fogarty, T. F. (1976). System concepts and the dimensions of self. In P. J. Guerin, Jr. (Ed.), *Family therapy* (pp. 144–153). New York: Wiley.

Framo, J. L. (1976). Family of origin as a therapeutic resource for adults in marital and family therapy: You can and should go home again. *Family Process, 15,* 193–210.

Gerson, M. J. (2010). *The embedded self: An integrative psychodynamic and systemic perspective on couples and family therapy* (2nd ed.). New York: Routledge.

Glickauf-Hughes, C. (1996). Sadomasochistic interactions. In F. W. Kaslow (Ed.), *Handbook of relational diagnosis and dysfunctional family patterns* (pp. 270–286). Hoboken: NJ: Wiley.

Gold, J. (Ed.) (2001). Special issue: The integration of individual and system therapies. *Journal of Psychotherapy Integration, 11,* 285–410.

Gottman, J. M. (1994). *What predicts divorce? The relationship between marital processes and marital outcomes.* Hillsdale, NJ: Lawrence Erlbaum Associates.

Hamamura, T. (2012). Are cultures becoming individualistic? A cross-temporal comparison of individualism–collectivism in the United States and Japan. *Personality and Social Psychology Review, 16,* 3–24.

Hardy, K. V., & Laszloffy, T. A. (1995). The cultural genogram: Key to training culturally competent family therapists. *Journal of Marital and Family Therapy 21,* 227–237.

Hargrove, D. S. (2009). Psychotherapy based on Bowen family systems theory. In J. H. Bray & M. Stanton (Eds.), *The Wiley-Blackwell handbook of family psychology* (pp. 286–299). West Sussex, UK: Wiley.

Harvey, J. H., Pauwels, B. G., & Zickmund, S. (2005). Relationship connection: The role of minding in the enhancement of closeness. In C. R. Snyder & S. J. Lopez (Eds.), *Handbook of positive psychology* (pp. 423–433). New York: Oxford University Press.

Harvey, J. H., Wenzel, A., & Sprecher, S. (Eds.) (2004). *Handbook of sexuality in close relationships.* Mahwah, NJ: Lawrence Erlbaum Associates.

Haworth-Hoeppner, S. (2000). The critical shapes of body image: The role of culture and family in the production of eating disorders. *Journal of Marriage and the Family, 62,* 212–227.

Hennon, C. B., & Wilson, S. M. (Eds.) (2008). *Families in a global context*. New York: Routledge.

Henriques, G. R. (2003). The Tree of knowledge system and the theoretical unification of psychology. *Review of General Psychology, 7*, 150–182.

Henriques, G. R. (2004). Psychology defined. *Journal of Clinical Psychology, 60*, 1207–1221.

Henriques, G. (2011). *A new unified theory of psychology*. New York: Springer Press.

Hewitt, J. P. (2005). The social construction of self-esteem. In C. R. Snyder & S. J. Lopez (Eds.), *Handbook of positive psychology* (pp. 135–148). New York: Oxford University Press.

Hong, Y., Morris, M. S., Chiu, C., & Benet-Martinez, V. (2000). Multicultural minds: A dynamic constructivist approach to culture and cognition. *American Psychologist, 55*, 709–720.

Hsu, J. (2001). Marital therapy for intercultural couples. In W. Tseng & J. Streltzer (Eds.), *Culture and psychotherapy: A guide to clinical practice* (pp. 225–242). Washington, DC: American Psychiatric Press.

Jacobson, N. S., & Margolin, G. (1979). *Marital therapy: Strategies based on social learning and behavior exchange principles*. New York: Brunner/Mazel.

Johnson, S. J., & Whiffen, V. (Eds.). (2003). *Attachment processes in couple and family therapy*. New York: Guilford.

Jones, S. E., & LeBaron, C. D. (2002). Research on the relationship between verbal and nonverbal communication: Emerging integrations. *Journal of Communication, 52*, 499–521.

Karpel, M. A. (1994). *Evaluating couples: A handbook for practitioners*. New York: Norton.

Kelly, A., Fincham, F. D., & Beach, S. R. H. (2003). Emerging perspectives on couple communication. In J. O. Greene & B. R. Burlson (Eds.), *Handbook of communication and social interaction skills* (pp. 723–752). NJ: Lawrence Erlbaum Associates.

Kiecolt-Glaser, J. K., & Newton, T. L. (2001). Marriage and health: His and hers. *Psychological Bulletin, 127*, 472–503.

Kiesler, D. J. (1982). Interpersonal theory for personality and psychotherapy. In J. C. Anchin & D. J. Kiesler (Eds.), *Handbook of interpersonal psychotherapy* (pp. 3–24). New York: Pergamon.

Kiesler, D. J. (1996). *Contemporary interpersonal theory and research: Personality, psychopathology, and psychotherapy*. New York: Wiley.

Kiesler, D. J. (1999). *Beyond the disease model of mental disorders*. Westport, CN: Praeger.

Kleinman, A. (2004). Culture and depression. *New England journal of medicine, 351*, 951–953.

Lee, S. A., & Farrell, M. (2006). Is cultural competency a backdoor to racism? *Anthropology News, 47*(3), 9–10.

Le Roux, J. (2002). Effective educators are culturally competent communicators. *Intercultural Education, 13*, 37–48.

Lewis, J. M., Beavers, W. R., Gossett, J. T., & Phillips, V. A. (1976). *No single thread: Psychological health in family systems*. New York: Brunner/Mazel.

Litzinger, S., & Gordon, K. C. (2005). Exploring relationships among communication, sexual satisfaction, and marital satisfaction. *Journal of Sex & Marital Therapy, 31*, 409–424.

Lopez, S. R., & Guarnaccia, P. J. (2005). Cultural dimensions of psychopathology: The social world's impact on mental illness. In J. E. Maddux & B. A. Winstead (Eds.), *Psychopathology: Foundations for a contemporary understanding* (pp. 19–37). Mahwah, NJ: Lawrence Erlbaum Associates.

Loue, S., & Sajatovic, M. (Eds.). (2008). *Diversity issues in the diagnosis, treatment, and research of mood disorders.* New York: Oxford University Press.

Magnavita, J. J. (2000). *Relational therapy for personality disorders.* Hoboken, NJ: Wiley.

Magnavita, J. J. (2005). *Personality-guided relational therapy: A unified approach.* Washington, DC: American Psychological Association.

Magnavita, J. J. (2012). Advancing clinical science using system theory as the framework for expanding family psychology with unified psychotherapy. *Couple and Family Psychology: Research and Practice, 1,* 3–13.

Mahoney, M. J. (1991). *Human change processes: The scientific foundations of psychotherapy.* New York: Basic Books.

Manusov, V., & Patterson, M. (Eds.). (2006). *The SAGE handbook of nonverbal communication.* Thousand Oaks, CA: Sage Press.

Markus, H. R., & Kitayama, S. (1991). Culture and the self: Implications for cognition, emotion, and motivation. *Psychological Review, 98,* 224–253.

McLemore, C. W., & Hart, P. P. (1982). Relational psychotherapy: The clinical facilitation of intimacy. In J. C. Anchin & D. J. Kiesler (Eds.), *Handbook of interpersonal psychotherapy* (pp. 227–247). New York: Pergamon.

McNulty, J. K., & Fincham, F. D. (2012). Beyond positive psychology? Toward a contextual view of psychological processes and well-being. *American Psychologist, 67,* 101–110.

Miller, G. (2012). *Fundamentals of crisis counseling.* Hoboken, NJ: Wiley.

Minuchin, S. (1974). *Families and family therapy.* Cambridge, MA: Harvard University Press.

Nichols, W. C. (1988). *Marital therapy: An integrative approach.* New York: Guilford.

Nichols, W. C. (2005). The first years of marital commitment. In M. Harway (Ed.), *Handbook of couples therapy* (pp. 28–43). Hoboken, NJ: Wiley.

Olson, D. H. (1996). Clinical assessment of treatment interventions using the family circumplex model. In F. W. Kaslow (Ed.), *Handbook of relational diagnosis and dysfunctional family patterns* (pp. 59–101). Hoboken, NJ: Wiley.

Olson, D. H., & Gorall, D. M. (2003). Circumplex model of marital and family systems. In F. Walsh (Ed.), *Normal family processes* (3rd ed., pp. 514–547). New York: Guilford.

Papp, L. M., & Witt, N. L. (2010). Romantic partners' individual coping strategies and dyadic coping: Implications for relationship functioning. *Journal of Family Psychology, 24,* 551–559.

Paris, J. (2004). Sociocultural factors in the treatment of personality disorders. In J. J. Magnavita (Ed.), *Handbook of personality disorders: Theory and practice* (pp. 135–147). Hoboken, NJ: Wiley.

Pasley, K., & Olmstead, S. B. (2009). Changing landscape of American family life. In J. H. Bray & M. Stanton (Eds.). *The Wiley-Blackwell handbook of family psychology.* (pp. 53–67). West Sussex, UK: Wiley.

Pequegnat, W., & Bray, J. H. (1997). Families and HIV/AIDS: Introduction to the special section. *Journal of Family Psychology, 11,* 3–10.

Perry, B. D. (2009). Examining child maltreatment through a neurodevelopmental lens: Clinical application of the neurosequential model of therapeutics. *Journal of Loss and Trauma, 14,* 240–255.

Rasoal, C., Eklund, J., & Hansen, E. M. (2011). Toward a conceptualization of ethnocultural empathy. *Journal of Social, Evolutionary, and Cultural Psychology, 5,* 1–13.

Revenson, T. A., Kayser, K., & Bodenmann, G. (Eds.). (2005). *Couples coping with stress: Emerging perspectives on dyadic coping.* Washington, DC: American Psychological Association.

Ridley, C. R., & Lingle, D. W. (1996). Cultural empathy in multicultural counseling: A multidimensional process model. In P. B. Pedersen & J. G. Draguns (Eds.), *Counseling across cultures* (4th ed., pp. 21–46). Thousand Oaks, CA: Sage.

Rosenstein, C. (2009, July). Cultural development and city neighborhoods. *Charting civil society* (No. 21). Washington, DC: The Urban Institute. Retrieved March 13, 2013, from http://www.urban.org/publications/411937.html

Scott, Z., & Mcloughlin, C. (2012). *Topic guide on political systems.* University of Birmingham, UK: Governance and Social Development Resource Centre. Retrieved March 17, 2013, from http://www.gsdrc.org/go/topic-guides/political-systems

Sherif Trask, B., & Hamon, R. R. (Eds.). (2007). *Cultural diversity and families: Expanding perspectives*. Thousand Oaks, CA: Sage Publications.

Smith, T. B., Domenech Rodriguez, M., & Bernal, G. (2011). Culture. In J. C. Norcross (Ed.), *Psychotherapy relationships that work: Evidence-based responsiveness* (2nd ed., pp. 316–335). New York: Oxford University Press.

Sprecher, S., & Cate, R. M. (2004). Sexual satisfaction and sexual expression as predictors of relationship satisfaction and stability. In J. H. Harvey, A. Wenzel, & S. Sprecher (Eds.), *The handbook of sexuality in close relationships* (pp. 235–256). Mahwah, NJ: Lawrence Erlbaum Associates.

Stanton, M., & Welsh, R. (2012). Systemic thinking in couple and family psychology research and practice. *Couple and Family Psychology, 1,* 14–30.

Sternberg, R., & Hoijat, M. (Eds.) (1997). *Satisfaction in close relationships*. New York: Guilford.

Sue, D. (2005). Asian American masculinity and therapy: The concept of masculinity in Asian American males. In G. E. Good & G. R. Brooks (Eds.), *The new handbook of psychotherapy and counseling with men: A comprehensive guide to settings, problems, and treatment approaches* (rev. and abridged edition, pp. 357–368). San Francisco: Jossey-Bass.

Sue, N., & Zane, N. (2005). How well do both evidence-based practices and treatments as usual satisfactorily address the various dimensions of diversity? Ethnic minority populations have been neglected by evidence-based practices. In J. C. Norcross, L. E. Beutler & R. F. Levant (Eds.), *Evidence-based practices in mental health: Debate and dialogue on the fundamental questions* (pp. 329–337). Washington, DC: American Psychological Association.

Swidler, A. (1986). Culture in action: Symbols and strategies. *American Sociological Review, 51,* 273–286.

Terkelsen, K. G. (1980). Toward a theory of the family life cycle. In B. A. Carter & M. McGoldrick (Eds.), *The family life cycle: A framework for family therapy* (pp. 21–52). New York: Gardner Press.

Thomas, A. J. (1998). Understanding culture and worldview in family systems: Use of the multicultural genogram. *The Family Journal: Counseling and Therapy for Couples and Families, 6,* 24–32.

Thompson, S. Z. (2005). The role of personal control in adaptive functioning. In C. R. Snyder & S. J. Lopez (Eds.), *Handbook of positive psychology* (pp. 202–213). New York: Oxford University Press.

Tov, W., & Diener, E. (2007). Culture and subjective well-being. In S. Kitayama & D. Cohen (Eds.), *Handbook of cultural psychology* (pp. 691–713). New York: Guilford.

Twenge, J. M., Campbell, W. K., & Foster, C. S. (2003). Parenthood and marital satisfaction: A meta-analytic review. *Journal of Marriage and Family, 65,* 574–583.

Vangelisti, A. L. (2004). Preface. In A. L. Vangelisti (Ed.), *Handbook of family communication* (pp. x–xii). Mahwah, NJ: Lawrence Erlbaum Associates.

von Scheve, C., & von Luede, R. (2005). Emotion and social structure: Towards an inter-disciplinary approach. *Journal for the Theory of Social Behaviour, 35*, 303–328.

Walsh, F. (2002). A family resilience framework: Innovative practice applications. *Family Relations, 51*, 130–137.

Walsh, F. (2003). Family resilience: A framework for clinical practice. *Family Process, 42*, 1–18.

Wang, Y.-W., Davidson, M. M., Yakushko, O. F., Savoy, H. B., Tan, J. T., & Bleir, J. K. (2003). The scale of ethnocultural empathy: Development, validation, and reliability. *Journal of Counseling Psychology, 50*, 221–234.

Weeks, G. R., & Treat, S. (2001). *Couples in treatment: Techniques and approaches for effective practice* (2nd ed.). Philadelphia: Brunner-Routledge.

Zimmer, D. (1983). Interaction patterns and communication skills in sexually distressed, maritally distressed, and normal couples: Two experimental studies. *Journal of Sex & Marital Therapy, 9*, 251–265.

Part III

TREATMENT COMPONENTS

Principles and Techniques of Unified Psychotherapy

This final part of the volume focuses on treatment strategies of unified psychotherapy. As noted earlier, the contemporary state of affairs in psychotherapy parallels the status of the discipline at large. Daniel Robinson (1995), an eminent historian of psychology, wrote: "In its current form, psychology is so various, so partitioned into separate provinces, that the nonspecialist might pardonably conclude that there is no unified subject at all" (pp. 3–4). Equivalent fragmentation in the field of psychotherapy has resulted in part from the development and emergence of many approaches and modalities of treatment over the first century of clinical science and psychotherapy—necessary, in fact, to the evolution of clinical science and psychotherapy. However, given the field's diversity at this juncture in its development, we believe that arranging components of clinical science in an organized fashion has many benefits to the field and clinical practitioners. Accordingly, in casting its gaze at the different rungs of the total ecological system (TES) and their interconnectedness, a unifying psychotherapeutic lens is interested in ways in which patients' maladaptations may express themselves across the intrapsychic–biological, interpersonal–dyadic, relational–triadic, and sociocultural–familial levels, and, within the context of that evolving understanding, in deciding on the optimal systems level(s) and modes of intervention. Thus, whereas many texts in the field present couple and family therapy as approaches to treatment distinctly separate from individual psychotherapy or from community-level interventions, from the perspective of the four-level framework we have presented couple or family therapy not as a separate approach but as part of working at a certain level in the system. Thus, as we shall present in the final chapter, we believe couples and family therapy are best conceptualized as modalities of treatment that often contain specialized techniques depending on the couple or family therapy approach at play, but that also encompass certain commonalities in method as well.

In pursuing unification of the vast array of extant therapeutic approaches and techniques, an important step entails recognizing that they target different levels and subsystem components of the total system. We have adopted the term *restructuring* to organize and describe all the methods and techniques encompassed by contemporary psychotherapeutics (Magnavita, 2012). *Webster's Ninth New Collegiate Dictionary* (1985) defines restructure as follows: "to change the makeup, organization, or pattern of" (p. 1006). Extrapolating from this definition, the concept of restructuring thus conveys the action of psychotherapeutic techniques as altering the content, self-organized patterns, and processes characterizing the given system level (e.g., interpersonal-dyadic) and subsystems (e.g., cognitive–affective schema of self and others) of interest. It is useful in this context to bear in mind the proposed distinction between "two basic forms of knowledge restructuring: 'weak' and 'radical.' The former involves relatively minor adjustments in domain-specific knowledge, while radical restructuring entails dramatic shifts in core constructs and their relations" (Mahoney, 1991, p. 148). As with many sharp distinctions drawn within the realm of human processes, weak and radical restructuring can be conceived as anchoring two ends of a continuum, such that clinically it is most realistic to think in terms of varying degrees of system-level and subsystem restructuring.

Before we begin this part, we also think it important to provide our perspective on the place of technique in unified psychotherapeutics. We view techniques to be vital components of the treatment process, but also believe clinicians are well served by maintaining a balanced perspective on their relative contribution to therapeutic change processes. On the one hand, we believe it important to not *over*estimate their importance. Thus, we share Mahoney's (1991) concern about "technolatry and the possible tyranny of techniques" (p. 286). Hans Strupp (1978) wrote "techniques per se are inert unless they form an integral part of the therapist as a person" (p. 314), reminding us that psychotherapy is a fundamentally interpersonal enterprise. Thus, whether characterized as "ritualized methods of human relatedness and communication" (Mahoney, 1991, p. 387) or "relational acts" (Safran & Muran, cited in Norcross & Lambert, 2011, p. 5), techniques are entwined elements of the interpersonal process that *is* psychotherapy. As Grawe's (2007) observations suggest, with experience psychotherapy becomes more than just a matter of selecting the appropriate techniques:

> … even—or specifically—experienced therapists have a renewed, intensive desire to understand (even more about) mental disorders and the function of psychotherapy. The prefabricated truisms of the therapy schools don't impress them anymore; they are beyond that stage. They have learned to work with the tools acquired from the therapy schools—the thought patterns and action repertoires—but they know about the limitations of these tools. They tend to work either eclectically or they have a pronounced interest in the integration of these methods that they have experienced as valuable and effective. For such therapists, integration attempts that mesh with their experience or that provide entirely "fresh," not yet overused perspectives are particularly attractive to extend their therapeutic expertise. (pp. 11–12)

LeDoux (2002) brings still another perspective to techniques, underscoring that "psychotherapy is fundamentally a learning process for its patients, and as such is a way to rewire the brain. In this sense, psychotherapy ultimately uses biological mechanisms to treat mental illness" (p. 299).

This having been said, we also believe it important that the role of techniques in psychotherapy not be *under*estimated. Techniques are potentially potent, systematic ways of making therapeutic things happen (Anchin, 2003), and some six decades of research firmly indicate that they indeed contribute to the outcomes of psychotherapy (Norcross & Lambert, 2011). In this light, we appreciate the rich compendium of techniques that has been developed over the course of contemporary psychotherapy and believe that being adept and skillful with a wide range of techniques is critical for the unified psychotherapist (cf. Marquis, 2009; Melchert, 2013). Grawe (2007) wrote: "Once the various therapeutic strategies and processes have been uncoupled from their original theoretical backgrounds, the question of therapeutic effectiveness can be asked afresh" (p. 13). The next part of this volume attempts this "uncoupling" in the service of what Grawe seemed to be attempting in his work, which shares much in common with the path we have taken in ours.

Chapter 8

UNIFYING PSYCHOTHERAPEUTICS

Intrapsychic and Dyadic Levels

In this chapter on unifying psychotherapeutics, we begin at the *intrapsychic level,* or the *individual personality system,* followed by a description of working at the *dyadic level.* We show how to orient one's clinical work and navigate flexibly among the four levels using our unified framework, and offer clinical suggestions. Although we separate these four levels for heuristic and pedagogical purposes, they are interrelated levels. In this chapter (linking the intrapsychic–biological and the interpersonal–dyadic), it is important to underscore the necessity of approaching these two levels from a dialectical perspective. In other words, even when we are focused on what is occurring at the intrapsychic level, we are cognizant of the fact that we conduct our therapeutics in dyadic, triadic, or larger relational units. We may toggle our perspectives back and forth as we are working among the various levels, in that our attention may shift to one domain or another, but all are operative at some level of systemic activation. For example, even if one is addressing intrapsychic defenses, one is operating within the dyadic context of the therapeutic relationship (upper left-hand corner of the triangle—Figure 5.2) and thus one cannot separate the impact that addressing defenses will have on the therapeutic alliance. Said differently, at one level the intervention is targeting the patient's defenses, but at another level that intervention is itself a verbal and nonverbal process occurring between the therapist and patient, and therefore may impact on the nature and quality of the therapeutic alliance. With practice, this ability to think in terms of different levels and their intersections becomes implicit learning and not always an actively conscious process. With continued practice and mindfulness, holding multiple perspectives becomes an intuitive way of working and thinking—less left-brain conscious decision-making and more in coherence and "flow" (Csikszentmihalyi, 1991) with the patient. In other words, one is in sync with the patient's personality system, work is effortless and natural, and time passes without awareness.

As emphasized throughout preceding chapters, personality is a complex system (Block, 2002; Magnavita, 2005; Mayer, 1998) and as clinicians we enter the system at various levels, thus becoming an active part. In this manner, through entering and joining a system, we can effect change. We seek to discover the system's fulcrum points—that is, the domain level that is most likely to shift the system to a higher level of differentiation and integration; the former entails modifying components in ways that therapeutically enhance their structuralization and functioning, while the latter involves different ways of improving the interplay of different components in ways that benefit the functioning and experience of the system-as-a-whole. For example, a couple enters marital therapy, but among clinical findings during initial assessment is that the husband is clearly suffering from severe emotional and cognitive dysregulation. Therefore, before starting or in conjunction with marital work, a psychopharmacological consultation might be very beneficial to see if neurobiological intervention in the service of inducing changes in neural underpinnings of emotional regulation processes is appropriate (see, e.g., Green, Cahill, & Mahli, 2007; Gross, 2002; Silvers, Buhle, & Ochsner, in press). In another case, a couple with marital disturbance is malfunctioning because of unresolved sexual trauma in one member of the dyad, so we consider a trauma-focused therapy for that individual and then reconvene the dyadic work. We believe that using a personality-guided approach enhances all therapeutic work (Magnavita, 2005; Millon, 1999); the personality configuration guides and illuminates the clinical process and determines the focus of treatment and the restructuring methods and techniques that are selected from Psychotherapedia™.

METHODS AND TECHNIQUES OF
UNIFIED PSYCHOTHERAPY

The methods and techiques of unified psychotherapy include the entire range of those offered by contemporary clinical science. Viamontes and Beitman (2009) believe that *"Psychotherapy theory is in conceptual disarray. There are too many schools, too many theories, and too many strategies and techniques"* (p. 783). Lebow (2008), in his volume, *Twenty-First Century Psychotherapies: Contemporary Approaches to Theory and Practice*, presents the most prominent approaches: behavioral, cogntive, experiential, mindful-ness- and acceptance-based, postmodern/poststructural, psychoanalytic, existential, feminist, and integrative (technical eclecticism, common factors and mulimodal). We agree that there indeed are too many "stand-alone" theories that oftentimes work at cross purposes; unified psychotherapy is an attempt to address the disarray alluded to by Viamontes and Beitman by providing a framework that can enhance practitioners' capacity to *draw* from the richness of approaches, methods, and techniques in the field.

In the present approach the vast array of psychotherapeutic techniques are divided into four major categories of *restructuring* methods based on the specific systemic domain level the techniques are designed to target and in which its primary mutative action occurs. Specifically, coordinated with the four domain levels of the biopsychosocial system, these methods entail submethods and techniques for achieving (a) *intrapsychic restructur-ing* (IR)—healing the mind/brain, (b) *dyadic restructuring* (DR)—healing self and others, (c) *triadic restructuring* (TR)—healing triads and family systems, and (d) *mesosystem restructuring* (MR)—healing larger systems. In turn, each of these categories contains groups of restructuring methods, which are specific techniques or action sequences, each of which with particular foci, modes of action, and mechanisms of change. These submethods further differentiate the four main methods into finer categories, which generally target a specific domain such as defensive, cogntive, or affective restructur-ing. These submethods are often specific to a particular approach.

Psychotherapedia

Psychotherapedia is an organized framework of methods and techniques that derive from unified psychotherapy (Magnavita, 2012). At each of the four levels of the system, there are *methods* and *submethods*, which include categories of *techniques*, which emerge from a comprehensive review of the literature. One of the goals of the Unified Psychotherapy Project (UPP) is to catalogue the techniques of psychotherapy in this organizing tax-onomy. We believe this will advance clinical science by offering an orga-nized evolving framework that can continue to accrue techniques as they are developed. Currently, various methods and techniques are sequenced into a formal *approach*, and in the case of empirically supported treatments the clinical methodology is characteristically presented in a treatment manual to demonstrate how these technical interventions should prog-ress. Nevertheless, while "the information from randomized clinical trials of manual-guided therapies tends to be useful at the beginning of therapy (it helps if you know where to start) … it does not provide guidance once the treatment process goes outside of the bounds of the manual or is not effective" (Pinsof, Goldsmith, & Latta, 2012, p. 253). We believe, especially in difficult cases, manualized treatment provides a useful guide when working in a particular domain, but its utility decreases when there is greater complexity reflective of multiple system-level dysfunctions. While particularly over the past 30-plus years there has been a valuable, inexorable shift entailing increased integration of various approaches (Anchin & Magnavita, 2006, 2008), currently, as discussed in Chapter 1, there are growing indications of a trend toward unification in that there seems to be a convergence toward recognition of the major component domains that we have outlined in this volume. Since we are starting our clinical presentation with Level I of the total ecological system (TES), which is primarily concerned with the individual personality system, it is useful to provide a brief review highlighting a number of important aspects of personality dysfunction and disorders. Subsequently, we discuss the expression of symptoms in the personality system.

AN OVERVIEW OF PERSONALITY SYSTEMATICS AND THE TREATMENT OF PERSONALITY DYSFUNCTION

All those who enter treatment have an operating personality system and can be placed on the structural continuum: *normal–neurotic–borderline–psychotic*. Some will have a more differentiated self-system: *greater emotional capacity and self–other differentiation*, integral to an adaptive personality system, and will therefore be more resilient and at a higher level of functioning. Yet others, falling at different points along the continuum, will be less resilient and lower functioning. Some will channel their anxiety primarily to one pathway, for example, and others multiple pathways: *smooth muscles–cognitive processes–character defenses–striated muscles*. Clinicians who develop expertise in the treatment and management of personality dysfunction will be able to go beyond treating symptom disturbances and make a major impact by altering the way the personality system operates (Livesley, 2001, 2003; Magnavita, 2004, 2010; Millon, 1999). Personality, when it becomes chronically dysfunctional, becomes a disorder, which represents a fairly ubiquitous condition for those patients seen in mental health and behavioral settings. Approximately 50% of patients seen in clinical practice are diagnosed with a comorbid (co-occurring) personality disorder (Merikangas & Weissman, 1986). Many patients with personality disturbances place excessive demands on medical providers, and succeed in alienating them, as their personality issues often interfere with their ability to access and effectively utilize services and care. They often enact behavioral patterns that are unhealthy, expressed in such forms as drug addiction, smoking, and high-risk behaviors (Magnavita, Powers, Barber, & Oltmanns, 2013).

Personality disorder reflects chronic dysfunction in the personality system of the individual and may be expressed in any mixture of levels—that is, at the *intrapsychic* (e.g., problems in affect regulation, impulse control, defensive functioning, identity, regulation of self-esteem, cognitive beliefs), *dyadic* (e.g., disturbances in interpersonal relationships, self–other differentiation, capacity for intimacy and closeness), *triadic* (e.g., deficient differentiation, tendencies to triangulate others), *familial* (e.g., dysfunctional family process and maladaptive structural configurations, multigenerational transmission), and *sociocultural* (e.g., participation in dysfunctional cultural and political subsystems). Individuals with personality dysfunction often express their maladaptive patterns in multiple matrices indicative of systemic homeostasis (difficulty adapting to changing environmental demands because of ineffective attempts at keeping the system in equilibrium). For example, they may have difficulty with emotional regulation and use primitive defenses at the intrapsychic level, be prone to interpersonal conflict at the dyadic level, and triangulate others at the triadic level. This often results in family dysfunction evident at the sociocultural–familial level. Thus, they often experience difficulties in ego adaptation, self-image, interpersonal relationships, and in family, work, and societal contexts. Their difficulties are manifested in repetitive maladaptive behaviors, for example, self-defeating interpersonal patterns that occur and recur, often without the benefit of self-awareness, including lack of awareness of their self-sabotaging aspects.

Etiology and Pathogenesis. The etiology and pathogenesis of personality dysfunction is multifactorial; there is no single developmental pathway, but rather convergent processes that include genetic, temperamental, developmental, familial, and cultural factors (Livesley, 2001; Magnavita, 2004, 2010; Magnavita, Powers, Barber, & Oltmanns, 2013). There is ample evidence to show that much personality dysfunction is caused by early trauma, especially physical and sexual abuse in the case of more severe personality dysfunction, but also implicated as causal factors are loss, emotional abuse, neglect, and narcissistic use (Bierer et al., 2003; Donaldson-Pressman & Pressman, 1994; Gabbard, 2005; Sperry, 2003; Yen et al., 2002).

Issues With Classification. The classification of personality disorders was enhanced with the use of the multiaxial diagnostic system, which placed personality on Axis II of the *Diagnostic and Statistical Manual of Mental Disorders*, fourth edition (*DSM-IV*; American Psychiatric Association, 1994). And although the *DSM-5* (American Psychiatric Association, 2013) has replaced the multiaxial with a single axis system, the latter will continue to include the diagnosis of personality disorder(s)—along with all other mental disorders (*DSM-IV*'s Axis I) and medical diagnoses (*DSM-IV*'s Axis III)—that may pertain to a given patient. By the same token, there has been controversy about the *DSM*'s categorical approach to diagnosis of personality disorders, which is continued in *DSM-5*—for example, diagnosing personality disorder on the basis of a dichotomous presence-or-absence criterion (see Shedler & Westen, 2004). Directly addressing this major drawback, McWilliams (2011) captured the heart of the problem: "From a practitioner's standpoint, the often-lamented fact that a person diagnosed with one personality disorder frequently meets criteria for four to six other disorders (Blais & Norman, 1997; Grilo, Sanislow, & McGlashan, 2002; Watson & Sinha, 1998) does not indicate a need for greater accuracy about what defines one disorder and rules out another; it is evidence that personality is inherently complex, interpenetrating, and multidimensional" (p. 115). In this respect, the importance of theory in guiding what is often a highly complex process of clinical assessment, understanding, and treatment decision making cannot be underestimated.

Child and Adolescent Personality Dysfunction. Another area of controversy is the conceptualization and diagnosis of children and adolescents with personality disorders. Following guidelines from the early versions of the *DSM*, a personality disorder diagnosis in some circumstances may be given to children. Many clinicians believe that this does a disservice and is overly stigmatizing. However, there are those who believe child and adolescent personality disorders should be identified so that appropriate treatment can be offered as early as possible (Bleiberg, 2001; Freeman & Reinecke, 2007; Kernberg, Weiner, & Bardenstein, 2000). Most clinicians who treat children and adolescents are likely to have seen many cases where there is clear evidence for early personality dysfunction that if untreated might become more enduring. Clinical evidence and empirical findings suggest that personality dysfunction has its origins in part in dysfunctional personologic systems, which transmit dysfunctional patterns and show signs of a multigenerational transmission process (Magnavita, 2000, 2007; Magnavita & MacFarlane, 2004); in this light, the appearance of personality dysfunction prior to adulthood is not surprising.

Central Processes Common Among Patients With Personality Dysfunction

There are a number of critical processes that are characteristic of maladaptive and dysfunctioning personality systems. As the personality system becomes more dysfunctional there is an increasing positive feedback loop in many components of the personality system, providing continual reinforcement and expression of the underlying neural circuits, internal psychological processes, and behavioral systems. Consequently, these habits (see Henriques, 2011, pp. 234–235) and the neural networks in which they are encoded become highly fixed (Cozolino, 2002). These processes can be difficult to distinguish without having pattern recognition tools, which allow us to clearly perceive and ascertain these system malfunctions. Only then is it possible to alter or effectively restructure these processes.

Clinical theorists suspect that these patterns are driven by a number of factors; examples include identification with destructive attachment figures, nonmetabolized guilt that requires self-punishment, dysfunctional ways of communicating painful aspects of experience, rigid agentic and communal motives, and particular patterns of self-protection that were once adaptive but that have lost their adaptive value in the current life sphere. Some of the most commonly encountered of these include reenactments, repetitive maladaptive behavior patterns, and self-sabotage. *Enactment–reenactment* (Jacobs, 1986) is both a defense against unbearable feeling and an attempt to communicate one's untold story. "Unable to communicate through language, the traumatized, severely disturbed patient may draw the therapist into situations that symbolize his or her traumatic experience. The interaction mirrors the patient's past and may evoke the patient's disowned, dissociated feelings and conflicts in the therapist, inducing the therapist to respond in ways that feel alien" (Brown & Lane, 2000, pp. 71–72). *Repetitive maladaptive behavior patterns* represent yet another process indicative of personality system malfunctions. In this recursive process, individuals, couples, and families seem caught in maladaptive loops of intrapsychic and/or interpersonal behaviors, which result in destructive or symptomatic occurrences. *Self-sabotage* is yet another process that tends to be a hallmark of many patients with personality dysfunction. Self-sabotage refers to an individual's tendency to prevent him- or herself from accomplishing a sought-after goal, or being unable to savor the joys of one's family life or accomplishments, or any number of other expressions of an internal need to punish oneself and suffer. Interestingly, these processes often seem to be outside the individual's awareness—that is, they are *ego-syntonic*—until they are pointed out. A significant component of treatment, where indicated, is to make that which is ego-syntonic *ego-dystonic,* that is, something of which the patient is painfully aware. To do so, the clinician needs to serve in a *pattern recognition function,* achieved through continually identifying and bringing the patient's attention to these patterns, as well to the limitations they impose and the costs they exact.

This progression, consisting of restructuring what is ego-syntonic (out of awareness and causing virtually no anxiety to the person) to the state of being ego-dystonic (the awareness creates discomfort), is a precursor to change that can be readily linked to Prochaska, DiClemente, and Norcross's (1992, cf. Prochaska, Norcross, & DiClemente, 1994; Norcross, Krebs, & Prochaska, 2011) transtheoretical model of change. In this model, change is viewed as a process that progresses through a series of six stages: (a) *precontemplation,* in which the patient is unaware of his or her dysfunctionalities and consequently there is no intention to change; (b) *contemplation,* in which the patient is aware that problems exist and is thinking about changing, but is ambivalent about undertaking the action(s) necessary for change to occur; (c) *preparation*, in which the patient intends in the very near future to undertake change-related action(s) and may have taken very initial steps in this direction; (d) *action*, in which the patient is actively working on changing dysfunctional intrapsychic, interpersonal, and/or behavioral processes and patterns; (e) *maintenance*, in which the patient works to sustain and consolidate gains and to prevent relapse; and (f) *termination*, wherein change has become well established and there is no fear of relapse. In order to move to the contemplative stage of change, one must be cognizant of the roles that self-defeating patterns play in the maintenance of symptomatic and dysfunctional behavior, as well as in relational disturbances.

The Integrity of the Personality System

An important initial function of treatment, in addition to assessing the patient's stage of change, is to assess the integrity of the patient's personality system, regardless of the approach (e.g., cognitive, psychodynamic, experiential) or the modality of treatment (e.g., individual, couples, family, group) offered. An excellent resource for those not familiar with depth-oriented, intrapsychic personality assessment is the *Psychodynamic Diagnostic Manual* (PDM Task Force, 2006), which—along with a special issue of the *Journal of Personality Assessment* focusing on the *PDM* (Huprich & Meyer, 2011)—we highly recommend. In accord with perspectives articulated in the present volume, the *PDM*

> is the first psychological diagnostic classification system that considers the whole person in various stages of development.... The resulting nosology goes from the deep structural foundation of personality to the surface symptoms that include the integration of behavioral, emotional, cognitive, and social functioning.... The *PDM* does not look at symptom patterns described in isolation, as do the *International Classification of Diseases* (ICD) and the *Diagnostic and Statistical Manual* of the American Psychiatric Association (*DSM*). Research on brain development and the maturation of mental processes suggests that patterns of behavioral, emotional, cognitive, and social functioning involve many areas working together rather than in isolation. (Gordon, 2010, p. 1312)

It is important to note as well that "although it is based on psychodynamic theory and supporting research, the *PDM* is not doctrinaire in its presentation. It may be used in conjunction with the ICD or *DSM*. The *PDM* Task Force made an effort to use language that is accessible to all the schools of psychology. It was developed to be particularly useful in case formulation that could improve the effectiveness of any psychological intervention" (Gordon, 2010, p. 1312). In this context, we underscore that it is much better for the clinician to be on solid ground when engaging in any treatment than it is to find oneself in the position of having selected an approach that does not match the requirements of the patient's personality system. In the following case example, the integrity of the patient's individual personality system was fairly good and the level of family dysfunction very high.

CASE EXAMPLE: THE TRIANGULATED COLLEGE STUDENT

The patient is a 20-year-old female with a history of psychiatric hospitalization for depression and panic. She attends a university where her mother is a professor of psychology, and although the patient is very gifted intellectually, she begins a semester with good intentions and then halfway through "runs out of gas" and stops attending, despite the fact that her mother encourages attending her classes. The patient has been on a variety of psychotropic medications in the past, which seemed to have made things worse. She also has a recent history of being sexually assaulted and since that time has been more withdrawn. Her individual personality system is relatively well functioning most of the time. Her level of emotional differentiation is somewhat low and her defenses are at times primitive. She has cut and burned herself. Although there are some features of borderline personality, she does not have many of the features. Individual psychotherapy was initiated along with psychopharmacological treatment. In her individual work it became clear that the family system was highly dysfunctional, with both parents suffering from personality dysfunction. Her father was on disability and stayed home, complaining to his daughter how much his wife didn't care and only cared about her career. The patient was clearly triangulated and felt responsible for her parents' well-being. She was afraid to differentiate because of fear that her parents' marriage would collapse and her father might commit suicide. The parents were resistant to coming into treatment together and each one meet with one of the clinicians on the treatment team. In this case, a dysfunctioning personality system in the identified patient was not structurally deficient, but seemed to be the result of a disturbed parental dyad and a high level of triangulation preventing her from

(continued)

CASE EXAMPLE *(continued)*

being appropriately launched into an independent life. Her parents, although sophisticated, continued to undermine her attempts at moving away by encouraging her to return to the university where her mother taught, and for the third time taking another class with her. Treatment focused on addressing her internal belief that she was responsible for her father's emotional state and belief that she could never be good enough for her mother. A history of developmental emotional and some physical neglect were also addressed as she became more highly differentiated and assertive about her needs.

OPERATING AT THE INTRAPSYCHIC LEVEL I

Regardless of the integrity of the intrapsychic system and whether the goals of treatment are symptomatic reduction, relational disturbance, or personality restructuring, methods and techniques of IR are central to most contemporary forms of and approaches to psychotherapy. Unified psychotherapy combines an understanding of relational principles, skill with various approaches to treatment, facility with different modalities of treatment, and the ability to seamlessly combine methods to achieve the goals of the patient; we will devote more time explaining how to combine these various components of treatment in the final chapter. It is useful to have some way of organizing the compendium of techniques that are offered by contemporary approaches to psychotherapy so we can select from this powerful armamentaria of techniques. We present this organization scheme momentarily, but it is important to keep in mind that, while techniques are the action sequences psychotherapists utilize, having knowledge of these alone will not make one a competent psychotherapist. Unified psychotherapy is not a technical process, but rather a complex set of relational skills and knowledge sets.

Methods and Techniques of IR

IR comprises those methods, submethods, and techniques that are primarily aimed at the intrapsychic level of the system. Each therapist will have a preference for techniques he or she utilizes based on the therapist's own personality, training, and indications of appropriateness from the patient. Some may prefer more nondirective techniques and others more active ones. The art of differential treatment selection and therapeutics (Frances,

Clarkin, & Perry, 1984) is central to unified psychotherapy, which draws from multiple approaches. At the same time, given feedback and feedforward circuits of interconnectedness between subsystems composing the intrapsychic–biological level of the personality system, changes effected through interventions targeting a given intrapsychic subsystem will invariably impact other intrapsychic structures and processes. For example, while explicit emphasis at a given point in treatment may be on the patient's defenses or schema, restructuring either of the latter will in turn exert influence on the patient's affective experiencing.

There are a number of subtypes of IR that are useful when working at the intrapsychic level. These include:

1. *Defensive restructuring*—the focus is on defensive operations (Cramer, 2006; Davanloo, 1980; Reich, 1933), which are unconscious psychological processes that protect the individual from the discomfort or distress that would accompany subjectively experiencing internal stimuli—for example, feelings, thoughts, physical sensations, motives, needs, and/or desires—that, accurately or not, carry threatening and otherwise dangerous meanings to the individual. In this respect, in relation to their function vis-à-vis *internal* stimuli, defenses are essentially the psychological equivalent of behavioral avoidance vis-à-vis threatening *external* stimuli: An individual can potentially prevent or avoid contact with a threatening facet of his environmental surround through *behavioral* avoidance, but he cannot physically take flight from threatening internal stimuli—however, he can do so psychologically. Defenses serve this self-protective purpose. However, in addressing the patient's defenses, it is critical to bear in mind that their use at a given point in time may be adaptive or maladaptive, and that this assessment is based on consideration of a number of parameters, including the situational context in which a given defense is being used, the content being defended against (e.g., the nature of a specific emotion or wish), a given defense's relative level of maturity (e.g., humor; suppression) or immaturity (e.g., projection), and duration of its usage over a given time frame (see, e.g., Cramer, 2000; McWilliams, 2011). A host of techniques have evolved that can be used to address the patient's defensive constellation, for example, identification of defenses, educating the patient about defenses, and challenging defenses (see Magnavita, 2005, pp. 175–183; cf. McCullough Vaillant, 1997; McCullough, Kuhn, Andrews, Kaplan, Wolf, & Hurley, 2003), in the service of salutary defensive restructuring and in turn enhancing psychosocial adaptation. An important point to bear in mind is that some techniques of defensive restructuring can dramatically increase anxiety, while others are more effective

at stabilizing the defense system or strengthening a faltering one, for example, through supporting the adaptive value of the patient's defenses.

2. *Cognitive restructuring*—The focus is on cognitive schema and beliefs (Beck, Rush, Shaw, & Emery, 1979; Beck, Freeman, & Associates, 2004; Beck & Weishaar, 2008; Young, 1999; Young, Klesko, & Weishaar, 2003), with emphasis on identifying and modifying maladaptive automatic and core thoughts and beliefs about self and about others—and through these cognitive change processes, fostering constructive changes in the patient's internal, subjective experience (e.g., moods and emotional states; personal and relational goals; views of self and others) and overt functioning (e.g., relationally; job functioning; leisure time activities). Illustrative examples of cognitive-restructuring techniques include labeling and challenging distortions (e.g., overgeneralization, dichotomous/black–white thinking, personalization, magnification/minimization), collaboratively examining available evidence that supports and that disconfirms the given thought or belief in question, and developing alternative interpretations of and meanings attached to specific actions on the part of self and/or other(s) in the context of specific interpersonal situations and events (see, e.g., Anchin, 2003, 2006; Anchin & Pincus, 2010; J. Beck, 2011; Freeman, Pretzer, Fleming, & Simon, 2004; Riso, du Toit, Stein, & Young, 2007; Young, 1999). These restructuring methods tend to elicit less intense levels of anxiety than defensive or affective restructuring and are excellent techniques for novice psychotherapists to learn and incorporate before moving on to some of the more technically demanding ones.

3. *Affective restructuring*—The focus is on affective experience and processing relative to dysfunctionalities in affectivity, which can take numerous forms; exemplars include problems in the realms of emotional regulation (underregulation or overcontrol; Aldao, 2013; Gross, 2002; Greenberg & Paivio, 1997; Shedler & Westen, 2004), emotional experiencing (Fosha, 2008), differentiation of affective states (Magnavita, 2005), affect tolerance (e.g., Linehan, 1993; McWilliams, 2011), metabolization of affect (Fosha, 2004a; Magnavita, 2005); experiencing of positive emotional states (Fosha, 2004b), and drawing meanings embedded in emotional states (Anchin, 2003; Greenberg & Paivio, 1997). Overarchingly, affective restructuring centers on optimizing the patient's experiencing, regulation, use, and communication of emotion in ways that distinctly benefit her adaptation to life's stressors and challenges, goal pursuits, functioning in the interpersonal as well as other life realms (e.g., vocationally; leisure activities), and psychological and emotional well-being.

Experiential, humanistic, existential, narrative, and psychodynamic approaches to treatment provide an abundance of procedures and techniques directly focused on different facets and components of affective restructuring; an illustrative sampling of approaches includes Greenberg and Paivio's (1997) emotionally focused therapy process, entailing the three phases of bonding, evoking and exploring, and emotion restructuring; the highly relational, restructuring, and experiential–affective strategies and techniques of accelerated experiential–dynamic psychotherapy developed by Fosha and colleagues (e.g., Fosha, 2000, 2008; Fosha & Yeung, 2006; Lamagna, 2011; Lipton & Fosha, 2011; Prenn, 2011); methods of Gestalt therapy (e.g, Brownell, 2010; Mann, 2010; Perls, 1973; Perls, Hefferline, & Goodman, 1951); Gendlin's (1996) focusing-oriented techniques; Bugental's (1987) existential–humanistic treatment methods; and teaching distress tolerance skills, a key component of dialectical behavior therapy (Linehan, 1993), as well as other approaches to enhancing emotion regulation (see, e.g., Kring & Sloan, 2010). These techniques can raise anxiety in those who have a low capacity for affective experience and/or by virtue of placing a demand on intimacy and closeness. Hence, as a cautionary note, we underscore that restructuring affect directly and too quickly can flood the patient and lead to an exacerbation of symptoms.

4. *Cognitive–behavioral restructuring*—The focus is on conditioned affective responses and re-learning. These methods are especially, although by no means exclusively, used in the treatment of posttraumatic stress disorder and extinction of phobic responses, which can include affect phobias (McCullough, 2003). Techniques entail diverse forms of exposure treatment (e.g., Barlow, 1988; Foa, Hembree, & Rothbaum 2007; Hossack & Bentall, 1996; Paunovic, 2002, 2003; Robjant & Fazel, 2010; Schauer, Neuner, & Elbert, 2012; Shapiro, 2001), while also encompassing relaxation methods, breathing exercises, and mindfulness-based practices (Hayes, Villatte, Levin, & Hildebrandt, 2011; Treanor, 2011).

5. *Neurobiological restructuring*—The focus is on neurobiological systems. These techniques are excellent for reducing anxiety and include various types of biofeedback, neurofeedback, transcranial magnetic stimulation, and pharmacotherapy. While these methods focus directly on restructuring neurobiological processes, it is important to also take note of the ever-growing consensus that, in undertaking any of the aforementioned forms of intrapsychic restructuring, by virtue of the mind/brain interconnection the clinician is simultaneously restructuring the patient's neurobiology (Cozolino, 2010; Schore, 2012; Viamentes & Beitman, 2009).

Symptoms—Emergent Phenomena of the Personality System

We turn our attention to a unifying perspective on the treatment of symptomatic expressions, more or less the equivalent of *DSM-IV-TR* Axis I clinical syndromes. The clinical process with an individual entering psychotherapy characteristically begins with the patient's report of troubling symptoms, which may be expressed in relatively vague terms, for example, "I feel lousy all the time; I feel down and just don't feel like doing anything," or conversely, in terms that are very circumscribed, for example, "I have a panic attack whenever I go into an elevator." However vague or circumscribed, and whatever domains (e.g., troubling thoughts, feelings, somatic phenomena, and/or facets of interpersonal functioning) encompassed by the patient's reported symptoms, the latter are articulations of his or her *phenomenology*, how the patient subjectively experiences and perceives distress. While these are often initial representations of the patient's psychopathology, they are also the first expressions of the patient's *personality system*. Nevertheless, in our experience, therapists tend to overlook the latter, to no small degree a function of the hegemony of the *DSM*, which, by virtue of its descriptive emphasis, has strongly encouraged clinicians to remain highly symptom-oriented in assessing the patient, arriving at a diagnosis (or set of diagnoses), and selecting interventions to be implemented. McWilliams (2011) beautifully captured the dilemma: "Practitioners find it hard to resist intense pressures to narrow our clinical gaze to phenomena that the *DSM* can describe. Having become widely accepted as the standard taxonomy by researchers, in an era when research evidence is demanded in support of clinical treatments, the *DSM* has inevitably structured our sense of how to think about psychological problems" (p. 114).

However, symptoms, even when they cluster into definable clinical syndromes, are not a sufficient basis for comprehensively, and therefore fully accurately, understanding the patient and formulating optimal directions for treatment. Others have touched on the issues at play. For example, Kagan (2012), commenting on the *DSM-5*, pointed out that, like those preceding it, the latter

> will [be] use[d] to decide who has a mental disorder and what disorder he or she has. Unfortuntately … this guide, like the four before it, ignores the origin of a symptom and relies primarily on the feelings and behaviors patients describe as salient in their consciousness. This definition of mental illness is flawed, because every symptom in the current handbook has more than one origin. Most of these illness categories are analogous to complaints of headaches or cramps. Physicians can decide on the best treatment for a headache only after they have determined its cause. The symptom alone is an insufficient guide. (p. xx)

The important question of a symptom's origins speaks to one facet of the broader problem that suffuses the symptom focus of the *DSM*, and this is its inability to address the crucial issue of meaning (Anchin, 2006). For example, while descriptively a given patient's clinical depression may be characterized in terms of a cluster of discernible cognitive, emotional, and vegetative symptoms, this diagnostic designation imparts only a partial understanding of his psychopathology and distress; it tells us nothing about the originating context and hence idiosyncratic meaning of the patient's depression. As underscored by McWilliams (2011), "clinicians must assess whether a depression expresses grief over loss, helplessness in the face of others' control, oversensitivity to criticism, self-defeating relational patterns, failure to meet internal standards, an anniversary reaction, or something else (Carter, 2006; Goodheart, 2004)" (p. 114). Context is crucial to meaning (Anchin, 2006; McNulty & Fincham, 2012), and in the clinical realm, across patients the same symptom is likely to have heterogeneous meanings depending on an array of contextual factors. This consideration was fundamental to the rationale for developing the *PDM*: "A shared and motivating experience of the contributors to the *PDM* was dismay at how the dominance of a narrow, descriptive-psychiatry model has promoted the decline of the empirically sound and clinically valuable idiographic tradition, in which clients' difficulties are conceptualized *in the context of* their unique personalities, developmental challenges, and life contexts" (McWilliams, 2011, p. 112, emphasis added). As succinctly crystallized by Bornstein (2011), "in this way the *PDM* provides the clinician with a more complete picture of the patient, not just the patient's pathology" (p. 148).

Unified psychotherapy's emphasis on the whole person accords with this sensibility, viewing symptomatic expressions as "outbreaks" of dysfunction in the patient's personality system, that is, in his or her recurrent pattern of motivation, thinking, feeling, acting, and/or reacting in response to environmental stressors with which the patient is ineffectively coping. In this regard, consistent with the centrality of the relational matrix in a unified approach, "by far the most important class of stressors are social or interpersonal ... [that is,] stress ... socially induced as a result of interactions between people (Moss, 1973)" (Kiesler, 1999, p. 126; see also Kiesler, 1996). However, as Kiesler (1999) pointed out, stressful environments or events can also involve the patient's physical–impersonal environment (e.g., noise, starvation, disasters), societal factors (e.g., work, socioeconomic status, political circumstances), and distinctly cultural factors (i.e., factors associated with racial, ethnic, and cultural diversity). The following case illustrates this holistic systemic framework for understanding symptomatic expressions and its unified treatment implications.

CASE EXAMPLE: SYMPTOMATIC EXPRESSION

A 24-year-old female enters psychotherapy with the primary present-ing complaint of ongoing feelings of anxiety, severe panic attacks (e.g., in addition to experiencing extremely intense anxiety, she reports rapid heartbeat, difficulty breathing, dizziness, and chills), the strong belief at such times she is "going crazy," and ensuing fear about expe-riencing still another such attack. While these are the symptoms most prominent in the patient's subjective experience, biopsychosocial assessment reveals that this distressing symptomatology can be most comprehensively understood as an expression of multiple causal fac-tors, in particular the strong probability of an inherited predisposition to physiological overreactivity (suggested by a family history of anxi-ety disorders); chronic feelings of inferiority, inadequacy, and anxious-ness; living in a small apartment (which she cannot afford to move out of) with a roommate who continuously disparages and criticizes her and will not cease despite the patient's assertive requests; being caught in the middle between two frequently quarreling divorced parents, both of whom she loves but is also angry with; and, consonant with the value system of her cultural group, striving for high levels of achieve-ment, which in turn contributes to perfectionistic self-expectations that she nevertheless perceives as not being met, due most recently to frequent errors that she has been making at her job—which, given her magna cum laude graduation from a well-known national university, she perceives to be far below her potential. Historical data reveal that the patient was also sexually abused on two different occasions dur-ing her youth, and a year and a half prior to entering treatment she ended an emotionally abusive relationship.

Organizing and consolidating these factors within a unified frame-work, the patient's panic disorder is thus a symptomatic expression of a pernicious, reciprocally interacting mixture of causal and maintaining factors anchored in the biopsychosocial matrix of her life: These factors can be categorized as *intrapsychic–biological* (an inherited predisposi-tion to heightened physiological reactivity, affectively laced memories of being abused, chronic anxiousness, the belief that she is "going crazy," worry, repressed anger, unmet perfectionistic self-expectations, feelings of inadequacy and inferiority), *interpersonal–dyadic* (presently living with a critical roommate), *triadic–relational* (caught in the middle between her quarreling divorced parents, each of whom expresses their negative feel-ings about the other to the patient), and *sociocultural* (the nature of her job and the cultural group that serves as her frame of reference).

Using this case as a working illustration, a principal strategy in the unified psychotherapy of symptomatic expressions is to foster reduction in the patient's presenting symptomatology as among initial goals of treatment, since these symptoms in and of themselves characteristically lie at the center of the patient's subjective distress and not infrequently also impair psychosocial functioning. Consistent with the principles of evidence-based practice of psychology (EBPP), therapist selection of treatment interventions in ameliorating the patient's symptomatic expression is informed by best available research (e.g., empirical support for the effectiveness of cognitive-behavior therapy [CBT] in the treatment of panic [Woody & Ollendick, 2006]), clinical expertise (e.g., in the present case, skill that the therapist has developed in incorporating solution-focused, strength-based interventions into treating this particular form of symptomatic expression), and patient factors (e.g., concurrent personality pathology; see Newman, Crits-Christoph, Gibbons, & Erickson, 2006). On the basis of this tripartite set of EBPP considerations, the initially formulated treatment package will directly target the patient's panic in part through the empirically supported CBT techniques of applied relaxation training (to address affective and physiological components of the patient's panic) and cognitive restructuring techniques (to modify the patient's misconceptions about her panic, e.g., her belief that she is "going crazy," and associated fears of having another panic attack). Additionally, the therapist will pursue neurobiological restructuring of physiological underpinnings and components of the patient's anxiety and panic through discussing referral to a psychiatrist, who will undertake an evaluation for the appropriateness of psychotropic medication(s).

Directly intervening in the patient's symptomatic expression is a necessary but not sufficient component of a unified approach to treating this form of psychopathology. In line with the conception of symptomatic expressions as "outbreaks" of personality dysfunction vis-à-vis negative environmental circumstances and events, the therapist must also decode meanings about the multiple levels of the biopsychosocial matrix contributing to the symptomatic expression. Thus, in addition to making rapid therapeutic inroads on the patient's symptomatology, a second major strategy of unified psychotherapy of symptomatic expressions is to identify and intervene in salient *stressor–reaction constellations*, defined as social–environmental triggers and the patient's covert and overt reactions to them that have been instrumental in activating and/or maintaining the patient's symptomatology. Recall in this context that, in the present case, during assessment the patient had identified two of the ongoing stressors—her critical roommate and quarreling parents—that contributed to the pulsing reservoir of anxiety serving as the cauldron of her panic attacks. Asked during the course of her opening narrative how she dealt with each of these stressors, the patient indicated that she had actually recently begun to tell herself to not get caught up in these respective individuals' negativity—constructive self-talk that she implemented, in the case of her roommate, by walking away and focusing her attention and actions on a given activity that were in the interest of her own well-being (e.g., calling a friend), and in the case of her parents, by assertively telling them to stop as soon as they begin talking about the other parent. Through "guided discovery" (Freeman et al., 2004), she saw more clearly that these recent reactions to her roommate and parents were indeed effective in reducing feelings of anxiety and stress—and that she also felt more empowered when enacting them. The patient had thus self-initiated actions that were effective in achieving interpersonal–dyadic and triadic–familial restructuring, respectively, yielding positive consequences at the biological–intrapsychic level.

Reflecting the manner in which a unified approach's flexible, multiparadigmatic framework can illuminate significant processes that might otherwise pass under the therapist's radar and that can be incorporated into the individualized treatment package, the therapist took note of the patient's salutary reactions to her roommate and parents through the lens of a strength-based, solution-focused perspective (Anchin, 2003; Bertolino, Kiener, & Patterson, 2009; O'Connell, 1998). The strength-based component of this perspective encourages the therapist to ascertain patient strengths and constructive processes that may already be in motion, while the solution-focused component capitalizes on these processes through straightforward interventions that explicitly highlight their effectiveness as solutions and encourage their implementation as consistently as possible. These solution-focused interventions will thus be integrated into the treatment package as tactics for implementing the second unified treatment strategy noted above.

In addition to directly targeting the patient's symptomatology and intervening in salient stressor–reaction constellations, a third strategy of unified psychotherapy in addressing symptomatic expressions entails intervening in selected aspects of the patient's personality system implicated in the nonlinear chain of biopsychosocial processes that precipitate symptom outbreaks. Indeed, of direct pertinence to the present case, available research indicates that treatment prognosis is worse for anxiety-disordered patients with a comorbid personality disorder (Newman, Crits-Christoph, Gibbons, & Erickson, 2006). Consequently, rather than allowing the free reign, as it were, of maladaptive personality processes as potential impediments to the effectiveness of interventions targeting the symptomatic expression, over time a unified approach to treating this patient will proactively layer into the therapeutic process interventions designed to restructure relevant aspects of her personality dysfunction. In the present case, consistent with psychodynamic and cognitive theory and practice (e.g., A. Beck et al., 2004; Busch, Milrod, & Singer, 1999; Milrod, Leon, Barber, Markowitz, & Graf, 2007; Shear, Cooper, Klerman, Busch, & Shapiro, 1993), dysfunctional components of the patient's self-schema—specifically, chronic feelings of inferiority, inadequacy, vulnerability, and perfectionistic self-expectations—are hypothesized to be key interrelated personality processes associated with her anxiety and proneness to panic.

The working formulation guiding intervention at this level is that the patient's perfectionistic strivings constitute a defense that serves the purpose of overcompensating for her deep-seated negative self-identity and intimately related painful feelings of inferiority, inadequacy, and unworthiness, but that this dynamic is in fact a self-defeating vicious circle in several ways (Blatt, 1995): (a) Her pursuit of perfection is itself attended by feelings of anxiousness; (b) achieving perfection is virtually impossible due to the excessively high, unrealistic level of her self-standards, and hence inevitably she falls short in her own eyes, which only serves to reinforce her feelings of anxiety, inadequacy, and inferiority, which are all the more heightened when she observes herself making errors or receives negative feedback from significant others; (c) even when near-perfection is achieved (e.g., in her appearance; in her job performance), it is extremely difficult to maintain these levels on a highly consistent basis by virtue of the intrinsic variability of human systems; and (d) because of the ingrained nature of her negative self-identity and feelings of inadequacy, inferiority, and unworthiness and their multiple sources, high-level achievement only assuages these deeply painful self-feelings on a temporary basis, akin to putting a bandage on a deep wound, while failing to heal them in a significant, enduring way, thereby unwittingly enabling them to persist and to continue to drive her overcompensatory yet anxiogenic quest for perfection.

Therapeutic work designed to foster meaningful, salutary changes in these maladaptive facets of the patient's enduring self-schema will integrate concepts and techniques from several schools of thought, including psychodynamic and experiential psychotherapies (e.g., to foster intellectual and emotional insight into these dynamics—e.g., her perfectionism as a defense against painful feelings of inadequacy and inferiority—and their self-defeating psychological and emotional consequences); interpersonal psychotherapy (e.g., to understand her negative self-identity and intimately related feelings of inadequacy, inferiority, and unworthiness as introjective consequences of the sexual and emotional abuse perpetrated by significant others); cognitive therapy (e.g., to facilitate cognitive restructuring of her perfectionistic self-expectations in more realistic and flexible directions); and schema-focused therapy (e.g., to foster development of a more positive, integrated, and realistic self-identity and integrally associated feelings of worthiness).

As this example illustrates, a unified approach thus conceptualizes symptoms in the context of the complex biopsychosocial matrix of the patient's life. To summarize, in the present case a three-tiered approach to treatment ensues, entailing (a) interventions to foster symptom reduction and management, (b) identification and intervention in salient stressor–reaction constellations, with emphasis on fostering modifications in specific covert and overt reactions that have played an instrumental role in activating and/or maintaining the patient's symptomatology, and (c) interventions directed at restructuring relevant aspects of personality dysfunction that operate as the infrastructure undergirding, and in a sense "driving," the patient's maladaptive reactions to the difficult circumstances of her life (cf. Westen, Gabbard, & Blagov, 2006). Over the course of treatment, the ongoing selection, pacing, and sequencing of specific interventions for implementing this multilevel set of strategies will be informed by a variety of considerations, for example, the relative rapidity of symptom reduction, the amount of skill building needed to cultivate healthier reactions to salient stressors, and the degree of personality pathology. Moreover, it should also be noted that therapeutic work will incorporate the unified treatment strategy of "working the loop" (Anchin, 2003), whereby the therapist capitalizes on constructive change occurring in one domain of functioning to actively promote change in other domains of the patient's personality and relational functioning. For example, when the patient enacts constructive actions vis-à-vis her roommate or parents, she will also be encouraged to make experiential contact with the concomitant feeling of empowerment and, in session, the patient and therapist will "feed" this feeling back into the patient's cognitive–affective–motivational system by examining specific ways in which the patient can actively utilize this empowered feeling state to make a positive difference in maladaptive aspects of her self-schema (e.g., in her thoughts and feelings of inadequacy and vulnerability) and in the confidence with which she pursues her goals.

Restructuring the Personality System

All treatment, to some degree or another, exerts impact on the personality system. However, when constituting the primary focus of treatment, personality disorders and trait disturbances remain some of the most challenging clinical presentations. There are various frameworks for conceptualizing, assessing, and treating personality disorders, the most prominent of which are the categorical, dimensional, structural, and factor models (Magnavita, 2004a; *PDM* Task Force, 2006; Widiger & Costa, 2013). Some approaches will enhance personality functioning by increasing skills (e.g., regulation of emotions) or building resources, and others will more actively address key components of the personality configuration (e.g., faulty schemas of self and others; rigid defenses; maladaptive interpersonal patterns) as the primary foci of treatment. Accumulating evidence demonstrates that personality disorders can be effectively treated (Dimaggio & Livesley, 2012), and a number of approaches that incorporate distinct evidence-based constructs and techniques have been developed primarily for treating this class of complex disorders. These include cognitive therapy (Beck et al., 2004), schema-focused therapy (Young, 1999; Young et al., 2003), interpersonal reconstructive therapy (Benjamin, 1996, 2003), transference-focused therapy (Clarkin, Yeomans, & Kernberg, 1999; Yeomans, Clarkin, & Kernberg, 2002), dialectical behavior therapy (Linehan, 1993; Robins, Rosenthal, & Cuper, 2010), short-term dynamic therapy (Davanloo, 1980; cf. Clarkin, Fonagy, & Gabbard, 2010), and mentalization-based treatment (Bateman & Fonagy, 2006), while a number of additional approaches to treating personality dysfunction containing robust evidence-based components can be found in Magnavita (2010). We also urge the reader in the direction of Critchfield (2012; Critchfield & Benjamin, 2006), Clarkin (2012), Dimaggio, Salvatore, Fiore, Carcione, Nicolò, and Semerari (2012), Livesley (2012), and Magnavita (1997, 2005, Chapter 7) for valuably instructive treatment guidelines and principles for restructuring personality dysfunction.

OPERATING AT THE DYADIC LEVEL II

Symptoms and personality dysfunction are expressed in a relational context. Many patients enter treatment because of concerns about how either they or other family members are reacting to others. Issues of intimacy and closeness are often a manifestation of these disturbances. In some modalities of treatment such as couple and marital therapy, the dyad is often addressed in vivo—in "real time"—as they process and work on their issues in the presence of the therapist. The dyadic processes will differ to some degree among different modalities of treatment, which we discuss in the last chapter. Suffice it to say that, across different dyadic pairings, dyadic processes have similar elements and are derived from interpersonal and relational science. In individual therapy the patient–therapist dyad is the primary relational unit of change. In couples therapy we now have a dyad (the couple) and a threesome (couple with therapist).

Couples therapy has become an important modality of treatment due to the increasing number of couples who are experiencing marital and relational difficulties (Lebow & Gasbarrini, 2009). Marital distress is associated with more work and health problems, as well as problems with children. John Gottman (1994, 1999) is one of the most influential couples researchers whose work is solidly empirically grounded. Regardless of whether one is trained in providing marital therapy, it is imperative to have a basic appreciation of some of Gottman's findings so that appropriate referrals can be made when indicated. Gottman identified four character-istics predictive of chronic marital problems and eventual divorce. These he termed "The Four Horsemen": defensiveness, criticism, contempt, and stonewalling. When these are present in the couple dyad, the situation is generally toxic for the dyad and those in proximity.

Sue Johnson (2004) has developed an evidence-based approach to treating distressed couples, termed emotionally focused couple therapy, that essentially works at the level of self–other and emotional differen-tiation in the dyad. Her approach emphasizes restructuring the emo-tional system and the partners' attachment to one another. Lebow and Gasbarrini (2009) summarize a number of current approaches for work-ing with the marital/couple dyad, while more detailed presentations may be found in Gurman (2008). It is beyond the scope of this volume to pres-ent a detailed guide to treating the marital/couple dyad, but we hope that a basic understanding of the centrality of the latter will alert clinicians to the fact that this subsystem needs to be addressed when other members in the family system are experiencing psychological distress or behavioral disturbances. Some clinicians believe that the power of relational restruc-turing lies in having the couple engage in their process in the presence of a trained therapist who can actively facilitate dyadic restructuring.

Methods and Techniques of Dyadic Restructuring

There are a number of submethods of dyadic restructuring. The first two methods we describe—expected–transactive and self–other—occur in the context of the patient–therapist dyad. The third type occurs in a dyadic relationship with a therapist. Although there are many techniques that can be used interchangeably, three dyadic interventions have emerged from two distinct modalities of psychotherapy—individual and marital. These three methods include:

1. *Expected–transactive restructuring*—The focus is on the expected relationship with the therapist or the *transference*. This method of restructuring also includes the *countertransference* that is engen-dered in the therapist (Wolf, Goldfried, & Muran, 2013). This is the primary dyadic focus in individual therapy. This form of restructuring is in vivo in that the re-enactment patterns and transference issues that the patient brings with him- or herself to treatment are inevitably going to "come alive." The expected rela-tionship or transference–countertransference response is probably one of the most important pattern recognition tools. The thera-peutic work of individual psychotherapy is very much a product of the patient–therapist dyad. In a sense, this dyad as it unfolds provides abundant information by providing a sample of the patient's interpersonal functioning (Goldfried & Davison, 1976).

2. *Self–other restructuring*—The focus is on the real relationship with the therapist (Gelso, 2009, 2011). Emphasized here is differentiation from the therapist (McCullough Valliant, 1997). The identification, acknowledgment, and repair or processing of therapeutic ruptures is a major aspect of most dyadic processes (Safran & Muran, 2000). The main techniques of self–other restructuring are those techniques that are used for rupture repair, self-disclosure, and dyadic regulation (Fosha, 2003).

3. *Relational restructuring*—The focus is on a dyadic relationship other than the therapist–patient dyad, such as a marital, couple, or partner relationship. The most common techniques of relational restructuring are utilized in couples therapy (Gottman, 1999; Gottman & Gottman, 2013; Johnson, 2004). In "gridlocked couples—two fists in opposition" (p. 99), there are generally core issues that prevent couples from establishing intimacy. Gottman's research shows: "Behind each person's gridlocked position lies something deep and meaningful—something core to that person's belief system, needs, history or personality. It may be a strongly held value or perhaps a dream not yet lived" (Gottman & Gottman, 2013, p. 100). The individual personality system is connected to the dyad; the dyad is connected to the triad—family and social system.

Basics of Dyadic Restructuring

Regardless of whether the focus of the dyadic restructuring is on the patient–therapist dyad or the relational dyad, the goal is to enhance differentiation and integration. Keeping this in mind allows the clinician to select from a rich array of dyadic-restructuring techniques to enhance self–other differentiation processes. We want to move the individual developmentally along a path toward more capacity to identify and express oneself and thus reduce blaming, projection, and other defenses that interfere with intimacy and closeness.

CASE EXAMPLE: SELF–OTHER RESTRUCTURING— WORKING IN THE PATIENT–THERAPIST DYAD IN THE CONTEXT OF A DEPLETED FAMILY SYSTEM

The patient is an 18-year-old male who entered treatment because of chronic behavioral problems and substance abuse for which he

(continued)

CASE EXAMPLE *(continued)*

had spent time in jail and was on probation. He presented with severe depression, which was unresponsive to various psychopharmacological agents. He had done poorly in high school even though he was gifted, and had lost a job for stealing. His parents turned him into the authorities for using drugs. He spent 3 days in jail. The prosecutor informed him that if he had a positive urine screen for drugs he would return to jail for a longer stay. He was defiant and oppositional and tested the system. He continued to use drugs, and even though he had begun community college and was doing well, the prosecutor believed he should be returned to jail and spent 3 months incarcerated. He witnessed a number of violent events in prison that traumatized him. He appeared very disengaged, lethargic, prone to explosive outburst, and felt that he would be better off dead. After he was released from jail he believed his life was over because he was convinced that he was now a convicted felon, so why bother applying for a job? He spent most of the day in bed or playing videogames. His parents were invited into treatment and it was clear that his father was entirely disengaged and unable to meet the patient on the most basic level, reacting with rage and wishing his son would return to jail and "learn his lesson." His relationship with his mother was somewhat enmeshed and she seemed to feel more of an emotional connection to her son than her husband. Interestingly, the patient was committed to treatment and with few exceptions over the course of 4 years attended individual treatment. In his case, his capacity for relatedness was quite low, and yet with patience he developed an increasing mentalizing capacity. Over the course of the treatment he lessened his substance abuse and began to show some signs of coming to life. Behavioral activation was used to encourage him to initiate activity. Although his motivation was minimal he finally found a part-time job and then a full-time job where he continues to work. He returned to community college but was unable to sustain the effort required and dropped out. The main focus of this treatment completed in a dyad with the therapist included work on self and self–other differentiation. He was also treated with an exposure-based trauma treatment to reduce his posttraumatic stress disorder from his prison experiences. There were a few family sessions where he confronted his father and attempted to make a connection, but his father was not able to respond and the patient came to terms with his father's severe limitations.

This is a case of a young man with some antisocial personality features who, with unified treatment, was able to advance his level of differentiation and progress developmentally. Much of the therapeutic efforts could be classified as self–other restructuring. The real relationship with the therapist provided an experience of attachment with a noncontrolling and nonintrusive attachment figure with whom he was able to establish a secure attachment while he began the arduous process of differentiation.

Relational Restructuring

As Gottman and Gottman (2013) emphasize: "Individual therapy requires that only an individual and therapist be present in the consulting room; in relationship therapy, however, it is assumed that the two people appearing in the consulting room not only know one another but also have some sort of a relationship" (p. 101). Couples therapists use techniques of relational restructuring often by teaching and having couples practice their relational skills in the session and outside the consulting room.

Relational Elements and Principles

The dyadic level encompasses the relational skills and principles necessary for therapeutic effectiveness regardless of the therapeutic approach or modality utilized. Some of the important elements that are essential include development of a collaborative therapeutic alliance, the communication of empathy, openness and exploration, and the quality of the therapists' interpersonal skills (Horvath & Bedi, 2002). Psychotherapy is difficult work. Therapists often work with very disturbed individuals who may be in extreme states of distress and act in very self-destructive ways. The converging evidence suggests that our ability to manage and metabolize our own negative reactions to patients while maintaining compassion is an essential aspect of unified psychotherapy, regardless of the modality or domain level in which one is operating (Magnavita, 2013).

CASE EXAMPLE: RELATIONAL RESTRUCTURING

The couple—a man in his late 60s and woman in her late 50s—entered treatment after a 7-year relationship that became increasingly contentious and conflictual, resulting in the man's children "refusing to allow me to see Sally." There had been an escalation of Sally becoming triangulated with Sam's grown children, with a number of highly charged fights occurring between Sally and Sam's

(*continued*)

CASE EXAMPLE *(continued)*

children resulting in them separating. Sally initially entered treatment and had a low level of differentiation, blaming Sam's children and Sam for mistreating her. Sam was invited to attend a couples consultation and agreed. Sally immediately became emotionally dysregulated and Sam silent. Apparently, their relationship consisted of Sally attempting to "get Sam to stand up to his adult children who control him." Sam declared he felt pulled apart between his children and Sally, who expected to be "number one" to him. The first stage of relational restructuring followed the principles of couples therapy, which is to create a safe space to begin a differentiated communication. Following this phase Sally was able to begin to listen to Sam's feelings of being pulled apart by his children, to whom he felt he needed to remain loyal, and Sally's feelings of not being number one. As they began to explore the reality of their relationship they began to understand one another in a deeper fashion, and Sally developed some empathy for Sam, whose wife had died before they began dating and who he unrealistically thought Sally would replace.

SUMMARY

In this chapter the benefits of adopting a unifying framework when operating at the intrapsychic and dyadic levels of the personality system are illustrated. Restructuring the personality system of an individual benefits from utilizing a wide array of methods and techniques of contemporary clinical science. Various methods, submethods, and techniques of psychotherapy are organized into a compendium and correspond to the four levels of the personality system, and clinicians can select techniques to address the various dysfunctioning domain systems. Developing an understanding of the various techniques and the major domains that they address afford clinicians the opportunity to be more precise and focused in our interventions. Applying principles of personality systematics allows us to understand how the individual personality system operates at the intrapsychic level and is expressed dyadically, shaping and being shaped by our relationships. Symptoms expressions are representations of a personality system, and by selecting the most effective forms of restructuring can be altered in a more focused and systematic manner.

REFERENCES

Aldao, A. (2013). The future of emotion regulation research: Capturing context. *Perspectives on Psychological Science, 8,* 155–172.

American Psychiatric Association. (1994). *Diagnostic and statistical manual of mental disorders* (4th ed.). Washington, DC: Author.

Anchin, J. C. (2003). Cybernetic systems, existential phenomenology, and solution-focused narrative: Therapeutic transformation of negative affective states through integratively oriented brief psychotherapy. *Journal of Psychotherapy Integration, 13,* 334–442.

Anchin, J. C. (2006). A hermeneutically informed approach to psychotherapy integration. In G. Stricker & J. Gold (Eds.), *A casebook of psychotherapy integration* (pp. 261–280). Washington, DC: American Psychological Association.

Anchin, J. C., & Magnavita, J. J. (2006). The nature of unified clinical science: Implications for psychotherapeutic theory, practice, training, and research. *Psychotherapy Bulletin, 41*(2), 26–36.

Anchin, J. C., & Magnavita, J. J. (2008). Toward the unification of psychotherapy: An introduction to the journal symposium. *Journal of Psychotherapy Integration, 18,* 259–263.

Anchin, J. C., & Pincus, A. L. (2010). Evidence-based interpersonal psychotherapy with personality disorders: Theory, components, and strategies. In J. J. Magnavita (Ed.), *Evidence-based treatment of personality dysfunction: Principles, methods, and processes* (pp. 113–166). Washington, DC: American Psychological Association.

Barlow, D. (1988). *Anxiety and its disorders: The nature and treatment of anxiety and panic.* New York: Guilford.

Bateman, A. W., & Fonagy, P. (2006). *Mentalization-based treatment for borderline personality disorder: A practical guide.* New York: Oxford University Press.

Beck, J. (2011). *Cognitive behavior therapy: Basics and beyond* (2nd ed.). New York: Guilford.

Beck, A. T., Freeman, A., Davis, D. D., & Associates. (2004). *Cognitive therapy of personality disorders* (2nd ed.). New York: Guilford.

Beck, A. T., Rush, A. J., Shaw, B. F., & Emery, G. (1979). *Cognitive therapy of depression.* New York: Guilford.

Beck, A. T., & Weishaar, M. E. (2008). Cognitive therapy. In R. J. Corsini & D. Wedding (Eds.), *Current psychotherapies* (8th ed., pp. 263–294). Belmont, CA: Brooks/Cole.

Benjamin, L. S. (1996). *Interpersonal diagnosis and treatment of personality disorders* (2nd ed.). New York: Guilford.

Benjamin, L. S. (2003). *Interpersonal reconstructive therapy: Promoting change in nonresponders.* New York: Guilford.

Bertolino, B., Kiener, M., & Patterson, R. (2009). *The therapist's notebook on strengths and solution-based therapies.* New York: Routledge.

Bierer, L. M., Yehuda, R., Schmeidler, J., Mitropoulou, V., New, A. S., Silverman, J. M., & Siever, L. J. (2003). Abuse and neglect in childhood: Relationship to personality disorder diagnoses. *CNS Spectrums, 8,* 737–740, 749–754.

Blatt, S. J. (1995). The destructiveness of perfectionism: Implications for the treatment of depression. *American Psychologist, 50,* 1003–1020.

Bleiberg, E. (2001). *Treating personality disorders in children and adolescents: A relational approach.* New York: Guilford.

Block, J. (2002). *Personality as an affect-processing system: Toward an integrative theory.* Mahwah, NJ: Lawrence Erlbaum Associates.

Bornstein, R. F. (2011). From symptom to process: How the PDM alters goals and strategies in psychological assessment. *Journal of Personality Assessment, 93,* 142–150.

Brown, J. A., & Lane, R. C. (2000). Enactment, classical and relational perspectives: Definition, conceptualization, usefulness, and role in the therapeutic process. *Journal of Psychotherapy in Independent Practice, 1,* 71–87.

Brownell, P. (2010). *Gestalt therapy: A guide to contemporary practice.* New York: Springer Publishing.

Bugental, J. F. T. (1987). *The art of the psychotherapist.* New York: Norton.

Busch, F. N., Milrod, B. L., & Singer, M. B. (1999). Theory and technique in psychodynamic treatment of panic disorder. *Journal of Psychotherapy Practice and Research, 8,* 234–242.

Clarkin, J. P. (2012). An integrated approach to psychotherapy techniques for patients with personality disorders. *Journal of Personality Disorders, 26,* 43–62.

Clarkin, J. F., Fonagy, P., & Gabbard, G. O. (Eds.). (2010). *Psychodynamic psychotherapy for personality disorders: A clinical handbook.* Arlington, VA: American Psychiatric Publishing.

Clarkin, J. F., Yeomans, F. E., & Kernberg, O. F. (1999). *Psychotherapy for borderline personality.* New York: Wiley.

Cozolino, L. (2002). *The neuroscience of psychotherapy: Building and rebuilding the human brain.* New York: Norton.

Cozolino, L. (2010). *The neuroscience of psychotherapy: Healing the social brain* (2nd ed.). New York: Norton.

Cramer, P. (2000). Defense mechanisms in psychology today: Further processes for adaptation. *American Psychologist, 55,* 637–646.

Cramer, P. (2006). *Protecting the self: Defense mechanisms in action.* New York: Guilford.

Critchfield, K. L. (2012). Tailoring common treatment principles to fit individual personalities. *Journal of Personality Disorders, 26,* 108–125.

Critchfield, K. L., & Benjamin, L. S. (2006). Integration of therapeutic factors in treating personality disorders. In L. G. Castonguay & L. E. Beutler (Eds.), *Principles of therapeutic change that work.* (pp. 253–271). New York: Oxford University Press.

Csikszentmihalyi, M. (1991). *Flow: The psychology of optimal experience.* Scranton, PA: Harper Collins.

Davanloo, H. (Ed.). (1980). *Short-term dynamic psychotherapy.* New York: Jason Aaronson Press.

Dimaggio, G., & Livesley, W. J. (2012). Introduction to the special feature on the integrated treatment of personality disorder. *Journal of Personality Disorders, 26,* 1–6.

Dimaggio, G., Salvatore, G., Fiore, D., Carcione, A., Nicolò, G., & Semerari, A. (2012). General principles for treating personality disorder with a prominent inhibitedness trait: Towards an operationalizing integrated technique. *Journal of Personality Disorders, 26,* 63–83.

Donaldson-Pressman, S., & Pressman, R. M. (1994). *The narcissistic family: Diagnosis and treatment.* New York: Lexington Books.

Foa, E. B., Hembree, E. A., & Rothbaum, B. O. (2007). *Prolonged exposure therapy for PTSD: Emotional processing of traumatic experiences: Therapist guide.* New York: Oxford University Press.

Fosha, D. (2000). *The transforming power of affect: A model for accelerated change.* New York: Basic Books.

Fosha, D. (2003). Dyadic regulation and experiential work with emotion and relatedness in trauma and disordered attachment. In M. F. Solomon & D. J. Siegel (Eds.), *Healing trauma: Attachment, mind, body, and brain* (pp. 221–281). New York: Norton.

Fosha, D. (2004a). Brief integrative therapy comes of age: A commentary. *Journal of Psychotherapy Integration, 14*, 66–92.

Fosha, D. (2004b). "Nothing that feels bad is ever the last step:" the role of positive emotions in experiential work with difficult emotional experiences. Special issue on *Emotion,* L. Greenberg (Eds.), *Clinical Psychology and Psychotherapy, 11,* (pp. 30–43).

Fosha, D. (2008). Transformance, recognition of self by self, and effective action. In K. J. Schneider (Ed.), *Existential-integrative psychotherapy: Guideposts to the core of practice* (pp. 290–320). New York: Routledge.

Fosha, D., & Yeung, D. (2006). Accelerated experiential-dynamic psychotherapy: The seamless integration of emotional transformation and dyadic relatedness at work. In G. Stricker & J. Gold (Eds.), *A casebook of psychotherapy integration* (pp. 165–184). Washington DC: American Psychological Association.

Frances, A., Clarkin, J. F., & Perry, S. (1984). *Differential therapeutics in psychiatry: The art and science of treatment selection.* New York: Brunner/Mazel.

Freeman, A., Pretzer, J., Fleming, B., & Simon, K. M. (2004). *Clinical applications of cognitive therapy* (2nd ed.). New York: Kluwer Academic/Plenum Press.

Freeman, A., & Reinecke, M. A. (Eds.). (2007). *Personality disorders in childhood and adolescence.* Hoboken, NJ: Wiley.

Gabbard, G. O. (2005). Mind, brain, and personality disorders. *American Journal of Psychiatry, 162,* 648–655.

Gelso, C. J. (2009). The real relationship in a postmodern world: Theoretical and empirical explorations. *Psychotherapy Research, 19,* 253–264.

Gelso, C. J. (2011). *The real relationship in psychotherapy: The hidden foundation of change.* Washington, DC: American Psychological Association.

Gendlin, E. T. (1996). *Focusing-oriented psychotherapy: A manual of the experiential method.* New York: Guilford.

Goldfried, M. R., & Davison, G. C. (1976). *Clinical behavior therapy.* New York: Holt, Rinehart & Winston.

Gordon, R. M. (2010). The psychodynamic diagnostic manual (PDM). In I. Weiner & E. Craighead (Eds.), *Corsini's Encyclopedia of Psychology* (4th ed., Vol. 3, pp. 1312–1315). Hoboken, NJ: Wiley.

Gottman, J. M. (1994). *What predicts divorce? the relationship between marital processes and marital outcomes.* Hillsdale, NJ: Lawrence Erlbaum Associates.

Gottman, J. M. (1999). *The marriage clinic: A scientifically based marital therapy.* New York: Norton.

Gottman, J. M., & Gottman, J. S. (2013). Difficulties with clients in gottman method couples therapy. In A. W. Wolf M. R. Goldfried & J. C. Muran (Eds.), *Transforming negative reactions to clients: From frustration to compassion* (pp. 91–112). Washington, DC: American Psychological Association.

Grawe, K. (2007). *Neuropsychotherapy: How the neurosciences inform effective psychotherapy.* New York: Psychology Press.

Green, M. J., Cahill, C. M., & Malhi, G. S. (2007). The cognitive and neurophysiological basis of emotion dysregulation in bipolar disorder. *Journal of Affective Disorders, 103,* 29–42.

Greenberg, L. S., & Paivio, S. C. (1997). *Working with emotion in psychotherapy.* New York: Guilford.

Gross, J. I. (2002). Emotion regulation: Affective, cognitive, and social consequences. *Psychophysiology, 39,* 281–291.

Gurman, A. S. (Ed.). (2008). *Clinical handbook of couple therapy* (4th ed.). New York: Guilford.

Hayes, S. C., Villatte, M., Levin, M., & Hildebrandt, M. (2011). Open, aware, and active: Contextual approaches as an emerging trend in the behavioral and cognitive therapies. *Annual Review of Clinical Psychology, 7,* 141–168.

Henriques, G. (2011). *A new unified theory of psychology.* New York: Springer Press.

Horvath, A. O., & Bedi, R. P. (2002). The alliance. In J. C. Norcross (Eds.), *Psychotherapy relationships that work: Therapists contributions and responsiveness to patients* (pp. 37–69). New York: Oxford University Press.

Hossack, A., & Bentall, R. P. (1996). Elimination of posttraumatic symptomatology by relaxation and visual-kinesthetic dissociation. *Journal of Traumatic Stress, 9,* 99–110.

Huprich, S. K., & Meyer, G. J. (2011). Introduction to the JPA special issue: Can the psychodynamic diagnostic manual put the complex person back at the center-stage of personality assessment? *Journal of Personality Assessment, 93,* 109–111.

Jacobs, T. S. (1986). On countertransference enactments. *Journal of the American Psychoanalytic Association, 34,* 289–307.

Johnson, S. M. (2004). *The practice of emotionally focused couple therapy: Creating connection.* New York: Brunner/Routledge.

Kagan, J. (2012). *Psychology's ghosts: The crisis in the profession and the way back.* New Haven, CT: Yale University Press.

Kernberg, P., Weiner, A., & Bardenstein, K. (2000). *Personality disorders in children and adolescents.* New York: Basic Books.

Kiesler, D. J. (1996). *Contemporary interpersonal theory and research: Personality, psychopathology, and psychotherapy.* New York: Wiley.

Kiesler, D. J. (1999). *Beyond the disease model of mental disorders.* Westport, CN: Praeger.

Kring, A. M., & Sloan, D. M. (Eds.). (2010). *Emotion regulation and psychopathology: A transdiagnostic approach to etiology and treatment.* New York: Guilford.

Lamagna, J. (2011). Of the self, by the self, and for the self: An intra-relational perspective on intra-psychic attunement and psychological change. *Journal of Psychotherapy Integration, 21,* 280–307.

Lebow, J. L. (Ed.). (2008). *Twenty-first century psychotherapies: Contemporary approaches to theory and practice.* Hoboken, NJ: Wiley.

Lebow, J. L., & Gasbarrini, M. F. (2009). Couples therapy. In G. O. Gabbard (Ed.), *Textbook of psychotherapeutic treatments* (pp. 533–552). Washington, DC: American Psychiatric Press.

LeDoux, J. (2002). *Synaptic self: How our brains become who we are.* New York: Penguin Books.

Linehan, M. M. (1993). *Cognitive-behavioral treatment of borderline personality disorder.* New York: Guilford.

Lipton, B., & Fosha, D. (2011). Attachment as a transformative process in AEDP: Opertionalizing the intersection of attachment theory and affective neuroscience. *Journal of Psychotherapy Integration, 21,* 253–279.

Livesley, W. J. (Ed.). (2001). *Handbook of personality disorders: Theory, research, and treatment.* New York: Guilford.

Livesley, W. J. (2003). *Practical management of personality disorder.* New York: Guilford.

Livesley, W. J. (2012). Integrated treatment: A conceptual framework for an evidence-based approach to the treatment of personality disorder. *Journal of Personality Disorders, 26,* 17–42.

Magnavita, J. J. (1997). *Restructuring personality disorders: A short-term dynamic approach.* New York: Guilford.

Magnavita, J. J. (2000). *Relational therapy for personality disorders.* Hoboken, NJ: Wiley.

Magnavita, J. J. (2004). Toward a unified model of treatment for personality dysfunction. In J. J. Magnavita (Eds.), *Handbook of personality disorders: Theory and practice* (pp. 528–553). Hoboken, NJ: Wiley.

Magnavita, J. J. (2005). *Personality-guided relational therapy: A unified approach.* Washington, DC: American Psychological Association.

Magnavita, J. J. (2007). A systemic family perspective on child and adolescent personality disorders. In A. Freeman & M. Reinecke (Eds.), *Personality disorders in children and adolescents* (pp. 131–181). Hoboken, NJ: Wiley.

Magnavita, J. J. (2010). Methods, components, and strategies of unified treatment: Using evidence and personality systematics to enhance outcome. In J. J. Magnavita (Eds.), *Evidence-based treatment of personality dysfunction: Principles, methods, and processes* (pp. 253–285). Washington, DC: American Psychological Association.

Magnavita, J. J. (2012). Mapping the clinical landscape with psychotherapedia™: The unified psychotherapy project. *Journal of Unified Psychotherapy and Clinical Science, 1,* 21–36.

Magnavita, J. J. (2013). Pattern recognition in the treatment of narcissistic disorders: Countertransference from a unified perspective. In A. W. Wolf M. R. Goldfried & J. C. Muran (Eds.), *Transforming negative reactions to clients: From frustration to compassion* (pp. 221–244). Washington, DC: American Psychological Association.

Magnavita, J. J., & MacFarlane, M. M. (2004). Family treatment of personality disorders: A historical overview and current perspectives. In M. M. MacFarlane (Ed.), *Family treatment of personality disorders: Advances in clinical practice* (pp. 3–39). New York: The Haworth Clinical Practice Press.

Magnavita, J. J., Powers, A. D., Barber, J. P., & Oltmanns, T. F. (2013). Personality disorders. In L. G. Castonguay & T. F. Oltmanns (Eds.), *Psychopathology: From science to clinical practice.* New York: Guilford.

Mahoney, M. J. (1991). *Human change processes: The scientific foundations of psychotherapy.* New York: Basic Books.

Mann, D. (2010). *Gestalt therapy: 100 key points and techniques.* New York: Routledge.

Marquis, A. (2009). An integral taxonomy of therapeutic interventions. *Journal of Integral Theory and Practice, 4,* 13–42.

Mayer, J. D. (1998). A systems framework for the field of personality. *Psychological Inquiry, 9,* 118–144.

McCullough, L., Kuhn, N., Andrews, S., Kaplan, A., Wolf, J., & Hurley, C. L. (2003). *Treating affect phobia: A manual for short-term dynamic psychotherapy.* New York: Guilford.

McCullough Valliant, L. (1997). *Changing character: Short-term anxiety-regulating psychotherapy for restructuring defenses, affects, and attachment.* New York: Basic Books.

McNulty, J. K., & Fincham, F. D. (2012). Beyond positive psychology? toward a contextual view of psychological processes and well-being. *American Psychologist, 67,* 101–110

McWilliams, N. (2011). The *psychodynamic diagnostic manual*: An effort to compensate for the limitations of descriptive psychiatric diagnosis. *Journal of Personality Assessment, 93,* 112–122.

Melchert, T. P. (2013). Beyond theoretical orientations: the emergence of a unified scientific framework in professional psychology. *Professional Psychology: Research and Practice, 44,* 11–19.

Merikangas, K., & Weissman, M. (1986). Epidemiology of DSM-III Axis II personality disorders. In A. FrancesHales (Eds.), *Psychiatry update* (pp. 258–278). Washington, DC: American Psychiatric Press.

Millon, T. (with Grossman, S., Meager, S., Millon, C., & Everly, G.). (1999). *Personality-guided therapy*. Hoboken, NJ: Wiley.

Milrod, B. L., Leon, A. C., Barber, J. P., Markowitz, J. C., & Graf, E. (2007). Do comorbid personality disorders moderate panic-focused psychotherapy? an exploratory examination of the American Psychiatric Association practice guideline. *Journal of Clinical Psychiatry, 68*, 885–891.

Newman, M. C., Crits-Christoph, P., Gibbons, M. B. C., & Erickson, T. M. (2006). Participant factors in treating anxiety disorders. In L. G. Castonguay & L. E. Beutler (Eds.), *Principles of therapeutic change that work* (pp. 121–154). New York: Oxford University Press.

Norcross, J. C., Krebs, P. M., & Prochaska, J. O. (2011). Stages of change. In J. C. Norcross (Eds.), *Psychotherapy relationships that work: Evidence-based responsiveness* (2nd ed., pp. 279–300). New York: Oxford University Press.

Norcross, J. C., & Lambert, M. J. (2011). Evidence-based therapy relationships. In J. C. Norcross (Eds.), *Psychotherapy relationships that work: Evidence-based responsiveness* (2nd ed., pp. 3–21). New York: Oxford University Press.

O'Connell, B. (1998). *Solution-focused therapy*. Thousand Oaks, CA: Sage.

Paunovic, N. (2002) Prolonged exposure counterconditioning (PEC) as a treatment for chronic post-traumatic stress disorder and major depression in an adult survivor of repeated child sexual and physical abuse. *Clinical Case Studies, 1*, 148–169.

Paunovic, N. (2003) Prolonged exposure counterconditioning as a treatment for chronic posttraumatic stress disorder. *Journal of Anxiety Disorders, 17*, 479–499.

Perls, F. (1973). *The Gestalt approach and eyewitness to therapy*. Palo Alto, CA: Science and Behavior Books.

Perls, F. S., Hefferline, R. F., & Goodman, P. (1951). *Gestalt therapy: Excitement and growth in the human personality*. New York: Julian Press.

Pinsof, W. M., Goldsmith, J. Z., & Latta, T. A. (2012). Information technology and feedback research can bridge the scientist–practitioner gap: A couple therapy example. *Couple and Family Psychology: Research and Practice, 1*, 253–273.

Prenn, N. (2011). Mind the gap: AEDP interventions translating attachment theory into clinical practice. *Journal of Psychotherapy Integration, 21*, 308–329.

Prochaska, J. O., DiClemente, C. C., & Norcross, J. C. (1992). In search of how people change: Applications to addictive behaviors. *American Psychologist, 47*, 1102–1114.

Prochaska, J. O., Norcross, J. C., & DiClemente, C. C. (1994). *Changing for good: The revolutionary program that explains the six stages of change and teaches you how to free yourself from bad habits*. New York: W. Morrow.

PDM Task Force. (2006). *Psychodynamic diagnostic manual*. Silver Spring, MD: Author.

Reich, W. (1933). *Character analysis*. Leipzig, DE: Verlag.

Riso, L., du Toit, P. L., Stein, D. J., & Young, J. E. (Eds.). (2007). *Cognitive schemas and core beliefs in psychological problems: A scientist-practitioner guide*. Washington, DC: American Psychological Association.

Robjant, K., & Fazel, M. (2010). The emerging evidence for narrative exposure therapy: A review. *Clinical Psychology Review, 30*, 1030–1039.

Robins, C. J., Rosenthal, M. Z., & Cuper, P. F. (2010). Dialectical behavior therapy. In J. J. Magnavita (Eds.), *Evidence-based treatment of personality dysfunction: Principles, methods, and processes* (pp. 49–78). Washington, DC: American Psychological Association.

Robinson, D. N. (1995). *An intellectual history of psychology* (3rd ed.). Madison, WI: University of Wisconsin Press.

Safran, J. D., & Muran, J. C. (2000). *Negotiating the therapeutic alliance: A relational treatment guide.* New York: Guilford.

Schauer, M., Neuner, F., & Elbert, T. (2012). *Narrative exposure therapy: A short-term treatment for traumatic stress disorders* (2nd, rev. and expanded ed.). Gottingen, DE: Hogrefe Publishing.

Schore, A. N. (2012). *The science of the art of psychotherapy.* New York: Norton.

Shapiro, F. (2001). *Eye movement desensitization and reprocessing: Basic principles, protocols and procedures* (2nd ed.). New York: Guilford.

Shear, M. K., Cooper, A. M., Klerman, G. L., Busch, F. N., & Shapiro, T. (1993). A psychodynamic model of panic disorder. *American Journal of Psychiatry, 150,* 859–866.

Shedler, J., & Westen, D. (2004). Dimensions of personality pathology: An alternative to the five-factor model. *American Journal of Psychiatry, 161,* 1743–1754.

Silvers, J. A., Buhle, J. T., & Ochsner, K. N. (in press). The neuroscience of emotion regulation: Basic mechanisms and their role in development, aging and psychopathology. In K. N. Ochsner & S. M. Kosslyn (Eds.), *The Oxford handbook of cognitive neuroscience* (Vol. 2). New York: Oxford University Press.

Sperry, L. (2003). *Handbook of the diagnosis and treatment of DSM-IV-TR personality disorders* (2nd ed.). Philadelphia: Brunner-Routledge.

Strupp, H. H. (1978). The therapist's theoretical orientation: An overrated variable. *Psychotherapy, 15,* 314–317.

Treanor, M. (2011). The potential impact of mindfulness on exposure and extinction processes in anxiety disorders. *Clinical Psychology Review, 31,* 617–625.

Viamontes, G. I., & Beitman, B. D. (2009). Brain processes informing psychotherapy. In G. O. Gabbard (Ed.), *Textbook of psychotherapeutic treatments* (pp. 781–808). Washington, DC: American Psychiatric Press.

Webster's Ninth New Collegiate Dictionary. (1985). Springfield, MA: Merriam-Webster Inc.

Westen, D., Gabbard, G. O., & & Blagov, P. (2006). Back to the future: Personality structure as a context for psychopathology. In R. F. Krueger & J. L. Tackett (Eds.), *Personality and psychopathology* (pp. 335–384). New York: Guilford.

Widiger, T. A., & Costa, P. T., Jr. (Ed.). (2013). *Personality disorders and the five-factor model of personality* (3rd ed.). Washington, DC: American Psychological.

Wolf, A. W., Goldfried, M. R., & Muran, J. C. (Eds.). (2013). *Transforming negative reactions to clients: From frustration to compassion.* Washington, DC: American Psychological Association.

Woody, S. R., & Ollendick, T. H. (2006). Technique factors in treating anxiety disorders. In L. G. Castonguay & L. E. Beutler. (2006). (Eds.), *Principles of therapeutic change that work.* (pp. 167–186). New York: Oxford University Press.

Yen, S., Shea, M. T., Johnson, D. M., Zlotnick, C., Dolan-Sewell, R., Skodol, A. E., ... & McGlashan, T. H. (2002). Traumatic exposure and posttraumatic stress disorder in borderline, schiozotypal, avoidant, and obsessive-compulsive personality disorders: Findings from the collaborative longitudinal personality disorder study. *Journal of Nervous and Mental Disease, 190,* 510–518.

Yeomans, F. E., Clarkin, J. F., & Kernberg, O. F. (2002). *A primer of transference-focused psychotherapy for borderline patients.* Oxford, UK: Jason Aaronson.

Young, J. E. (1999). *Cognitive therapy for personality disorders: A schema-focused approach* (3rd ed.). Sarasota, FL: Professional Resource Press.

Young, J. E., Klosko, J. S., & Weishaar, M. (2003). *Schema therapy: A practioner's guide.* New York: Guilford.

Chapter 9

UNIFYING PSYCHOTHERAPEUTICS

Triadic, Family, and Sociocultural Domains

A family seeking assistance for a troubled child and a couple experiencing an extramarital affair cannot be fully understood at the intrapsychic and dyadic level. Moving beyond the intrapsychic and dyadic levels to the triadic, family, and sociocultural are essential to unifying psychotherapy. Familiarity engaging intrapsychic and interpersonal systems and processes, using various restructuring methods and techniques, are essential but not sufficient. In this chapter, we continue to describe and illustrate how to orient treatment using unified principles, methods, and techniques at Level III—*relational–triadic* and Level IV—*sociocultural–familial*. In the previous chapter we explained how the *intrapsychic system—* individual personality, and the *dyadic—interpersonal* systems are central domains of many contemporary treatment approaches. We illustrated how dyads are formed through affective processes, fueling our attachment bonds, which when dysfunctional lead to clinical syndromes and behavioral and relational disturbances. These dyads, which are important relational molecules, tend to be unstable-forming threesomes, or under stress become pathological or triangulating, impeding growth and development in individuals, couples, and families. By expanding our range of operation to relational units beyond the dyad we can develop a much greater facility in understanding and strategizing treatment, incorporating the techniques from Psychotherapedia™ that will maximize treatment effects. In this chapter we illustrate some of the basic principles of how to flexibly work in triads, families, and larger relational systems. We use "relational" to describe systems beyond the twosome, the focus of interpersonal perspectives. We begin with principles, processes, methods, and techniques for working with triads, then move to family systems, and then finally to larger relational domains such as the social, political, and cultural system.

OPERATING AT THE TRIADIC LEVEL III

The lower the levels of integrity of the individual personality system and of differentiation in primary dyadic relationships, the greater the likelihood that triadic processes are in operation in a dysfunctioning system. Loyalties that may work at cross-purposes are established or maintained over generations. A woman abused by a family member may remain locked in a triangle of loyalty with her deceased parents who betrayed her. A relatively minor event, such as a financial or career setback, may disrupt a fixed system, creating a tipping point that results in escalating dysfunction. It is critical to recognize and track these systemic perturbations. Triadic as well as dyadic configurations represent the dialectic in humans between the need for change and the desire for stability. Fixed or rigid triangles, which have become triangulated, impede change, whereas flexible ones allow growth and autonomous functioning. Whether the goals of treatment are symptomatic reduction, relational disturbance, or personality restructuring, methods and techniques of *triadic restructuring (TR)* are important elements of unified treatment when working at the triadic–relational level.

Methods and Techniques of Triadic Restructuring (TR)

As we have presented, unstable dyads, which are characterized by low levels of differentiation in the individual personality system, are prone to triangulate others, most notably children and vulnerable others, such as in extramarital affairs. Again, nonmetabolized feelings over unresolved conflict leads to anxiety, which, when poorly regulated at the intrapsychic or dyadic level, leads to triangulation. When healthy, dyads are excellent anxiety-regulating systems—for example, when we are hurt or in distress, connecting and receiving an empathic response from another person can help us restore our psychic equilibrium. Guerin et al. (1996) pointed out, "It's important to remember that the essence of a triangle is to lower anxiety in the individual and tension in the twosome by shifting to the discussion of a third person or issue" (p. 49). They suggest that the clinician should be alert to the following triadic functions: (a) stabilization of unstable dyad, (b) displacing dyadic anxiety, and (c) avoiding intimacy and closeness. Triadic restructuring encompasses a number of techniques that allow for structural changes in fixed triangulated relationships.

TR is a method of psychotherapy that emphasizes the enhancement of processes and reorganization of structures, which occur in a three-person system or multiple overlapping triangular configurations (Bowen, 1976; Minuchin, 1974; Guerin et al., 1996). The focus of triadic restructuring is the relational-triadic subsystems that are three-person relational configurations (Bowen, 1976; Minuchin, 1974). The following submethods are included in this category:

1. *Relational–triadic restructuring* (Magnavita, 2005). In this submethod of TR, the focus is on techniques and processes that serve to de-triangulate an individual from a fixed triad. Techniques that encourage self-focus and prevent blaming of others are subsumed under relational triadic restructuring (Guerin et al., 1996). Minuchin (1974) pioneered many useful structural techniques vis-à-vis relational triangles. As indicated elsewhere (Magnavita, 2004), "Many of his interventions consisted of blocking transactions to restructure hierarchy in a family and actively rearranging family members to restructure their preferred relational patterns" (p. 546).

2. *Symbolic–relational restructuring* (Magnavita, 2005). In this submethod of TR triadic differentiation is undertaken without the presence of one or two members of the triadic configuration. Individual modalities of treatment may serve this function by emphasizing the triadic schema in which a person has participated. Educating an individual about the purpose and functions of triangles provides awareness of his or her power and improves the chance of not being drawn into these configurations.

Recognizing triangulated relationships serves as a useful pattern recognition tool for the clinician, alerting us to powerful dynamic forces operative within a system. Guerin et al. (1996) described this process:

...developmental and situational stress trigger anxiety and depression in the individual. This state of emotional arousal often results in behavior patterns that produce conflict in relationships and support dysfunction in the individuals. This process inevitably activates surrounding relationship triangles and becomes embedded in them. These triangles in turn reinforce pathology in the individuals and conflict in their relationships. (p. 37)

The reader can imagine that in the relational–triadic matrix (Figure 6.1), the flow of anxiety between the dyad is so intense that it seeks the third corner of the triangle to absorb some of this attention by shifting the focus. For example, if one of the parents is in an addictive process that threatens to destabilize or destroy a marriage, the couple's child may develop some physical, somatic, or emotional problem that diverts attention and allows the couple to continue without addressing the issue that is creating anxiety in both parties.

Using a unified perspective allows us to adopt the pattern recognition tools that help us see the complexity and interrelatedness of clinical phenomena. If the reader has not been introduced to the concept of relational triangles, it will become readily apparent that once this construct is assimilated, it is extremely helpful in tracking many dynamic processes in various therapeutic modalities.

The Dialectic of Holding a Parsimonious and Complex Perspective

Effective clinicians have the capacity to live in a dialectic world where opposing forces and perspectives must be held simultaneously. In unified psychotherapy, the process is to find the most parsimonious understanding, while having a grasp of the enormous complexity of each system we encounter; where to focus attention is the most challenging aspect of unified treatment; where our clinical attention alights is what is honored in the system and where the energy and information exchange takes place. So it is important to shine the light of our attention where it is most illuminating to the change process. Attempting to see the situation through multiple lenses and then intervening in as focal a manner as possible is the goal. It is important not to become overly fixated in any domain without good reason to do so.

Rapidly Identifying and Mapping the Spectrum of Triadic Configurations

It is beyond the scope of this volume to present in detail the scope of triadic conceptualizations, but it is useful to have a triadic map handy to use as another pattern recognition tool. Readers who are not familiar with relational triangles are strongly advised to read Guerin et al.'s (1996) *Working with Relationship Triangles: The One-Two-Three of Psychotherapy*. This is an excellent volume on working triadically. The authors provide a comprehensive review of two common categories of triangular configurations: *extrafamilial* and *intrafamilial*. These are important to be cognizant of because of their ubiquity in clinical practice. Extrafamilial triangles include (a) extramarital affairs, (b) social network triangles—for example, boys at a local bar, and (c) occupational triangles—that is, excessive devotion and escape into work. Intrafamilial triangles include: (a) in-law triangles, which entail overinvolvement with family of origin, (b) triangles with children, which may cross generational boundaries, (c) spouse and sibling triangles, involving overinvestment in the sibling system, and (d) primary parental triangles, entailing a primary triangle brought to a new relationship and re-enacted. The point is to use the lens of the triadic level to ferret out dynamic configurations that may have existed for a substantial period of time or are evolving and becoming problematic.

Having worked over the years with countless couples who have been in triangulated relationships underscores a common theme that when aware of becomes obvious. Couples who are in triangulated relationships often seem on the verge of destruction and in some cases can maintain these stable-chaotic states for years. These couples and/or individuals seem to walk close to the abyss and may incite within the therapist countertransference reactions of worry and feeling burdened by an eminent catastrophe "on one's watch."

CASE EXAMPLE: TRIADIC RESTRUCTURING: WALKING AROUND HOLDING A HAND GRENADE WITH THE PIN OUT

Cindy, a woman in her 30s, phoned the therapist asking for an appointment, saying that she was very worried about her husband Lew, a 36-year-old executive who she said was spending all his time working and sometimes sleeping at the office. She came in for the initial session and outlined her concerns, including concerns about his drinking. She was asked to invite him into the next session, which he attended. He reported that he was in fairly severe distress and for about a year was engaged in a sexual affair with his secretary at work. Shortly afterward the wife discovered this when she saw their text messages to each other. Couples work was suggested and Lew said that he did not want a divorce and would stop the affair. Cindy said that she wanted to preserve the marriage. They had three young boys and she still loved him, although she did not know how much longer she could take his deception and betrayal. Lew was seen for some individual work where he reported that he was a victim of rather extensive trauma as a child and was told by his father that all men suffer and then die. He engaged in a brief course of trauma-focused treatment with some benefit. In his individual sessions Lew became aware of how he took a passive position in his marriage, as did his father. He also reported extreme mood

(continued)

CASE EXAMPLE (*continued*)

variability and demonstrated episodes of emotional dysregulation in the sessions at the slightest criticism from his wife when she was present. Lew said he wanted to stop the affair but on a number of occasions resumed his relationship, thereby threatening the marriage. The course of treatment was quite stormy during this phase and talk of separation and divorce ensued. Cindy began to get closer to a single male who was interested in her, stimulating an intense jealous reaction from Lew who called the man and told him to back off. The focus of the individual treatment was on his wish to destroy his marriage and family and start over with his girlfriend, but every time he came close to "blowing it all up" he expressed ambivalence and did not want to be separated from his children while raising his girlfriend's child. In both individual and couples sessions Lew was told that in order to work on the marriage he would have to discontinue his extramarital relationship, which caused him much distress. As he became committed to this path, his level of distress in his relationship with his wife escalated. He became very despairing and suicidal, believing he could not get what he needed from his wife and only tentatively approaching her because of his rejection sensitivity. He was also placed on psychotropic medication to help with his depression and emotional dysregulation, which provided some help. At his wife's urging he was able to help his secretary leave for another position. The marriage stabilized and they discontinued treatment. He returned about 3 months later saying the marriage was now stabilized but that he was beginning to fall into the same pattern with his new "attractive" secretary. It became clear in that session that he did not have much in the way of self-care and put all his energy into his career (another triangle) because this is where he felt affirmed. He was able to discuss the developing extramarital relationship and then talked through the sequence of what would happen if he wound up following his fantasy and living with her. We discussed how he walked around with a hand grenade with the pin out and that he could easily blow up his life, destroying his marriage and career in one final act of destructiveness. The next phase of work focused on his lack of differentiation and his fear of getting his needs met from his wife.

In these cases where the triangulated relationships are unstable it is imperative to foster stabilization to the fullest extent possible while the therapeutic process can proceed. Working too rapidly can result in highly destructive forces being unleashed, and unfortunately the patterns will reconfigure in future relationships, usually at a less differentiated level. In this case, in which multimodal therapy was offered, it is easy to identify one of multiple domain systems to account for the relational and personality disturbance. One might say that Lew is someone with a need for high stimulation and is dopamine deficient. However, while there is some truth to this, from the perspectives provided by a unifying framework one can see that in fact multiple domain levels interacting from the past and present are shaping this trajectory. Finally, Lew began to work on his lack of assertiveness in his marriage and his belief that he deserved to identify and meet some of his own needs, such as taking family vacations without his in-laws (another triangle that was addressed in the couples work).

Regulating and Shifting Triadic Pathways of Anxiety

It is important when conducting triadic restructuring to assess the level and pathways of anxiety, and when making a structural shift to be careful that too much anxiety gets diverted, which may be difficult to modulate and may flood the system. For example, in one case a man with a history of violence was having a 7-year affair with a woman who began to put pressure on him to leave his wife. When it became clear that she was going to hold her ground he became increasingly emotionally dysregulated as his abandonment fears were activated. His ambivalence was so intense that he continued to pay for her living expenses even while she started seeing other men. His relationship with his wife also worsened during this period as he became even more preoccupied with his mistress. Although very resistant at first, he agreed to a course of trauma-focused therapy to process some violent events he had been involved in, and this seemed to increase his tolerance of his mistress separating. A focus on his ability to regulate his emotions and a restructuring of his negative believes allowed him to navigate this period without resorting to violence, which was part of his adaptational strategy when feeling threatened.

CASE EXAMPLE: TRIADIC RESTRUCTURING OF THE SIBLING–PARENTAL SUBSYSTEM

The couple with severe marital dysfunction was at a stalemate. The wife believed that unless her husband stopped drinking and using pornography she would not have anything to do with him. Feeling more abandoned and rejected fed the husband's destructive cycle. The family was seen with all the children and the wife's therapist. It was clear that the father was marginalized and took a passive

(continued)

CASE EXAMPLE (*continued*)

position. During the session some structural interventions were suggested and followed up on. The couple's young-adult male children were brought into treatment for consultation. The father and his two sons were seen in an attempt to strengthen this subsystem, which seemed the healthiest in the system. The young college-age students were parentified in that they stepped up and assumed care-taking roles for two special-needs adopted children that the couple took on to stabilize their highly conflicted marital dyad. During the session the father asked one of his sons if he should come home from work earlier, as he avoided the emotional conflict in the marraige by working as much as possible to be out of the house. Before leaving for the session, the mother said to one son: "You don't love me anymore." He was preparing to return to school after semester break and would not be available for providing daycare for his younger adopted siblings. This type of powerful force exerted in family systems exerts pressure on other members that may result in their development becoming impeded. In this case it was suggested that the young men could set a boundary with their mother and, except in special circumstances, verbally communicate to her that she and their dad had decided to adopt and they were not going to be doing childcare. The father supported this stance and all three of them expressed fear that "Mom might go crazy" if they set boundaries. She had a breakdown in the past and they were worried that it would happen again. They were able to articulate their feelings about being "held hostage" by their mother's needs and expressed anger at their father for retreating into his work to escape the anxiety.

OPERATING AT THE MESOSYSTEM LEVEL IV

The mesosystem includes the interrelationship among the individual, family, and sociocultural systems. We can impact the mesosystem by changing any critical element, but this level represents the most complex interplay of the various domains of the TES and is most prone to chaos, which can be created by small perturbations in almost any part of the system.

Treatment Strategies and Principles for the Mesosystem Domains

Treatment strategies for the mesosystem in effect subsume all the methods presented in this volume as well as all the techniques of contemporary clinical science. However, it is useful to underscore some of the strategies of the various domain systems and get a sense of how it all works—which, as likely has become apparent by this point, is often chaotic and far from predictable.

Individual Personality System

As we have discussed in detail, the individual personality system in a sense is the smallest relational unit that interacts with the family and larger systems. Our personality system is constantly interacting with and being responded to by the systems in which we are embedded, an essential one of which is the family system into which we are born, or adopted, and raised.

Family System

We believe that the family is a central domain of personality systematics and it behooves all clinicians to have a basic familiarity with family processes and structures, regardless of the treatment model that is preferred. The family system is a somewhat flexible relational unit, which is shaped by social, cultural, political, economic, multigenerational, and ecosystem factors. The family unit is the main relational system responsible for socialization and the shaping of one's personality system. A network of interacting relational units,

> [t]he family, or any other relationship system, can be viewed structurally as a network of potential triangles that interlock with one another. (For instance, the husband and wife in a family are two points with connections to each of their children, various in-laws, friends, and others.) These triangles are dormant when the level of emotional arousal in the individuals and the tension in the relationship are low. Stress triggers emotional arousal with the individual, thereby increasing the tension in the relationship dyad. The combination of these factors (stress, emotional arousal, and tension) activates the triangle. (Guerin et al., 1996, pp. 55–56)

Clinicians generally do not encounter functional families in their work. The more common experience is of dysfunctional families experiencing chronic states of distress, which can be a pathway for personality dysfunction, clinical syndromes, and relational disturbances. Characteristics of dysfunctional families have been discussed in Chapter 7. Research indicates that "both a negative emotional environment and a disturbed attachment between parents and their child may contribute to the development and maintenance of severe psychopathology and to recurrent relapse" (Doane & Diamond, 1994, p. 35). Untreated stress can lead to an intergenerational spiral where unresolved core issues or trauma can be reactivated in family members and create a bionegative state that becomes chronic, leading to a multigenerational deterioration of family members. Generally, dysfunctional family systems seem to be more likely to experience chaos than stable functional families (Evans & Wachs, 2010).

Dysfunctional families cut across all socioeconomic levels. Families from different socioeconomic levels may cope with different challenges and the resulting pathological adaptations may be expressed differently. Families from lower socioeconomic levels may evidence various "dimensions of chaos: crowding and density, noise and confusion, clutter and messiness, fluidity and instability of residents, lack of predictability and routines, [and] low supervision and monitoring" (Brooks-Gunn, Johnson, & Leventhal, 2010, p. 156).

General Family Treatment Goals

The basic goals of treatment will naturally vary from family to family and should be determined after assessment of each family system and the related domain levels active in the disturbance. The general goals of treatment include the following: (a) improved communication, (b) enhanced emotional capacity and strengthening of emotional regulation among various relational components, (c) creation of functional family hierarchies, (d) development of higher-level defenses, (e) enhanced capacity for intimacy or enhancing capacity for attachment, (f) enhanced capacity to accommodate different family members' evolving needs for autonomy, (g) improved problem-solving capacity, (h) greater capacity for tolerating anxiety without triangulation, and (i) ability to flexibly navigate life cycle transition periods and adapt to new family demands, for example launching young adults, accepting new family members, and dealing with aging parents (Magnavita, 2005).

Sociocultural Systems

Social systems strongly influence how personality develops; a person's relationships and the people he or she associates with on a still-broader scale continuously shape and influence how his or her personality is expressed. "The world we live in is a complex amalgam of meanings and practices. Stories about ourselves, others, and social institutions such as the family and the workplace, and about the past and the future of our countries and the world as a whole, fill the space in which we live or lives" (Kitayama, Conway, Pietromonaco, Park, & Plaut, 2010, p. 561). Even the city or region where we reside says something about our personality. Researchers are beginning to study the effects that physical environments, such as living in cities, have on character strengths (Park & Peterson, 2010), and others are examining the impact that regional differences have on our personality (Rentfrow, 2010). Research demonstrates the influence the sociocultural system has on shaping character, supporting the multidimensional nature of the TES. Various hypotheses about how regional differences affect personality have been put forth. These differences may be the result of "selective migration patterns—that people migrate to places that satisfy and reinforce their basic psychological needs" (Rentfrow, 2010, p. 551). An alternative explanation is "that regional personality differences emerge as a result of social influence—individuals' thoughts, feelings, and behaviors are affected by the people around them" (p. 551), and another possibility is that "differences are a result of ecological influence—aspects of the physical environment affect how people interact as well as the types of activities in which they engage" (p. 551). Rentfrow (2010) believes that "these three hypotheses are not mutually exclusive but probably work in concert" (p. 551). Relative to these influences, we believe it is important to be clinically alert to the "goodness-of-fit" individual and family systems have with their geographical location. When there is incongruity it is likely that the system will be operating under increased stress, which may lead to individual and systemic disturbances. As the world becomes increasingly more diverse and migration patterns amplify as a result of geopolitical conflict, these influences are even more important to bear in mind when conducting clinical work with displaced families and groups.

Rapid advances in technology have led to a new era, which is dramatically changing social systems through the introduction of the internet, computer technology, and social networking. These trends are in effect changing how social interactions are conducted in industrialized countries, influencing and shaping the character of those who use this technology. The stories we construct and the narratives that are formed are in part scripted by our national and sociocultural experiences, which serve as "generative schemas for reflecting on the past and planning for the future, guiding and motivating the behaviors of every individual who shares them. These behaviors are often conventionalized, scripted, and widely shared in the group" (Kitayama et al., 2010, p. 561).

Cultural systems shape the way in which individuals are neurobiologically encoded by providing the preferred personality attributes that the culture requires to perpetuate itself. Kitayama et al. (2010) describe the implication of their "production-adoption model of cultural change":

> One striking implication of the model is that contemporary American culture is simultaneously highly homogeneous over its territory and remarkably diverse across its regions. As we argue, the culture is unified in terms of its *implicit* ethos (defined by both tacit practices and associated mental habits). At the same time, it is quite diverse across regions in terms of its *explicit* ethos (defined by both explicitly held values and the behaviors that

are guided by them). Both aspects of culture are important in achieving a truly comprehensive understanding of the dynamic process of cultural maintenance and change. (p. 559)

In terms of human rights and equality, some cultures/societies show more signs of cultural pathology than others. These pathological cultural forces have tremendous impact on the members of that society (see, e.g., Bauder, 2002; Gottschall, 2004). Unified psychotherapeutics requires an understanding of the cultural influences that are operative in any patient system.

Political Systems

The study of political processes has become a burgeoning area of interest in psychology. We can depict the political processes as a fractal of our culture. Through policies and laws, political systems contribute to the shaping and nuancing of cultural memes.

Methods and Techniques of Mesosystem Restructuring (MR)

The focus of MR is the sociocultural–familial subsystem. The restructuring of the mesosystem includes the following submethods:

1. *Familial restructuring* (Magnavita, 2000, 2005). This includes techniques directed toward altering the processes, communication, and structure of the nuclear and extended family system (Bowen, 1976; Minuchin, 1974).
2. *Social restructuring* (Magnavita, 2005, 2006). This includes strategies for addressing dysfunctional aspects of social systems.
3. *Political restructuring*. These are activities that individuals and groups undertake to change political systems. During the writing of this volume, following the Newtown, Connecticut, mass murder, a major political restructuring has been evident. Whether this will be successful, and to what degree, in reducing gun violence in the United States is still uncertain.

Dysfunctional Personologic Family Systems

In a previous volume, Magnavita (2005, pp. 161–165) presented a typology of dysfunctional family systems that have a higher likelihood of producing members with personality dysfunction. These families typically revolve around themes representative of unresolved trauma or the effects of generational patterns of addictive behavior. To illustrate, one type that was offered was of a developmentally delayed family. These seem to be more common in clinical practice as the economic conditions for the middle class in the United States have worsened.

CASE EXAMPLE: A DEVELOPMENTALLY DELAYED PERSONOLOGIC SYSTEM

A young woman in her late 20s was seen for consultation. Still residing at home with her parents, she reported that she could not move out of her parents' home because she was not earning enough money. History revealed that her two brothers, one younger and one older, also lived at home and were not employed. A family consultation was offered first with her parents, who were in a high-conflict marriage with high levels of Gottman's indicators of a faltering marriage. They were living separate lives and were unwilling to divorce because of their cultural beliefs. This family fit the description of a developmentally delayed, dysfunctional personologic system. Assessment revealed a low level of differentiation among the parents and a severely triangulated younger son who was emotionally enmeshed with his mother and cut off from his father. Both parents undermined his efforts to become autonomous. They paid for his care and insurance even though they themselves were of limited means. In fact, he had not worked for 4 years and showed no effort to attain a job. His behavior in the sessions with his parents was highly regressed and his personality system was characterized by an avoidant and dependent style.

Another illustration of a dysfunctional family system is one in which family functioning is dominated by medical illness and processes.

CASE EXAMPLE: A MEDICALLY ILL DYSFUNCTIONAL PERSONOLOGIC SYSTEM

Janet, a patient with a history of extreme childhood sexual trauma, suffered from fibromyalgia and chronic fatigue syndrome. She was diagnosed with multiple psychiatric disturbances, including bipolar disorder. Over the course of a number of years, her functioning deteriorated to the point that she had trouble engaging in the basic activities of life. She left her job as an administrative assistant and qualified for disability. Her husband was employed full-time and their four children were relatively high functioning. The family's functioning increasingly revolved around Janet's physical condition. A course of treatment included individual psychotherapy using multiple methods, including intrapsychic restructuring using trauma-based

(*continued*)

> ### CASE EXAMPLE (*continued*)
>
> therapy to address the childhood abuse and behavioral activation to address her depression and somatic disturbances. Her husband was also included in the treatment to strengthen the marital dyad. Over the course of 40 sessions she was able to resume some functional life, spending some time traveling and working part time.

Societal Problems

There is an increasing awareness that behavioral problems are having a major negative impact on the population. These problems include obesity, smoking, gun violence, and bullying.

Mass Murder in Newtown, Connecticut—The Mesosystem in Chaos

On December 14, 2012 a mass murder occurred in Newtown, Connecticut, in the same state where the first author resides. We can use our unified framework to examine this horrific event, which has had profound effects on the United States that are reverberating throughout the country's cultural, political, economic, and social structures, as well as the individual personality systems of the entire populace. Briefly, a 20-year-old male entered the Sandy Hook Elementary School with an assault weapon owned by his mother. He killed his mother, then drove to Sandy Hook Elementary School and shot his way through the front door, killing the principal and school psychologist who bravely attempted to stop him. The mayhem continued as he repeatedly shot and murdered 20 young children and 4 other adults. Due in part to the age of the victims and unexplainable nature of this event, the country was profoundly shaken.

There are many perspectives and multiple levels with which we can attempt to understand this massacre and the ensuing events that seem surreal to a country plagued by gun violence. We can discern from preliminary reports that the young man who committed this atrocity may have been suffering from some type of neurobiologically based mental disorder. We do not know the nature of his disturbance at the intrapsychic–biological level, as this young man committed suicide and was not able to be examined psychologically, which might have added to our understanding. From history we can assume he likely had a neurobiological or structural issue with his brain. At the microlevel we might therefore say that the issue is ensuring that psychologically disturbed young men are identified and effectively treated. We may also wonder what his level of attachment was to his mother, whom he murdered, and whether he had suffered psychologically or had even been traumatized. From what we learned from public reports it was suspected that he had some type of "developmental disorder" and was considered "odd" and a "loner." At the triadic level, his parents divorced and his father remarried. He remained in residence with his mother and there was some indication that he was having difficulty transitioning to college even though he was apparently very intelligent. Apparently he was estranged from his father.

Unfortunately, his mother was a gun owner and took her son to the shooting range. According to news reports she was very fond of her guns, which unfortunately included a Bushmaster semi-automatic assault weapon used by the military and capable of firing a frightening number of high-velocity bullets in seconds. We don't know what went on in the deadly interaction with his mother or how he came into possession of this weaponry, but we do know that he seemed intent on murder and mayhem—as has been the case with a number of other young North American upper middle-class individuals who have committed mass murders.

What are the factors that have led to this type of violence and what can be done to prevent future occurrences? This is where we observe the process from the sociocultural level. Shortly after the Newtown massacre, a Presidential Commission headed by Vice President Joe Biden was formed to address these questions. The Commission made recommendations, which were met with tremendous resistance by the gun lobby, and in April 2013, formal gun-control legislation prompted by the Newtown shootings was defeated in the Senate. There are many stakeholders involved. The National Rifle Association (NRA) has taken the position that any gun control is ineffective and that assault rifles and clips that allow for rapid firing without reloading should not be banned. Instead they are laying blame on the computer game industry that produces and markets violent video games to children and adolescents. From this perspective, this and the fact that "lunatics" are getting guns is the problem. Their solution is that more "good guys" should have guns and the CEO of the NRA recommended an armed guard at every school as well as arming teachers and principals.

This is a tragic example of the sociopolitical and economic system dysfunctioning to the point that there is a severe polarization among many citizens of the United States. Many people believe that President Obama and his administration are intent on doing away with the Second Amendment. The controversy rages, but if and how the system will reconfigure is not certain. After reading this volume we hope that it is easier to see how the complexity of our larger system often borders on chaos and at times there are outbreaks of extreme systemic disturbance where there is a confluence of factors that result in unimaginable and senseless tragedy.

SUMMARY

In this chapter there is a focus on Level IV, the sociocultural–familial system, and the methods and techniques that are useful for clinicians to understand when working in any domain of the patient system. The mesosystem encompasses the interaction among the individual personality system, family system, and sociocultural structures. The system is shaped and modified by complex processes that occur among these subsystems and domains. Identifying the various components that are dysfunctioning gives us a much greater appreciation for the scope of the change process and where to intervene. Unified treatment encourages a multidimensional perspective. Selecting techniques and methods of mesosystem restructuring consistent with the domain level in which we have some locus of influence focalizes our work and adds precision to our case formulation and treatment planning.

REFERENCES

Bauder, H. (2002). Neighbourhood effects and cultural exclusion. *Urban Studies, 39,* 85–93.

Bowen, M. (1976). Theory in the practice of family therapy. In P. J. Guerin, Jr. (Ed.), *Family therapy: Theory and practice* (pp. 42–90). New York: Gardner Press.

Brooks-Gunn, J., Johnson, A. D., & Leventhal, T. (2010). Disorder, turbulence, and resources in children's homes and neighborhoods. In G. W. Evans & T. D. Wachs (Eds.), *Chaos and its influence on children's development: An ecological perspective* (pp. 155–170). Washington, DC: American Psychological Association.

Doane, J. A., & Diamond, D. (1994). *Affect and attachment in the family: A family-based treatment of major psychiatric disorder.* New York: Basic Books.

Evans, G. W. & Wachs, T. D. (Eds.). (2010). *Chaos and its influence on children's development: An ecological perspective.* Washington, DC: American Psychological Association.

Gottschall, J. (2004). Explaining wartime rape. *The Journal of Sex Research, 41,* 129–136.

Guerin, P. J., Fogarty, T. F., Fay, L. F., & Kautto, J. G. (1996). *Working with relational triangles: The one-two-three of psychotherapy.* New York: Guilford.

Kitayama, S., Conway, L. G., Pietromonaco, P. R., Park, H., & Plaut, V. C. (2010). Ethos of independence across regions in the United States. *American Psychologist, 65,* 559–574.

Magnavita, J. J. (2000). *Relational therapy for personality disorders.* Hoboken, NJ: Wiley.

Magnavita, J. J. (2004). Toward a unified model of treatment for personality dysfunction. In J. J. Magnavita (Ed.), *Handbook of personality disorders: Theory and practice* (pp. 528–553). Hoboken, NJ: Wiley.

Magnavita, J. J. (2005). *Personality-guided relational therapy: A unified approach.* Washington, DC: American Psychological Association.

Magnavita, J. J. (2006). In search of the unifying principles of psychotherapy: Conceptual, empirical, and clinical convergence. *American Psychologist, 61,* 882–892.

Minuchin, S. (1974). *Families and family therapy.* Cambridge, MA: Harvard University Press.

Park, N., & Peterson, C. (2010). Does it matter where we live? The urban psychology of character strengths. *American Psychologist, 65,* 535–547.

Rentfrow, P. J. (2010). Statewide differences in personality: Toward a psychological geography of the United States. *American Psychologist, 65,* 548–558.

Chapter 10

FORMULATION OF UNIFIED TREATMENT PACKAGES

Clinical Decision Making in Unified Therapeutics

In this final chapter of the volume, we present the basic components of treatment planning, emphasizing the decision-making processes essential to unified therapeutics. We describe how these essential components, which are the concrete building blocks of unified treatment (manualized approaches, modalities, format, methods, and so forth) are the tools and processes in our "clinical toolkit." Clinicians select from these tools when they develop treatment packages tailored to the characteristics and features of the patient system. We either do treatment planning systematically and thoughtfully, utilizing the best information and decision-making processes, or we operate from a lack of information, habit, and bias. Knowing what these tools are and the basics of how they work will enhance your clinical efficacy. An analogy is a mechanic who possesses a full set of automobile repair tools, who knows the basic procedures of how they are used yet cannot repair your car. Much more is required of mechanics and clinicians. Familiarity with one evidence-based approach or another, although important, does not provide a sufficient foundation for unified therapeutics. All clinicians at some point believe they have learned an effective treatment only to find that the "operation was a success"—we applied the treatment by the manual—"but the patient died"—dropped out of treatment, got worse, or didn't improve because they didn't comply with the requirements. In this volume, we have reviewed many of the theoretical and clinical pattern recognition tools that we find to have clinical utility. Treatment planning is where the "rubber meets the road" and everything that one knows, and doesn't know, is pulled together in a process that requires decision making in complex situations, often with incomplete information and with limited empirical evidence to draw upon. "Treatment planning and formatting constitutes the art and science of developing and presenting to the client the essential algorithms most appropriate to him or her" (Magnavita, Critchfield, & Castonguay, 2010, p. 287).

The First Step—Engagement and Assessment

Clinicians must be able to rapidly and comprehensively assess patients and the systems in which they are embedded. However, there is no assessment unless the clinician effectively engages the patient system in a therapeutic process. Developing assessment skills is beyond the scope of this volume, which assumes a basic level. There are some critical aspects of any therapeutic assessment process that should be considered. Marques (2008) provides a useful summary for us: "It is imperative that clinicians pay attention to how clients experience and assess themselves—what they consider their primary problems, the duration of their problems and any precipitating events, why they are seeking help at this point in time, how they classify themselves, how they relate to themselves, what they see as their strengths and weaknesses, whether they have had therapy before and what their experience of it was like, their assessments of the likelihood of changing for the better, and how they think they can best achieve their desired outcomes and goals" (pp. 4–5). We begin to use our pattern recognition skills as soon as a patient contacts us. Mahoney (2003) wrote:

> The complexity of human change processes merits appreciation. Human development rarely follows a simple, linear path. It is more often a zigzag course, with frequent sticking points, repetitive circles, occasional regressions, and a few startling leaps and falls. The particulars may seem dizzying in their diversity, yet there are patterns. Patterns suggest principles. Understanding principles of human development is essential to the task of psychotherapy. (pp. 9–10)

As Mahoney points out, it is imperative to keep in mind that each patient, couple, family, and larger system is progressing along a developmental path and at each point in time the system is reconfiguring the manner in which it operates, sometimes flexibly but typically more chaotic or rigidly. We have the privilege of entering the patient system and in doing so we inevitably will become an important component at whatever level we are operating.

While engaging the patient system, the clinician must formulate a treatment protocol in collaboration with the patient/system and weave together a number of important elements of treatment acceptable to the patient. These initial treatment recommendations based on a unified case conceptualization then become the agreed upon treatment contract. Once treatment ensues the clinician must be able to evaluate the effectiveness of the intervention, test by gathering evidence from various data streams, and make a determination regarding effectiveness. If the treatment is not proceeding along the expected course, then, in collaboration with the patient, modifications are made and re-contracting takes place. On a daily basis clinicians are faced with enormously complex situations, which require an ability to effectively make decisions. Parents seeking consultation for a child might convincingly make a case that their child who they suspect has attention deficit disorder should be referred to a pharmacotherapist immediately because the family issues are noncontributory. A rapid determination has to be made and the risks and benefits assessed.

CLINICAL DECISION MAKING

Most readers have probably seen the reports of various treatment guideline committees and societies that address a clinical issue, review the literature, and then often present clinical decision-making trees, which are usually logically derived and provide useful guidance. These decision trees are based on clinical algorithms that weigh certain choice points and suggest where to go. For example, a patient presenting with a chronic and severe clinical depression who has been treatment refractory and unresponsive to a variety of pharmacological approaches and psychotherapy might be considered a candidate for electroconvulsive therapy (ECT) following one decision tree. These decision trees can be excellent heuristic devices to codify some of the decision points in clinical practice. In this volume, we presented a framework for organizing the various domains and levels of potential focus for making clinical decisions, but how does this really come together in our offices? We believe that this is one of the most important challenges for clinical science. It is wonderful to have the compendium of methods, techniques, and relational principles that constitute clinical science, but it is another thing to know how these fit together for each case. It is a very confusing situation for clinicians. Different theories and approaches may have greater or lesser relevance based on many factors such as developmental stage, socioeconomic level, educational level, ethnic background, and so forth. Clinical wisdom is hard earned and comes from seeing multiple cases and learning both rapid, intuitive decision making and slower, more methodical decision making. Recent advances in decision-making theory represent an important contribution to clinical science and an exciting area for future development.

The Basic Domains of Clinical Decision Making

Clinical decision making rests on three essential domains, like a three-leg stool that remains solid when all three legs are intact and can bear the weight. These elements, derived from the American Psychological Association Presidential Task Force (2006), include the best "available research, clinical expertise, and patient characteristics, culture, and preferences)" (Norcross, Hogan, & Koocher, 2008, p. 5). We agree with the authors "that clinical practice should be predicated on the best available research integrated with the clinician's expertise within the context of a particular patient "(or patient system)" (Norcross, Hogan, & Koocher, 2008, p. xi). We also concur that evidence-based practice is important but not sufficient for a unified clinical science, which requires convergent evidence from many sources to have clinical utility. The knowledge of the empirical research that shows cognitive-behavioral therapy (CBT) is superior to relaxation training for the treatment of trauma is a very useful starting point, but much broader domains are required of the practitioner to show how to navigate the complexities of the patient system.

Characteristics of Clinical Decision Making

Drawing from literature of decision making, there are characteristics that when understood, just as our theoretical framework, can serve as another unifying force for clinical science and psychotherapy. Difficult decisions often involve uncertainty, complexity, high-risk consequences, alternatives, and interpersonal issues. Decision making in clinical practice requires, in most cases, multiple strategies to be successful. At times, rapid intuitive responses are called for, and at other times deliberate and contemplative ones are the best way to proceed.

Fast or Slow Processing. In his book *Thinking, Slow and Fast*, Daniel Kahneman (2011), the Nobel Prize–winning psychologist and behavioral economist, describes two systems that account for the way we process information to make decisions. In what he calls *System 1*, decisions are made fast, emotionally, intuitively, and subconsciously, similar to what Gladwell (2005) describes as thin slicing. *System 2* is deliberate, methodical, slower, logical, and conscious. Many clinicians believe that their work is more of the System 1 nature and the researchers whom we have met seem to be more

System 2 processors. Both systems seem necessary for the complexity of clinical practice. Keith Stanovich (2011) also describes a similar two-type processing system, which essentially is logical versus emotional (cf. Epstein, 2003). Which system best serves as a guide to information processing and decision making in unifying psychotherapy?

Simplifying Complexity—The Benefits of Checklists

When a physician frequently washes his or her hands he or she significantly reduces the probability of a poor outcome. In his book, *The Checklist Manifesto: How to Get Things Right*, Gwande (2010), a Harvard surgeon and innovator, offers useful guidance in how to prevent error in medicine. Gwande's use of lists to reduce error is actually a System 2 approach that offers us excellent advice. Whenever possible we should develop checklists to make sure we have not missed something crucial. A checklist allows us to be certain we are not going to overlook a certain element of treatment that is of importance. Much of what should be put on our checklist centers on questions that are essential for gathering important information. Some of these include checking whether there is a history of substance abuse, traumatic experiences, suicide attempt or plan, violence, or addictions. When we fail to ask these questions there is a danger that treatment will not be on the mark and important information essential to treatment planning will be overlooked.

Thin-Splitting

In *Blink*, Gladwell (2005) reports on the research of John Gottman whose work we previously discussed. Gottman (1999b) can accurately predict which marriages will last six years, and surprisingly, can do so by watching a three-minute video of a couple talking. Most clinicians have met other clinicians who seem to be able to accurately read relational systems with an instinctive sense for what is called for in each clinical situation. Gladwell describes the adaptive unconscious as part of our brain that acts like a giant computer responsible for rapid decision making. Some of our iconic therapists, such as Milton Erickson, Fritz Perls, Carl Rogers, and others, seem to possess a natural skill at figuring out what is needed in their work. The work of a number of researchers is giving credence to the concept that certain individuals are deeply intuitive and can make use of this in therapeutic relationships, reading the system and responding in novel ways. In their classic work, *Systematic Treatment Selection*, Beutler and Clarkin (1990), from whom we have derived much of our thinking about treatment planning, wrote: "An effective therapist intuitively is able to respond to the unique characteristics and needs of the patients, and in this process to apply a variety of interventions that encourage movement and enhance the persuasive power of the interpersonal experience of psychotherapy" (p. 265).

Bias Influences in Clinical Decision Making

There are many aspects of decision-making theory and research that we can incorporate into our clinical process with the goal of increasing mindfulness, to hone our clinical decision-making skills. The more aware we are of these cognitive and perceptual traps that can influence our thinking, the better chance we have to avoid them. Cognitive science and psychological theory have made many important contributions useful for understanding decision-making processes and for building a theoretical model. There are two basic ways that humans make decisions: rational and emotional (Lehrer, 2009). The first is using rationality, such as we have discussed when looking at decision trees in treatment guidelines, and the other is emotional or intuitive. Many neuroscientists have discussed left-brain thinking, which tends to be more rational, language-based, and linear, and right-brain processing, which tends to be more emotional, intuitive, and enabling the "thin-slicing" alluded to above. Gladwell (2005) writes: "Truly successful decision making relies on a balance between deliberate and instinctive thinking" (p. 141).

Insufficient or Overabundant Information

We might think that the best way to make a sound clinical decision is to have an abundance of clinical information from patient interviews, collaborative interviews with family members, results from reliable and valid psychometric instruments, and so on. However, too much information may be a problem. Gladwell (2005) discusses the research of Stuart Oskamp (1965), who found that the diagnostic accuracy of a group of psychologists asked to examine a case and respond to a questionnaire did not improve in the accuracy of their judgment with more information. He successively gave the psychologists more case information to process and found that their confidence in their diagnostic formulation increased. However, Oskamp found that even though their certainty increased with each new data set, their overall accuracy remained the same. This has been described as the *dilution effect* in that the more nondiagnostic information available, the greater the tendency not to appropriately weigh more critical data. Gladwell opines that our desire for confidence may actually undermine our clinical accuracy. Why does this occur? There are various elements of the decision-making process that can highjack us and make us more prone to error:

- *Confirmation bias*: A tendency to honor information that confirms our belief. Selectively gathering data that support our bias and interpreting the data in a manner that confirms this bias can affect our decision making. For example, there was a phase in the history of psychotherapy where many clinicians trained in treating survivors of sexual abuse would often ask questions supporting their belief system. In one instance a psychotherapist in supervision had a bias that most women who sought treatment were sexually molested, which matched her own schema in that she had experienced this type of trauma. Some of her patients later reported that she asked leading questions that assumed sexual trauma must have occurred to explain certain symptom constellations. When patients responded saying they had no memory of such events the therapist would use this as evidence that the person surely repressed this information.

- *Overconfidence*: Research has shown that we tend to be overly confident of our own knowledge and accuracy in decision making. We are generally over confident in how effective we are, which may impede our judgment; even when receiving feedback to the contrary we hold our high self-regard. Lambert's (2010) research clearly demonstrated that clinicians suffer from overconfidence in their ability, and he was surprised by how often clinicians failed to predict negative treatment outcomes. He describes this phenomenon as the Lake Woebegone Effect from Garrison Keillor's program, *A Prairie Home Companion*, in which he describes all the children as being above-average and the women good looking. Results from Walfish, McAlister, O'Donnell, and Lambert (2012) revealed that when a group of therapists were asked to rate their skill level, 25% assessed themselves at the 90% level compared to their peers and none as below average. Lambert's research shows that paying attention to patient feedback is critical to reducing our overconfidence. Even if we believe things are going well, if the patient has a different perception then it behooves us to pay attention.

- *Self-serving bias*: We are all vulnerable to the moral hazard of believing what we are doing is positive and thinking highly of ourselves. We tend not to be so accurate at assessing ourselves. We tend to exaggerate our positive attributes and rationalize and blame external events for things that go awry. Clinicians are vulnerable, as are all humans, to this type of bias. When treatment goes poorly or a patient has a negative result we often say the patient was "unmotivated," "treatment refractory," "difficult," or, worse, a "malignant borderline." We may assume that our "failed" cases are the result of bad luck. We have found that a way to keep this bias in check is to seek out professional and peer supervision. We also find that showing videotapes is a humbling experience for even the most experienced therapists, and we recommend that therapists regularly tape their sessions for review by a peer group or colleague.

- *Difficulty dealing with complexity*: Another potential bias results from the challenge of dealing with complexity and wanting to simplify phenomenon that are not often understood in a linear fashion. For example, a patient who suffered from borderline personality, complex posttraumatic stress disorder (PTSD), and mood disturbance was seen with her husband, who asked if her difficulties were best explained by a neurotransmitter imbalance. The best way to address this complexity bias is to learn more about chaos and complexity theory. There are many situations that call for a parsimonious decision or action in clinical practice and others where bearing the dialectic tension of the complexity is essential. Knowing which is called for requires knowledge and experience.

- *Status quo effects*: This entails an irrational preference for the familiar. For example, we indicate below that the standard duration of a psychotherapy session is 45 to 50 minutes, yet we could find no evidence that this duration has any clinical superiority over any other duration. Why does clinical science continue to favor this length of session? The status quo effect seems to be operative in this case. It is easy for us to embrace what we find familiar. A good way to counteract this tendency to accept the status quo is by seeking out new training experiences or other activities that create an openness to experience.

- *Narrative fallacy bias*: We tend to tell stories to explain "facts" that may support our bias. This type of bias is based on finding *illusory correlations* or relationships that do not really exist (Hamilton & Gifford, 1976). These narratives then can be attractor states for selectively encoding data that support this narrative. Psychoanalysis has been accused of this type of bias, wherein explanations that were spun into narratives were "validated" by selectively drawing examples from clinical practice.

- *Anchoring effects*: At times we tend to rely on a particular type of information even if it is not relevant to our decision making. It tends to be the first piece of evidence that we process (Tversky & Kahneman, 1974). In one case, a woman in her early 30s wanted to have children and was concerned about the fact that she was on a mood stabilizer prescribed 8 years earlier when she was hospitalized by the inpatient psychiatrist. She was maintained on this mood stabilizer until she consulted with a new psychopharmacologist who questioned the initial diagnosis. She was seen for a consultation and psychometric testing, suggesting the possibility that this diagnosis might not be substantiated. A decision was made to discontinue the mood stabilizer while closely monitoring her response. After 6 months it seemed that her initial reaction and hospitalization was the result of unidentified trauma. The original psychotherapists and pharmacotherapist were anchored to the preliminary diagnosis and the implication that without medication she would relapse. Anchoring is often also seen in the way original diagnostic formulations are carried forth over time.

Countering Bias—Seeking to Maintain an Open Frame and a Mindful Position

There are no easy cures for allowing our biases to influence us, but we can increase our mindfulness. Being more cognizant of how bias influences our judgment and decision making can enable us to be more mindful of traps to which we are prey when we are working. Our bias might be expressed in our preferred approaches to treatment or favoring a modality we were trained in when another might be indicated. When reviewing the elements of treatment in the next section, take some time and notice how you assess and value each component, notice which elements you favor or prefer, and ask yourself why you might overlook a particular element.

Steps in Clinical Decision Making

In addition to being cognizant of common ways that bias affects our clinical decisions, it is also worthwhile to follow basic steps for any clinical decision making:

1. *Specify the treatment objectives.* Do this as early in the process as possible and make these objectives measurable in some fashion so that they can be used for gathering data. The Subjective Units of Distress Scale (SUDS) is a simple tool with clinical utility. Essentially, the patient is asked to rate his or her distress on a scale of 0 to 10, with 10 representing the highest level of distress and 0 the absence of distress. There are many other psychometric instruments that are easy to administer, reliable, and valid (see, e.g., Antony & Rowa, 2005; Beevers, 2011; Lopez & Snyder, 2003; Strack, 2010; Whipple & Lambert, 2011).

2. *Rank ordering treatment priorities.* Once the patient's objectives are operationalized and a list is developed, they should be ranked ordered so the treatment begins with the one most important to the

patient system. For example, an individual with depression, anxiety, personality dysfunction, and substance dependence might benefit if motivated to address the addictive process or addressing the anxiety with techniques to lower the threshold. The list may shift as more information is gathered and more awareness gained. A couple with a problematic child who is triangulated might come to the realization that they have unresolved marital conflict and thus the treatment may be reformatted to include the marital modality.

3. *Treatment options are offered and discussed.* These elements are presented in the following section of this chapter. This step will specify these elements such as individual psychotherapy, using a short-term format, with specific methods elaborated. Other treatment options should also be proposed and explored as to their cost benefit and fit. The clinician should develop some sense of what level of the system he or she will be operating in, which will to a great degree determine the methods and format selected.

4. *Conduct a cost–benefit analysis.* A useful process in most cases is to weigh the costs and benefits of alternatives in terms of time, resources, potential outcome, potential harm, and so on.

5. *Select the best-fit treatment package.* In collaboration with the patient system, the best alternative option is selected.

6. *Assessing treatment progress.* In the next stage, information is gathered to make a determination if the treatment package is effectively working toward the desired outcome or whether changes need to be made, such as introducing another modality, or intensifying the treatment by using more frequent or longer sessions.

Once we are cognizant of our biases we can use these decision-making steps to begin the process of developing a treatment package for each patient system, maintaining awareness that any treatment package is our first attempt to capture the elements of the patient system that need to be addressed and offer a preliminary plan to achieve the objectives. It is good to keep in mind that diagnosis and treatment planning evolve and should be modified over time as the system changes or doesn't. It is imperative to have an appreciation of the building blocks that are part of the treatment package.

BUILDING BLOCKS OF CLINICAL SCIENCE AND UNIFIED PSYCHOTHERAPEUTICS

In examining the many aspects of clinical science on which unified psychotherapy is based, it is essential to delineate the various components of unified clinical science. These then are the elements of treatment that converge to form an individualized treatment package and include:

Treatment Approaches: A treatment approach usually has a theoretical foundation, a set of methods and techniques, as well as a suggested sequence for carrying out procedures of the approach. Formal approaches generally have manuals or texts to describe all the essential theory, elements, and procedures. Many of these have been subjected to empirical investigation, which supports their use. Clinicians can select various formal treatment approaches depending on their educational and training experiences. These approaches tend to focus their interventions primarily on one domain level. However, research shows that there is an inexorable movement toward eclectic and integrative approaches. There are over 100 manualized treatments that clinicians can use to guide their work (Duncan & Miller, 2006). How can clinicians possibly select the most effective from these? Lambert (2010) believes the field is in a state of chaos with so many potential interactive effects that it is not possible to use clinical trials to compare psychotherapies or to guide practice. Something different is required. Lambert (2010) writes: "In routine care, judgments and treatment decisions are made by individual clinicians 'informed by evidence,' expertise, and patient considerations" (p. 22).

Advantages of "Pure Form Treatment Approaches." Formalized or "pure form" treatment approaches, often referred to as evidence-based treatment (EBT; Chambless, 1996) offer manuals for treatment that can be taught and implemented with a certain degree of integrity. These are important tools for training and skill acquisition.

Disadvantages of "Pure Form Treatment Approaches." There are some limitations to relying upon evidence-based treatment approaches. They may be constraining and not allow the flexibility needed to navigate complex systems. When exclusively relied on, the results may not be optimal. Over adherence to a manualized treatment may result in poorer treatment outcomes.

When an approach that focuses primarily at one level of the system or on a specific domain is not achieving the desired results, then shifting therapeutic attention to another level might be helpful. Over the course of our careers we have sought training in many of the latest approaches and have often found the training extremely valuable. Training in various approaches to treatment seems to be a necessary part of professional development. An awareness of the therapeutic action and scope of different approaches is important to ascertain.

Treatment Methods: Treatment methods are smaller component units of various treatment approaches that include sequences of techniques. For example, as described in Chapter 8, there are various techniques of cognitive, affective, and defensive restructuring with different sequences of specific technical interventions. Likely the most important aspect of any method is to understand the desired effect on the system so it is appropriately applied. As we have discussed, the therapeutic action of some methods is to heighten affect and anxiety and others to lower anxiety. For example, utilizing methods of defensive restructuring with a fragile patient system may create iatrogenic disturbance. It is always important to attain supervision and advanced training when acquiring new therapeutic skills. Some methods are more consistent with a particular approach or theory of psychotherapy. For example, interpretation, free association, and taking a neutral stance are hallmark techniques of psychoanalytic therapy. Newer forms of psychodynamic psychotherapy often use methods that require higher levels of interpersonal engagement and therapist activity. Methods are important skills that can be used to keep the level of arousal within an optimal window. "If arousal level is optimal, it will facilitate self observation, disconfirmation of pathogenic beliefs, and cognitive change" (Beutler & Clarkin, 1990, p. 272).

Treatment Techniques: Techniques are the "specific procedures" of psychotherapy (Beutler & Castonguay, 2006, p. 8) that are usually depicted by a structured series of verbal interactions, such as challenging dysfunctional beliefs, a cognitive restructuring technique. One of the goals of the Unified Psychotherapy Project is to produce a compendium of techniques in an organized fashion to advance clinical science. Techniques are interpersonal, cognitive, and technical operations that are the mainstay of psychotherapeutics. We know very little about the taxonomy or action of techniques. Certain techniques may cluster together into a method that suggests a sequence of techniques that are similar to learning a style of dance with the various steps and movements being the technical aspect. The effect of various techniques should be understood before they are utilized. A critical aspect of any technical intervention concerns whether the technique may increase anxiety or distress, or serve to lower it. Beutler and Clarkin (1990) nicely break down techniques into two different classes: procedures that reduce distress and those that increase emotional arousal:

- *Decreased Distress/Arousal*: (1) ventilation, (2) reassurance, (3) relaxation and distraction, (4) reflection, (5) advice and teaching, (6) hypnosis, (7) breath control, (8) focus on sensations, and (9) counterconditioning.

- *Increased Arousal*: (1) confrontation, (2) encounters with significant others, (3) two-chair dialogues around unfinished business, (4) directed-forced fantasies, (5) analysis of transference and defense, (6) interpretation, (7) silence, and (8) questions. (p. 274)

Other clinical theorists have suggested useful steps in increasing or decreasing emotional arousal (Davanloo, 1980; McCullough, 2003). It is useful to bear in mind the notion of channels of anxiety as a useful way to track and modulate anxiety.

Sequencing and Combining—techniques, methods, and modalities: All of the technical elements of psychotherapeutics may be arranged in sequences or combined. Techniques may be sequenced in a logical fashion such as that used to build a therapeutic alliance (empathic attunement with techniques of verbal affirmation, reflection of feeling and content, etc.) followed, for example, by interpretation, active cognitive restructuring, and processing of affect. Methods may be sequentially arranged into a standard approach to treatment. Treatment modalities may also be offered sequentially. The first course of treatment might be family, followed by individual psychotherapy, and then a support group.

Combining various techniques, methods, and modalities may also be indicated. Again there are few empirical data to guide these treatment decisions but there is clinical evidence to show that combining certain approaches or modalities may augment treatment. For example, a patient who is receiving dialectical behavior therapy for emotional regulation may also benefit from a trauma-focused approach.

Relational Factors: Relational factors are essential components of all psychotherapeutics and are concerned with the quality and management of the therapeutic relationship. These include the therapeutic alliance, cohesiveness in group therapy, empathy, goal consensus and collaboration, positive regard, congruence/genuineness, feedback, repair of alliance ruptures, self-disclosure, management of countertransference, and quality of relational interpretations (Norcross, 2011). The personality characteristics of the therapist combined with preferred attitudes about how one conducts oneself in the therapeutic frame represents the stance that is taken by the therapist. There is a wide range of therapeutic styles and stances. Some therapists are much more active and engaging and others more cognitive and neutral in their interactions. Regardless of the manifesto of any approach, there is no evidence that any one personality style or approach is superior. What is likely most important are patient–therapist matching factors. The goodness-of-fit seems to be a critical aspect of treatment that needs further attention. We usually make this explicit with our patients, informing them of the research that underscores the power of a therapeutic match. The therapeutic relationship is the interpersonal conduit for delivering various treatment interventions. There continues to be debate in the field concerning the importance of these factors, with some coming down on the side of the debate that maintains the relationship is the curative component.

Treatment Modalities

We refer to treatment modality as the relational unit in which treatment is delivered, basically corresponding to levels of our framework: individual—intrapsychic; marital/couples—dyadic; family—triadic. An important area for clinical science is to develop a better understanding of the differential functions and effects of various treatment modalities. In lieu of empirical evidence, clinical decision making is necessary with incomplete data. The following are the main modalities of treatment from which clinicians develop treatment packages.

Individual Psychotherapy. Individual psychotherapy remains the main modality, other than pharmacotherapy, for delivery of mental health care. Individual psychotherapy is indicated for many expressions of clinical symptoms, behavior disorders, and personality dysfunction. Individual psychotherapy, although the preferred modality, is the most expensive as it requires the presence of a highly trained professional clinician. It seems to be warranted especially in cases where focal work is needed and where other modalities might dilute the process.

Group Psychotherapy. Group psychotherapy was developed as an alternative to individual psychotherapy and has many advantages in that it can maximize the healing aspects of larger systems to effect change. It tends to be an underutilized modality in spite of having a substantial evidence base (Piper, 2008). Beutler and Clarkin (1990) identify three advantages of group psychotherapy: (1) It allows for identification and modeling with peers, (2) it makes use of support and advice, and (3) it allows for the practice of newly developed skills in a social environment that more closely approximates the reactions that are encountered outside of the group. Group therapy may be provided by a trained psychotherapist or delivered as support groups led by facilitator members, as in self-help groups such as Alcoholics Anonymous. Group psychotherapy is a cost-effective modality of treatment because one or sometimes two psychotherapists can address the needs of a number of people in an efficient format.

Couples/Marital Psychotherapy. This modality of treatment is primarily the way in which methods of dyadic restructuring are carried out. There has been significant progress made in advancing understanding of this modality of treatment. We believe that working with couples is an essential clinical skill for which it is well worth attaining both basic and advanced training. So many of the problems encountered in clinical populations either emerge from dysfunction in primary relationships or significantly impact them. For example, there is accumulating evidence that untreated spousal depression is an important factor in marital dissatisfaction. Conversely, dysfunctional marriages and partnerships may lead to depression in one or both members of a dyad.

Family Psychotherapy. Family psychotherapy seems to offer many benefits for a spectrum of disturbances (see, e.g., Carr, 2009a, 2009b; Diamond & Josephson, 2005) and requires advanced training.

Treatment Settings

As part of any clinical decision-making process, a decision must be made about the most appropriate treatment setting in which the treatment will be delivered. Each level of care has advantages and disadvantages and a systematic review of these needs to be completed before a decision is made—except, of course, in extreme emergencies where a higher or more restrictive level of care is necessary to preserve life.

Outpatient Treatment. Most mental health and behavioral treatment is provided on an outpatient basis, usually in a private office, clinic, or other facility.

Inpatient Hospitalization. Usually considered a more intensive setting for treatment, many patients will require an increased level of care when in danger or in a relapsing condition.

Partial Hospitalization and Day Treatment. Partial hospital and day-treatment programs serve an important need for patients who need a more intensive level of care than can be provided in outpatient therapy, but who do not require the most restrictive care such as that provided in hospitals.

Residential and Community Settings. Other settings to be considered are residential community settings and community care settings, which are usually provided by community mental health systems for those individuals who need supervision or longer periods of step-down care.

Treatment Formats

The format includes the manner in which the treatment is delivered and is an essential component of the treatment package. There is limited empirical evidence to guide the clinician in determining how to adjust these components of effective treatment.

Duration of Session. The length of the session is a critical variable of all treatment that frames the approach and intervention in a unit of time. Typically the duration of the session has been 45 to 50 minutes, which was based on the psychoanalytic model of treatment and has been carried forth by most approaches. Group modalities often are longer in duration. Over the past two decades there has been more acceptance of utilizing extended sessions of 90-minute duration, or in some cases even longer blocks of treatment with breaks between sessions.

Frequency of Sessions. The number of sessions provided within a period of time is another important factor to consider when developing treatment packages. We determine the frequency of sessions in collaboration with patients, letting them know that we can adapt the frequency as circumstances require or change. We let patients know that they can pace the treatment. If they want to accelerate or need more support we can increase the frequency or adjust the length of the sessions. As treatment progresses, we also space the sessions out to allow more between-session time to test out new learning. Some patients seem to benefit from the structure of regular weekly appointments, or in severe cases, with intensive outpatient treatment almost daily, to function at their optimal level of adaptation. Other patients seem to benefit when sessions are spaced at longer intervals to allow for metabolizing of feelings and to provide sufficient time to practice the new skills and patterns that they are trying to develop. There is scant research on making these decisions. A general rule of thumb is that increasing the frequency or length of sessions intensifies the treatment experience but also may allow more time for incorporating the changes that are being made.

Length of Treatment. The length of treatment varies from a single session to long-term and maintenance formats. We generally begin treatment with the goal of using a short-term format, and then if the clinical situation and patient response to treatment indicates that a longer-term treatment is needed, we recontract with informed consent and a discussion of why we might be changing the format. Finding the best fit for each patient is a matter of informed decision making and experimentation. Generally seeking to provide the least restrictive level of care is the goal and is generally a cost-effective approach.

Principles of Treatment

Clinical researchers have begun to systematically distill from the empirical evidence principles of effective treatment common to all therapeutic approaches (Castonguay & Beutler, 2006; Critchfield, 2012). Some important principles culled from the literature by Castonguay and Beutler (2006) include:

- Therapy outcome is likely to be enhanced if the client is willing to engage in the treatment process.

- The therapist is likely to increase his or her effectiveness if he or she demonstrates attitudes of open-mindedness, flexibility, and creativity.

- The positive impact of therapy is likely to be increased if the therapist is comfortable with long-term, emotionally intense relationships.

- The benefits of therapy may be enhanced if the therapist is able to tolerate his or her own negative feelings regarding the patient and the treatment process.

- The therapist is likely to be more effective if he or she is patient.

- Therapy is likely to be beneficial if a strong working alliance is established and maintained during the course of treatment.

- Therapists should relate in an empathic manner characterized by caring, warmth, acceptance, congruence, and authenticity (pp. 357–359).

The research on principles of therapeutic change and specific facets of the therapy relationship associated with positive outcomes (cf. Norcross, 2011) is informative regardless of the specific treatment approach that is determined to be optimal in each case.

Factors That Should Determine the Appropriate Treatment

In *Restoring Psychotherapy as the First Line Intervention in Behavioral Care*, Cummings and O'Donohue (2012) suggest the following factors be considered when developing a treatment package: (1) therapies that are safe; (2) therapies that are effective; (3) therapies that are efficient; (4) therapies designed with consideration of patient preferences; (5) therapies that encourage active participation in management of health; (6) therapies that prioritize patient problems and don't miss severe threats to well-being and functioning; (7) therapies delivered in a timely manner; and (8) therapies that the therapist is competent to provide (pp. 6–16).

Guiding Principles of Unified Psychotherapy

A central guiding principle of unified psychotherapy is that, springboarding from the patient's presenting complaints, the therapist's understanding of the patient's dysfunctionality and distress is based on assessment of pathogenic and pathological processes across all four levels of the multicomponent biopsychosocial systems model of personality and psychopathology (i.e., the individual, dyadic, familial, and sociocultural levels) and formulation of the nature of their reciprocal interplay. No domain can be ignored or the therapist risks failing to consider the nature and weighting of its contribution to maintaining a system in a state of dysfunction and pain. In gathering these data, the therapist is encouraged to use multiple methods of assessment, including not only interview data, but also relevant self-report measures, information from pertinent significant others (e.g., during early assessment, meeting with the patient's spouse or partner to obtain his or her perspectives), and direct observation (e.g., having other family members attend a session with the patient in order to observe dysfunctional family processes linked to the patient's problems). Based on the understanding of the patient's disorder(s) derived through comprehensive assessment, and informed by additional essential considerations discussed above (e.g., collaborative decision making with the patient), the therapist develops a preliminary individualized treatment package.The latter includes (a) the specific goals of treatment, (b) the modality to be used (e.g., individual psychotherapy, couple therapy, family therapy, group therapy, day treatment, and so forth)—and if more than one modality is indicated, the concurrence and/or sequencing of these modalities, (c) within a given modality, specific treatment methods and techniques considered to be most effective, and (d) the treatment format (i.e., length of treatment, frequency of sessions, length of sessions). Importantly, the initial treatment package is an organic composition, subject to modification and revision over the course of therapy as a function of such key considerations as the acquisition of additional significant clinical data and the degree of therapeutic change achieved by the patient; realistically, over the course of treatment, assessment and treatment compose an ongoing, mutually informing dialectic.

Ethical Decision Making—Above All, Do No Harm and, Where Possible, Do Good

Inherent in any clinical decision-making process is the necessity of ethical decision making and the mandate to "do no harm" (Magnavita, 2010).

Quadratic Decision Making

We are many decades away from having clinical algorithms to make these complex treatment decisions. A risk–benefit analysis—looking at the possible results of answers to two sets of questions in a quadratic formulation—can be used as a guide to enhance ethical clinical decision making when empirical data are scarce.

Ethical treatment of patients using a unifying framework can be guided by questions addressing the risk–benefit of various clinical decisions to safeguard the treatment process and optimize outcomes by weighing different options (cf. Barnett, in press). No definitive answers will be forthcoming, but the path to ethical treatment will be safeguarded and the patient's care will be honored. It is evident that clinicians who operate in a unified framework must be able to manage working with incomplete information and uncertainty. Any treatment decision can be assessed if the clinician can ask two sets of risk–benefit analysis questions concerning treatment decision making with a focus on analyzing potential risk and harm. The first two questions are, *"What are the risks if I treat the patient using specific treatment plan A—*approach or modality and so on?" and the opposite, *"What are the risks if I don't pursue this treatment plan?"* In answering the first series of questions, the psychologist might respond, "The risk of pursuing treatment plan A—an intensive restructuring personality approach with extended sessions—is that the results might be less than optimal because it is likely that the patient will drop out of treatment because it might not be tolerated." The answer to the second question of not pursuing treatment plan A might lead to the application of a treatment approach less optimal than evidence-based treatment and a continuation of certain self-destructive personality patterns.

Proceeding in our risk–benefit analysis, the next set of questions then considers the alternative choice. *"What are the benefits of pursuing treatment plan A?"* and the corollary, *"What are the benefits of not proceeding with treatment plan A?"* In answering the second two questions, the psychologist might respond, "Proceeding with treatment plan A has a greater likelihood of optimal outcome if tolerated and completed" and, in addressing the final question, "The potential benefit of not proceeding with treatment plan A is that a it might allow time for the development of a positive therapeutic alliance, increasing collaboration and increasing motivation to withstand the challenges of intensive treatment approach."

Shattering Sacred Icons and Challenging the Reification of Ritualized Clinical Practices

Although there is burgeoning research evidence to guide the practitioner, in many regards psychologists have surprisingly little empirical evidence that can be used to inform their practices and clinical decision making. There are a number of treatment approaches that have a reasonable research base. However, there is no ideal approach for every patient. Blindly following a protocol for an empirically based approach may in itself be unethical. In one case (in which JJM was the therapist), the patient asked for hypnosis to help him stop drinking. After being told there was no empirical evidence that this would be productive, the patient, at the end of what appeared to be a very productive session, announced she wasn't coming back. In this case, one might quote the old adage, "The operation was a success, but the patient died," as one of my early supervisors used to remind us fledgling therapists. Rather, the complexity of the disorder may require an eclectic approach (Stone, 2009). Much of what we accept as standard practice, such as length of sessions, frequency of sessions, boundary issues, and multiple therapeutic relationships (when the same psychologist combines multiple treatment modalities) are best characterized as clinical lore and ritual, often without any substantive body of evidence supporting the continuation of these practices. In the era of evidence-based treatment it seems unlikely that any one approach might fit all. In fact, there are many practices that are reified by psychotherapists and yet may be contraindicated. For example, the 50-minute session, which has been the mainstay of most psychotherapy, may not be optimal for those whose defenses are entrenched, as we see in many patients with personality disorders. Longer sessions may allow sufficient time to restructure defenses and address core issues. Flexibility might necessitate experimenting with the most efficacious treatment format and then altering it, depending on patient response to treatment. The practice of unified psychotherapy is based on a foundation of empirically determined principles, such as clinician flexibility and creativity (Castonguay & Beutler, 2006), combined with continual ethical informed decision making, even when there may be little in the way of empirical data on which to base these clinical decisions.

SUMMARY

In this final chapter we have discussed the basic components of treatment planning and formatting in a unifying approach to psychotherapy. Emphasis has been placed on different elements of the clinical decision-making process, including biases that can heighten a therapist's proneness to error, ways of countering these biases, and basic steps to guide clinical decision making. This was followed by a discussion of building blocks of clinical science and unified psychotherapeutics, which included considerations pertaining to treatment approaches, methods, and techniques; sequencing and combining of techniques, methods, and modalities; relationship factors; the various treatment modality options; treatment settings; and the format of treatment. A number of central treatment principles, factors to consider in determining the appropriate treatment, and basic guiding principles of unified psychotherapy were also indicated. The fundamental importance of ethics in any clinical decision making, including incorporation of a quadratic approach to addressing the risk–benefit of various clinical decisions, was also presented.

REFERENCES

American Psychological Association Presidential Task Force on Evidence-Based Practice (2006). Evidence-based practice in psychology. *American Psychologist, 61,* 271–285.

Antony, M. M., & Rowa, K. (2005). Evidence-based assessment of anxiety disorders in adults. *Psychological Assessment, 17,* 256–266.

Barnett, J. E. (in press). Ethics and the unified psychotherapy movement. *Journal of Unified Psychotherapy and Clinical Science.*

Beevers, C. G. (2011). Introduction: Evidence-based practice for major depressive disorder. In D. W. Springer, A. Rubin & C. G. Beevers (Eds.), *Treatment of depression in adolescents and adults* (pp. 1–20). Hoboken, NJ: Wiley.

Beutler, L. E., & Castonguay, L. G. (2006). The task force on empirically based principles of therapeutic change. In L. G. Castonguay & L. E. Beutler (Eds.), *Principles of therapeutic change that work* (pp. 3–10). New York: Oxford University Press.

Beutler, L. E., & Clarkin, J. (1990). *Systematic treatment selection: Toward targeted therapeutic interventions.* New York: Brunner/Mazel.

Carr, A. (2009a). The effectiveness of family therapy and systemic interventions for child-focused problems. *Journal of Family Therapy, 31,* 3–45.

Carr, A. (2009b). The effectiveness of family therapy and systemic interventions for adult-focused problems. *Journal of Family Therapy, 31,* 46–74.

Castonguay, L., & Beutler, L. E. (2006). Common and unique principles of therapeutic change: What do we know and what do we need to know? In L. G. Castonguay & L. E. Beutler (Eds.), *Principles of therapeutic change that work* (pp. 353–369). New York: Oxford University Press.

Chambless, D. L. (1996). In defense of dissemination of empirically supported psychological interventions. *Clinical Psychology: Science and Practice, 3,* 230–235.

Critchfield, K. L. (2012). Tailoring common treatment principles to fit individual personalities. *Journal of Personality Disorders, 26,* 108–125.

Cummings, N. A., & O'Donohue, W. T. (Eds.). (2012). *Restoring psychotherapy as the first line intervention in behavioral healthcare.* Dryden, NY: Ithaca Press.

Davanloo, H. (Ed.). (1980). *Short-term dynamic psychotherapy.* New York: Jason Aaronson Press.

Diamond, G., & Josephson, A. (2005). Family-based treatment research: A 10-year update. *Journal of the American Academy of Child and Adolescent Psychiatry, 44,* 872–887.

Duncan, B. L., & Miller, S. D. (2006). Treatment manuals do not improve outcome. In J. C. Norcross, L. E. Beutler & R. F. Levant (Eds.), *Evidence-based practices in mental health: Debate and dialogue on the fundamental questions* (pp. 140–149). Washington, DC: American Psychological Association.

Epstein, S. (2003). Cognitive-experiential self-theory of personality. In T. Millon & M. J. Lerner (Eds.), *Handbook of psychology: Vol. 5. Personality and social psychology* (pp. 159–184). Hoboken, NJ: Wiley.

Gwande, A. (2010). *The checklist manifesto: How to get things right.* New York: Holt Books.

Gladwell, M. (2005). *Blink: The power of thinking without thinking.* New York: Little, Brown and Company.

Gottman, J. M. (1999b). Predicting divorce among newlyweds from the first three minutes of a marital conflict discussion. *Family Process, 38,* 293–301.

Hamilton, D., & Gifford, R. (1976). Illusory correlation in interpersonal perception: A cognitive basis of stereotypic judgments. *Journal of Experimental Social Psychology, 12,* 392–407.

Kahneman, D. (2011). *Thinking fast and slow.* New York: Farrar, Strauss and Giroux.

Lambert, M. J. (2010). *Prevention of treatment failure: The use of measuring, monitoring, and feedback in clinical practice.* Washington, DC: American Psychological Association.

Lehrer, J. (2009). *How we decide.* New York: Houghton Mifflin Harcourt.

Lopez, S., & Snyder, C. R. (Eds.). (2003). *Positive psychological assessment: A handbook of models and measures.* Washington, DC: American Psychological Association.

Magnavita, J. J. (2010). Methods, components, and strategies of unified treatment: Using evidence and personality systematics to enhance outcome. In J. J. Magnavita (Ed.), *Evidence-based treatment of personality dysfunction: Principles, methods, and processes* (pp. 253–285). Washington, DC: American Psychological Association.

Magnavita, J. J., Critchfield, K. L., & Castonguay, L. G. (2010). Treatment planning and formatting: Combining science and art in implementing the framework of therapy. In J. J. Magnavita (Ed.), *Evidence-based treatment of personality dysfunction: Principles, methods, and processes* (pp. 287–305). Washington, DC: American Psychological Association.

Mahoney, M. J. (2003). *Constructive psychotherapy: A practical guide.* New York: Guilford.

Marquis, A. (2008). *The integral intake: A guide to comprehensive idiographic assessment in integral psychotherapy.* New York: Routledge.

McCullough, L. (2003). *Treating affect phobia: A manual for short-term dynamic psychotherapy.* New York: Guilford.

Norcross, J. C. (Ed.). (2011). *Psychotherapy relationships that work: Evidence-based responsiveness* (2nd ed.). New York: Oxford University Press.

Norcross, J. C., Hogan, T. P., & Koocher, G. P. (2008). *Clinician's guide to evidence-based practices: Mental health and the addictions.* New York: Oxford University Press.

Oskamp, S. (1965). Overconfidence in case-study judgments. *Journal of Consulting Psychology, 29,* 261–265.

Piper, W. E. (2008). Underutilization of short-term group therapy: Enigmatic or understandable? *Psychotherapy Research, 18,* 127–138.

Stanovich, K. E. (2011). *Rationality and the reflective mind.* New York: Oxford University Press.

Stone, M. H. (2009). Perspective: Pitfalls in the psychotherapy of borderline personality or the triumph of faith over fact. *Journal of Personality Disorders, 23,* 3–5.

Strack, S. (2010). Evidence-based assessment and instrumentation for personality disorders. In J. J. Magnavita (Ed.), *Evidence-based treatment of personality dysfunction: Principles, methods, and processes* (pp. 19–48). Washington, DC: American Psychological Association.

Tversky, A., & Kahneman, D. (1974). Judgment under uncertainty: Heuristics and biases. *Science, 185,* 1124–1130.

Walfish, S., McAlister, B., O'Donnell, P., & Lambert, M. J. (2012). An investigation of self-assessment bias in mental health providers. *Psychological Reports, 110,* 639–644.

Whipple, J. L., & Lambert, M. J. (2011). Outcome measures for practice. *Annual Review of Clinical Psychology, 7,* 81–111.

INDEX